globalization

and

education

critical perspectives

Social Theory
Education
& Cultural Change

Series Editors

Carlos Alberto Torres
    Director, Latin American Center
    University of California at Los Angeles

Raymond Allen Morrow
    Department of Sociology
    University of Alberta

Critical Theories in Education:
Changing Terrains of Knowledge and Politics

   Thomas S. Popkewitz and Lynn Fendler

Globalization and Education:
Critical Perspectives

   Nicholas C. Burbules
   and Carlos Alberto Torres

```
          : : ; - ; - ~ + C 4 C 1 : .
        ; 1 = C + I 1 I ~ + - - ; ; I + = 1 I + C 1 - :
       : I X C = 1 ~ I I 1 I 1 1 - X 1 I + = = = 1 X = C C + + ~ :
      : I X C C X + 1 I 1 I I ~ ~ I 1 1 1 1 = X = 1 I = ~ ~ ~ + = = X I :
     . ~ + X = C S C + X = 1 ~ + X D % S S O O 8 D 8 O S D D C = = X 1 1 = = I .
    ; I + 1 + + X X X = = + ~ 1 D % % C I = C D D D O = + 4 O 4 X S O I X C 4 X I :
   + = + 1 = + = X C X X C I 1 C D O % S O + 1 C % % % 4 X % $ 8 4 8 S + X % % % O + :
  X S = = C 4 C S D S S 4 C 1 = D D C S D $ 8 1 I S % D D $ $ $ % 4 1 ; : : I = + I + + :
  1 % C X D $ $ % D % $ $ S 4 4 = S D S % $ $ $ + + 4 % % % % $ % X I - ; ; - 1 ~ ~ ; ~ + X :
  : % % X 8 % 8 % D D $ $ % 8 % C C C D % $ $ $ D X % $ $ $ $ $ $ + - ; ; ; ; - ; ; = I 1 + =
  = $ $ 8 4 X D % $ O 8 8 D % % % D O globalization $ = ; : : : : ; ; ; - ~ : ~ - X -
  S % D $ D 8 C % % $ D 4 C C C S O $ $ $ $ $ % % $ $ $ $ % $ $ 4 = = + 1 I - ~ ~ ~ I 1 I 1 X 1
.D D $ $ $ $ D D 8 C X X C X O % % $ $ D O S 8 and $ $ $ $ $ % D S C = X X X X C C C C C X =
 : 4 D $ $ D D C 4 X X X X X X C O O S S 8 % % $ % % $ $ $ $ $ $ $ $ % S X C O D O S C 4 1 + X X
 : % % $ $ O S D 4 1 1 = + = X = X X X C 4 education $ % $ $ $ D X X D % $ C X C C 1 = H
  D $ $ $ % D 8 X = X X X = X X = I + X X X X C = C % D S D C S C 8 O X = = O 8 S 4 C = = C C C =
  X $ $ $ D % D + I = C C C X = I 1 I 1 1 1 X X X C X C D % $ % D % 8 O D C 4 C C = 4 X X X X X -
 : D % % D % $ 4 I = X C X C critical perspectives 8 S C S S X = C X X + +
  I 8 % % % % % C + X = C C X I = X X - - 1 = 4 % $ % $ $ % % D % $ % % D % $ % S + 1 + + + :
   = $ $ $ $ % % X S = = X C = + 1 X + I 1 X + 8 $ $ $ $ $ $ % $ $ % $ $ $ % % O 1 X = + ;
    X $ $ $ $ $ % 8 X X C 4 = I ~ ~ = C D C X 4 % % $ $ $ $ $ $ $ $ $ $ $ % C ~ + 1 :
     I % $ $ $ $ $ % S X C X X = I ~ + % D D % $ D $ $ $ % $ $ % $ % % % $ $ C 4 1 :
      : C $ $ $ $ D 4 S X X = O 4 X ~ X % $ $ $ % % % D % $ % $ % D % % $ D 8 ~
       ; C % $ $ % 8 X X = % D S = + + O % $ % % % % % % % % % $ D 8 % 8 = :
        : + O % $ % O C S C 8 % % % 4 4 8 S O % % % % D D 4 4 = ~ .
         : ~ X O 8 D % % % % % D D 8 S 4 S 8 O 8 4 1 I .
          : ; - - I X X X 1 - I I I ; : .
```

edited by

nicholas c. burbules
carlos alberto torres

Routledge

New York   London

Published in 2000 by
Routledge
29 West 35th Street
New York, NY 10001

Published in Great Britain by
Routledge
11 New Fetter Lane
London EC4P 4EE

Copyright © 2000 by Routledge

Printed in the United States of America on acid-free paper.

Globalization and education: critical perspectives / Nicholas C. Burbules and
Carlos Alberto Torres, eds.
    p.   cm. — (Social theory, education, and cultural change)
    Includes bibliographical refrerences and index.
    ISBN 0-415-92048-5 (hard). — ISBN 0-415-92047-7 (pbk.)
    1. Education—Social aspects. 2. Education—Economic aspects. 3. Education
and state. 4. International economic relations. 5. International education. 6.
Critical pedagogy. I. Burbules, Nicholas C. II. Torres, Carlos Alberto. III. Series.
LC191.G545   1999
370.11'5—dc21   99-23276   CIP

globalization and education

critical perspectives

All systems are false, that of Marx
no less than Aristotle's—however
much truth both may have seen.[1]

Globalization and Education:
An Introduction

Nicholas C. Burbules and Carlos Alberto Torres

**From Education in the Enlightenment to Globalized Education:
Preliminary Thoughts**

This book brings together an outstanding group of international authors to discuss the topic of how globalization is
affecting educational policy in nation-states around the
world. The authors have quite different views of "globalization." For some of these authors, the term refers to the emergence of supranational institutions whose decisions shape
and constrain the policy options for any particular nation-
state; for others, it means the overwhelming impact of global

economic processes, including processes of production, consumption, trade, capital flow, and monetary interdependence; for still others, it denotes the rise of neoliberalism as a hegemonic policy discourse; for some it primarily means the emergence of new global cultural forms, media, and technologies of communication, all of which shape the relations of affiliation, identity, and interaction within and across local cultural settings; and for still others, "globalization" is primarily a *perceived* set of changes, a construction used by state policymakers to inspire support for and suppress opposition to changes because "greater forces" (global competition, responses to IMF or World Bank demands, obligations to regional alliances, and so on) leave the nation-state "no choice" but to play by a set of global rules not of its own making. Of course, each of the authors cites the complex interplay of these various factors with different weights and in different relations.

We asked each author to focus on a concept that we thought was central to understanding the particular impact of globalization on educational policy and practice, concepts that are being rethought and redefined in this (real or perceived) global context. These concepts include: "neoliberalism," "the state," "restructuring," "reform," "management," "feminism," "identity," "citizenship," "community," "multiculturalism," "new social movements," "popular culture," and "the local" (as opposed to/in relation to "the global"). Clearly, these reflect not only changing concepts but also changing relations, practices, and institutional arrangements. This book's focus is how the rethinking of these key ideas suggests fundamental changes to the way societies are forming educational policy and practice. While this is primarily a work of theory, these discussions contain specific and concrete implications for how education is changing, and will need to change, in response to new circumstances. The work here is critical to the extent that the authors refuse to accept as given the particular forms that globalization is taking, and ask skeptical questions about the winners and losers by this new set of rules. To the extent that "globalization" (conceived in a particular way) has become an ideological discourse driving change because of a perceived immediacy and necessity to respond to a new world order, we want to present a corrective to the enthusiasts of globalization and suggest that even as these changes occur, they can change in different, more equitable, and more just ways. In our view, educators in particular must acknowledge the force of these trends and see their implications for shaping and constraining the choices available to educational policies and practices while also resisting the rhetoric of "inevitability" that so often drives particular policy prescriptions.

One way to reexamine the apparent inevitability of globalization is to situate the contemporary debate in an historical framework. Something, indeed, does seem to be changing in the field of education, and these changes have been at work for a long period of time. From the perspective of the Enlightenment, nothing could be more personalized, more intimate and local, than the educational process in which children and youth come of age in the context of acquiring and learning their family, regional, and national culture. Before the institution of public education, the education of the elite was carried out by tutors working with their pupils in a highly personalized manner. Education of the mind, of the capacities and talents of the individual, was a basic principle. In a different class context, for children of rural or working families, education or upbringing was also a personal affair, governed by families and local communities. Fitting into a community, whether a local or national culture and way of life, can be seen as the educational imperative cutting across these contexts.

Later, when schooling as a public institution took shape, this notion of local and familial responsibility for upbringing remained. The idea that schools acted *in loco parentis,* reinforced by policy structures supporting community control over schooling, situated the learner in a relation to immediate and familiar learning needs: needs of identity, affiliation, citizenship, and work roles that responded to a context already close at hand. Even in more centralized, nationalized public school systems the same dynamic can be seen at work, invoked at a different level: policies enforce conformity and identification with a national tradition, a larger community, and a broader context of citizenship and work responsibility, but still one in which the conditions of affiliation are based on relative proximity and homogeneity (although here fissures between the local and the national can—and still do—crack open).

The implications of this educational process, especially as it becomes a public concern, go well beyond the aim of developing the individual self. As the economics of education tell us, the education of the public has costs and benefits for the society at large and therefore is not only an expenditure but also an investment. Thus, the political implications of education surpass the conditions of an individual to be educated and constitute a strategic set of decisions that affect society at large, hence the importance of education as public policy and the role of the state (see Raymond Morrow and Carlos Torres, in this volume).[2]

This dialectical process of forming the individual as a self and as a member of a larger community implies, as a premise in the Western tradition, the need to preserve the treasures of the civilization within the process of socializing the members of each new generation. This becomes even more of an imperative as the nation-state becomes the site, surrounded by borders, in which the pedagogical process is governed. Organized systems of education operate under the aegis of a nation-state that controls, regulates, coordinates, mandates, finances, and certifies the process of teaching and learning. Not surprisingly, a principal purpose of the educational system so designed is to create a loyal and competent citizen.

The question we face now is: To what extent is the educational endeavor affected by processes of globalization that are threatening the autonomy of national educational systems and the sovereignty of the nation-state as the ultimate ruler in democratic societies?[3] At the same time, how is globalization changing the fundamental conditions of an educational system premised on fitting into a community characterized by proximity and familiarity? The origins, nature, and dynamics of the process of globalization are, therefore, a focus of concern for educational philosophers, sociologists, curriculum workers, teachers, policymakers, politicians, parents, and many others involved with the educational endeavor. The processes of globalization, however defined, seem to have serious consequences for transforming teaching and learning as they have been understood within the context of educational practices and public policies that are highly national in character.

Many further questions recur in such reflections. How can globalization be defined? Is globalization "real" or merely an ideology? If globalization is an inexorable trend, how does this affect the political economy of countries and, in turn, their culture and education? How are moves toward economic restructuring affecting educational systems worldwide? Is there an international educational organization and agenda that could create a new hegemony in curriculum, instruction, and pedagogical practices, in general, as well as in policies concerning school financing, research, and evaluation? Are these factors and outcomes symmetrical or homogeneous in their implications for all countries and regions? How does globalization relate to the ongoing process of political struggle in different societies? These are some of the central questions that the contributors to this book have undertaken to answer.

Economic Restructuring and the Trend toward Globalization

> In order to capture the gist of social action, we must recognize the onto-logical complicity, as Heidegger and Merleu-Ponty suggested, between the agent (who is neither a subject or a consciousness, nor the mere exe-cutant of a role or the carrier of a function) and the social world (which is never a mere "thing" even if it must be constructed as such in the objectivist phase of research). Social reality exists, so to speak, twice, in things and in minds, in fields and in habitus, outside and inside of agents. And when habitus encounters a social world of which it is the product, it finds itself "as a fish in water," it does not feel the weight of the water and takes the world about itself for granted.[4]

The patterns of global economic restructuring, which emerged in the late seventies, went hand in hand with the implementation of neoliberal policies in many nations. At that time, capitalist management was caught in a profit squeeze, with labor fighting to keep wages high and foreign competitors pressing them to keep prices down. As the economy slowed, state revenues failed to keep pace with social expenditures, and taxpayers began to express resentment toward those who benefited the most from state revenues (the state bureaucracy, welfare recipients, institutions receiving state subsidies, and so on). This led to a breakdown of consensus around the viability and value of the welfare state. The state withdrew from its role as an arbiter between labor and capital, allying itself with capital and pushing labor into a defensive position.[5]

Economic restructuring reflected a world trend characterized by at least the following elements:

1. the globalization of the economy in the context of a new international division of labor and economic integration of national economies (such as emerging common markets and trade agreements)[6];

2. the emergence of new exchange relations and arrangements among nations, and among classes and social sectors within each country, and the emergence of new areas, especially in developed countries, where information and services are becoming more important than manufacturing;

3. the increasing internationalization of trade, reflected in the increasing capacity to connect markets on an immediate basis and to move capital across national frontiers (currently 600 major multinational corporations [MNCs] control 25 percent of the world economy and 80 percent of world trade);

4. the restructuring of the labor market, with the hourly wage being replaced in many settings by piecework remuneration, and the power of unions undermined by a relaxation or nonenforcement of labor legislation;

5. the decrease in capital-labor conflict, mainly due to such factors as the increase of surplus workers (unemployed or underemployed), the intensification of competition; the decrease of profit margins, less protective labor contracts, and the institutionalization of "team concept" strategies;

6. the shift from a rigid Fordist model of production to a model based upon increased flexibility in the use of the labor force, inventories, labor processes, and labor markets, and upon the declining costs and increasing speed of moving products and information from one location of the globe to another;

7. the rise of new forces of production, with industry shifting from an industrial-mechanical model to one governed by the microchip, robotics, and automatic, self-regulating machines, which in turn has led to the emergence of a high-tech information society based on the computer;

8. the growing importance of capital-intensive production, which results in the de-skilling or redundancy of large sections of the workforce, a situation that leads to a polarized labor market composed of a small, highly skilled, and well-paid sector on the one hand, and a large, low-skilled, and low-paid sector on the other;

9. the increase in the proportion of part-time and female workers, many of them now working out of their homes;

10. the increase in the size and importance of the service sector, at the

expense of primary and secondary ones; and

11. the ever-increasing financial, technological, and cultural gap between more-developed and less-developed countries, with the only exception being the "newly industrialized countries" (NICs).[7]

Economic restructuring also has reflected a deep fiscal crisis and budget reductions affecting the public sector have resulted in the reduction of the welfare state and increased privatization of social services, health, housing, and education. There has been a restructuring of the state/worker relationship in such a way that the social salary (public expenditure distributed in the form of social benefits) diminishes at the expense of individual salaries. As a result of this, society has been segmented into two sectors: one protected or included by the state, and the other unprotected and excluded.[8] Economic restructuring has led to a model of exclusion that leaves out large sectors of the population, particularly women living in poverty in developed and developing countries.

These elements of economic restructuring have been concomitant with the trend toward globalization. Contrary to Marx and Engels's prediction, the globalization of the economy has produced a unification of capital on a world scale, while workers and other subordinate groups have become more fragmented and divided. In fact, neoliberal restructuring is operating through the impersonal dynamic of capitalist competition in a progressively deregulated common market, enhancing the local impact of global trends. Nation-states have become increasingly internationalized, in the sense that their agencies and policies become adjusted to the rhythms of the new world order.

As we have pointed out, economic restructuring has led to an increasing proletarianization and de-skilling of jobs. Although high technology is presented as the solution to many economic problems, it has not contributed to raising the standard of living of most people. Even if some jobs are being created in high-tech industries, these jobs are mostly in clerical and assembly work, which pay below-average wages and do not require high skills, or in personal services jobs. Not surprisingly, the most important category of job creation in the United States in the last decade has been in the realm of personal services, including job categories as varied as physical and health trainers to private security services.[9]

Another evident change is that, with the implementation of neoliberal policies, the state has withdrawn from its responsibility to administer public resources to promote social justice. This is being replaced by a blind faith in the market (for example, in calls for increased school privatization, "choice," and vouchers) and the hope that economic growth will generate a spillover to help the poor, or that private charity will pick up what state programs leave out. Despite calls from the Right to dismantle or reduce the size of the state, skeptical observers of state reduction argue that the main issue is not the state's size, or its expenditures, but the *type* of its interventions and investments, whether promoting welfare and equality, on the one hand, or subsidizing corporate growth through tax incentives or through the rubric of "military spending," on the other. The neoliberal state, particularly in the more developed societies, and in the developing countries striving to emulate them, is characterized by drastic cutbacks in social spending, rampant environmental destruction, regressive revisions of the tax system, loosened constraints on corporate growth, widespread attacks on organized labor, and increased spending on military "infrastructure."

Corporations are becoming so powerful that many are creating their own postsecondary and vocational education programs. Burger King has opened "academies" in fourteen U.S. cities, and IBM and Apple are contemplating the idea of opening schools for profit. Whittle Communications (a corporation largely owned by Time Warner and the British Associated Newspapers) not only provides satellite dishes and TV sets in exchange for advertisement to more than ten thousand schools (the Channel One project) but also it is planning to open one thousand profit-making schools serving two million children within the next ten years.[10] Moreover, U.S. corporations are spending nearly $40 billion each year, approaching the total annual expenditures of all U.S. four-year and graduate colleges and universities, to train and educate their current employees. Even as early as the mid-eighties, Bell and Howell had thirty thousand students in its postsecondary network, and ITT had twenty-five postsecondary proprietary institutions.[11] It has been reported that AT&T alone performs more education and training functions than any university in the world.[12]

This process of privatizing education is occurring in the context of new relations and arrangements among nations, characterized by a new global division of labor, an economic integration of national economies (common markets, free trade, and so forth), the increasing concentration of power in supranational organizations (such as the World Bank, IMF, UN, E.U., and

G-7), and what we have called the "internationalization" of nation-states.

The mobility of capital gives capitalists, particularly financial speculators, a great deal of leverage over the nation-state, itself a product of the industrial revolution, and one unequipped in many ways to cope with the basic demands of the postindustrial world. Speculation in national currencies and the self-fulfilling prophecy of international "credit" legitimacy have contributed to an ever-shifting terrain for countries attempting to get their economic houses in order. The days leading up to the preparation of this book have seen serious currency crises in Russia, the Philippines, Malaysia, and other emerging Asian economies, which suddenly found the rules of the global economic game changing even as they were trying to play by them.

As argued by Korten, corporate influence over the nation-state is exercised indirectly, through intellectual leadership, instilling in policymakers a new set of values and setting limits on the nation-state's range of options, which is a more effective strategy in changing policy priorities than the explicit threat of punitive sanctions.[13] These new values, aptly reflected in the neoconservative and neoliberal agendas (see Michael W. Apple, in this volume),[14] promote less state intervention and greater reliance on the free market, and more appeal to individual self-interest than to collective rights. David Held claims, "The internationalization of production, finance and other economic resources is unquestionably eroding the capacity of any individual state to control its own economic future . . . . Multinational corporations may have a clear national base, but their interest is above all in global profitability. Country of origin is of little consequence for corporate strategy."[15] Clearly, the growing integration of the economy pushes toward a borderless world and provides considerable evidence for the reduced ability of national governments to control their own economies or to define their own national economic aims.[16]

In summary, there are changes at the economic, political, and cultural levels of society that tend to promote and reinforce a more global perspective on social policy. At an economic level, these factors include changes in *trade* relations (groups such as GATT, or G-7, that promote the reduction of import taxes, tariffs, and regulations; and the formation of "free-trade" regions such as NAFTA or the E.U.); changes in *banking and credit* processes (world credit systems such as Visa, ATMs, currency exchange, and capital flow and financial markets that are truly globalized); the presence of *international lending agencies* (such as the IMF and World Bank); changes in the factors of *production* that have led to the rise of new "post-Fordist" industries (the knowledge economy, the service sector, tourism, and culture industries); the presence of *global corporations* not tied to (or loyal to) any national base or boundary; the *mobility of labor* and the *mobility of companies*, which have thrown labor unions on the defensive; new *technologies* (for the transmission of data, capital, and advertising); and new patterns of *consumption* (sometimes termed the "McDonaldization" of taste—fast, standardized, and oriented to convenience over quality), along with new advertising and marketing strategies that promote what George Ritzer calls the "means of consumption" (shopping malls, television buying channels, on-line purchasing, and easy credit).[17]

At the political level, the nation-state survives as a medial institution, far from powerless, but constrained by trying to balance four imperatives: (1) responses to transnational capital; (2) responses to global political structures (for example, the United Nations) and other nongovernmental organizations; (3) responses to domestic pressures and demands, in order to maintain its own political legitimacy[18]; and (4) responses to its own internal needs and self-interests. Most policy initiatives, including educational policies, are formed in the matrix of these four pressures, centered on the nation-state conceived no longer as a sovereign agent, but rather as an arbiter attempting to balance a range of internal and external pressures and constraints. Economic factors, such as external debt, the fiscal crisis of the state, or the creation of regional entities such as the European Union are having profound political-economic implications.[19] In this context, the pressures on the nation-state have sharpened a long-standing question of political theory: Is the state a pluralist sphere for the contest of competing interest groups, or is it a nonneutral terrain, reflecting a set of constraints and preoccupations that give special weight to the demands of specific social interests? It is clear to us that there has been a pronounced shift in the terms of such a question, moving beyond purely statist views of politics to include a focus on new terrains of political contestation, new political actors, such as global social movements (what Falk calls "globalization from below"), and the constitution of what are, in effect, transnational civil societies (see Douglas Kellner, in this volume).[20]

Finally, in cultural terms, changes in global media (cable, satellite, CNN, the Internet); commercial culture (McDonalds, Nike, the colors of Benneton); increased mobility, with vastly enlarged travel and tourism sectors; changes in communications technologies; worldwide distribution of film, television, and music products; an increased presence and visibility of global religions that change local rituals into transnational ones; or the global world of sports, both in terms of competitive events (and spectacles) like the Olympics or World Cup and also, significiantly, in terms of sports marketing (apparel, footwear, equipment), sponsosrhip/advertising, and global betting and gambling, all show the challenges that confront societies attempting to reconcile their own local and traditional values with the growing globalization of cultures not of their making.

These undeniable changes notwithstanding, however, the effects of globalization are also sometimes exaggerated. Any good observer or world traveler will have noticed that the so-called process of globalization is not so global. Vast segments of the world are almost untouched by many of these globalization dynamics. What we are seeing is a segmentation (worldwide) between a globalized culture—for instance, the prevalence of an urban, cosmopolitan habitus—and the rest of the world, which sees few of the benefits (to the extent that there are such) of access to the global market or to cosmopolitan cultures. Likewise, as noted previously, the assertion of something called "globalization" is often used to reinforce its "inevitability" and so to suppress attempts to resist it, yet many attempts to counteract globalization processes are well in place around the world, as in the fields of ecology and resource management, for example.[21]

Critical Issues

> Knowledge does not itself conquer uncertainty but produces uncertainties that no one has had any historical experience in dealing with before.[22]

Although the overall shape and direction of the changes just noted are hardly matters of dispute any longer, there still remain significant disagreements about the nature and extent of this thing called "globalization." The more that we know about it, the greater the uncertainties about the consequences it brings with it. These questions become even more challenging as we attempt to move from the kind of macrolevel changes we have been surveying to specific areas of policy and practice such as education. We have grouped together here several critical issues which, as Giddens reminds us, reflect the new uncertainties that discussions of globalization have brought to light. They serve to introduce several central themes that will be taken up by the various chapters in this book.

What are the Origins of Globalization?   Theoretically, a central dilemma is whether to place the origins of contemporary globalization around 1971–1973, with the petroleum crisis that prompted several important technological and economic changes directed toward finding replacement sources for strategic raw materials and searching for new forms of production that would consume less energy and labor. Alternatively, one may, as some authors in this book have done, pinpoint the origins of globalization more than a century ago with changes in communication technologies, migration patterns, and capital flows (for instance, as these affected the process of colonization in the Third World).

An important question for many observers is whether we are facing a new historical epoch, the configuration of a new world system, or whether these changes are significant but not unprecedented, paralleled for example by similar changes in the late Middle Ages. But in our view this issue is not a matter of either/or. We are in a new historical epoch, a new global order in which the old forms are not dead but the new forms are not yet fully formed. David Held has suggested in his *Democracy and Global Order*, for instance, that we are in a new "global Middle Ages," a period reflecting that while the nation-states still have vitality, they cannot control their borders and therefore are subject to all sorts of internal and external pressures.

Furthermore, even if this new global order shows the end of the sovereignty of the nation-state, this situation nevertheless has differential impacts on states according to their position in the world order: states unified in regional alliances, such as NAFTA or the E.U.; emerging or intermediate states, such as Brazil, Korea, India, and China; less-developed states, such as Argentina, Hungary, Chile, and South Africa; developing states, including many in Latin America, Asia, and Africa; and underdeveloped states mired in an extreme state of dependency, such as Haiti, some Central American states, Mozambique, Angola, and Albania. Not only is the meaning and impact of "globalization" unsettled, but also it may operate differently in different parts of the world and, in some contexts, have little impact at all. Here, again, globalization is not itself a unified, global phenomenon.

Hence while globalization may reflect a set of very definite technological, economic, and cultural changes, the shape of its significance and its future trends are far from determined. As we have just noted, the historical specificity of this process does not necessarily guarantee a symmetrical or homogeneous impact worldwide. This account of globalization is quite different from the neoliberal account, a discourse about progress and a rising tide that lifts all boats, a discourse that takes advantage of the historical processes of globalization in order to valorize particular economic prescriptions about how to operate the economy (through free trade, deregulation, and so on)—and by implication, prescriptions about how to transform education, politics, and culture.

Beyond Dichotomous Accounts of Globalization. Certain dualities recur in the literature on this subject. In one widely influential distinction, there are two primary forces at work in the rise of globalization: globalization from above, a process that primarily affects the elites within and across national contexts, and globalization from below, a popular process that primarily draws from the rank-and-file in civil society.[23] This contrast highlights an important political dynamic (and it makes for a handy, hopeful picture of struggle and resistance on a world scale), but its widespread use obscures the ways in which these two trends are not entirely independent of one another. For example, the groups from "above" and "below" tend to merge in certain nongovernmental organizations; and the popular movements "from below" may still be perceived in certain local contexts as an imposition "from above."

Still other dualities prevail: between the global and the local; between economic and cultural dimensions of globalization; between globalization viewed as a trend toward homogenization around Western (or, even more narrowly, around American) norms and culture, and globalization viewed as an era of increased contact between diverse cultures, leading to an increase in hybridization and novelty; and between the material and rhetorical effects of globalization—or, as it might be put, between globalization and "globalization." Finally, there is the question of whether globalization is a "good thing": Is globalization beneficial to the cause of economic growth, equality, and justice, or is it harmful? Does it promote cultural sharing, tolerance, and a cosmopolitan spirit, or does it yield only the illusion of such understanding, a bland, consumerist appreciation, as in a Disney theme park, which elides issues of conflict, difference, and asymmetries of power?

For us, none of these either/ors captures the subtlety or difficulty of the issues at stake. Each replicates an easy choice between polar alternatives, "good" and "bad" kinds of globalization, rather than a conflicted situation of sustained tensions and difficult choices. A reconsideration of, and in many cases a direct challenge to, these sorts of easy dichotomies will recur throughout this book. It is, in our view, central to understanding globalization in all its complexity and ambiguity.

What are the Crucial Characteristics of Globalization? In light of these many debates, it could be extremely risky to advance a description of the characteristics of globalization that most closely affect education, but these seem to include, at the very least:

- in *economic terms*, a transition from Fordist to post-Fordist forms of workplace organization; a rise in internationalized advertising and consumption patterns; a reduction in barriers to the free flow of goods, workers, and investments across national borders; and, correspondingly, new pressures on the roles of worker and consumer in society;

- in *political terms*, a certain loss of nation-state sovereignty, or at least the erosion of national autonomy, and, correspondingly, a weakening of the notion of the "citizen" as a unified and unifying concept, a concept that can be characterized by precise roles, rights, obligations, and status (see Capella, in this volume);

- in *cultural terms*, a tension between the ways in which globalization brings forth more standardization and cultural homogeneity while also bringing more fragmentation through the rise of locally oriented movements. Benjamin Barber characterized this dichotomy in the title of his book, *Jihad vs. McWorld*[24]; however, a third theoretical alternative identifies a more conflicted and dialectical situation, with both cultural homogeneity and cultural heterogeneity appearing simultaneously in the cultural landscape. (Sometimes this merger, and dialectical tension, between the global and the local is termed "the glocal."[25])

Globalization and the State-Education Relationship

In *educational terms*, there is a growing understanding that the neoliberal version of globalization, particularly as implemented (and ideologically defended) by bilateral, multilateral, and international organizations, is reflected in an educational agenda that privileges, if not directly imposes, particular policies for evaluation, financing, assessment, standards, teacher training, curriculum, instruction, and testing. In the face of such pressures, more study is needed about local responses to defend public education against the introduction of pure market mechanisms to regulate educational exchanges and other policies that seek to reduce state sponsorship and financing and to impose management and efficiency models borrowed from the business sector as a framework for educational decisionmaking.[26] These educational responses are mostly carried out by teacher unions, new social movements, and critical intellectuals, often expressed as opposition to initiatives in education such as vouchers or publicly subsidizing private and parochial schools.

This poses a peculiar problem for analysis. Because the relationships between state and education vary so dramatically according to historical epochs, geographical areas, modes of governance, and forms of political representation, and between the differential demands of varied educational levels (elementary, secondary, higher education, adult, continuing, and non-formal education), any drastic alteration of modes of governance (for instance, the installation of a military dictatorship that may rule for several years before yielding back to democracy) can have multiple, complex, and unpredictable effects on education. This situation calls for a more nuanced historical analysis of the state-education relationship. This problematic is made more difficult by the trend we have discussed above: the erosion in the autonomy of the nation-state in all matters, including educational policy matters.[27]

For example, let us consider briefly the situation in Latin America. From the moment in which civil wars were ended, more than a century and a half ago (culminating in the process of national organization in the 1880s), educational systems were created alongside the establishment of borders for countries. The constitution of the nation-states included the creation of strong armies and the promulgation of national constitutions based on principles drawing from the British Magna Carta, the American Revolution, and the French Revolution, and therefore expressing a strongly liberal underpinning. Thus, at least three primary state formations predominated in the Latin American experience during the last century and a half. (The exceptions to this trend have been, of course, periods of military intervention, military dictatorship, and revolution, all of which alter the liberal-democratic state form.) These three forms of the state include the *liberal* state promoting liberal education (say, from the 1880s until the crisis of 1929 in some countries, or until around the Second World War in most countries); the *developmentalist* state (around the 1950s until the 1980s), in which there is a consistent pattern of modernization (though sometimes "forced" modernization through authoritarian regimes), with a central role played by educational reforms based on the human capital model; and the constitution of different forms of the *neoliberal* state and neoliberal educational policy.[28]

In short, from a historical perspective, this complex connection between education and the state poses a problem for the analysis of the state-education relationship. There is no single way in which these institutions are associated, and so no single way in which they will be affected by the conditions of globalization. Economically, the pressures of externally imposed austerity conditions (for example, as a condition of IMF loans) may lead to savage reductions in expenditures on education; in other contexts, the desire for increased economic competitiveness and productivity may lead to increased expenditures on education. Politically, some national contexts will organize education around a revitalized conception of nationalism and citizen loyalty (perhaps in reaction to tribal or other fractious loyalties); in other contexts, a notion of cosmopolitan citizenship may prevail, one encouraging travel, foreign language study, and multicultural tolerance. Culturally, some nations will accept, even encourage, an increased reliance on the media, popular culture, or new communication and information technology as a window through which to understand one's place in a global world; in other contexts these same trends will give rise to an increase in insularism, suspicion, and resistance to external influences. A book such as this can only begin the process of exploring the diversity of such responses to globalization, across varied national contexts, and the diversity of state-education relationships that generate educational principles, policies, and practices in light of these new conditions.

The Dilemmas of Globalization

Is globalization merely deleterious, or are there positive features associated with its practices and dynamics? We have already tried to challenge such an easy frame of judgment. Two features that might be termed "positive" are the globalization of democracy or, at least, a peculiar form of liberal democracy (more a democracy of method than a democracy of content);[29] and the prevalence and expansion of a belief in "human rights" and the growth of organizations attempting to monitor and protect them. For those fortunate enough to be living in certain sectors of society, globalization is associated with a higher standard of living, not only in the availability of consumer goods but also in occasions for travel and for enriching contact with other world cultures.

The most obvious "evils" of globalization are structural unemployment, the erosion of organized labor as a political and economic force, social exclusion, and an increase in the gap between rich and poor within nations and, especially, worldwide. Some people associate globalization with an increase in urban insecurity due to growing urban violence, with the growing presence of extraterritorial, extrastate movements that thwart international development and may pose serious threats to security, peace, stability, and development (such as drug trafficking, mafias, merchants of weapons of mass destruction, or terrorist organizations).

But is it possible to sort out the benefits from the evils? Indeed, are "benefits" from one standpoint "evils" from the standpoint of others? In one sense, the framework of such judgments needs to be not simply a matter of whether globalization is "really happening" or not, but of globalization *in what respects* and *on whose terms*? A number of developing countries, such as China or Malaysia, have become increasingly suspicious of globalization and have tried to find ways to constrain its effects on their national way of life. Yet, at the same time they desire some of the benefits of participation in a global economy and exchange of goods and information. A major question today is the extent to which societies will be able to pick and choose the ways in which, and the degree to which, they can participate in a global world; or whether, as with other Faustian bargains, there is no halfway alternative.

Similarly, both below and beyond the national level, there are clearly regional and traditional movements for whom globalization is something to be resisted vigorously. The rise of some new social movements and the role of local and international nongovernmental organizations exert an influence that may be termed *counterglobalization*. In some instances these groups are equally "global" in character (international human rights organizations, such as Amnesty International; environmental organizations, such as Greenpeace; or labor organizations, such as the ILO). In other cases they are *antiglobalization*, profoundly resistant to the economic, political, and cultural interpenetration of different societies and cultures (for example, regionalist and fundamentalist groups of various types). While globalization is clearly happening, its form and shape are being determined by patterns of resistance, some with more progressive intentions than others.

Is it possible, then, to give general answers to the question of how globalization is affecting educational policy and practice worldwide? As indicated by our earlier discussion, we believe that there can be no single answer; national and local economic, political, and cultural changes are affected by, and actively responding to, globalizing trends within a broad range of patterns. Indeed, because education is one of the central arenas in which these adaptations and responses occur, it will be one of the most myriad of institutional contexts. Hence, the answers developed will require a careful analysis of trends in education, including:

- the currently popular policy "buzz words" (privatization, choice, and decentralization of educational systems) that drive policy formation in education and prevailing research agendas based in rational organization and management theories (see Michael Peters, James Marshall, and Patrick Fitzsimons, in this volume);

- the role of national and international organizations in education, including teacher unions, parent organizations, and social movements (see Bob Lingard, in this volume);[30]

- the new scholarship on race, class, gender, and the state in education (which raises concerns about multiculturalism and the question of identity in education, critical race theory, feminism, postcolonialism, diasporic communities, and new social movements (see Jill Blackmore; Douglas Kellner; Allan Luke and Carmen Luke; Cameron McCarthy and Greg Dimitriadis; Fazal Rizvi; and Stephen Stoer and Luiza Cortesão, all in this volume).

Questions about the role of participatory action research, popular education, and multicultural democratic struggle emerge as central in these debates. From these critical perspectives might emerge new educational models to confront the winds of change, including education in the context of new popular cultures and nontraditional social movements (and hence the role of cultural studies to understand them); new models of rural education for marginalized areas and the education of the poor; new models for migrant education, for the education of street children, for the education of girls and women, in general, but particularly in the context of traditional societies and cultures that have suppressed women's educational aspirations; new models of partnerships for education (between state, NGO, third-sector, and in some instances religious or private organizations); new models for adult literacy and nonformal education; new models of university/business relationships; and new models for educational financing and school organization (for instance, charter schools).

Some reform initiatives have been actively supported by UNESCO and other UN agencies. These include, for instance, reforms toward universal literacy and universal access to education; educational quality as a key component of equity; education as lifelong education; education as a human right; education for peace, tolerance, and democracy; eco-pedagogy, or how education can contribute to sustainable ecological development (and hence to an eco-economy); and educational access and new technologies of information and communication (see Nicholas C. Burbules, in this volume). Thus, the influence of globalization upon educational policies and practices can be seen to have multiple, and conflicting, effects. Not all of these can be classified simply as beneficial or not, and some are being shaped by active tensions and struggles. The essays in this book illuminate such dilemmas in all their complexity.

Conclusion: Dilemmas of a Globalized Education System

We hope by now that the main purposes of this book have become clear: first, to identify, characterize, and clarify some of the debates surrounding the phenomenon of globalization; and second, to try to understand some of the multiple and complex effects of globalization on educational policy and policy formation. In summarizing some of the consequences of globalization for educational policy, we will follow the previous organization divided into three parts: tracing some of the economic impacts, the political impacts, and the cultural impacts.

At the economic level, because globalization affects employment, it touches upon one of the primary traditional goals of education: preparation for work. Schools will need to reconsider this mission in light of changing job markets in a post-Fordist work environment; new skills and the flexibility to adapt to changing job demands and, for that matter, changing jobs during a lifetime; and dealing with an increasingly competitive international labor pool. Yet, schools are not only concerned with preparing students as producers; increasingly, schools help shape consumer attitudes and practices as well, as encouraged by the corporate sponsorship of educational institutions and of products, both curricular and extracurricular, that confront students every day in their classrooms. This increasing commercialization of the school environment has become remarkably bold and explicit in its intentions (as in the case of Chris Whittle's project, Channel One, discussed previously, which admits quite openly that it offers schools free televisions so as to expose children to a force-fed diet of commercials in their classrooms every day).

The broader economic effects of globalization tend to force national educational policies into a neoliberal framework that emphasizes lower taxes; shrinking the state sector and "doing more with less"; promoting market approaches to school choice (particularly vouchers); rational management of school organizations; performance assessment (testing); and deregulation in order to encourage new providers (including on-line providers) of educational services.[31]

At the political level, a repeated point here has been the constraint on national/state policy making posed by external demands from transnational institutions. Yet, at the same time that economic coordination and exchange have become increasingly well regulated, and as stronger institutions emerge to regulate global economic activity, with globalization there has also been a growing internationalization of global conflict, crime, terrorism, and environmental issues, but with an inadequate development of political institutions to address them. Here, again, educational institutions may have a crucial role to play in addressing these problems, and the complex network of intended and unintended human consequences that have followed from the growth of global corporations, global mobility, global communication, and global expansion. In part, this awareness may help to foster a more critical conception of what education for "world citizenship" requires.

Finally, global changes in culture deeply affect educational policies, practices, and institutions. Particularly in advanced industrial societies, for instance, the question of "multiculturalism" takes on a special meaning in a global context. How does the discourse of liberal pluralism—which has been the dominant framework for multicultural education in developed societies learning to live with others within a compact of mutual tolerance and respect—extend to a global order in which the gulf of differences becomes wider, the sense of interdependence and common interest more attenuated, and the grounding of affiliation more abstract and indirect (if it exists at all)? With the growing global pressures on local cultures, is it education's job to help preserve them? How should education prepare students to deal with the terms of local, regional, national, and transnational conflict, as cultures and traditions whose histories of antagonism may have been held partly in suspension by strong, overarching nation-states break loose when those institutions lose some of their power and legitimacy? To the degree that education can help support the evolving construction of the self and, at a more general level, the constitution of identities, how can multiculturalism as a social movement, as citizenship education, and as an antiracist philosophy in curriculum intervene in the dynamics of social conflict emerging between global transformations and local responses?

In this context, for example, current debates over bilingualism in the United States are surprisingly limited both in their theoretical content and their political foresight. From a theoretical perspective, it really makes no sense to argue *against* the teaching and learning of multiple languages; if anything, students need to develop even more proficiency than just bilingualism. The European experience with youth who are proficient in several languages finds that such skills facilitate interpersonal, academic, and social communication, expand intellectual horizons, and encourage appreciation and tolerance for different cultures.

In this and other respects, the global context presents a fundamentally different sort of challenge to education than in the Enlightenment framework. Whereas previously education was more focused on the needs and development of the individual, with an eye toward helping the person fit into a community defined by relative proximity, homogeneity, and familiarity, education for life in a global world broadens the outlines of "community" beyond the family, the region, or the nation. Today the communities of potential affiliation are multiple, dislocated, provisional, and ever-changing.[32] Family, work, and citizenship, the main sources of identification in Enlightenment education, remain important, certainly, but they are becoming more ephemeral, compromised by mobility (whether voluntary or diasporic) and competition with other sources of affiliation, including the full range of what can be termed, in Benedict Anderson's phrase, "imagined communities."[33] Whereas schools or (before that) tutors acted *in loco parentis*, preparing learners for a relatively predictable range of future opportunities and challenges, schools today confront a series of conflicting, and changing, ad hoc expectations, directed to unpredictable alternative paths of development and to constantly shifting reference points of identification. As a result, educational aims that have more to do with flexibility and adaptability (for instance, in responding to rapidly changing work demands and opportunities), with learning how to coexist with others in diverse (and hence often conflict-riven) public spaces, and with helping to form and support a sense of identity that can remain viable within multiple contexts of affiliation, all emerge as new imperatives.

In closing, we believe that the manner in which such new educational imperatives get worked out in particular national and cultural settings depends upon two overarching sets of issues. The first is whether, given the decreasing role and influence of the nation-state in unilaterally determining domestic policies, and given the fiscal crisis of public revenues in most societies, there will be a corresponding decline in the state's commitment to educational opportunity and equality, or whether there will simply be a greater turn toward the market, privatization, and choice models that regard the public as consumers who will only obtain the education they can afford. More broadly, will these changes produce an overall decline in the civic commitment to public education itself?

The second key issue is whether the troubles that educational systems experience today, which are not all related to the processes of globalization, signal a more deeply felt and decisive dilemma in developed and developing societies: the question of governability in the face of increasing diversity (and an increased awareness of diversity); permeable borders and an explosion in worldwide mobility; and media and technology that create wholly new conditions shaping affiliation and identification. What is the role of education in helping to shape the attitudes, values, and understandings of a multicultural democratic citizen who can be part of this increasingly cosmopolitan world?

At least some of the manifestations of globalization as a historical process are here to stay. Even if the particular form of "globalization" presented by the neoliberal account can be regarded as an ideology that serves to justify policies serving particular interests but not others, the fact is that part of this account is based in real changes (and to be fair, real opportunities, at least for certain fortunate people). The particular ways in which people talk about globalization today may end up being a passing fad. But as the chapters in this book make clear, at a deeper level something is changing in the areas of economy, politics, and culture that will fundamentally alter the terrain of public and private life. Public education today is at a crossroads. If it carries on as usual as if none of these threats (and opportunities) existed, it runs the risk of becoming increasingly superseded by educational influences that are no longer accountable to public governance and control. In our view, nothing less is at stake today than the survival of the democratic form of governance and the role of public education in that enterprise.

Notes

1. Max Horkheimer, *Eclipse of Reason* (New York: Seabury, 1974), 198.
2. Roger Dale, *The State and Education Policy* (Philadelphia: Open University Press, 1989).
3. Boaventura de Sousa Santos, *Reinventar a Democracia: Entre o Pré-contratualism e o Pós-contratualismo* (Universidade de Coimbra: Centro de Estudos Sociais, Portugal, 1998).
4. Pierre Bourdieu, quoted in Loïc J. D. Wacquant, "Toward a Reflexive Sociology: A Workshop with Pierre Bourdieu," in *Social Theory and Sociology: The Classics and Beyond*, ed. Stephen P. Turner (Cambridge, Eng.: Basil Blackwell, 1996), 213–229.
5. Robert B. Reich, *Education and the New Economy* (Washington, D.C.: National Education Association, 1988); and Robert Reich, *The Work of Nations: Preparing Ourselves for 21st Century Capitalism* (New York: Vintage Books, 1992).
6. Andrew Sayer and Richard Walker, *The New Social Economy: Reworking the Division of Labor* (Cambridge and Oxford, Eng.: Blackwell, 1992).
7. Daniel Schugurensky and Carlos Alberto Torres, "Higher Education, Globalization and Exclusion: Latin America and the Caribbean in Comparative Perspective" (paper delivered at the Conference on Public Policy and Higher Education: Cuba, The Dominican Republic, Puerto Rico, and New York, Centro de Estudos

Puertorriqueños, Hunter College of the City of New York and CUNY Dominican Institute, 22–26 April 1997); Daniel García Delgado, *Estado-Nación y Globalización. Fortalezas y Debilidades en el Humbral del Tercer Milenio* (Buenos Aires: Ariel, 1998); Roland Robertson and Habib Haque Khondker, "Discourses of Globalization: Preliminary Considerations," *International Sociology* 13, no. 1 (1998): 25–41; Ray Kiely, "Globalization, Post-Fordism and the Contemporary Context of Development," *International Sociology* 13, no. 1 (1998): 95–116; and Peter Beyer, "Globalization Systems, Global Cultural Models and Religion(s)," *International Sociology* 13, no. 1 (1998): 79–94.

8. Claus Offe, *Disorganized Capitalism* (London: Hutchinson, 1985); and David Harvey, *The Conditions of Postmodernity* (Oxford, Eng.: Basil Blackwell, 1989).

9. Reich, *The Work of Nations.*

10. Michael W. Apple, *Official Knowledge: Democratic Education in a Conservative Age* (New York and London: Routledge, 1993).

11. Daniel C. Levy, *Higher Education and the State in Latin America: Private Challenges to Public Dominance* (Chicago and London: University of Chicago Press, 1986).

12. Schugurensky and Torres, "Higher Education, Globalization, and Exclusion" and Roberto Rodriguez, "Universidad y globalización en América Latina," *Educación Superior y Sociedad* 6, no. 2 (1995): 143–58.

13. David C. Korten, *When Corporations Rule the World* (West Hartford, Conn.: Berrett-Koehler Publishers, Kumarian Press, 1995).

14. Geoff Whitty, "New Right and New Labour: Continuity and Change in Education Policy" (paper delivered at the Annual Conference of the German Association for the Study of British History and Politics, Mülheim, Ruhr, 21–22 May 1998).

15. David Held, ed., *Political Theory Today* (Stanford: Stanford University Press, 1991), 216, 214.

16. Stuart Holland, *Towards a New Bretton Woods: Alternatives for the Global Economy* (Nottingham, Eng.: Spokesman and Associates Research in Economy and Society, 1994); William Peaff, "Get Ready for the Euro to Rock the U.S. Boat," *Los Angeles Times*, 31 Jan. 1998, sec. B-11; and John-Thor Dalburg, "11 Nations Launch Euro in Historic Bid for Unity," *Los Angeles Times*, 1 Jan. 1999, sec. A-1, A21–24. The $1 trillion a day that is now traded around the clock has tripled the figure of 1986. The value of world trade in 1993 was about $8 trillion, a figure twenty times greater in real terms than it was in 1950, and equal to one-third of the gross world product. Foreign direct investment, amounting to some $2 trillion worldwide, is courted by countries throughout the world. The regular flow of companies, technologies, products, and parts between countries undermines the ability of national governments to control their economies or even to define national economic goals. In the new global economy, the "nationality" of products and firms is difficult to assess. See Robert Reich, *The Work of Nations.*

17. George Ritzer, "Globalization, McDonaldization, and Amercianization," in *The McDonaldization Thesis* (London: Sage, 1998), 81–94.

18. Nicholas N. Kittrie, *The War against Authority: From the Crisis of Legitimacy to a New Social Contract* (Baltimore and London: Johns Hopkins University Press, 1995).

19. William Peaff, "Get Ready for the Euro to Rock the U.S. Boat"; and Dalburg, "11 Nations Launch Euro in Historic Bid," second reference.

20. Susan Eckstein, ed., *Power and Popular Protest: Latin American Social Movements* (Berkeley, Los Angeles, and London: University of California Press, 1989); and Richard Falk, "The Making of Global Citizenship," in J. Brecher, J. B. Childs, and J. Cutler, eds., *Global Visions: Beyond the New World Order* (Montreal: Black Rose Books, 1993), 39–50.

21. Jonathan A. Fox and L. David Brown, *The Struggle for Accountability: The World Bank, NGOs, and Grassroots Movements* (Cambridge: MIT Press, 1998); Jerry Mander and Edward Goldsmith, *The Case against the Global Economy and for a Turn toward the Local* (San Francisco: Sierra Club, 1996); and Korten, *When Corporations Rule.*

22. Rita Caccamo, "The Transition to Late Modern Society: A Conversation with Anthony Giddens," *International Sociology* 13, no. 1 (1998): 128.

23. Carlos Alberto Torres, *Education, Democracy and Multiculturalism: Dilemmas of Citizenship in a Multicultural Society* (Ladham, Md.: Rowman and Littlefield, 1998); Falk, "The Making of Global Citizenship"; see also Douglas Kellner, in this volume.

24. Benjamin Barber, *Jihad vs. McWorld* (New York: Ballantine Books, 1995).

25. See Robert Arnove and Carlos Alberto Torres, eds., *Comparative Education: The Dialectic of the Global and the Local* (Lahman, Md.: Rowman and Littlefiield, 1999).

26. Joel Samoff, *Coping with Crisis: Austerity, Adjustment, and Human Resources* (London and New York: Cassell, 1994); William C. Ayers and Janet L. Miller, eds., *A Light in Dark Times: Maxine Greene and the Unfinished Conversation* (New York: Teachers College Press, 1998); Fox and Brown, *The Struggle for Accountability*; see also Michael W. Apple, in this volume.

27. Sousa Santos, *Reinventar a Democracia*; see also Raymond A. Morrow and Carlos Alberto Torres, in this volume.

28. There were, of course, revolutionary state experiences and socialist experiences, the most important one being the Cuban Revolution, which altered the principles of democratic governance. Every typology is tentative and tries to encapsulate patterns of generalization or rules in the context of historical productions, rather than the exceptions that, sometimes, and particularly in education, have given birth to the most exciting educational experiences in the region. [Carlos Alberto Torres and Adriana Puiggrós, eds., *Latin American Education: Comparative Perspectives* (Boulder: Westview, 1997); Carlos Alberto Torres, "The State, Nonformal Education, and Socialism in Cuba, Nicaragua, and Grenada," *Comparative Education Review* 35, no. 1 (1991): 110–30; and M. Carnoy and Carlos Alberto Torres, "Education and Social Transformation in Nicaragua (1979–1989)," in *Education and the Social Transition in the Third World: China, Cuba, Tanzania, Mozambique and Nicaragua*, ed. M. Carnoy and J. Samoff, with A. M. Burris, A. Jonhston, and Carlos Alberto Torres (Princeton: Princeton University Press, 1990), 315–57.] For more on the neoliberal state, see Raymond A. Morrow and Carlos Alberto Torres, in this volume.

29. Torres, *Education, Democracy and Multiculturalism.*

30. Juan Pravda, "Educational Decentralization in Latin America, Lessons Learned," (Washington, D.C.: Human Resources Division, Technical Department, Latin America and the Caribbean, the World Bank, 15 Dec. 1991), mimeographed.

31. Geoff Whitty and Tony Edwards, "School Choice Policies in England and the United States: An Exploration of their Origins and Significance," *Comparative*

Education 34, no. 2 (1998): 211–27.

32. See Nicholas C. Burbules, in this volume.

33. Benedict Anderson, *Imagined Communities* (New York: Verso, 1991).

The State, Globalization, and Educational Policy

Raymond A. Morrow and Carlos Alberto Torres

What is Globalization?

Whatever its other merits, the preoccupation with postmodernist theory has had two disabling effects. On the one hand, in its challenge to traditional forms of social science, it has distracted attention away from attempting to understand the structural forces that continue to drive social change. On the other hand, in focusing on the supposed autonomy, spontaneity, and contested character of postmodern culture, it has often glossed over the continuing strategic role of the state in the context of cultural policy. The problematic of globalization potentially provides a useful framework for addressing the weaknesses of so-called "postmodern" approaches, especially in the context of education and educational policy studies.[1]

Our position here is somewhat paradoxical in that we simultaneously acknowledge that globalization has a long history, and yet we also are concerned with the novel features of more recent developments. At least three basic stances have been taken with respect to the origins of globalization. Some have argued that its origins lie with that of human civilization generally, hence it is part of a process that is now more than five centuries old. In this formulation, the problematic of globalization originates with the emergence of universalistic religions that established the universal-particular dichotomy that culminates in the contemporary problematic of globalization.[2] A second, more influential, approach—world-systems theory—links globalization with the origins of capitalism, culminating in the sixteenth-century emergence of a global economy.[3] But a third perspective—which has exploded in the 1990s as the most typical form of "globalization theory"—considers globalization a more recent phenomenon, dating at the earliest from the mid-twentieth century or perhaps the last two decades. Anticipations of this type of analysis can be found in the theories of postindustrial society that emerged in the 1960s. But the decisive shift came with the literature in the 1970s and 1980s on the so-called "post-Fordist" transformation of production processes as a global process, as well as related accounts of an information society, cultural globalization, or a postmodern culture.[4]

Our discussion of the relationship between education and globalization takes as foundational the globalizing processes unleashed by capitalism as a world system. Such accounts take as their focus of analysis the role of educational systems in the formation and reproduction of the capitalist nation-states,[5] as well as the theme of colonialism and imperialism in the context of the contradictory universalism of European "Enlightenment."[6] But our focus here is on the more recent phase of the formation of a world system, one in which the notion of globalization has taken on new and distinctive connotations with differential implications for "First," "Second," "Third," and "Fourth" Worlds. As we will see, one of the most fundamental implications of contemporary globalization centers around the changed relationship between education and the state. While the rhetoric of neoconservatism and neoliberalism calls for a diminishing role of the state and the de facto de-statization of civil societies, the role of the state has remained key in the articulation of social interests and the representation of groups and classes that benefit or suffer from the processes of modernization and public policy formation. Nevertheless, it is also clear that globalization dramatically alters many of the ways in which states mediate power at both the substate and transnational levels.

Globalization has been defined as "the intensification of worldwide social relations which link distant localities in such a way that local happenings are shaped by events occurring many miles away and vice versa."[7] David Held suggests, among other things, that globalization is the product of the emergence of a global economy, expansion of transnational linkages between economic units creating new forms of collective decision making, development of intergovernmental and quasi-supranational institutions, intensification of transnational communications, and the creation of new regional and military orders. The process of globalization is seen as blurring national boundaries, shifting solidarities within and between nation-states, and deeply affecting the constitution of national and interest-group identities.

It is useful for introductory purposes to distinguish globalization processes in the contexts of economic, political, and cultural life.[8] But with respect to education, it is the interplay between the economic and political contexts of globalization that has driven most discussions of the need for educational reform. Although the important question of cultural globalization overlaps with the problematic of multiculturalism in education, space limitations preclude taking these issues up in this essay.[9]

The Network Society Thesis

Three distinct but overlapping literatures have illuminated various aspects of the process of globalization in its most recent—and some would argue, revolutionary—phase. The earlier postindustrial society literature stressed the evolution of the economy toward the production of services and the primacy of knowledge in production.[10] Closely related theories of the information society shifted the focus to the role of communication and computerization as part of the knowledge complex underlying postindustrial transformation.[11] These theories share an analysis of the development of capitalism based on three major technological thresholds or "revolutions": the initial eighteenth-century revolution based on the steam engine;

the late-nineteenth-century transformation based on advances in electrical and chemical industries; and the third revolution based on control and communications technologies, culminating in the computer revolution.[12] The third body of literature concerned with post-Fordism reinterprets the evidence analyzed by postindustrial and information society theories, but shifts the focus of analysis from the "forces" of production (that is, technologies) to the "relations" of production. In contrast to the centrally organized assembly line of Fordist industrial organization, post-Fordist production is organized around strategies of flexible production, which allow shorter runs of more differentiated goods.[13]

From a post-Fordist perspective, the new global economy is very different from the former national economy. What is most novel is not the expansion and volume of trade or the international division of labor as such. As critics of simplistic theories of globalization have pointed out, the current quantitative trends in global movement of goods and people can be traced back to the nineteenth century; moreover, multinational corporations have not necessarily evolved into "transnational" ones that undermine the older system of national economies as bases of politics and economic power.[14]

The more significant shifts have taken place in the organization of production and its relation to knowledge and information. National economies were previously based on standardized mass production, with a few managers controlling the production process from above and a great number of workers following orders. This economy of mass production was stable as long as it could reduce its costs of production (including the price of labor) and retool quickly enough to remain competitive at the international level. Because of advances in communications and transportation technology and the growth of service industries, production has become fragmented around the world. The new global economy is more fluid and flexible, with multiple lines of power and decision-making mechanisms, analogous to a spider's web, as opposed to the static pyramidal organization of power that characterized the traditional capitalist system.[15]

One of the most theoretically ambitious and empirically detailed accounts of globalization that synthesizes themes based on information society theory and post-Fordist theories of production has recently been published by Manuel Castells in the three volumes of *The Information*

Age: Economy Society and Culture. As he concludes:

> A new economy has emerged in the last two decades on a worldwide
> scale. I call it informational and global to identify its fundamental
> distinctive features and to emphasize their intertwining. It is *infor-*
> *mational* because the productivity and competitiveness of units or
> agents in this economy (be it firms, regions, or nations) fundamen-
> tally depend upon their capacity to generate, process, and apply effi-
> ciently knowledge-based information. It is *global* because the core
> activities of production, consumption, and circulation, as well as
> their components . . . are organized on a global scale. . . . It is infor-
> mational *and* global because, under the new historical conditions,
> productivity is generated through and competition is played out in a
> global network of interaction.[16]

For Castells, this informational economy is distinct from the world economy that emerged in the sixteenth century:

> A global economy is something different: it is an economy with the
> capacity to work as a unit in real time on a planetary scale. While the
> capitalist mode of production is characterized by its relentless expan-
> sion, always trying to overcome limits of time and space, it is only in
> the late twentieth century that the world was able to become truly
> global on the basis of the new infrastructure provided by information
> and communication technologies.[17]

A central characteristic of this highly globalized capitalism, which has
heavily affected labor markets, is how the factors of production are no
longer located in close geographic proximity. Furthermore, the marginal
profit rates are growing because of the continued increase in per capita
productivity (whose rate of growth continues to increase in some countries
of advanced capitalism) and a reduction of costs (via layoffs, intensification of production, replacing more expensive workers with less expensive
ones, and the replacement of labor with capital). With the growing segmentation of labor markets, in which the primary markets offer more
income, stability, and perquisites, there has been an increasing replacement
of hourly wages by payment for piecework. This creates a clear distinction

between the nominal and real salaries and wages of workers and the social wage via indirect loans and state actions. At the same time, this set of transformations implies the decline of the working class and a reduction of the power of organized labor in negotiating economic policies and in the constitution of the social pact.

These changes in the global composition of labor and capital are taking place at a time when there is an abundance of labor and when the conflicts between labor and capital are decreasing. The increase of supernumerary workers is also associated with an increase in international competition and the conviction on the part of the working class and labor unions that it is not possible to pressure the companies in search of more and better social services or salaries. This is impossible because of the abundance of labor, and because the falling profit margins of companies in the transnational and competitive environment has resulted in job losses and the accelerated migration of capital from regional markets in advanced capitalistic countries to areas where labor is highly skilled and poorly paid. One of the most dramatic consequences has been the stagnation or decline of real wages for the majority of the work population in the United States during the past two decades, as well as major increases in wealth and income for the top two deciles.[18]

The threat of regional free-trade agreements such as NAFTA or the new arrangements proposed by the World Trade Organization mark the limits of protectionist policies. Well-known examples are: trained engineers and computer experts from India entering the payroll information of North American companies in databases for a fraction of the cost of employing American white-collar workers; the low-cost mass production by Chinese workers, sometimes subject to forced labor; and young Indonesian girls working in the production of athletic shoes for Nike at a pay rate of ten cents an hour.

In order to deal with falling rates of profit, transnational capitalism seeks more productivity per capita or the reduction of the actual costs of production, as well as the transfer of production activities to tax-free zones where there is cheap and highly skilled labor, limited organized labor, easy, efficient, and cheap access to natural resources, favorable political conditions, access to better infrastructure and national resources, larger markets, and tax incentives.[19]

It is imperative to situate the new national and regional realities within the context of the global economic, political, social, and cultural changes of the past twenty-five years. The current regional situation is affected by innumerable changes including: the rise of the newly industrialized countries in Asia and the Pacific Rim (and its impact on the models of economic development until the financial fiasco of the summer of 1997); the promise of consolidating regional economic markets in the context of political globalization and regionalization (for example, the European Economic Community, NAFTA, and MERCOSUR, as well as the International Monetary Fund and the World Bank); the intensification of competition among the major industrial powers of Germany, Japan, and the United States; the opening of Eastern Europe; and the resurgence of regional ethnic and religious conflicts. And finally, under the heading of cultural globalization these changes are linked with a global popular culture and complex processes of neocolonial imposition, hybridization, and resistance.[20]

Work, the Occupational Structure, and Education. While the public education system in the old capitalist order was mostly oriented toward the production of a disciplined and reliable workforce—although there was resistance to systemic reproduction and other radical political responses even in these school settings—the new global economy requires workers with the capacity to learn quickly and to work in teams in reliable and creative ways.[21] The most productive workers in a global economy are those Robert Reich calls "symbolic analysts," who will make up the most productive and dynamic segments of the labor force.[22]

Along with the segmentation of labor markets, globalization implies that full-time workers have been replaced with part-time workers (with a substantial reduction in the cost of labor due to fewer employer contributions to health, education, and social security), an increase in female participation in labor markets, a systematic fall in real salaries, and a growing gap that separates salaried workers from the dominant sectors of society and from self-subsistence wage earners. A similar international phenomenon can be identified in the growing social and economic gap between developing countries and advanced capitalist nations.

The implications of the global informational economy model for occupational structures and educational demands is significantly different from those proposed by "postindustrial society" models. The latter, based primarily on linear extrapolations of data from the first half of the century, emphasize the shift of the locus of productivity by occupation sectors, arguing for a shift from primary to secondary, then tertiary (for example, services) activity. But as Castells argues on the basis of detailed comparative analysis, "The appropriate distinction is not between an industrial and a postindustrial economy, but between two forms of knowledge-based industrial, agricultural and services production. . . . Therefore, I propose to shift the analytical emphasis from *postindustrialism* . . . . to *informationalism.*"[23] Based on comparative analysis of trends from the past two decades and future projections, Castells describes the complex resulting occupational shifts as follows:

- the steady decline of traditional manufacturing employment;
- the rise of both producer services and social services, with the emphasis on business services in the first category and health services in the second category;
- the increasing diversification of service industries as a source of jobs;
- the rapid rise of managerial, professional, and technical jobs;
- the formation of a "white-collar" proletariat, made up of clerical and sales workers;
- the relative stability of a substantial share of employment in retail trade;
- the simultaneous increase of the upper and lower levels of the occupational structure; and
- the relative upgrading of the occupational structure over time, with an increasing share of those occupations that require higher skills and advanced education proportionately higher than the increase of the lower-level categories.[24]

As Castells warns, this "somewhat upgraded" occupational structure has no necessary relationship to "upgrading" society as a whole or increasing income or equality. From this perspective, as well, there is no single model of an informational society; different G-7 countries have pursued somewhat different strategies.[25] The relative success of Germany and Japan in the 1970s and 1980s, for example, was based in part on embedding information processing into material production or handling goods, "instead of being disjointed in a stepped up technical division of labor."[26] The result is two distinctive patterns of informational economy: the "service economy model," represented by the United States and Canada, and the "industrial production model," found in Japan and Germany.

A crucial implication of this line of analysis for education is that the advent of the informational economy does not imply—despite much popular hype to the contrary—any radical or dramatic shift of employment patterns beyond tendencies that have already been evident for the past couple of decades. Although these changes do not preclude continuing attempts to link job training to projections about globalization, the general effectiveness and significance of such strategies are likely to be muted and limited. If this line of argument is valid, then the more significant impact of a global and informational economy on education will lie elsewhere.

We would argue that the more decisive implications of globalization and post-Fordism for education lie in three areas: (1) most fundamentally, the changed role of the state in the global, informational (that is, post-Fordist) economy in response to the failures of the previous welfare-state, Keynesian model of development; (2) neoliberal pressures to develop educational policies that attempt to restructure postsecondary educational systems along entrepreneurial lines in order to provide flexible educational responses to the new model of industrial production; and (3) a related call for the reorganization of primary and secondary education and teacher education along lines that correspond to the skills and competencies (hence educational qualifications) ostensibly required by workers in a globalizing world.

We will consider the question of the state separately in the next section. After that we will examine several contexts of transformation that are suggestive of the impacts on educational settings: international education, global distance education, the shift toward "academic capitalism" in higher education, and calls for changes in teacher education and curricula that are adapted to the supposed imperatives of the new "flexible" worker.

Education and the State in the Context of Globalization

The Traditional System. In terms of education, the public education system in the old capitalist order was oriented toward the construction of "citizens" for the nation-state, as well as the production of a disciplined and reliable workforce of the type now characterized as "Fordist" production processes.[27] In the context of intensified globalization, the very nationalism linked with traditional citizenship training has been called into question. As a consequence, a new impetus has been given to a more cosmopolitan conception of citizenship of the type earlier promoted in the context of the role of "international studies" in a liberal arts curriculum.[28] More ominously, the new post-Fordist global economy seems to require new kinds of workers who are adaptable to flexible work regimes and insecure employment, a process with profound implications for the "functions" of educational institutions. From this perspective, teachers' organizations serve primarily as an obstacle to adapting educational systems to these new imperatives.

But the most dramatic arguments for the impact of globalization on education have been developed in the name of "postmodern" claims about the obsolescence of the nation-state. In the provocative formulation of one "postmodernist" critic:

> Does the national educational system have a future at all? Postmodernism would suggest that it does not. . . . Indeed the whole logic of postmodern and globalization theory is that the national educational system *per se* is now defunct, at once irrelevant, anachronistic and impossible. Governments no longer have the power to determine their national systems. They increasingly cede control to regional and international organizations on the one hand . . . and to consumers on the other. . . . With growing social diversity and cultural fragmentation they become increasingly privatized and individualistic, shorn of their public and collective associations. As the national state becomes a marginal force in the new world order so education becomes an individualized consumer good delivered in a global market and accessed through satellite and cable links. National education ceases to exist.[29]

Even if such extreme formulations must be rejected, it is clear that the tasks of education in the formation of national citizenship will necessarily change significantly in the direction of a greater recognition of global diversity and interdependence. But the underlying flaw in such arguments about the irrelevance of national educational systems stems from a simplistic account of the implications of globalization for the autonomy of national states.

The State: Powerless or Interdependent? Celebration and condemnation of the supposed decline of the welfare state can be found in many different ideological and analytical forms. But most of these analyses fail to address the more precise question of how the waning of state powers has potentially grave consequences given the logic of globalization. Moreover, many commentators confuse a loss of sovereignty with a loss of power, as opposed to its changed forms. As Castells argues:

> While global capitalism thrives, and nationalist ideologies explode all over the world, the nation-state, as historically created in the Modern Age, seems to be losing its power, although, and this is essential, *not its influence*. . . . Indeed the growing challenge to state's sovereignty around the world seems to originate from the inability of the modern nation-state to navigate the uncharted, stormy waters between the power of global networks and the challenge of singular identities. The instrumental capacity of the nation-state is decisively undermined by globalization of core economic activities, by globalization of media and electronic communication, and by globalization of crime.[30]

Neoliberalism versus the Challenge of Globalization. The neoliberal challenge to the welfare state has provided the most influential ideological grounds for welcoming this weakening of central state powers. But the rise of neoliberalism stems from more than its ideological appeal; its very success was closely related to the pressures of globalization that emerged in the 1970s. The fiscal crisis of the state produced by the classical Keynesian strategies of the welfare state did not produce a crisis of legitimation of the type that led to the revival of democratic socialism as hoped for by many on the Left.[31] Rather, Thatcherism and Reaganism became the ideological reference points for a vast process of restructuring that reduced demands on welfare states and provided a more flexible regulatory environment within which globalizing economic processes could proceed with fewer obstacles.

Paradoxically, however, these policies oriented toward a smaller, more business-oriented state were also implicated in some contexts (for example, Britain and Australia) with the use of massive state power to coerce the reorganization of educational systems. For instance, in a recent interview with one of the authors, Noam Chomsky perceptibly argues that universities have always been parasitic institutions insofar as they depend upon public and private funds, and indeed, the overall process of funding poses severe limits to the autonomy of universities in advanced capitalist societies:

> Universities are parasitic institutions. They do not generate their own funds. We don't really have a market society. To the extent that it is a market society—limited, guided market society—the universities aren't in the market. So they don't support themselves by tuition, they support themselves by funding from somewhere. Some of their funding is public. You can call it different names: you can call it scholarships, you can call it research grants. But one of the sources is the public through the government. Another source is rich people making endowments. A third source is corporate sponsorship of research, and so on. Those are basically the funding sources. Now the universities have the serious problem that, in fact, individuals in departments within them have microcosms of this problem of maintaining intellectual independence and integrity in the face of a parasitic existence. And that is not an easy line to walk . . . serious universities—and that is a serious statement—have to face a conflict between the sources of their existence and funding which is going to be overwhelmingly supportive of existing systems of power and authority. It can't be otherwise.[32]

Chomsky seems to agree with the implicit assumption of Castells that the state may be weakened by a number of processes, globalization being one of them, but that its influence is not weakened. Indeed, the traditional function of state subsidies for corporations has not been abandoned under neoliberal policies. Chomsky would argue that, in the past, industrial policy was simply and clearly outlined in the function of the military: "The function of the military is to subsidize mass technology, they don't really care about the military application. Their role is to create a technological and scientific basis for the next generation of corporate profit . . . it is called industrial policy."[33]

Indeed, for Chomsky, the present neoliberal condition is not so different from the past if one looks at military research funding and the implications for one of the growing and most popular business tools, the Internet:

> Actually, one of the most recent examples of this is the Internet, which

is now considered the great business opportunity, the triumph of free enterprise, and all of this grew out of a defense research agency. They got most of the ideas in software, they gave the initial funding. . . . Throughout thirty years the intellectual initiative and funding came overwhelmingly from the state sector: the Pentagon, the National Science Foundation. Finally, a couple of years ago it was handed over to corporations. And now they are using it as a tool for their tremendous profits, so that's a dramatic case with almost every useful technology.[34]

Globalization and Local Dialectics: Implications for Educational Policy

Introduction: The Local, the Global, and Commodification. The educational changes linked to the globalization of capitalism cannot readily be summarized in general theses, because education is implicated in broader cultural changes that are essentially contradictory. As Kellner insightfully argues, "Culture is an especially complex and contested terrain today as global cultures permeate local ones and new configurations emerge that synthesize both poles, providing contradictory forces of colonization *and* resistance, global homogenization *and* local hybrid forms and identities."[35] As a consequence, simplistic versions of dependency theory and cultural imperialism are not adequate to explain the emerging patterns relating the local and the global.

In the context of education, however, it is possible to identify a crucial, pervasive structural effect that defines the specific, neoliberal form of globalization taking place: commodification. Historically, the state retained considerable autonomy in constructing mass public educational systems and extensively regulating private, especially profit-oriented, educational ventures. Although theories of cultural reproduction emphasized the ways in which this use of state autonomy contributed indirectly to the perpetuating of the existing class systems, they retained the assumption that the state should exercise this directive responsibly, but on a more equitable basis. Moreover, globalization in principle includes the possibility that such radicalized educational planning could take on international forms, addressing cross-national inequalities.

What the earlier theories of cultural reproduction did not anticipate, however, was the possibility that there might be a massive privatization and commodification of educational activities that would be rationalized in terms of the inevitable "logic" and imperatives of globalization taken as a deterministic process. In this respect the advent of globalization provides a rationale for reorganizing the "correspondence principle" that links, according to structuralist Marxists, the economy and educational systems. But this linking of "competitiveness" with privatization and a market orientation in education is more an expression, we would argue, of neoliberal ideology than any inherent or invariant imperatives stemming from globalization. That is the reason that a basic assumption of this chapter is to differentiate neoliberal globalization, as an ideology, from the globalization of the economy, politics, and eventually culture as a historical and structural process.

The original creation of mass education as a public good was based on a fundamental insight into the strengths and weaknesses of markets as a means of organizing social activities. Above all, in strongly class-divided societies, there is a profound discrepancy between educational "needs" and the capacity to pay, as well as societal requirements for long-term planning that cannot be met by short-term, individualistic, highly fluctuating market decisions. Despite the importance of a critique of educational expertise in the context of state planning,[36] this should not be confused with arguments for the abandonment of public responsibility to market forces.[37]

Finally, it should be acknowledged that under the right conditions markets may be selectively used to open up and pluralize ossified public educational systems. This possibility is particularly attractive in societies with weak, unstable democratic institutions incapable of initiating effective public-sector reforms. But the chronic danger of such strategies is that they simply reinforce educational inequalities by encouraging the wealthy sectors of society to create a private educational system, thus eroding commitments of the dominant elites to the public system.

Broadly speaking, the emergence of the globalization problematic in education has contributed to a reconfiguration of political positions with respect to educational policy.[38] The political positions of the Left have been increasingly defensive, for example, in defending the more traditional humanistic values and face-to-face methods of instruction of traditional education.[39] In this defensive context, many of the earlier leftist criticisms of the effects of schools on reproducing class, race, and gender inequalities are inevitably set aside. Furthermore, the agenda of educational reform in response to globalization has been largely dominated by the neoliberal right, and by optimistic prophets of the power of the integration of new, computer-based technologies to transform educational delivery.

At this point, it is instructive to turn from the broader canvas of relations between globalization, education, and the state by addressing some specific contexts of transformation. Several such contexts of globalization in education can be identified: new developments in cross-cultural education (for example, international education and global distance education); the impact of structural adjustment policies imposed by international agencies on developing countries in the name of creating a global economy; the rise of entrepreneurial universities in response to the pressures of globalization; and attempts to reform primary and secondary curricula and teacher training in the name of globalization, stressing the imperatives of flexible production required for international competitiveness.

Cross-Cultural Education. Aspects of the more recent globalization tendencies in education have their origins in older cross-cultural problematics that have taken on new meanings. On the one hand, the increasing perception of interdependency has given new life to the humanistic notion of "cosmopolitan education" as part of a strategy of breaking down cultural difference and miscommunication. On the other, this new situation has created the technological means and demand—deriving primarily from marginalized and peripheral societies and regions—for access to the "global" knowledge dominated by the cosmopolitan centers, for example, in the context of global distance education.

International Education. In one of its more constructive, if marginalized, forms, "global talk" has given a new impetus to the older notion of "international" education as the foundation of a liberal arts curriculum. Rather than being directly driven by the economic imperatives of global competition, this pedagogical tradition has its origins in a humanistic conception of cultural diversity, a theme reinforced by contemporary notions of multiculturalism, as well as cultural and postcolonial studies.[40] Perhaps even more important than the laudable objective of creating intercultural understanding, these new forms of international education need to confront head-on the negative aspects of globalization, especially as they affect educational institutions. But such critical approaches tend to be marginalized given the philanthropic origins of much of the funding of such global education projects, as well as their links with creating uncritical, mobile trainees for international business.

Yet the internationalization of education seems to be a key element of the contemporary educational landscape. "Diploma mill" universities in the United States, for instance, which cannot capture a sizable portion of the country's university market given their poor reputation, have expanded overseas with distance education programs, dramatically increasing their enrollment, particularly of middle-class students in the developing and emergent countries. Fund-raising has acquired an international dimension as universities appeal to alumni in emerging countries—although the growing trend of academic fundraising in Asia has somewhat slowed with the crisis of the last two years. Teachers' unions are moving into more active international exchanges among peers, with the creation of more hemispheric teacher union organizations. Sister-school relationships have sprung up in the last three decades, with a growing membership. International organizations of education have increased their membership and action in their fields of competence in recent decades (for example, the World Council of Comparative Education and Fulbright programs). Educational standards are being established by specific international organizations and are considered landmarks in many educational domains. For instance, the Organization for Economic Cooperation and Development (OECD) has developed "certification teams" to evaluate, at the request of the host country or the host institution, the conditions of research universities in developing countries, and their recommendations carry substantial weight in local funding, accreditation, and institutional evaluation. Not only has this OECD process been fundamental in reshaping higher education in some developing countries, but "OECD has become a major force in producing information and stimulating analysis of a comparative, transnational, and global kind."[41] Indeed, there is another kind of social movement emerging, particularly in advanced countries, with a growing network of educators and associations linked to global education as an attempt to expand the "global mindedness" of students.

Global Distance Education. Another context in which globalization has had an even more significant impact is the burgeoning field of "global" distance education. Although driven in part by technological advances such as the Internet, global distance education has successfully responded to cutbacks in public education and targeted those in need of access to resources outside of their home countries. The arguments for such global education include: the advantages of a more diverse student clientele; increased access (a theme defining the origins of, and now the global expansion of, the Open University in the United Kingdom); making the highest levels of expertise available to larger audiences; and responding to an educational curriculum that is inherently global in nature (for example, environmentalism, peace studies, and even business).[42] But there are also some important arguments that call into question such developments: the cognitive limitations of electronic delivery and computer-based systems of information retrieval based on fragmentation of knowledge; the loss of the critical, reflective side of education in a context driven by individualized packaging and marketing of skills; the contribution of global education to the further breakdown of local communities and educational systems; and the role of global education as part of a broader process of cultural invasion, especially from the developed to the "underdeveloped" parts of the world.[43] While these developments in industrial advanced societies are important and affect quite dramatically educational policy, the changes wrought by globalization in developing countries are even more daunting.

Developing Countries: Structural Adjustment and Educational Policy. The most visible impact of globalization on education in developing societies stems from the imposition of structural adjustment policies. Structural adjustment policies are directly linked to globalization to the extent that all strategies of development are now linked to the imperatives of creating stability for foreign capital. In other words, given the insurmountable obstacles to raising sufficient capital internally, there is no other choice than adapting to policies that systematically undercut the capacity of governments to construct educational policies that enhance educational equality or seek to develop some degree of national autonomy in the context of research and development. In this context, bilateral and multilateral organizations (most importantly in education the role of the World Bank and UNESCO) have a strong presence in the formulation of educational policy, more so under contexts of financial austerity and structural reforms of the economies.

A number of critical analyses of the international presence in educational policy emphasize that the presence of external donors may lead to a process of public policy planning through marketing, rather than rational public choice and planning (that is, selecting the kinds of projects more likely to be financed by external donors and making them the central components of a given public policy[44]). Such critical studies examine how the presence of external agencies such as the World Bank or UNESCO condition, and in some cases determine, the way educational reform is conducted; priorities are assigned; research is designed, implemented, and used in educational reform; and policy initiatives are selected, evaluated, or set forth. Certain public policy options have been granted such widespread legitimacy and financial support that they have become virtually hegemonic.[45]

For instance, a number of debates and educational financing initiatives, such as vouchers or charter and magnet schools, which were developed in the United States and England,[46] are now being discussed and implemented in several developing societies; and a central discussion about the presence of international organizations in the formulation of educational policies are being described by some as the struggle for "accountability."[47] Perhaps no place has been more subject to these processes of internationalization and globalization than the university.

Globalization and Universities: Academic Capitalism. In highly developed societies, the most dramatic impact of globalization on educational policy has occurred in those contexts where the real or imagined challenge of globalization has been implicated with fundamental restructuring of post-secondary educational institutions.[48] As Slaughter and Leslie argue in *Academic Capitalism*, contemporary changes in the academy—based on their study of Britain, the United States, Australia, and Canada—compare in significance to those during the last quarter of the nineteenth century. Whereas the industrial revolution of that period created the wealth that made possible the modern university system,

> so the globalization of the political economy at the end of the twentieth century is destabilizing patterns of university professional work developed over the past hundred years. Globalization is creating new structures, incentives, and rewards for some aspects of academic

careers and is simultaneously instituting constraints and disincentives for other aspects of careers.[49]

As Slaughter and Leslie conclude:

> Despite the very real differences in their political cultures, the four countries developed similar policies at those points where higher education intersected with globalization of the postindustrial political economy. Tertiary education policies in all countries moved toward science and technology policies that emphasized academic capitalism at the expense of basic or fundamental research, toward curricula policy that concentrated moneys in science and technology and fields close to the market . . . , toward increased access at lower government cost per student, and toward organizational policies that undercut the autonomy of academic institutions and of faculty.[50]

But it would be dangerous to draw hasty conclusions about the overall implications of these findings. Although the authors conclude that this "convergence is best explained by globalization theory" (that is, by the imperative of the breakdown of the Keynesian model of growth and international competition), this pattern has not been widely found in extreme forms in other advanced societies. Even the Canadian case—where universities have effectively resisted such structural change despite increased targeting of funding and the reduction of costs per student—deviates in important respects. This difference is attributed to the extreme decentralization of education, although it is argued that high levels of public debt may require such changes in the future.[51]

The problem here involves distinguishing more clearly between the fiscal crisis of the welfare state (which forces a reduction of expenditures irrespective of ideological leanings) and the presumed pressures of globalization that entail a reorganization of the production process and the subordination of education to it. It should not be taken for granted that these specific responses to globalization follow some kind of inexorable logic based on economic imperatives, as opposed to an ideological convergence—most notable in the English-speaking world—upon neoliberal educational recipes as a specific response to globalization and international competition. To be sure, the failure of the Left effectively to propose alternative strategies in response to globalization (for example, policies oriented more toward global cooperation than neo-Darwinian competition) has left the impression that the neoliberal options were the only ones available.[52]

Nor should it be forgotten that local responses to globalizing pressures have paradoxical, even contradictory, implications. For example, in the case of California, the global phenomenon of immigration has been met with the political decisions of Propositions 187 and 209, which, in effect, make a diverse society (a trait of globalization) more difficult to achieve and maintain in the context of the perennial struggle for equality and representation. Similarly, the outlawing of bilingual education in some states in the United States, much like the treatment of guest workers in Europe or Japan, reflects a popular defensiveness vis-à-vis globalization that indicates the disjunction of the local and global in the everyday lives of most people.

Globalizing Primary and Secondary Education: Job and Teacher Training. Although the principle of training for the globalized economy is central to the agenda of neoliberal postsecondary reforms, this issue is complicated by the broader dynamic of reorganizing research and development in the context of the considerable autonomy of post secondary institutions. Furthermore, the high level of skill and creativity required of students at this level makes it easier to challenge simplistic notions of technical training oriented toward emerging job markets. At the primary and secondary level, however, it is considerably easier to introduce an agenda that might involve the redefinition of the role and preparation of teachers, as well as a complementary curriculum oriented toward the formation of the new kind of worker that is needed by the global economy. In part, this requires making a sharp distinction between academic and vocational routes, thus reversing previous movements against streaming and tracking, developed in the name of educational equity.[53] Some of the most dramatic and self-conscious reforms of this kind have been undertaken in Britain, and especially in Australia.[54]

In many ways the image of the new worker suggested by post-Fordist theory appears attractive. The imperatives of flexible production require workers capable of high levels of autonomy and group participation linked to broadly based skills training. But as Soucek has persuasively demonstrated, the appearances of more democratic participation are contradicted by three problematic aspects of the post-Fordist industrial model: (1) in practice the introduction of new production concepts only involves a small minority of workers; (2) hence the continuities with Fordism in this context remain central to the logic or production; and (3) even those that might be involved in post-Fordist production are confronted by a new economy of time and control that calls into question many of the presumed benefits of autonomy and participation, at least for the individual worker:

> Post-Fordist flexibility is thus a double-edged weapon—on the one hand, it promises worker autonomy, democratic participation and training; on the other, it tends to deliver those promises in packages whose contents do not correspond to the attached labels. Worker autonomy has thus become a willingness to work harder, democratic participation means to think of new ways of intensifying labor effort, and training has come to mean to learn less about more.[55]

To drastically overhaul educational systems on the basis of such problematic assumptions about the post-Fordist workplace may be in the immediate interests of many types of employers, but it is not clear that it will effectively serve the broader interests of society, let alone workers in general. The overall effect is to shift education toward competence-based skills at the expense of the more fundamental forms of critical competence required for autonomous learning and active citizenship.

The flip side of post-Fordist neoliberal educational policy calls for transformation of the professionalism and accountability of teachers. Again, this agenda has some superficially appealing features, such as accountability to the student as client. Hence, traditional forms of teacher professionalism are challenged on the assumption that education cannot be left to teachers and researchers if it is to be accountable. But beneath the rhetoric there is considerable ambiguity with respect to who is the client (students or potential employers) and who should define the nature of the service.[56] As Soucek concludes, what underlies this model is the reduction of teaching to the model of the industrial workplace. Many critics of neoliberal policies have insightfully shown how standardization of teaching and curriculum is closely linked to de-skilling of teachers and the logic of technical control in education.[57]

Making teachers accountable for the employability of students is contradicted by studies that question whether excessive unemployment is caused by the mismatch between schools and jobs. Moreover, long-term labor market success as measured in terms of income and satisfaction is closely bound up with a number of competencies and personal qualities that cannot be conceptualized within the framework of this post-Fordist model of the worker and teacher.[58] Although globalization clearly has implications for educational reform, the argument for a neoliberal strategy of subordinating educational institutions to the logic of a new industrial process falters in decisive ways.

Countermovements: Contesting the New Global Order

Review of the Argument So Far. To this point we have presented the problematic of globalization primarily in the structural contexts of the interplay between economic change, the changing role of states at the national level, and the impact of these on educational institutions and educational policy. For the most part these relations have been described as the outcome of these structural changes, whether endured passively or anticipated proactively (as in the case of some types of educational reform). While taking seriously the claim that these developments do indeed represent remarkable changes in the world order and the role of nation-states, we have remained skeptical with respect to various claims and projections made in the name of globalization. Only with time and more conclusive research will it be possible to assess what has been happening and what are the future directions of change. Above all, however, we have been concerned with questioning some of the neoliberal claims about the "necessary" adaptation of educational policies to sustain international competitiveness. Such claims reflect both contestable claims about the nature of globalization and the supposed benefits to be derived from importing the flexible production model into the domain of education.

But the prophets of globalization need to be questioned in another way: it is also important to consider how these changes have created new forms of inequality, poverty, and social exclusion, increasingly disrupted processes of identity formation, and set into motion proactive and reactive social movements.

The Victims of Globalization: The Rise of the Fourth World. One of the tragic paradoxes of oppression and powerlessness is that the positions of the victims of social change and political domination have no necessary relationship to the forms of consciousness that might facilitate effective resistance to these processes. With the benefit of a problematic theory of history, orthodox Marxism postulated that the objective status of the working classes within the capitalist mode of production guaranteed the formation of a universal consciousness and sense of collective self-interest that would guide emancipation. One of the central themes of postmodernist conceptions of politics, in contrast, is a celebration of the diversity of standpoints for reflecting about oppression, especially in the context of identity politics. But from a critical global perspective, the diversity of the victims of globalization poses major problems with respect to the potential bases of shared identity and collective resistance.

In the more recent period, the meanings of the terms First, Second, and Third World have changed dramatically and suggested the need for the notion of a "Fourth World." The statist world of bureaucratic collectivism has collapsed, partly because it could not master the challenges of a global information world. The term "Third World" has become problematic because it refers to such diverse contexts of development that it has little descriptive value. While the notion of the First World retains some plausibility as the locus of informational capitalism, its identity is threatened by the "Fourth World," the dark side of the very globalizing processes it brought into being:

> Because of [globalization] a new world, the Fourth World, has emerged, made up of multiple black holes of social exclusion throughout the planet. The Fourth World comprises large areas of the globe, such as Sub-Saharan Africa, and impoverished rural areas of Latin America and Asia. But it is also present in literally every country, and every city, in this new geography of social exclusion. It is formed of American inner-city ghettos, Spanish enclaves of mass youth unemployment, French banlieues warehousing North Africans, Japanese Yoseba quarters, and Asian mega-cities' shanty towns. And it is populated by millions of homeless, incarcerated, prostituted, criminalized, stigmatized, sick, and illiterate persons. They are the majority in some areas, the minority in others, and a tiny minority in a few privileged contexts. But, everywhere, they are growing in number, increasing in visibility, as the selective triage of informational capitalism, and the political breakdown of the welfare state, intensify social exclusion. In the current historical context, the rise of the Fourth World is insepa-

rable from the rise of informational, global capitalism.[59]

The question of a critical pedagogy of such a Fourth World remains to be developed, despite the pathbreaking formulations of Paulo Freire's *Pedagogy of the Oppressed.*[60] The conception of social transformation underlying Freire's analysis was still framed within the assumptions of the nation-state and the possibility of overcoming dependency through a socialist strategy of national development. Yet as recent events in Brazil have underscored, the dominant groups have realistically (and cynically) allied with the imperatives imposed by the global economic order, leaving Brazil's own Fourth World to provide the victims for further "structural adjustment."

Opposing Globalization: The Disjunction of the Local and the Global. Although it is possible to signify the "Fourth World" as an analytical construct, it does not correspond to a probable form of collective consciousness among its victims. In the context of globalization, the shift of the locus of power and decision making away from the nation-state further erodes the capacity of marginalized groups to grasp the structural processes that determine their fate. Such marginalized groups are the least able to fend for themselves against global flows and pressures for structural adjustment. In this respect the new categories of the oppressed are in no position to take advantage of the forms of reflexive identity that have been hailed as a defining trait of high modernity (or postmodernity). Hence, the potentially liberatory possibilities of "reflexive life-planning" (a term used by Giddens) remain an option only for the few. As Castells suggests:

> This is because the network society is based on the systemic disjunction between the local and the global for most individuals and social groups. . . . Therefore, reflexive life-planning becomes impossible, except for the elite inhabiting the timeless space of flows of global networks and their ancillary locales. . . . Under such conditions, civil societies shrink and disarticulate because there is no longer continuity between the logic of power-making in the global network and the logic of association and representation in specific societies and cultures. The search for meaning takes place then in the reconstruction of defensive identities around communal principles. Most of social action becomes organized in the opposition between unidentified

flows and secluded identities. . . . While in modernity (early or late) project identity was constituted from civil society (as in the case of socialism on the basis of the labor movement), in the network society, project identity, if it develops at all, grows from communal resistance. This is the actual meaning of the new primacy of identity politics in the network society.[61]

Despite the rhetoric of inevitable evolutionary advancement associated with many of the prophets of economic globalization, it has not gone uncontested, any more than it has undermined what Castells refers to as the "powers of identity":

Along with the technological evolution, the transformation of capitalism, and the demise of statism, we have experienced, in the last quarter of the century, the widespread surge of powerful expressions of collective identity that challenge globalization and cosmopolitanism on behalf of cultural singularity and people's control over their lives and environment.[62]

The diversity of these movements and their marginal relationship with existing educational systems—especially those undergoing reform in the name of globalization—are indicative of the growing gap between "official" institutions and the everyday realities of those who do not fit into the economic logic of the new global order.[63]

Conclusion

In summary, we have argued that the history of the state and public education systems are fundamental elements of explaining public policy formation in education in the context of globalization. To be sure, the rise of a global, informational economy has weakened the state and reinforced neoliberal strategies of economic and social policy. The weakened position of the state has in turn opened the way for increased commodification of education, as well as calls for "reforming" education in response to the supposed imperatives of "globalization." Some responses, such as renewed calls for international education, have critical potential. Others, such as global distance education, remain ambiguous in their implications. Given the space constraints in this chapter, we have been unable to address in detail the implications of globalization for the growing multiculturalism of industrial advanced societies and, furthermore, the implications of globalization for multicultural education in promoting citizenship and democracy, a challenge that has been addressed elsewhere.[64]

While there are clearly opportunities for enhancement of educational access and for forming a global culture, such possibilities must not be uncritically celebrated and need to be subjected to a more differentiated and balanced assessment, as well as to international debate and perhaps regulation. In developing countries, where weak and impoverished democratic regimes have not yet been able to extend the basic benefits of mass public education on an equitable basis, structural adjustment policies have been imposed as part of the globalization of development options. Clearly, redressing North-South inequalities in education requires new kinds of proactive strategies that could be justified in terms of a rather different vision of globalization. Further, the entrepreneurial university is touted as necessary for competitiveness in global informational capitalism, rather than also being viewed as an ideologically driven strategy for reducing the autonomy of education and deflecting its critical potential. In this politicized context, it becomes difficult to analyze and evaluate the kinds of reforms that may indeed enhance flexibility and meaningful choice, without undermining the longer-term goals and necessary autonomy of educational institutions. Similarly, the rhetoric of globalization is used to guide strategies of primary and secondary educational reform whose agenda is based more on ideology than on empirically justifiable analyses of the benefits of a "flexible production" model that undercuts the larger cultural and humanistic tasks of education. Paradoxically, the political Left has assumed a "conservative" position in defending these traditional goals of education, but has largely yielded the agenda of educational experimentation and reform to neoliberal calls for "choice" and "flexibility."

Furthermore, the rhetoric of globalization used to promote the neoliberal agenda ignores the downside of globalization, or rationalizes it away as a necessary evil. But the rise of a Fourth World that is closely connected to the expansion of globalization continues as a reminder of the new forms of inequality and social exclusion that have been created by the informational global economy. Although these same processes have unleashed new forms of resistance, the disjunction between local events and global flows makes it difficult to articulate social movement strategies that are more than defensive.[65]

But the future has not been written and no one can ever claim a definitive understanding of the current relationships between globalization, the state, education, and social change. For such reasons we anticipate this problem - atic will remain one of the most central occupations of educational scholarship for many years to come.

Notes

1. To be sure, there are theoretical approaches classified as "postmodern" that do not neglect structural issues and which are thus broadly complementary to the problematic of globalization that we develop in this chapter (for example, David Harvey, *The Condition of Postmodernity* [Oxford, Eng.: Basil Blackwell, 1989]; and Fredric Jameson, *Postmodernism, or, The Cultural Logic of Late Capitalism* [Durham, N.C.: Duke University Press, 1991].)
2. Roland Robertson, "Social Theory, Cultural Relativity and the Problem of Globality," in *Culture, Globalization and the World-Sytem: Contemporary Conditions for the Representation of Identity*, ed. Anthony D. King (Minneapolis: University of Minnesota Press, 1997), 69–90.
3. Immanuel Wallerstein, "World-Systems Theory," in *Social Theory Today*, ed. Anthony Giddens and Jonathan H. Turner (Stanford: Stanford University Press, 1987), 309–24.
4. Harvey, *The Condition of Postmodernity*; Krishnan Kumar, *From Post-Industrial to Post-Modern Society: New Theories of the Contemporary World* (Oxford and Cambridge, Eng.: Basil Blackwell, 1995); and Frank Webster, *Theories of the Information Society* (London and New York: Routledge, 1995).
5. Raymond A. Morrow and Carlos A. Torres, *Social Theory and Education: A Critique of Theories of Social and Cultural Reproduction* (Albany: SUNY Press, 1995).
6. Martin Carnoy, *Education as Cultural Imperialism* (New York: David McKay, 1974); John Willinsky, *Learning to Divide the World: Education at Empire's End* (Minneapolis and London: University of Minnesota Press, 1998); and Carlos Alberto Torres, *Democracy, Education and Multiculturalism: Dilemmas of Citizenship in a Global World* (Lanham, Md.: Rowman and Littlefield, 1998).
7. David Held, ed., *Political Theory Today* (Stanford: Stanford University Press, 1991), 9.
8. Malcolm Waters, *Globalization* (London and New York: Routledge, 1995).
9. Mike Featherstone, *Undoing Culture: Globalization, Postmodernism and Identity* (London and Thousand Oaks, Calif.: Sage, 1995); and Anthony D. King, ed., *Culture, Globalization and the World-System* (Binghamton, SUNY Press, 1997).
10. Daniel Bell, *The Coming of Post-Industrial Society: A Venture in Social Forecasting* (New York: Basic, 1976).
11. For example, Yoneji Masuda, *The Information Society as Post-Industrial Society* (Washington, D.C.: World Future Society, 1981); and Marc Uri Porat, "Global Implications of the Information Society," *Journal of Communication* 28 (1978): 70–80.

12. David Lyon, *The Information Society: Issues and Illusions* (Cambridge, Eng.: Polity Press, 1988); and Webster, *Theories*.

13. Aspects of this type of analysis are challenged by the "regulation school," which sees greater continuity, suggesting post-Fordism is merely an outcome of the logic of Fordism, as opposed to a qualitatively different form of organization. For an astute, detailed analysis of these debates, see Kumar, *From Post-Industrial to Post-Modern Society*.

14. Paul Hirst and Grahame Thompson, *Globalization in Question* (Cambridge, Eng.: Polity, 1996).

15. Adam Przeworski, *Democracy and the Market: Political and Economic Reforms in Eastern Europe and Latin America* (New York: Cambridge University Press, 1991); K. Ohmae, *The Borderless World: Power and Strategy in the Interlinked World Economy* (New York: Harper Business, 1990); K. Ohmae, *The End of the Nation State: The Rise of Regional Economies* (New York: Free Press Paperbacks, 1991); Robert B. Reich, *The Work of Nations* (New York: Vintage Books, 1991); L. Thurow, *Head to Head: The Coming Economic Battle among Japan, Europe, and America* (New York: William Morrow, 1992); and J. Mander and E. Goldsmith, eds., *The Case against the Global Economy and for a Turn Toward the Local* (San Francisco: Sierra Club Books, 1996).

16. Manuel Castells, *The Rise of the Network Society* (Oxford, Eng.: Blackwell, 1996), 66.

17. Ibid., 92.

18. Manuel Castells, *End of Millenium* (Oxford, Eng.: Blackwell, 1998), 130–45.

19. Daniel García Delgado, *Estado-nación y globalización: fortalezas y debilidades en el umbral del tercer milenio* (Buenos Aires: Ariel, 1998).

20. Michael Featherstone, ed., *Global Culture: Nationalism, Globalization and Modernity* (London: Sage, 1990); and Featherstone, *Undoing Culture*.

21. Wellford W. Wilms, *Restoring Prosperity: How Workers and Managers Are Forging a New Culture of Cooperation* (New York: Random House, 1996).

22. Reich, *The Works of Nations*.

23. Castells, *The Rise*, 204.

24. Ibid., 229.

25. The G-7 includes Canada, France, Germany, Italy, Japan, the United Kingdom, and the United States.

26. Castells, *The Rise*, 211.

27. Samuel Bowles and Herbert Gintis, *Schooling in Capitalist America: Educational Reform and the Contradictions of Economic Life* (New York: Basic Books/Harper, 1977); and John W. Meyer, Francisco O. Ramirez, Richard Rubinson, and John Boli-Bennett, "The World Educational Revolution, 1950–70," in *National Development and the World System: Educational, Economic, and Political Change, 1950–1970*, ed. John W. Meyer and Michael T. Hannan (Chicago and London: University of Chicago Press, 1979), 37–55.

28. Julia A. Kushigian, ed., *International Studies in the Next Millennium: Meeting the Challenge of Globalization* (Westport, Conn.: Praeger, 1998).

29. Andy Green, *Education, Globalization and the Nation State* (London: Macmillan, 1997), 3.

30. Manuel Castells, *The Power of Identity* (Oxford, Eng.: Blackwell, 1997), 243–44.

31. Jürgen Habermas, *Legitimation Crisis* (Boston: Beacon, 1975).

32. Conversation with Carlos Alberto Torres, MIT, Massachussetts, 9 Oct. 1998.

33. Ibid.

34. Ibid.

35. See Douglas Kellner, in this volume.

36. Thomas S. Popkewitz, *A Political Sociology of Educational Reform: Power/Knowledge in Teaching, Teacher Education, and Research* (New York and London: Teacher's College Press, 1991); Thomas S. Popkewitz and Marie Brennan, eds., *Foucault's Challenge: Discourse, Knowledge, and Power in Education* (New York and London: Teachers College Press, 1998).

37. Amy Stuart Wells and Jeannie Oakes, "Tracking, Detracking, and the Politics of Educational Reform: A Sociological Perspective," in *Sociology of Education: Emerging Perspectives*, ed. Carlos Alberto Torres and Ted Mitchell (New York: SUNY Press, 1998), 155–80; Torres, *Democracy*; Karen McClafferty, Carlos Alberto Torres, and Ted Mitchell, eds., *Challenges of Urban Education: Sociological Perspectives for the Next Century* (New York: SUNY Press, in press).

38. Martin Carnoy, "Globalization and Educational Reform," *Melbourne Studies in Education* 39, no. 2 (1998): 21–40; Torres, *Democracy*; and García Delgado, *Estado-nación*.

39. Paulo Freire, *Pedagogia da autonomia: Saberes necessários à prática educativa* (São Paulo: Paz e Terra, 1997).

40. Kushigian, *International Studies*; and Torres, *Democracy*.

41. Burkart Holzner and Mattew Harmon, "Intellectual and Organizational Challenges for International Education in the United States: A Knowledge System Perspective," in *International Education in the New Global Era*, ed. J. N. Hawkins, C. M. Haron, M. A. Kazanjian, G. W. Merkx, and D. Wiley (Los Angeles: International Studies and Overseas Programs, 1998), 36.

42. Robin Mason, *Globalising Education: Trends and Applications* (London and New York: Routledge, 1998), 4–5.

43. Ibid., 8–10.

44. Joel Samoff with Suleman Sumra, "From Planning to Marketing: Making Education and Training Policy in Tanzania," in *Coping with Crisis: Austerity, Adjustment and Human Resources*, ed. Joel Samoff (London and New York: Cassell, 1994), 134–72.

45. Martin Carnoy and Carlos Alberto Torres, "Educational Change and Structural Adjustment: A Case Study of Costa Rica," in *Coping with Crisis. Austerity, Adjustment and Human Resources*, ed. Joel Samoff (London and New York: Cassell, 1994), 64–99; Jonathan A. Fox and L. David Brown, *The Struggle for Accountability: The World Bank, NGO's and Grassroots Movements* (Cambridge and London: MIT Press, 1998); and Norma Paviglianiti, María Catalina Nosiglia, and Mónica Marquina, *Recomposición neoconservadora: Lugar afectado: la universidad* (Buenos Aires: IICE-UBA-Miño y Davila, 1996).

46. Geoff Whitty, "Creating Quasi Markets in Education," *Review of Research in Education* 22 (1997): 30–48.

47. Fox and Brown, *The Struggle*.

48. As noted previously, developing countries have been urged to follow similar strategies of reform in the context of structural adjustment.

49. Sheila Slaughter and Larry Leslie, *Academic Capitalism: Politics, Policies, and the Entrepreneurial University* (Baltimore and London: Johns Hopkins University Press, 1997), 1.
50. Ibid., 55.
51. Ibid., 61–62.
52. Carlos Alberto Torres and Daniel Schugurensky, "Globalización, neoliberalismo y educación superior," *Revista chilena de humanidades* no. 17 (1997): 37–46.
53. Jeannie Oakes, *Keeping Track: How Schools Structure Inequality* (New Haven, Conn.: Yale University Press, 1985).
54. Victor Soucek, "Public Education and the Post-Fordist Accumulation Regime: A Case Study of Australia: Parts One and Two," *Interchange* 26 (1995): 127–59.
55. Victor Soucek, "Educational Policy Formation in the Post-Fordist Era and its Impact on the Nature of Teachers' Work" (Ph.D. diss., University of Alberta, 1996), 215ff, 226–27.
56. Soucek, "Educational Policy," 288.
57. Michael W. Apple, *Official Knowledge: Democratic Education in a Conservative Age* (New York: Routledge, 1993); Michael W. Apple and Anita Oliver, "Becoming Right: Education and the Formation of Conservative Movements," in *Sociology of Education: Emerging Perspectives*, ed. Carlos Alberto Torres and Ted Mitchell (New York: SUNY Press, 1998), 91–120.
58. Shirley Walters, ed., *Globalization, Adult Education and Training* (London: Zed Books, 1997).
59. Castells, *End of Millenium*, 164–65.
60. Raymond A. Morrow and Carlos Alberto Torres, *Critical Social Theory and Education: Freire, Habermas and the Dialogical Subject* (New York: Teacher's College Press, in press); Torres, *Democracy*; and Freire, *Pedagogia*.
61. Castells, *The Power*, 11.
62. Ibid., 2.
63. Raymond A. Morrow and Carlos Alberto Torres, "The State, Social Movements, and Educational Reform," in *Comparative Education: The Dialectics of the Global and the Local*, ed. Robert Arnove and Carlos Alberto Torres (Lanham, Md.: Rowman and Littlefield, in press).
64. Torres, *Democracy*; and James A. Banks and McGee Banks, eds., *Multicultural Education: Issues and Perspectives* (Boston: Allyn and Bacon, 1989).
65. Morrow and Torres, "The State."

Between Neoliberalism and Neoconservatism: Education and Conservatism in a Global Context

Michael W. Apple

We have entered a period of reaction in education. Our educational institutions are seen as failures. High dropout rates, a decline in "functional literacy," a loss of standards and discipline, the failure to teach "real knowledge" and economically useful skills, poor scores on standardized tests—all of these are charges leveled at U.S. schools. And all of these, we are told, have led to declining economic productivity, unemployment, poverty, a loss of international competitiveness, and so on. Return to a "common culture," make schools more efficient, make them more responsive to the private sector: do this and our problems will be solved.

Behind all of this is an attack on egalitarian norms and values. Although hidden in the rhetorical flourishes of the critics, in essence "too much democracy"—culturally and politically—is seen as one of the major causes of "our" declining economy and culture. Similar tendencies are quite visible in other countries as well. The extent of the reaction is captured in the words of Kenneth Baker, former British secretary of education and science in the Thatcher government, who evaluated nearly a decade of rightist efforts in education by saying, "The age of egalitarianism is over."[1] He was speaking positively, not negatively.

The threat to egalitarian ideals that these attacks represent is not usually made quite this explicitly, since they are often couched in the discourse of "improving" competitiveness, jobs, standards, and quality in an educational system that is seen to be in total crisis.

It would be simplistic, however, to interpret what is happening as only the result of efforts by dominant economic elites. Many of these attacks do represent attempts to reintegrate education into a national and global economic agenda. Yet, they cannot be fully reduced to that, nor can they be reduced to being only about the economy. Cultural struggles and struggles over race and gender coincide with class alliances and class power.[2]

Education is a site of struggle and compromise. It serves also as a proxy for larger battles over what our institutions should do, who they should serve, and who should make these decisions. And yet, by itself it is one of the major arenas through which are worked resources, power, and ideology specific to policy, finance, curriculum, pedagogy, and evaluation in education. Thus, education is both cause and effect, determining and determined. Because of this, no one essay could hope to give a complete picture of this complexity. What I hope to do instead is to provide an outline of some of the major tensions surrounding education in the United States and other countries as they move in conservative directions. A key word here is directions. The plural is crucial to my arguments, since there are multiple and at times contradictory tendencies within the rightist turn.

It is impossible to understand current educational policy in the United States without placing it in its global context. Thus, behind the stress on higher standards, more rigorous testing, education for employment, and a much closer relationship between education and the economy in general, is the fear of losing in international competition and the loss of jobs and money to Japan and the "Asian Tiger" economies, to Mexico, and elsewhere—even given their current economic crises.[3] In the same way, the equally evident pressure in the United States to reinstall a (selective) vision of a common culture, to place more emphasis on the "Western tradition," on religion, on the English language, and similar emphases are deeply connected to cultural fears about Latin America, Africa, and Asia. This context provides a backdrop for my discussion.

The rightward turn—what I have elsewhere called the *conservative restoration*[4]—has been the result of the successful struggle by the Right to form a broad-based alliance. This new alliance has been so successful in part because it has been able to win the battle over common sense. That is, it has creatively stitched together different social tendencies and commitments and has organized them under its own general leadership in issues dealing with social welfare, culture, the economy, and education. Its aim in educational and social policy is what might best be described as "conservative modernization."[5]

There are four major elements within this alliance. Each has its own relatively autonomous history and dynamics, but each also has been sutured into the more general conservative movement. These elements include neoliberals, neoconservatives, authoritarian populists, and a particular fraction of the upwardly mobile new middle class. I shall pay particular attention to the first two groups since they—and especially neoliberals—are currently in leadership in this alliance to "reform" education. However, in no way do I want to dismiss the power of these latter two groups.

Neoliberals

Neoliberals are the most powerful element within the conservative restoration. They are guided by a vision of the weak state. Thus, what is private is necessarily good and what is public is necessarily bad. Public institutions such as schools are "black holes" into which money is poured—and then seemingly disappears—but which do not provide anywhere near adequate results. For neoliberals, there is one form of rationality more powerful than any other: economic rationality. Efficiency and an "ethic" of cost-benefit analysis are the dominant norms. All people are to act in ways that maximize their own personal benefits. Indeed, behind this position is an empirical claim that this is how *all* rational actors act. Yet, rather than being a neutral description of the world of social motivation, this is actually a construction of the world around the valuative characteristics of an efficiently acquisitive class type.[6]

Underpinning this position is a vision of students as human capital. The world is intensely competitive economically, and students—as future workers—must be given the requisite skills and dispositions to compete efficiently and effectively.[7] Further, any money spent on schools that is not directly related to these economic goals is suspect. In fact, as "black holes," schools and other public services as they are currently organized and controlled waste economic resources that should go into private enterprise. Thus, not only are public schools failing our children as future workers, but like nearly all public institutions they are sucking the financial life out of this society. Partly this is the result of "producer capture." Schools are built for teachers and state bureaucrats, not "consumers." They respond to the demands of professionals and other selfish state workers, not the consumers who rely on them.

The idea of the "consumer" is crucial here. For neoliberals, the world in essence is a vast supermarket. "Consumer choice" is the guarantor of democracy. In effect, education is seen as simply one more product like bread, cars, and television.[8] By turning it over to the market through voucher and choice plans, it will be largely self-regulating. Thus, democracy is turned into consumption practices. In these plans, the ideal of the citizen is that of the purchaser. The ideological effects of this are momentous. Rather than democracy being a *political* concept, it is transformed into a wholly *economic* concept. The message of such policies is that of what might best be called "arithmetical particularism," in which the unattached individual—as a consumer—is deraced, declassed, and degendered.[9]

The metaphors of the consumer and the supermarket are actually quite apposite here. For just as in real life, there are individuals who indeed can go into supermarkets and choose among a vast array of similar or diverse products. And there are those who can only engage in what can best be called "postmodern" consumption. They stand outside the supermarket and can only consume the image.

The entire project of neoliberalism nationally and internationally is connected to a larger process of exporting the blame from the decisions of dominant groups onto the state and onto poor people.[10] Yet, with their emphasis on the consumer rather than the producer, neoliberal policies need also to be seen as part of a more extensive attack on government employees. In education in particular, they constitute an offensive against teacher unions, which are seen to be much too powerful and much too costly. While perhaps not conscious, this needs to be interpreted as part of a longer history of attacks on women's labor, since the vast majority of teachers in the United States—as in so many other nations—are women.[11]

There are varied policy initiatives that have emerged from the neo-liberal segments of the new hegemonic alliance. Most have centered around either creating closer linkages between education and the economy or placing schools themselves into the market. The former is represented by widespread proposals for "school-to-work" and "education-for-employment" programs and by vigorous cost-cutting attacks on the "bloated state." The latter is no less widespread and is becoming increasingly powerful. It is represented by both national and state-by-state proposals for voucher and choice programs.[12] Behind this is a plan to subject schools to the discipline of market competition.[13]

Some proponents of "choice" argue that only enhanced parental "voice" and choice will provide a chance for "educational salvation" for minority parents and children.[14] Terry Moe, for instance, claims that the best hope for the poor to gain the right "to leave bad schools and seek out good ones" is through an "unorthodox alliance."[15] Only by allying themselves with Republicans and business—the most powerful groups supposedly willing to transform the system—can the poor succeed.

There is increasing empirical evidence around the world that the development of "quasi markets" in education has led to the exacerbation of existing social divisions surrounding class and race.[16] There are now increasingly convincing arguments that while the supposed overt goal of voucher and choice plans is to give poor people the right to exit public schools, among the ultimate long-term effects may be to increase "white flight" from public schools into private and religious schools and to create the conditions where affluent white parents may refuse to pay taxes to support public schools that are suffering more and more from the debilitating effects of the fiscal crisis of the state. The result is even more educational apartheid, not less.[17]

In his own review of evidence from the United States, England, New Zealand, and Australian experiences, Whitty argues that while advocates of choice assume that competition will enhance the efficiency and responsiveness of schools, as well as give disadvantaged children opportunities they currently do not have, this may be a false hope.[18] These hopes are not now being realized and are unlikely to be realized in the future "in the context of broader policies that do nothing to challenge deeper social and cultural inequalities." He continues, "Atomized decision-making in a highly stratified society may appear to give everyone equal opportunities but transforming responsibility for decision-making from the public to the private sphere can actually reduce the scope for collective action to improve the quality of education for all."[19]

This position is ratified by Henig, who states, "The sad irony of the current education-reform movement is that, through over-identification with school choice proposals, the healthy impulse to consider radical reforms to address social problems may be channeled into initiatives that further erode the potential for collective deliberation and collective response."[20] When this is coupled with the fact that such neoliberal policies in practice may reproduce traditional hierarchies of class, race, and gender, this should give us serious pause.[21]

There is a second variant of neoliberalism. This one *is* willing to spend more state and private money on schools, if and only if schools meet the needs expressed by capital. Thus, resources are made available for "reforms" and policies that further connect the education system to the project of making our economy more competitive. Two examples can provide a glimpse of this position. In a number of states, legislation has been passed that directs schools and universities to make closer links between education and the business community. In the state of Wisconsin, for instance, all teacher education programs must include identifiable experiences on "education for employment" for all of its future teachers; and all teaching in the public elementary, middle, and secondary schools of the state must include elements of education for employment in its formal curricula.[22]

The second example is seemingly less consequential, but in reality it is a powerful statement of the reintegration of educational policy and practice into the ideological agenda of neoliberalism. I am referring here to Channel One, a for-profit television network that is now broadcast into schools (many of which are financially hard-pressed given the fiscal crisis) enrolling more than 40 percent of all middle- and secondary school students in the nation. In this "reform," schools are offered a "free" satellite dish, two

VCRs, and television monitors for each of their classrooms by a private media corporation. They are also offered a free news broadcast for these students. In return for the equipment and the news, all participating schools must sign a three-to-five-year contract guaranteeing that their students will watch Channel One every day.

This sounds relatively benign. However, not only is the technology "hard-wired" so that *only* Channel One can be received, but broadcast along with the news are *mandatory advertisements* for major fast food, athletic wear, and other corporations that students—by contract—must also watch. Students, in essence, are sold as a captive audience to corporations. Since, by law, these students must be in schools, the United States is one of the first nations in the world consciously to allow its youth to be sold as commodities to those many corporations willing to pay the high price of advertising on Channel One to get a guaranteed (captive) audience. Thus, under a number of variants of neoliberalism not only are schools transformed into market commodities but so too now are our children.[23]

As I noted, the attractiveness of conservative restorational politics in education rests in large part on major shifts in our common sense—about what democracy is, about whether we see ourselves as possessive individuals ("consumers"), and ultimately about how we see the market working. Underlying neoliberal policies in education and their social policies in general is a faith in the essential fairness and justice of markets. Markets ultimately will distribute resources efficiently and fairly according to effort. They ultimately will create jobs for all who want them. They are the best possible mechanism to ensure a better future for all citizens (consumers).

Because of this, we of course must ask what the economy that reigns supreme in neoliberal positions actually looks like. Yet, far from the positive picture painted by neoliberals in which technologically advanced jobs will replace the drudgery and under- and unemployment so many people now experience, the reality is something else again. As I demonstrate in a much more complete analysis in *Cultural Politics and Education*, markets are as powerfully destructive as they are productive in people's lives.[24]

Let us take as a case in point the paid labor market to which neoliberals want us to attach so much of the education system. Even with the proportional growth in proportion of high-tech related jobs, the kinds of work that are and will be increasingly available to a large portion of the American population will not be highly skilled, technically elegant positions. Just the opposite will be the case. The paid labor market will increasingly be dominated by low-paying, repetitive work in the retail, trade, and service sector. This is made strikingly clear by one fact: there will be more cashier jobs created by the year 2005 than jobs for computer scientists, systems analysts, physical therapists, operations analysts, and radiologic technicians *combined*. Further, eight of the top ten individual occupations that will account for the most job growth in the next ten years include the following: retail salespersons, cashiers, office clerks, truck drivers, waitresses/waiters, nursing aides/orderlies, food preparation workers, and janitors. It is obvious that the majority of these positions do not require high levels of education. Many of them are low-paid, nonunionized, and part-time, with low or no benefits. And many are dramatically linked to, and often exacerbate, the existing race, gender, and class divisions of labor, nationally and globally.[25] This is the emerging economy we face, not the overly romantic picture painted by neoliberals who urge us to trust the market.

Neoliberals argue that by making the market the ultimate arbiter of social worthiness, this will eliminate politics and its accompanying irrationality from our educational and social decisions. Efficiency and cost-benefit analysis will be the engines of social and educational transformation. Yet among the ultimate effects of such "economizing" and "depoliticizing" strategies is a continued failure to interrupt the growing inequalities in resources and power that so deeply characterize this society.

Two of these effects are of particular import to my discussion of education. Many communities have indeed felt the severe consequences of exporting jobs to low-wage and largely nonunionized countries in terms of unemployment, downsizing, companies reneging on collective bargaining agreements, and so forth. The fiscal crisis this has caused—for example, through declining tax revenues, states and localities engaging in corporate givebacks to keep or attract industry, and so on—is all too visible in terms of the decaying educational infrastructure in cities and rural areas in many nations.[26] Yet there is a second effect that needs to be mentioned, one that is more ideological in terms of the formation of common sense. Global competition consistently frames public discussions of educational policy and practice. Reductive testing and accountability proposals, constant cost-cutting, marketization, closer links between education and the economy, and so much more are made to seem *inevitable*. Conservative discourses are naturalized by the "realities" of global competition.

How this naturalization is discursively constructed is important. Nancy Fraser illuminates the process in the following way:

> In male dominated capitalist societies, what is "political" is normally defined contrastively against what is "economic" and what is "domestic" or "personal." Here, then, we can identify two principal sets of institutions that depoliticize social discourses: they are, first, domestic institutions, especially the normative domestic form, namely the modern restricted male-headed nuclear family; and, second, official economic capitalist system institutions, especially paid workplaces, markets, credit mechanisms, and "private" enterprises and corporations. Domestic institutions depoliticize certain matters by personalizing and/or familializing them; they cast these as private-domestic or personal-familial matters in contradistinction to public, political matters. Official economic capitalist system institutions, on the other hand, depoliticize certain matters by economizing them; the issues in question here are cast as impersonal market imperatives, or as "private" ownership prerogatives, or as technical problems for managers and planners, all in contradistinction to political matters. In both cases, the result is a foreshortening of chains of in-order-to relations for interpreting people's needs; interpretive chains are truncated and prevented from spilling across the boundaries separating the "domestic" and the "economic" from the political.[27]

For Fraser, this very process of depoliticization makes it very difficult for the needs of those with less economic, political, and cultural power to be heard accurately and acted upon in ways that deal with the true depth of the problem. This is because of what happens when "needs discourses" get retranslated into both market talk and "privately" driven policies.

For our purposes here, we can talk about two major kinds of needs discourses. There are first *oppositional* forms of needs talk. They arise when needs are politicized from below and are part of the crystallization of new oppositional identities on the part of subordinated social groups. What was once seen as largely a "private" matter is now placed into the larger political arena. Sexual harassment, race, and sex segregation in paid labor, and affirmative action policies in educational and economic institutions provide examples of "private" issues that have now spilled over and can no longer be confined to the "domestic" sphere.[28]

A second kind of needs discourse is what might be called *reprivatization* discourses. They emerge as a response to the newly emergent oppositional forms and try to press these forms back into the "private" or the "domestic" arena. They are often aimed at dismantling or cutting back social services, deregulating "private" enterprise, or stopping what are seen as "runaway needs." Thus, reprivatizers may attempt to keep issues such as, say, domestic battery from spilling over into overt political discourse, and will seek to define it as purely a family matter. Or they will argue that the closing of a factory and moving it to another nation because of "cheaper" labor is not a political question, but instead is an unimpeachable prerogative of private ownership or an unassailable imperative of an impersonal "market mechanism."[29] In each of these cases, the task is to contest both the possible breakout of runaway needs and to depoliticize the issues.

In educational policy in the United States, there are a number of clear examples of these processes. In California, for instance, a recent binding referendum that prohibited the use of affirmative action policies in state government, in university admission policies, and so forth, was passed overwhelmingly because "reprivatizers" spent an exceptional amount of money on an advertising campaign that labeled such policies as "out of control" and as improper government intervention into decisions involving "individual merit." Voucher plans in education—where contentious issues surrounding whose knowledge should be taught, who should control school policy and practice, and how schools should be financed are left to the market to decide—offer another prime example of such attempts at "depoliticizing" educational needs. Both show the emerging power of reprivatizing discourses.

A distinction that is useful here in understanding what is happening in these cases is that between "value" and "sense" legitimation.[30] Each signifies a different strategy by which powerful groups or states legitimate their authority. In the first (value) strategy, legitimation is accomplished by actually giving people what may have been promised. Thus, the social democratic state may provide social services for the population in return for continued support. That the state will do this is often the result of oppositional discourses gaining more power in the social arena and having more power to redefine the border between public and private.

In the second (sense) strategy, rather than providing people with policies that meet the needs they have expressed, states and dominant groups attempt to *change the very meaning* of the sense of social need into something that is very different. Thus, if less powerful people call for "more democracy" and for a more responsive state, the task is not to give "value" that meets this demand, especially when it may lead to runaway needs. Rather, the task is to change what actually *counts* as democracy. In the case of neoliberal policies, democracy is now redefined as guaranteeing choice in an unfettered market. In essence, the state withdraws. The extent of acceptance of such transformations of needs and needs discourses shows the success of the reprivatizers in redefining the borders between public and private again and demonstrates how a people's common sense can be shifted in conservative directions during a time of economic and ideological crisis.

Neoconservatism

While neoliberals largely are in leadership in the conservative alliance, the second major element within the new alliance is neoconservatism. Unlike the neoliberal emphasis on the weak state, neoconservatives are usually guided by a vision of the strong state. This is especially true surrounding issues of knowledge, values, and the body. Whereas neoliberalism may be seen as being based in what Raymond Williams would call an "emergent" ideological assemblage, neoconservatism is grounded in "residual" forms.[31] It is largely, although not totally, based in a romantic appraisal of the past, a past in which "real knowledge" and morality reigned supreme, where people "knew their place," and where stable communities guided by a natural order protected us from the ravages of society.[32]

Among the policies being proposed under this ideological position are national curricula, national testing, a "return" to higher standards, a revivification of the "Western tradition," and patriotism. Yet, underlying some of the neoconservative thrust in education and in social policy in general is not only a call for "return." Also behind it—and this is essential—is a fear of the "other." This is expressed in its support for a standardized national curriculum, its attacks on bilingualism and multiculturalism, and its insistent call for raising standards.[33] As noted earlier, such proposals have become more strident as neoconservatives assail the "threats" of increased immigration and cultural blending posed by global mobility and interaction.

Behind much of this is a clear sense of loss—a loss of faith, of imagined communities, of a nearly pastoral vision of like-minded people who shared norms and values and in which the "Western tradition" reigned supreme. It is more than a little similar to Mary Douglas's discussion of purity and danger, in which what was imagined to exist is sacred and "pollution" is feared above all else.[34] We/they binary oppositions dominate this discourse, and the culture of "the other" is to be feared.

This sense of cultural pollution can be seen in the increasingly virulent attacks on multiculturalism (which is itself a very broad category that combines multiple political and cultural positions) in the denial of schooling or any other social benefits to the children of "illegal" immigrants, and even in some cases to the children of legal immigrants, in the conservative English-only movement, and in the equally conservative attempts to reorient curricula and textbooks toward a particular construction of the Western tradition.[35]

In this regard, neoconservatives lament the "decline" of the traditional curriculum and of the history, literature, and values it is said to have represented. Behind this complaint rests an entire set of historical assumptions about "tradition," about the existence of a social consensus over what should count as legitimate knowledge, and about cultural superiority.[36] Yet, it is crucial to remember that the "traditional" curriculum whose decline is lamented so fervently by neoconservative critics "ignored most of the groups that compose the American population whether they were from Africa, Europe, Asia, Central and South America, or from indigenous North American peoples."[37] Its primary and often exclusive focus was often only on quite a narrow spectrum of those people who came from a small number of northern and western European nations, in spite of the fact that the cultures and histories represented in the United States were "forged out of a much larger and more diverse complex of peoples and societies."[38] The mores and cultures of this narrow spectrum were seen as archetypes of "tradition" for everyone. They were not simply taught, but taught as superior to every other set of mores and cultures.[39]

As Lawrence Levine reminds us, a selective and faulty sense of history fuels the nostalgic yearnings of neoconservatives. The canon and the curriculum have never been static. They have always been in a constant process of revision, "with irate defenders insisting, as they still do, that change would bring with it instant decline."[40] Indeed, even the inclusion of such "classics" as Shakespeare within the curriculum of schools in the United States came about only after prolonged and intense battles, ones that were the equal of the divisive debates over whose knowledge should be taught today. Thus, Levine notes that when neoconservative cultural critics ask for a "return" to a "common culture" and "tradition," they are oversimplifying to the point of distortion. What is happening in terms of the expansion and alteration of official knowledge in schools and universities today "is by no means out of the ordinary; certainly it is not a radical departure from the patterns that have marked the history of [education]—constant and often controversial expansion and alteration of curricula and canons and incessant struggle over the nature of that expansion and alteration."[41]

Of course, such conservative positions have been forced into a kind of compromise in order to maintain their cultural and ideological leadership as a movement to "reform" educational policy and practice. A prime example is the emerging discourse over the history curriculum—in particular the construction of the United States as a "nation of immigrants."[42] In this hegemonic discourse, everyone in the history of the nation was an immigrant, from the first Native American population who supposedly trekked across the Bering Strait and ultimately populated North, Central, and South America, to the later waves of populations who came from Mexico, Ireland, Germany, Scandinavia, Italy, Russia, Poland, and elsewhere, to finally the recent populations from Asia, Latin America, Africa, and other regions. While it is true that the United States is constituted by people from all over the world—and that is one of the things that makes it so culturally rich and vital—such a perspective constitutes an erasure of historical memory. For some groups came *in chains* and were subjected to state-sanctioned slavery and apartheid for hundreds of years. Others suffered what can only be called bodily, linguistic, and cultural destruction.[43]

This said, however, it does point to the fact that while the neoconservative goals of national curricula and national testing are pressed for, they are strongly mediated by the necessity of compromise. Because of this, even the strongest supporters of neoconservative educational programs and policies have had to also support the creation of curricula that at least partly recognize "the contributions of the other."[44] This is partly due to the fact that there is an absence of an overt and strong national department of education and a tradition of state and local control of schooling. The "solution" has been to have national standards developed "voluntarily" in each subject area.[45] Indeed, the example I gave above about history is one of the results of such voluntary standards.

Since the national professional organizations in these subject areas—such as the National Council of Teachers of Mathematics—are developing such national standards, the standards themselves are compromises and thus are often more flexible than those wished for by neoconservatives. This very process acts to provide a check on conservative policies over knowledge. However, this should not lead to an exaggerated romantic picture of the overall tendencies emerging in educational policy. Since leadership in school "reform" is increasingly dominated by conservative discourses surrounding "standards," "excellence," "accountability," and so on, and since the more flexible parts of the standards have proven to be too expensive to implement, standards talk ultimately functions to give more rhetorical weight to the neoconservative movement to enhance central control over "official knowledge" and to "raise the bar" for achievement. The social implications of this in terms of creating even more differential school results are increasingly worrisome.[46]

Yet it is not only in such things as the control over legitimate knowledge where neoconservative impulses are seen. The idea of a strong state is also visible in the growth of the regulatory state as it concerns teachers. There has been a steadily growing change from "licensed autonomy" to "regulated autonomy" as teachers' work is more highly standardized, rationalized, and "policed."[47] Under conditions of licensed autonomy, once teachers are given the appropriate professional certification they are basically free—within limits—to act in their classrooms according to their judgment. Such a regime is based on trust in "professional discretion." Under the growing conditions of regulated autonomy, teachers' actions are now subjected to much greater scrutiny in terms of process and outcomes. Indeed, some U.S. states not only have specified the content that teachers are to teach but also have regulated the only appropriate methods of teaching. Not following these specified "appropriate" methods puts the teacher at risk of administrative sanctions. Such a regime of control is based not on trust, but on a deep suspicion of the motives and competence of teachers. For neoconservatives it is the equivalent of the notion of "producer capture" so powerful among neoliberals. For the former, however, the market will not solve this problem; rather a strong and interventionist state will see to it that only "legitimate" content and methods are taught. And this will be policed by statewide and national tests of both students and teachers.

As I have demonstrated elsewhere, such policies lead to the "de-skilling" of teachers, the "intensification" of their work, and the loss of autonomy and respect.[48] This is not surprising, since behind much of this conservative impulse is a clear distrust of teachers and an attack both on teachers' claims to competence and especially on teachers' unions.[49]

The mistrust of teachers, the concern over a supposed loss of cultural control, and the sense of dangerous "pollution" are among the many cultural and social fears that drive neoconservative policies. However, as I noted earlier, underpinning these positions as well is often an ethnocentric, and even racialized, understanding of the world. Perhaps this can be best illuminated through the example of Herrnstein and Murray's volume, *The Bell Curve*.[50] In a book that sold hundreds of thousands of copies, the authors argue for a genetic determinism based on race (and to some extent gender). For them, it is romantic to assume that educational and social policies can ultimately lead to more equal results, since differences in intelligence and achievement are basically genetically driven. Policymakers would be wise to accept this and plan for a society that recognizes these biological differences and does not provide "false hopes" to the poor and the less intelligent, most of whom will be black. Obviously, this book has reinforced racist stereotypes that have long played a considerable part in educational and social policies in the West.[51]

Rather than seeing race as it is—as a fully *social* category that is mobilized and used in different ways by different groups at different times[52]—positions such as those argued by Herrnstein and Murray provide a veneer of seeming scientific legitimacy for policy discourses that have been discredited intellectually many times before.[53] The sponsored mobility given to this book, in which it is reported that the authors received large sums of money from neoconservative foundations to write and publicize the volume, speaks clearly not only to the racial underpinnings of important parts of the neoconservative agenda but also to the power of conservative groups to bring their case before the public.

The consequences of such positions are not only found in educational policies but also in the intersection of such policies with broader social and economic policies, where they have been quite influential. Here too we can find claims that what the poor lack is not money, but both an "appropriate" biological inheritance and a decided lack of values regarding discipline, hard work, and morality.[54] Prime examples here include programs such as "Learnfare" and "Workfare," where parents lose a portion of their welfare benefits if their children miss a significant number of school days, or where no benefits are paid if a person does not accept low-paid work, no matter how demeaning, or even if child care or health care are not provided by the state. Such policies reinstall earlier "workhouse" policies that were so popular—and so utterly damaging—in the United States, Britain, and elsewhere.

Conclusion

Because of the complexity of educational politics in a global context, I have devoted most of this chapter to an analysis of the conservative social movements that are having a powerful impact on debates over policy and practice in education and in the larger social arena. I have suggested that the conservative restoration is guided by a tense coalition of forces, some of whose aims partly contradict others.

The very nature of this coalition is crucial. It is more than possible that the conservative modernization implied in this alliance can overcome its own internal contradictions and can succeed in radically transforming educational policy and practice. Thus, while neoliberals call for a weak state and neoconservatives demand a strong state, these apparently contradictory impulses can come together in creative ways. The emerging focus on centralized standards, content, and tighter control paradoxically can be the first and most essential step on the path to marketization through voucher and choice plans.

Once statewide or national curricula and tests are put in place, comparative school-by-school data will be available and will be published in a manner similar to the "league tables" on school achievement published in England. Only when there is standardized content and assessment can the market be set free, since the "consumer" can then have "objective" data concerning which schools are "succeeding" and which schools are not. Market rationality, based on "consumer choice," will insure that the supposedly good schools will gain students and the bad schools will disappear.[55]

When the poor "choose" to keep their children in underfunded and decaying schools in the inner cities or in rural areas (given the decline and expense of urban mass transportation, poor information, the absence of time, and their decaying economic conditions, to name but a few of the realities), *they* (the poor) will be blamed individually and collectively for making bad "consumer choices." Reprivatizing discourses and arithmetical particularism will justify the structural inequalities that will be (re)produced here. In this way, as odd as it may seem, neoliberal and neoconservative policies that are seemingly contradictory may mutually reinforce each other in the long run.[56]

Yet, while I have argued that the overall leadership in educational policy is exercised by this alliance, I do not want to give the impression that the elements under the hegemonic umbrella of this coalition are uncontested or are always victorious. This is simply not the case. As a number of people have demonstrated, at the local level throughout the United States and elsewhere there are scores of counterhegemonic programs and possibilities. It is crucial to remember, for example, that the processes and conflicts involved in globalization also constantly generate possibilities for other, more critical, engagements. On a larger level, these have included mobilizations around environmental issues, around international labor standards (Nike factories, for instance), around the repressive politics that often accompany global competition, and so on.[57] On an educational level, these realities also can and have been used to stimulate students and teachers to take such issues seriously as objects of critical inquiry in the curriculum. Indeed, the integration of these kinds of social issues has a long history in critical education in schools at all levels.[58] Many schools in many nations have shown remarkable resiliency in the face of the concerted ideological attacks and pressures from conservative restorational groups. And many teachers, community activists, and others have created and defended educational programs that are both pedagogically and politically emancipatory.[59]

Having said this, however, it is important to note the obstacles in creating the conditions for large-scale movements to defend and build progressive policies. We need to remember that there is no powerful central ministry of education in the United States. Teachers' unions are relatively weak at a national level (nor is there any guarantee that teachers' unions always act progressively). There is no consensus about an "appropriate" progressive agenda in educational policy here, since there is a vast multiplicity of compelling (and, unfortunately, at times competing) agendas involving race/ethnicity, gender, sexuality, class, religion, "ability," and so on. Thus, it is structurally difficult to sustain long-term national movements for more progressive policies and practices.

Because of this, most counterhegemonic work is organized locally or regionally. However, there currently are growing attempts at building national coalitions around what might best be called a "decentered unity."[60] Organizations in the United States such as the National Coalition of Educational Activists and the Rethinking Schools collective are becoming more visible nationally.[61] None of these movements have the financial and organizational backing that stands behind neoliberal and neoconservative groups. None have the ability to bring their case before the "public" through the media and through foundations in the ways that conservative groups have been able to do. And none have the capacity or the resources to mobilize quickly a large base of nationally directed membership to challenge or promote specific policies in the ways that the members of the conservative alliance can. Effective global or transnational coalitions around progressive educational concerns have proven even more elusive.

Yet, in the face of all of these structural, financial, and political dilemmas, the fact that so many groups of people have not been integrated under the conservative alliance's hegemonic umbrella, and have created scores of local examples of the very possibility of difference, shows us in the most eloquent and lived ways that educational policies and practices are not uni-dimensional. Even more important, these multiple examples demonstrate that the success of conservative policies is never guaranteed. This is crucial in a time when it is easy to lose sight of what is necessary for an education worthy of its name.

Notes

1. Madeleine Arnot, "Schooling for Social Justice" (unpublished paper, University of Cambridge, 1990).
2. Dennis Carlson and Michael W. Apple, eds., *Power/Knowledge/Pedagogy* (Boulder: Westview Press, 1998).
3. William Greider, *One World, Ready or Not* (New York: Simon and Schuster, 1997).
4. Michael W. Apple, *Official Knowledge* (New York: Routledge, 1993); and Michael W. Apple, *Cultural Politics and Education* (New York: Teachers College Press,

1996).

5. Roger Dale, "The Thatcherite Project in Education," *Critical Social Policy* 9 (1989): 4–19.

6. Ted Honderich, *Conservatism* (Boulder: Westview Press, 1990).

7. Given the current emphasis on this by neoliberals, it may be the case that while Bowles and Gintis's book, *Schooling in Capitalist America*, was reductive, economistic, and essentializing when it first appeared in 1976, oddly it may be more accurate today. See Samuel Bowles and Herbert Gintis, *Schooling in Capitalist America* (New York: Basic Books, 1976). For criticisms of their position, see Michael W. Apple, *Teachers and Texts* (New York: Routledge, 1988); Michael W. Apple, *Education and Power*, 2d ed. (New York: Routledge, 1995); and Mike Cole, ed. *Bowles and Gintis Revisited* (New York: Falmer Press, 1988).

8. Michael W. Apple, *Ideology and Curriculum*, 2d ed. (New York: Routledge, 1990).

9. Stephen Ball, *Education Reform* (Philadelphia: Open University Press, 1994).

10. See Apple, *Education and Power*. It is important to note as well that neoliberalism rests on a number of patriarchal assumptions. It is often based on an assumption that important social needs that are now met by the state in the areas of child care and caring for the elderly, health, and welfare will be taken up in the "domestic sphere." In essence, neoliberalism is dependent on both increasing the exploitation of the unpaid labor of women in the home and in communities and on the revivification of important aspects of the separation between the public and private spheres. For more on the ideological effects of this separation, see Nancy Fraser, *Unruly Practices* (Minneapolis: University of Minnesota Press, 1989).

11. Apple, *Teachers and Texts,* especially chap. 2 and 3; and Sandra Acker, "Gender and Teachers' Work," in *Review of Research in Education Volume 21*, ed. Michael W. Apple (Washington, D.C.: American Educational Research Association, 1995), 99–162.

12. See John Chubb and Terry Moe, *Politics, Markets, and America's Schools* (Washington, D.C.: Brookings Institution, 1990).

13. For further critical discussion of these plans, see Amy Stuart Wells, *Time to Choose* (New York: Hill and Wang, 1993); Kevin Smith and Kenneth Meier, eds. *The Case against School Choice* (Armonk, N.Y.: M. E. Sharpe, 1995); and Jeffrey Henig, *Rethinking School Choice* (Princeton: Princeton University Press, 1994).

14. Geoff Whitty, "Creating Quasi-Markets in Education," in *Review of Research in Education Volume 22*, ed. Michael W. Apple (Washington, D.C.: American Educational Research Association, 1997), 17. See also, Chubb and Moe, *Politics, Markets, and America's Schools*.

15. Quoted in Whitty, "Creating Quasi-Markets in Education," 17.

16. Geoff Whitty, Sally Power, and David Halpin, *Devolution and Choice in Education* (Bristol, Penn.: Open University Press, 1998).

17. I have discussed this at greater length in Apple, *Cultural Politics and Education*.

18. Whitty, "Creating Quasi-Markets in Education," 58.

19. Ibid.

20. Henig, *Rethinking School Choice*, 222.

21. See Apple, *Cultural Politics and Education*; and Whitty et al., *Devolution and Choice in Education*.

22. Many times, however, these initiatives are actually "unfunded mandates." That is,

requirements such as these are made mandatory, but no additional funding is provided to accomplish them. The intensification of teachers' labor at all levels of the education system that results from this situation is very visible.

23. Apple, *Official Knowledge*, 93–117. See also Alex Molnar, *Giving Kids the Business* (Boulder: Westview Press, 1996).
24. Apple, *Cultural Politics and Education*, 68–90.
25. Ibid. See also Greider, *One World, Ready or Not*, for a rich set of descriptions of the international implications of this.
26. See, for example, Apple, *Official Knowledge*; and Greider, *One World, Ready or Not*.
27. Fraser, *Unruly Practices*, 168.
28. Fraser, *Unruly Practices*, 172. See also the discussion of how gains in one sphere of social life can be "transported" into another sphere in Samuel Bowles and Herbert Gintis, *Democracy and Capitalism* (New York: Basic Books, 1986); and Apple, *Teachers and Texts*.
29. Fraser, *Unruly Practices*, 172.
30. Roger Dale, *The State and Education Policy* (Philadelphia: Open University Press, 1989).
31. Raymond A. Williams, *Marxism and Literature* (New York: Oxford University Press, 1977).
32. See Allen Hunter, *Children in the Service of Conservatism* (Madison: University of Wisconsin Institute for Legal Studies, 1988); and Apple, *Cultural Politics and Education*.
33. See, for example, E. D. Hirsch Jr., *The Schools We Want and Why We Don't Have Them* (New York: Doubleday, 1996).
34. Mary Douglas, *Purity and Danger* (London: Routledge and Kegan Paul, 1966).
35. See Cameron McCarthy and Warren Critchlow, eds., *Race, Identity and Representation in Education* (New York: Routledge, 1994); and Cameron McCarthy, *The Uses of Culture* (New York: Routledge, 1998).
36. See Apple, *Ideology and Curriculum*, for further analysis of the history and current status of these positions.
37. Lawrence Levine, *The Opening of the American Mind* (Boston: Beacon Press, 1996), 20.
38. Ibid.
39. Ibid.
40. Ibid., 15. Also see Apple, *Ideology and Curriculum*; and Herbert Kliebard, *The Struggle for the American Curriculum*, 2d ed. (New York: Routledge, 1995).
41. Levine, *The Opening of the American Mind*, 15.
42. Catherine Cornbleth and Dexter Waugh, *The Great Speckled Bird* (New York: St. Martin's Press, 1995).
43. See Apple, *Cultural Politics and Education*, 17.
44. This is often done through a process of "mentioning," where texts and curricula include material on the contributions of women and "minority" groups, but never allow the reader to see the world through the eyes of oppressed groups. Or, as is the case in the discourse of "we are all immigrants," compromises are made so that the myth of historical similarity is constructed at the same time as economic divides among groups grow worse and worse. See Apple, *Official Knowledge*, especially

chap. 3.

45. See, for example, Diane Ravitch, *National Standards in American Education* (Washington, D.C.: Brookings Institution, 1995).
46. For further discussion of this, see Michael W. Apple, "Do the Standards Go Far Enough?" *Journal for Research in Mathematics Education* 23 (Nov. 1992): 412–31; and Michael W. Apple, "Are Standards and Markets Democratic?" *Educational Researcher* 27 (Aug.–Sept. 1998): 24–28.
47. Dale, *The State and Education Policy*.
48. See Apple, *Teachers and Texts*; and Apple, *Education and Power*.
49. On the relationship between this and gender, see Acker, "Gender and Teachers' Work."
50. Richard Herrnstein and Charles Murray, *The Bell Curve* (New York: The Free Press, 1994).
51. See, for example, Michael Omi and Howard Winant, *Racial Formation in the United States* (New York: Routledge, 1994).
52. Ibid.
53. See Joe Kincheloe and Shirley Steinberg, eds., *Measured Lies* (New York: St. Martin's Press, 1996); and Steven Selden, *Inheriting Shame* (New York: Teachers College Press, 1999).
54. Rebecca Klatch, *Women of the New Right* (Philadelphia: Temple University Press, 1987). These kinds of assumptions are visible in a number of countries, often stimulated by the increasing power of neoliberal/neoconservative coalitions.
55. Whitty et al., *Devolution and Choice in Education*.
56. For further discussion of this, see Apple, *Cultural Politics and Education*, 22–41.
57. See, for example, the discussion of the Free Burma Campaign and the Coalition for Socially Responsible Investing in Zar Ni and Michael W. Apple, "Countering Capital on Campus," in *Campus Inc.*, ed. Geoffrey White (New York: Prometheus Books, in press).
58. See Ira Shor, *Critical Teaching and Everyday Life* (Boston: South End Press, 1980); Roger Simon, Don Dippo, and Arlene Schenke, *Learning Work* (New York: Bergin and Garvey, 1991); and Michael W. Apple, *Power, Meaning, and Identity* (New York: Peter Lang, 1999).
59. See especially Chris Searle, *None But Our Words* (Buckingham, Eng.: Open University Press, 1998); Michael W. Apple and James A. Beane, *Democratic Schools* (Washington, D.C.: Association for Supervision and Curriculum Development, 1995); and Greg Smith, ed., *Public Schools that Work* (New York: Routledge, 1993).
60. I have discussed the concept of "decentered unity," along with its companion concept "nonreformist reforms," in Apple, *Education and Power*; and especially, Apple, *Cultural Politics and Education*.
61. See, for example, the journal *Rethinking Schools*. It is one of the very best indicators of progressive struggles, policies, and practices in education. Information can be obtained from Rethinking Schools, 1001 E. Keefe Avenue, Milwaukee, Wisconsin, 53212, U.S.A.

It Is and It Isn't: Vernacular Globalization, Educational Policy, and Restructuring

Bob Lingard

Within the vernacular we sometimes describe the complexities of a social phenomenon by the use of: "Well, it is and it isn't." This seems to be a productive way to think about globalization generally, as well as its playing out in educational policy and restructuring. The recent restructuring of educational systems can aptly be explained by recourse to an understanding of globalization. However, we also need to understand the micro-histories, -cultures, and -politics of local practices of educational restructuring as they are implicated in the multiple flows of globalization.

The dominant reading of globalization within contemporary neoliberal or right-wing politics has been one of the supposed inevitability (and desirability) of market liberal ideology and its manifestation in both the structures and policies of governments. Paradoxically, some Left readings assume a similar inevitability, albeit more critically. There is an important distinction to be made between the ideological and empirical effects of globalization, particularly in policy terms, because policy is often concerned to construct policy problems in given ways. In this chapter the "myth of the powerless state"[1] in the face of globalization—indeed the reification of globalization as a causal explanation—is rejected. The nation-state still retains some capacity, if at times it lacks the will, to do more politically than simply facilitating economic globalization. Further, the argument here sees globalization and its specific manifestation within given nation-states, localities, and in educational restructuring as more nuanced than this and rejects any accounts that see globalization as simply resulting in top-down homogenization of both politics and culture. As Robertson notes, globalization has seen cultural tendencies for both homogenization and heterogenization in "mutually implicative" tension.[2] The stance in this chapter is to recognize the emergence of another period of laissez-faire economics and politics, albeit on a global scale, but mediated by history, politics, contingency, and complexity, along with these cultural tensions between homogenization and heterogenization and political tensions between integration (beyond nations) and fragmentation (within nations).[3]

In terms of educational restructuring then, it is and it isn't a result of globalization. The "big policies in a small world"—the apparent educational policy convergence across nations facilitated by greater global interconnectedness and a nascent global educational policy community—are mediated, translated, and recontextualized within national and local educational structures.[4] The cultural flows of globalization are experienced more directly by self-managing schools and their students, as well as in a mediated fashion via educational policy and restructuring. It is within schools in restructured educational systems that there is a tension between what Arjun Appadurai calls "context-productive" (top-down and policy driven) and "context-generative" (localized) practices, all nested within the flows of globalization.[5]

"Vernacular globalization" is the notion developed by Appadurai to pick up on these nuanced outcomes of the clash of the context-productive with context-generative practices and to reject globalization as meaning only Westernization, Americanization, commoditification, and homogenization. For Appadurai, context-generative micronarratives "allow modernity to be rewritten more as vernacular globalization and less as a concession to large-scale national and international policies."[6] Vernacular globalization in this sense carries resonances with the idea of "glocalization": the way local, national, and global interrelationships are being reconstituted, but mediated by the history of the local and the national and by politics, as well as by hybridization, an important resulting cultural feature of the multidirectional flows of cultural globalization and the tension between homogenization and heterogenization. While nations and cultures have to relativize their stance in relation to the capitalist West,[7] and while the most powerful economic interests have more capacity to affect global politics and cultures (out of the world's one hundred largest economies, forty-seven are multinational conglomerates[8]), globalization has seen a move beyond a center/periphery relationship in these matters, with multiple centers now across the globe and the periphery "speaking back" to these centers in a variety of (postcolonial) cultural and political ways. While mostly metropolitan elites (including policymakers) participate in global networks, there is broader recognition that "the constraints of geography are receding"[9] with "the phenomenal world" of most people, including policy elites and school students, being "truly global."[10]

In considering vernacular globalization in educational policy and restructuring, an analysis is provided of how the structures in which educational policy is produced and practiced have been reorganized, as political factors associated with the globalization of the economy pressure for a managerialist restructuring of the state, including education. Yeatman has argued that the transition from multinational to transnational capitalism in the sixties and seventies resulted in a disjunction between the "needs" of such a form of capital and the organizational structure and policy regime of the (nation-) state. She suggests that Keynesian-informed bureaucratic state structures and policies, which emphasized top-down expenditure as the solution to "social problems" resulting from the fallout of market economics and marked the end of the first period of laissez-faire, became "out of sync" with the emergent "needs" of transnational capital.[11] Michael Pusey likewise has noted how any move by national governments to "globalize" their economies "presupposes a closer functional incorporation of the 'political administrative' system (the state, and with it the obligatory conditions of elected governments) into an augmented economic system."[12] Habermas has made a similar observation to those proffered by Yeatman and Pusey concerning the implications of the globalization of the economy for state structures and policies:

> While the world economy operates largely uncoupled from any political frame, national governments are restricted to fostering the modernization of their national economies. As a consequence, they have to adapt national welfare systems to what is called the capacity for international competition.[13]

The politics surrounding the attempts to bring transnational capital and state organizational form into "sync" have seen the restructuring of the state in most Western societies, variously under the rubric of "new public management" or "corporate managerialism." State restructuring has been intimately implicated in the facilitation of a global economy by national governments. This development has been accompanied by talk in the literature of the emergent "evaluative,"[14] "competitive,"[15] "managerial,"[16] or "postmodern" state,[17] which takes as its chief policy focus the internationalizing of putative national economies; such economic restructuring has taken on "metapolicy" status, reframing educational policies in the process.[18] As a consequence, educational administration and policy have lost their erstwhile sui generis character and the voices of the profession have become somewhat muted, with teachers becoming the objects, rather than the subjects, of educational policy production. This chapter seeks to understand and analyze the resultant educational restructurings, that is, the playing out of vernacular globalization in what amounts to new forms of governance in education.

However, policy production in education is not only framed by these new structures within nations but also by the emergence of supranational political structures. Appadurai speaks of a number of cultural scapes of globalization, referring largely to the flows of people (for example, migrants, refugees, tourists, politicians, students, intellectuals, policy elites) and the rapid flow of media images and ideas via new technologies, and argues that, within diasporic public spheres, where politics are played out across national boundaries, we are seeing the emergence of a "postnational political order."[19] He believes that today in the context of cultural globalization the hyphen between the nation and the state has become somewhat attenuated, with each now the project of the other. While he overplays the demise of the nation-state, some other globalization theorists underplay the extent to which local, national, and global interrelationships are being reconstituted.[20] The position taken in this chapter is that the local, the national, and the emerging global structures sit in "mutually constitutive" relationships with each other.[21] Wiseman has suggested, "The processes of globalization are helping to create a world of 'nested locales' in which households, neighborhoods, cities, provinces, nations and regions sit inside the wider global relationships like Russian Babushka dolls."[22] A second focus in this chapter then deals with supranational policy production in education and an emergent global policy community,[23] drawing on a study that has sought to understand the mutual and interdependent relationships between the Organization for Economic Co-operation and Development (OECD), globalization, and educational policy production in Australia.[24] As such, this chapter makes a contribution to the study of the policy implications of globalization for supranational and transnational policy, a heavily underresearched and undertheorized domain.[25]

An Emergent Policy Settlement in Education

Within the sociology of education there has been broad agreement about the educational policy consensus in Western nations that accompanied the postwar boom period, the era of economic nationalism (1945–1973).[26] Education was seen as central to the production of economic prosperity and equality of educational opportunity within the nation. The organizational form of educational systems was the classical bureaucracy as defined by Weber, which was underpinned by technical rationality, whose pervasiveness was an element in social cohesion and control. Globalization has resulted in the "breakdown of economic nationalism" and the emergence of a new policy consensus globally within education.[27] The globalization of the economy has reduced the apparent policy tools of national governments, destabilized the postwar policy settlement, and witnessed the restructuring of the mechanisms for the delivery of a different range of policies. Brown and Lauder have suggested that what we have seen is a "global auction" in respect to investment by transnational corporations.[28] In respect to this auction, national governments have had to ensure the provision of infrastructure, including a suitably multiskilled and flexible workforce, reductions in corporate taxation levels, and a meaner and leaner welfare system. This call for international competitiveness has weakened the capacity of nation-states to provide social protection for their citizens.[29]

The rapidity of change, the move to post-Fordist production approaches, niche rather than mass production, service rather than manufacturing orientation, along with tighter budgets have waged a sustained attack on the state bureaucratic form that accompanied the Keynesian policy regime of demand management, evident in waves of educational restructuring. Whereas in the earlier period the bureaucratic paradigm was seen as the model of efficiency and fairness, the bureaucratic form came under strong critique as the globalized economy took hold and a new global educational policy consensus emerged. What was now required, so the argument went, was a flatter organizational arrangement geared toward the production of clearly stipulated outcomes at the lowest possible cost. This was also necessary given the speed of change; the sclerotic red-tapeism of the traditional state bureaucracies was deemed to be inappropriate in this context,[30] as was promotion according to seniority rather than merit. This has seen new private-sector management structures and practices incorporated into the public sector, reflecting what Waters calls a global "organizational ecumenism."[31] In education a new state form geared to delivering more narrowly defined goals at a cheaper cost has been the result.

However, and herein lies a paradox, while the structural formation of educational systems has been remade as flatter, leaner, and meaner, there is an emergent consensus that within the globalized economy the production of an educated workforce "judged according to international standards" is more important than ever, part of the state-provided infrastructure necessary to the competitive advantage of nations.[32] At the very moment that nations were losing some control over economic policies and were cutting expenditures, educational policy took on even greater significance. This renewed significance of education as an element of an effective (national) economic policy was reflected in the structures of its production and delivery, but not in expenditure terms.

Educational policy became an element of economic policy framed by a microeconomically focused and rearticulated version of human capital theory linked to the changing structure of the economies and labor markets in the postindustrialized nations of the globe. In the film *Primary Colors*, the President of the United States (a.k.a. Bill Clinton) talks to a group of manual workers about the way the U.S. economy is changing from being based on muscle power in manufacturing to being based on brainpower in the service sector as transnational corporations have relocated manufacturing work to the developing world. With this alignment between education and demand for a more highly skilled and flexible labor force, the politicization and min-isterialization of educational policy production has been one significant out-come, with policy production in education removed to a considerable extent from the policy grip of the educational policy community.[33]

One way to illustrate this new global educational policy consensus and vernacular globalization at work is to consider two Australian policy set-tlements, namely, that of social democratic Labor Party governments (1983–1996) and that of their successor coalition governments (1996–pre-sent). Both settlements were framed by the new global educational policy consensus. However, despite their broad discursive similarity, there were still differences between their responses, reflective basically of party ideo-logical differences and their differing electoral support bases—an indica-tion of vernacular globalization at play.

Labor governments under Bob Hawke and Paul Keating sought to cre-ate a nationally integrated education and training system geared toward the production of an upwardly skilled workforce. Given Australia's federal political structure and its high level of vertical fiscal imbalance—the fed-eral government has much greater revenue-raising capacity than the states, while the states are ostensibly responsible for the delivery of the expensive social services such as schools, hospitals, and policing—there was a com-plex politics at work in achieving a range of national educational policies, particularly in schooling. Schooling is constitutionally the responsibility of the states and jealously guarded by them. Despite that reality, Labor achieved a considerable range of national educational polices in schooling in the late eighties and early nineties.[34] These included equity-focused poli-cies such as the National Policy for the Education of Girls in Australian Schools and a National Aboriginal and Torres Strait Islander Education Policy. They also included some national policies that went more to the heart of schooling, such as National Goals for Australian Schools and National Curriculum Statements and Profiles, as well as those that were more economically focused such as the National Asian Languages and

Cultures Strategy, which was linked to the attempt to integrate the Australian economy more closely with that of the Asian region. Labor also sought more national control over technical and adult education through a national education and training reform agenda and attempted to integrate schooling and vocational training in the postcompulsory years. Given the federal government's financial and policy control over higher education, there was consolidation of the number of universities and very considerable expansion of university places, resulting in a move from elite to mass provision. However, these places were to be funded to an increasing extent by student fees, whereas from the mid-seventies until that time university education in Australia had been free. The government sought to improve retention to the end of secondary schooling and increase the numbers in both technical and adult education and in universities. This increased educational participation had two rationales: it was linked to the collapse of the teenage labor market and to the perceived need to upskill the workforce, with both sourced in different ways to the globalization of the economy. Labor's policy regime was thus a hybrid mix of social justice concerns and a tightening of the economy-education nexus with the introduction of user-pays practices in universities and technical and adult education.

Since the defeat of the Keating Labor government in 1996, the Howard Coalition governments have kept the broad framing of the Labor Party educational policy settlement (a specific manifestation of the global educational policy consensus), but reconstituted it through their party's ideological lens, including a more antagonistic relationship with the trade union movement. Equity concerns as articulated in Labor's hybrid approach have been considerably downgraded, while the concept of group disadvantage has been rejected as the basis for equity-focused policy interventions. Allan Luke has referred to the return of the individual deficit subject as the underpinning value of the Coalition's schooling policies, framed by an even stronger commitment to social disinvestment.[35] Welfare has been redefined as a privilege, rather than a right, within a framework of mutual obligation and the goal of individual self-sufficiency, rather than dependence on the "nanny state." Schooling policy at the national level has become narrower and more focused as part of a further hollowing out of state structures, and is very much outcomes oriented. Literacy testing and math testing have been introduced nationally. Technical and adult education has been pushed even further down the market track and there have been attempts to put schools, both public and private, in competition with each other. The fees for students in higher education have been increased and universities have been required to generate even more funds from nongovernment sources—from the sale of research, consultancies, and courses (often to international students). In contrast to Labor's facilitative relationship with the trade union movement, the Coalition has regarded the unions as an impediment to desired policy changes.

This comparative example is given to show how party ideology still mediates educational policy developments across party lines. However, it also illustrates the discursive shift from the conceptualization of education policy inherent in the Keynesian settlement in the era of economic nationalism to that of the era of the globalized economy. Contemporary Australian educational policy is and isn't a result of globalization.

Other examples could have been used to illustrate this point: for example, a cross-national one comparing the educational policies of Labor governments in Australia with the Thatcherite revolution in English education. Some good points of comparison would have been the more fulsome embrace of the market solution by Thatcher, or the way a unitary form of government "allows" political strategies different from those possible within a federal arrangement, but even more stark would have been the comparison between the hybrid equity/instrumentalism framing in Australia under Labor with the National Curriculum in England and Wales, following the Education Reform Act of 1988, with its resurrection of the "curriculum of the dead."[36] Labor sought to (post)modernize curriculum and integrate schooling and training, while the Thatcherite settlement wanted to return to a culture of little Englandism, one element of broader cultural restorationism (a dynamic similar to that of the United Kingdom can be seen in New Zealand).[37] One could also compare the policies in education that have resulted in the United States from President Clinton's claim that he wanted to be the "Education President" with those in England and Australia; in each context one would see in their different policies the playing out of the new global educational policy consensus. Comparative case studies of different systems and schools within and across those nations would demonstrate even more starkly this phenomenon, the generative intersection of micronarratives, -cultures, and -histories with the effects of globalization—vernacular globalization.

The analysis provided to this point has possibly been a little too deterministic in emphasizing the effects of economic globalization as mediated by state restructuring to the neglect of the cultural flows. The rapid flows of people associated with globalization, as well as the facilitation of diasporic public spheres across national boundaries by new technologies,[38] have also seen the development of hybrid cultural identities. Furthermore, economic globalization and the predominance of the neoliberal response to it have seen the meaner and leaner state less able to ameliorate the growing inequalities within the so-called "advanced" nations, the growing gap between "the haves" and "the have nots," the gap between those reveling in conspicuous consumption and those struggling with conspicuous deprivation. Capitalism in its globalized, disorganized form has dented the social security and cohesion that were the effects of the Keynesian settlement associated with economic nationalism. In contrast, we are experiencing today a "manufactured uncertainty"[39] and pervasive insecurity,[40] even among those who are currently employed, instabilities that are inherent in contemporary structures of feeling.

In this context, the progressive politics that have had most success in the last two decades have been those associated with the recognition of difference—identity politics—and new social movements,[41] rather than the politics of redistribution, which were central to the earlier Keynesian policy regime. Thus governments of various persuasions have introduced a range of affirmative action, equal opportunity, and antidiscrimination legislation. In Australia, where neoliberalism has been usually referred to as "economic rationalism," this range of recognition legislation has been called "social rationalization."[42] In a context where the two occur together—economic and social rationalization—where career preference is dependent upon educational success and credentialing for work in globalized primary labor markets, and where the gap between those so credentialed and those without has grown substantially, there have been a number of political backlashes. These have encompassed backlashes against affirmative action and the politics of difference and those against feminist policy gains. In Australia there has been the emergence of backlash national chauvinisms evident in the rise of the far-right-wing political party, One Nation, and echoes of such resentment politics around the world with, for example, Le Pen and the neo-Nazis in Europe and the right-wing white, male, working-class militias in the United States.

Schooling policy has thus become a site of culture wars in the last decade or so, a site of the politics of resentment,[43] manifest, for example, in attempts to redefine boys as the new disadvantaged in schooling,[44] and in debates about schooling and citizenship, related to Appadurai's point about the state and the nation now being the project of each other. In Australia, Labor governments at the national level (1983–1996) worked a politics of recognition through multiculturalism and attempted reconciliation with indigenous Australians. The subsequent conservative coalition governments have exploited backlashes against these Labor policies and sought to attract the vote of the disaffected white working-class men who traditionally have supported Labor governments. These coalition governments have hollowed out their involvement in schooling, emphasizing a narrower range of outcomes and rejecting affirmative action and concepts of group disadvantage. National literacy testing has been one response. However, the conception of literacy underpinning this government's literacy benchmarks appears to be underpinned by monoculturalism as opposed to a multicultural theorizing of multiliteracies necessary to effective citizenship in a globalized world. These abuses of literacy have been as much about creating a literacy crisis, justifying further social disinvestment in education, and imposing a rearticulated monoculturalism, as about literacy goals themselves.[45]

We are currently seeing the emergence in the policies of the Blair government in the United Kingdom, and in those of the European Union, the OECD, and UNESCO, of a concern for social inclusion, as national policy regimes give priority to internationalizing their economies. Thus they apparently have limited capacity to overcome unemployment and growing inequality. Calls for a "third way" in policy in the United Kingdom between the Keynesian welfare state and market liberalism are a further indication of increasing policy concern about growing inequalities, social exclusion, social disharmony, and their consequences.[46] George Soros, a doyen of the transnational capitalists, has also expressed concern at the implications of these social effects for future investment and economic development. Nonetheless, in terms of social policy and talk of the need for social inclusion, such concern appears to manifest itself in a focus on "employability," that is, the continual retraining of those made socially redundant, rather than with the creation of jobs and pursuit of equality through redistributive expenditure. In support of the vernacular globalization argument being put forth here, it is necessary to recognize that the third way carries different implications for various European countries. Think for example of what the third way might mean under Blair's New Labor Party built upon the deep and pervasive neoliberal market revolution of Thatcher and what it might mean in France, where there has been no such revolution.

There is another cultural element in educational policy that is linked to globalization and related hybridization and creolization of identities and cultures. The postmodern movement, a cultural effect of globalization, has been characterized by an epistemological critique of the rational subject and universalist bodies of knowledge,[47] a critique that recognizes the importance of the positionality of the knowledge producer in relation to the nature of the knowledge produced. All knowledge is deemed to be perspectival and claims to the universal are deemed to be appropriated as an exercise of power.[48] Thus the supposed neutrality of technical rationality endemic to bureaucracy, as well as dominant canons of knowledge, have been challenged. We have "no operative consensus concerning the ultimate or transcendental grounds of truth and justice"[49]—resulting in the foregrounding of what Lyotard calls a (postmodern) culture of performativity, which emphasizes the instrumental and operational, rather than truth claims.[50]

Restructured educational systems have been pervaded by this culture of performativity through the imposition of performance indicators as the new linking mechanisms between the "policy-producing center" and the "policy-practicing peripheries," which have been granted more autonomy to achieve preset goals.[51] As such, "Performativity is a systems-orientation: Instead of the state appearing as the enlightened and paternal command of shared community, the state is equated with the requirements of a system for ongoing integrity and viability."[52] Performativity is also symbiotic with the "needs" of the restructured state in the face of an increasingly complicated and diverse political environment. In this way, Yeatman suggests that performativity works as a "principle of selective closure in respect of the information overload and social complexity" that confronts the restructured state.[53] Specifically in relation to educational policy, the school-effectiveness literature has floated globally between nations (and supranationally) and seeks in a decontextualized and performative way to discover what schooling practices have desired effects (improved student performance on a range of skills), and as such is synergistic with the "needs" of restructured educational systems and policy.[54] This synergy is a specific example of Bourdieu's general point about the correlative relationship between the philosophy of the state and "demand for knowledge of the social world."[55] In that context, Ball speaks of the "magical solutions" offered by school effectiveness and other educational "policy entrepreneurs."[56]

The new hollowed-out structures and cultures of performativity within educational systems are "increasingly drained of normative and communal content." What we are left with is "an overarching shell of abstract instrumentalism" in the face of social disharmony and the hybridization of cultures and identities.[57] The OECD, UNESCO, APEC, and other supranational bodies have been important in instantiating the culture of performativity within restructured educational systems and support for a human capital conception of schooling within a neoliberal market ideology, to which they are complementary. However, Deacon et al. have argued that such supranational bodies also provide some potential for supranational policies of a more protective and socially progressive kind,[58] as an element of what David Held has called "cosmopolitan democracy."[59] It is to a consideration of supranational policy production that this chapter now turns, with a particular focus on the OECD.

Supranational Policy Production in Education

Within the educational policy literature there has been some analysis of policy borrowing across nations.[60] There is no doubt that the capacity for such cross-national policy borrowing has been greatly enhanced by the various flows of globalization. However, the literature on policy borrowing is fairly grounded in a preglobalization account of nations and the relations between them. While such borrowing continues in an enhanced fashion, there are also emergent postnational relationships within the educational policy community.

Appadurai argues that we are entering a postnational era in which there are serious disjunctions between economy, culture, and politics as they are affected by, and implicated in, globalization. To pick up on these disjunctions he speaks of a number of "scapes," including "ethnoscapes," "technoscapes," and "ideoscapes." These are useful as a way to move to some understanding of supranational and postnational policy flows or "policyscapes." Ethnoscapes refer to the large and rapid movement of peoples across the globe and between nations for a variety of reasons, evidencing the rhizomic and deterritorialized, rather than grounded and territorialized, nature of much of contemporary experience. This movement, "peoplescapes," includes politicians, policy elites, and policy intellectuals, with the effect of reducing the distance between elites. Technoscapes have allowed for instant communications as part of the time-space distanciation of globalization,[61] facilitating communication between policymakers and thus enhancing the likelihood of a global educational policy field and community. Ideoscapes refer to the rapid global flows of ideas—in our case, of educational policy ideas, contributing to the diaspora of key policy terms and concepts—recontextualized in different national and local contexts. Taken together these scapes indicate the emergence of a postnational educational policy community, consisting of globalizing bureaucrats,[62] senior public servants, policymakers, policy advisers, and policy intellectuals (and entrepreneurs). The policy ideas flowing globally are also linked to international political organizations, which will be considered below.

There is something of a disjunction between the way the global economy works today, with nation-states seen as complicating and mediating entities, and the way politics are organized, still largely within the boundaries of nations, despite talk of the emergence of postnational politics working in diasporic public spheres. Today national, cross-national, postnational, and supranational politics are occurring simultaneously as a result of globalization. Globalization has seen the creation of some supranational political organizations at the subglobal level, with the European Union being the best example. Other international organizations such as the World Bank, IMF, UN, UNESCO, and OECD are multilateral international organizations also being affected by globalization, as well as being, in some cases (such as the World Bank and IMF), largely "institutionalizing mechanisms" for market-liberal versions of global economics.[63] Some (such as NAFTA, APEC, and the E.U.) also represent the new regionalism emerging in global politics in response to the globalization of the economy. Together, these bodies constitute what Waters has referred to as "a complex and ungovernable web of relationships that extends beyond the nation state."[64]

Most of the literature on this ungovernable web of relationships has emphasized these bodies' support for neoliberal market economics on a global scale, unimpeded by national boundaries, which they seek to make more porous. The proposed Multilateral Agreement on Investment (MAI), initially sponsored by the OECD, exemplifies this argument. Yeatman suggests there is no other way to regard this agreement than "as the fruit of organised, concerted and conscious effort on the part of transnational corporate capital" as mediated by an international organization.[65] As Karl Polanyi once said, Laissez-faire was planned! The adoption of this agreement, strongly sponsored by the United States, would weaken even further the capacity of nations to control investment and protect social and environmental interests at the national and local levels. Yeatman explains its link to the OECD this way: "The reasoning behind the MAI, in starting with OECD or rich and developed nations, is that if they signed on, there would be much stronger leverage to bring the developing countries into a similar treaty regime."[66] She suggests that this is perhaps the best example of "a pro-transnational business or capitalist agenda" working at the likely expense "of national citizen communities and their sustainability."[67] There has nonetheless been opposition to the MAI and, at this point, it appears the OECD has failed to secure its adoption.

Care needs to be taken against being too deterministic and one-dimensional in the approach to international organizations while not denying their economic significance. The local institutionalization of their proposals often has unpredictable outcomes—manifest as vernacular globalization. Mention has already been made of the social disharmony resulting from the production of the socially redundant, as the capacity of nations to protect their populations has been reduced in the face of economic globalization and its sponsorship by some international organizations. However, there has also been recognition, at a number of political level, that the long-term interests of transnational capitalism will not be served by social ruptures and instabilities. Similarly, Deacon et al. call the emergence of global social policy enacted through supranational bodies in response to the globalization of the economy,[68] "cosmopolitan democracy" in an embryonic and inchoate form.[69] They talk of the possibility of supranational social policies of "regulation," "redistribution," and "provision,"[70] show how such policies along with supranational concepts of citizenship are beginning to emerge in the European Union, and argue the need for other international organizations to intervene in national politics in the interests of social protection. In their words, "The other side of the coin of the globalisation of social policy is the socialisation of global politics."[71] They note that there are such possibilities within the policy regimes and approaches of some other international organizations, even including those such as the IMF and World Bank, with a neoliberal economic focus. Such possibilities, they argue, are supported by the emergence of "global social reformists" who are working to counteract the influence of the "global laissez-faire economists," and to push an agenda of socially regulated capitalism globally.[72] In a somewhat optimistic but perhaps not unrealistic vein, they observe:

> The threat posed by global economic competition and global economic migration to the social democratic and social market economy achievements of Europe and elsewhere might impel an articulation of global reformism, just as the threat posed by the poor within one nation to the stability of capitalism-impelled national social reformism a century ago.[73]

Herein lies the contested complexity of postnational politics set against the globalization of the economy. In the remainder of this section of the chapter I will provide a brief account of the OECD as an illustrative example of how globalization has affected an international policy body, which itself has been an instrument of a contested conception of globalization in education.[74]

The Role of the OECD

The OECD is a globalizing institution developed in 1961 out of the Organization for European Economic Cooperation, which was created by the United States in the context of the cold war to reconstruct Europe through the Marshall Plan. The United States has taken a less prominent position since that time, perhaps playing a behind-the-scenes role in agenda setting, for example, in relation to the OECD's influential educational indicators project and in some senior appointments. However, it was the United States that strongly promoted and funded the Center for Cooperation with Economies in Transition, established within the OECD in 1990, to secure America's position of influence in the former Eastern bloc, following the end of the Cold War. Further, the United States, together with Japan, provides about half the funding of the organization.

At the overarching level, then, but always in a contested way, changing conceptions of United States market liberalism have been influential within the agenda setting of the organization. The attempt to achieve the MAI through OECD sponsorship is an exemplary case of this economic focus. Nonetheless, there are often tensions within OECD policy debates between Anglo-American neoliberalism and European social democracy. The organization also has social policy interests beyond the economic, but these are linked directly or indirectly to the causes and purposes of economic growth—the organizing principle of horizontality. Concerning educational policy, Papadopoulos argues that the OECD has "an inferred role for education, both for the contribution it can make to economic growth and as a means by which the purposes of such growth, namely an increase in general well-being, can be given reality."[75]

Unlike other international organizations, the OECD has no prescriptive mandate over its member countries, largely the rich countries of Europe, North America, Australia, New Zealand, and Japan, along with newer members such as Korea, Mexico (whose membership was sponsored by the United States), and the Czech Republic. The OECD describes itself as a kind of international think tank that helps governments "shape policy" by exerting influence through "mutual examination by governments, multilateral surveillance and peer pressure to conform or reform."[76] Thus the OECD works through suasion as a broker of policy ideas linked some way or other to economic concerns. There are two membership criteria: namely, a commitment to a market economy and to pluralistic democracy. Following the end of the Cold War many more nations meet these criteria and have been pushing for inclusion. In recognition of globalization, the organization expresses its commitment to promoting a "postindustrial age" whereby OECD economies are integrated into a "more prosperous and increasingly service-oriented world economy,"[77] which clearly reflects its orientation toward the concerns and interests of richer countries.

Organizationally, education is situated within the Directorate of Education, Employment, Labor, and Social Affairs (DEELSA). While the Education Committee of the OECD sets the broad program for education and represents the consensually negotiated interests of member nations, the Center for Educational Research and Innovation (CERI) works with the educational research community in a nongovernmental fashion and as such provides an alternative network of policy influence. The two other specialist education programs of Educational Buildings and Institutional Management in Higher Education work in different fashions again, with the former linking to provincial levels of government and the latter dealing directly with institutions. Education has no permanent status within the organization, with its work being mandated every five years by the council around an organizing theme. While the OECD is largely an intergovernmental organization, it is thus also linked in education to member countries in a nongovernmental way. The OECD is also part of the network of global organizations, with something of a global policy community operating in and across them in terms of careers and policy ideas. For instance, there have been connections between the OECD's educational indicators project and a similar project within APEC,[78] and a recent interest in lifelong learning across a number of international organizations.

While the major focus of the OECD is economic policy, Deacon et al. suggest it is not possible to ascribe to it "a meta-policy on economic and social matters,"[79] apart from its broad support for a liberalized world economy. They distinguish between the IMF-flavored economics secretariat and the social orientation of DEELSA. As the world economy has been globalized, the economics secretariat has become a stronger proponent of a neoliberal view of the world economy. This has fed into educational policy, but has been resisted to varying extents. Papadopoulos notes how, since the creation of DEELSA in 1974, education policy has had "to be 'protected' against narrow economic and instrumentalist perceptions of its role."[80] Context and dominant economic policy ideas have been important in the balance between the social and economic aspects of education, a balance affected also by which version of human capital theory has dominated. The changing balance between these two aspects within OECD policy formulations parallels that within many nations, namely, the move from the social democratic framing of education, linked to social goals and economic nationalism, to a focus more on the economic benefits of education to nations and individuals in the context of a globalized economy. The OECD stance here is both reflective and determinative of these national developments. The changing balance was obvious in the first OECD education ministers' conference held in 1978, "Future Educational Policies in the Changing Social and Economic Context," which strongly supported educational restructuring in the context of a globalizing economy. In 1988 at another OECD intergovernmental conference, "Education and

Economy in a Changing Society," the economic and social purposes of education were explicitly linked, with education now subsumed as an element of economic policy.

Deacon et al. document similar tensions within the social policy orientation of DEELSA, but indicate a recent shift in the opposite direction from a neoliberal view of social welfare as an expenditure burden to one of welfare as investment.[81] Overall, then, in terms of this economics/social tension, they suggest, "Taken together these orientations reflect that, in contrast to the U.S.-influenced IMF and World Bank, the economic and social policy of the OECD represents a much more balanced set of economic and social considerations typical of mainstream European social and economic policy."[82]

How then has OECD influence worked? One way is through its distinctive approach to educational policy, which Istance suggests has the following characteristics:

- educational policy making must be framed at least in part in relation to the other social and labor market policies that address people;
- focus on people is integral to economic prosperity apart from any social or cultural benefits;
- academic and political insights should be combined in "policy-relevant" analysis, rather than the educational community setting itself up in opposition to "politicians"; and
- national policies and practices should be informed through reference to those of other countries, learning from their achievements but not blindly copying.[83]

In this way, through an effective admixture of the subtly normative with the apparently disinterested, the OECD influences educational policy agenda setting and production within member nations. This OECD policy genre is also responsible for the social cachet contributing to its effectiveness.

In terms of influence, Papadopoulos suggests that the OECD has a "catalytic function"[84] in relation to educational policy production within its member nations, observing that it does not generate new ideas, but rather picks up on new ideas and agendas from members and the research community. Taylor's account of the OECD as a "knowledge mediator" has resonances with Papadopoulos's catalytic function.[85] The interdependence between the OECD's educational indicators project and a concern with efficiency and effectiveness in educational systems is a good case in point of the OECD serving a catalytic function and being a knowledge mediator.[86] More broadly, the OECD has sponsored neoliberal economic approaches and a microeconomically focused account of the role of education in ensuring the competitiveness of national economies. The indicators project ties in with such a framing ("How competitive are the educational outputs of member nations?") and links closely with the OECD's sponsorship of new public-sector managerialism.[87] The latter has contributed to overcoming the disjunction in member nations between state form and apparent needs of transnational capital.

For Papadopoulos, educational policy production remains largely a national activity. The veracity of his observation is being challenged, if the argument being put in this chapter carries any validity, and only holds today if we supplement his observation with the concept of vernacular globalization. In a somewhat similar but more global view of international organizations, McNeeley and Cha argue that they "have been an important catalyst in spreading world cultural themes and accounts" and that conceiving of them as "institutionalizing mechanisms" can provide useful insights.[88] Globally, the OECD has been an institutionalizing mechanism for neoliberal economics and the new managerialism. Its educational indicators project, while strongly supported and influenced by the United States, has sat in a synergistic relation to its support for new public management and has been one significant catalyst for the performativity now pervading restructured national educational systems. Most significant, however, has been the OECD's role (along with other international organizations) as an institutionalizing mechanism for the new global educational policy consensus, which stresses the centrality of an educated and multiskilled labor force to the competitive advantage of nations.

Archer has suggested that international organizations function as instruments of policy, as policy-making arenas, and as policy actors in their own right.[89] This is a useful way to think of the OECD and its relationship with member nations and to think further about how its policy influence might work. As a policy instrument the OECD's stance is used by some politicians in member nations to justify particular national or local policy developments. Vickers notes how this was the case in relation to higher education reforms in Australia in the late eighties.[90] OECD policy was basically used to legitimate policy developments in Australia, with globalization constructed as the contextual backdrop and justification for both policy narratives. The OECD also provides an arena in which nations can discuss policy issues and possible responses, while the OECD, as policy actor, can be a policy player in its own right through conferences, reports, and national and cross-national thematic reviews.

While the OECD has been an institutionalizing mechanism for economic globalization, the organization itself has been substantially affected by globalization,[91] as have its relationships with member countries, given the other sets of postnational networks now emerging. The E.U. is now a member of the OECD, which raises questions about the OECD's continuing significance to E.U. countries. Furthermore, the OECD has established relations with "the dynamic economies of Asia" and the "advanced economies of Latin America," and has also been involved in the Partners in Transition Program in Eastern Europe. The latter has precipitated a number of questions concerning the long-term function and purposes of the OECD in a globalized post-Cold War world: Is it a new Marshall Plan for former Eastern bloc countries serving American and transnational capital's interests or is it a policy think tank for the rich nations of the world? Globalization has also seen the emergence of new regional trading blocs, for example, APEC, "a government-led forum for facilitating private sector-led economic integration,"[92] and NAFTA. This raises questions about how the OECD can continue to meet the interests of all its members and where it sits in relation to these new regional identities and relationships. It was suggested earlier that all nations now must relativize their stance in relation to Western capitalism, raising questions about the extent to which globalization is a new form of Western hegemony, more specifically U.S. hegemony in a post-Cold War era, and what role the OECD plays in achieving and legitimating, or alternatively in contesting or mediating, such hegemony. When compared with other international organizations such as the IMF and World Bank, we can see that there has been some contestation of a straightforward human capital conception of education and concern now for the social disharmony that results from a particular form of national response to the globalization of the economy. However, it would appear that such concerns are also beginning to appear on the agendas of these organizations as well, because such disharmony is deemed to be against the interests of global capitalism, although this is still a long way from Deacon et al.'s "socialization of global politics."

Globalizing Educational Policy and Systems via the Vernacular

An account has been provided of the global and other factors precipitating the restructuring of educational systems and emergent educational policy settlements within the "developed" nations, resulting in apparent convergence across nations. These enabling factors, however, do not result in straightforward, top-down, context-productive outcomes. On the contrary: microhistories, -politics, -cultures, and context-generative practices within education at the national, provincial, and school levels result in hybridized effects in complex, mutually constitutive plays between nested locales within global relationships. Some of these plays are facilitated by supra- and postnational politics and the nascent global educational policy community. The outcome of the intersection of context-productive and context-generative policies and practices is divergence within and across national educational systems. The resultant hybrid outcomes are nonetheless an effect of globalization in all its economic, political, and cultural forms. They are framed by state restructuring that has been catalyzed by supranational political strategies, which in turn relate to the emergent disjunction between the workings of transnational or global capitalism and the earlier bureaucratic state form.

Within the new postbureaucratic state structures of education, policy now steers at a distance with changed center-periphery relations. The new state form, however, is no less important than its predecessor in educational policy production terms or as a site of political contestation. Rather, in a context of globalization it simply works in different ways through a regulatory/deregulatory mix toward narrower ends. These narrower goals are one element of an emergent global educational policy settlement, which is framed by the transition from education linked to a bounded economic nationalism to education conceived in relation to internationalizing national economies. Following that transition, education is constituted as one element of economic policy and deemed to be vital to the competitive economic advantage of nations. As a consequence, education elites have become less important in framing educational policy, but educators remain centrally important in generating local manifestations of this policy in practice.

Educational relationships have also changed within nations, which sit in mutually constitutive relationships with the multifaceted processes of globalization. For example, in Australia there have been ambitious attempts to reconstitute federalism so as to create an efficient national economic infrastructure in the context of a neoliberal reading of desirable responses to globalization of the economy. This strategy was evident in the moves toward national approaches in schooling, which still remains the constitutional prerogative of the states and territories. There have also been changes, for example, in the operation of federalism in the United States with respect to schooling policy, while a unitary form of government in New Zealand has seen perhaps the most substantial restructuring and deregulation of schooling in any nation. In England and Wales there has been the move to a national curriculum and testing and partial dismantling of local education authorities, all facilitated by a unitary form of government. The different playing out of these structural changes, and indeed of the new global educational policy consensus, is indicative of vernacular globalization at work.

In line with the argument of Taylor et al., this chapter has shown how globalization is now taken into account and used as a contextual justification in the establishment of educational policy priorities within national and provincial educational systems.[93] The way in which political organizations beyond the nation are also helping to frame such policies, through the example of the OECD, has also been demonstrated. A global educational policy community is emerging and is both an effect and facilitator of globalization and policy convergence across national education systems. Political organizations beyond the state and global policy community are potential sites for a challenge by global social reformers to the powerful influence of global laissez-faire economists. It seems that we are in a policy moment when there is at least some recognition that unfettered neoliberal economic policies result in growing inequality and social disharmony, while in contrast, social harmony is acknowledged as a necessary prerequisite for the growth of transnational capitalism—a situation propitious for the global social reformers. Finally, in depicting schools and educational systems as sites of culture wars, it has also been shown how globalization is affecting the cultural field within which educational policies and practices now operate.

What does all of this mean for theorizing educational policy? Taking as given a national, rather than globalized, context, Stephen Ball and his colleagues have developed a policy cycle approach to understand and explain policy relationships within restructured educational systems.[94] This recognizes three contexts in the policy cycle, namely: (1) the context of influence that works directly and indirectly on both the policy-producing center of the education state and schools; (2) the context of policy text production within that policy center; and (3) schools as the context of policy practices influenced by the other two contexts. A mutually interactive, nonlinear relationship is then postulated between state education policy and its rearticulation in the practices of schools. As Ball notes, "Policies are always incomplete insofar as they relate to or map on to the 'wild profusion' of local practice."[95]

Now, while we might want to quibble with the policy cycle's view that the three contexts have parity of power, this is nevertheless a useful way to reconceptualize what the traditional policy literature has seen as a linear and top-down relationship between policy production and implementation. In terms of the argument made throughout this chapter, however, modifications have to be made to the policy cycle account to acknowledge global processes and their varied effects and to recognize that the state remains important despite its restructuring. In effect, the policy cycle account has to be globalized because its initial formulation was grounded in the bounded space of the nation. Globalization in all its forms, but certainly globalization as mediated in the new global educational policy consensus, has affected these three policy contexts and their interrelationships. With respect to the latter, consider the way a quasi-market take-up of restructuring reconstitutes the relationships between parents and schools as they become consumers, rather than citizens. Think of how the globalized culture of performativity affects teachers' work and schools' relationships with their communities and educational systems. The effects of globalization on the state, educational policy, and schools are mediated yet again by local cultures, histories, and politics. Globalization maps onto local practice in contingent, contested, inflected, and thus unpredictable ways. Nonetheless, there is also a way in which globalization (an element of the context of influence) affects schools in a less-mediated fashion through their students—the new cyborgs and hybrids in the classroom, embryonic global citizens whose phenomenal world, certainly in the developed nations, is very much global.

While being affected by the state's new steering capacity, as well as by global action at a distance through postnational politics and international organizations, educational policy remains a palimpsest. It is always being reread and rearticulated against the micronarratives of schools and locales, which are nested within sets of mutually constitutive relationships globally. What is occurring in specific manifestations of educational restructuring and the new policy consensus is and isn't the effect of globalization; rather, this chapter has suggested that we are seeing the effect of vernacular globalization. Vernacular globalization is thus the conceptual device used throughout this chapter to account for both educational policy convergence and divergence, globally. While not denying the power of transnational capital and "McCulture," this analysis of vernacular globalization is suggestive of the multilayered ways political strategies need to be organized today—locally, nationally, globally—to ameliorate inequalities resulting from a neoliberal response and to work toward a reconceptualized version of social justice through schooling that seeks to pull together a politics of difference with a politics of redistribution.

Notes

1. Linda Weiss, "Globalisation and the Myth of the Powerless State," *New Left Review* 225 (1997): 3–27.
2. Roland Robertson, "Glocalisation: Time-Space and Homogeneity-Heterogeneity," in *Global Modernities*, ed. Mike Featherstone, Scott Lash, and Roland Robertson (London: Sage, 1995), 27.
3. Anna Yeatman, "Trends and Opportunities in the Public Sector: A Critical Assessment," *Australian Journal of Public Administration* 57, no. 4 (1998): 38–147.
4. Stephen Ball, "Big Policies/Small World: An Introduction to International Perspectives in Education Policy," *Comparative Education* 34, no. 2 (1998): 119–30.
5. Arjun Appadurai, *Modernity at Large: Cultural Dimensions of Globalization* (Minneapolis: University of Minnesota Press, 1996), 193.
6. Ibid., 10.
7. Malcolm Waters, *Globalisation* (London: Routledge, 1995).
8. Mark Latham, *Civilising Global Capital: New Thinking for Australian Labor* (Sydney: Allen and Unwin, 1998), 11.
9. Waters, *Globalisation*, 3.
10. Anthony Giddens, *Modernity and Self-Identity* (Cambridge, Eng.: Polity Press, 1991), 187.

11. Yeatman, "Trends and Opportunities."
12. Michael Pusey, *Economic Rationalism in Canberra: A Nation Building State Changes Its Mind* (Melbourne: Cambridge University Press, 1991), 210–11.
13. Jürgen Habermas, "The European Nation-State—Its Achievements and Its Limits: On the Past and Future of Sovereignity and Citizenship," in *Mapping the Nation*, ed. Gopal Balakrishnan (London: Verso, 1996), 292.
14. Guy Neave, "On the Cultivation of Quality, Efficiency and Enterprise: An Overview of Recent Trends in Higher Education in Western Europe, 1968–1988," *European Journal of Education* 23, no. 1–2 (1988): 7–23.
15. Philip Cerny, *The Changing Architecture of Politics: Structure, Agency and the Future of the State* (London: Sage, 1990).
16. John Clarke and Janet Newman, *The Managerial State Power, Politics and Ideology in the Remaking of Social Welfare* (London: Sage, 1997).
17. Bob Lingard, "Educational Policy Making in Postmodern State: An Essay Review of Stephen J. Ball's Education Reform: A Critical and Post-Structural Approach," *The Australian Educational Researcher* 23, no. 1 (1996).
18. Anna Yeatman, *Bureaucrats, Technocrats, Femocrats: Essays on the Contemporary Australian State* (Sydney: Allen and Unwin, 1990).
19. Appadurai, *Modernity at Large*, 22.
20. For example, Paul Hirst and Graham Thompson, *Globalisation in Question* (Cambridge, Eng.: Polity Press, 1996).
21. Carl Reus-Smit, "Beyond Foreign Policy: State Theory and the Changing Global Order," in *The State in Question: Transformations of the Australian State*, ed. Paul James (Sydney: Allen and Unwin, 1996), 161–95.
22. John Wiseman, *Global Nation? Australia and the Politics of Globalisation* (Cambridge, Eng.: Cambridge University Press, 1998), 14.
23. Leslie Sklair, "Conceptualising and Researching the Transnational Capitalist Class in Australia," *The Australian and New Zealand Journal of Sociology* 32, no. 2 (1996): 1–19.
24. Miriam Henry, Bob Lingard, Fazal Rizvi, and Sandra Taylor, *The OECD, Globalisation and Education Policy Making* (Oxford, Eng.: Pergamon Press, forthcoming).
25. Bob Deacon with Michelle Hulse and Paul Stubbs, *Global Social Policy, International Organisations and the Future of Welfare* (London: Sage, 1997), 1.
26. Phillip Brown, A. H. Halsey, Hugh Lauder, and Amy Stuart Wells, "The Transformation of Education and Society," in *Education Culture Economy Society*, ed. A. H. Halsey, Hugh Lauder, Phillip Brown, and Amy Stuart Wells (Oxford: Oxford University Press, 1997), 1–44.
27. Ibid.
28. Phillip Brown and Hugh Lauder, "Education, Globalization, and Economic Development," in *Education Culture Economy Society*, ed. A. H. Halsey, Hugh Lauder, Phillip Brown, and Amy Stuart Wells (Oxford: Oxford University Press, 1997), 172–92.
29. Deacon et al., *Global Social Policy*.
30. Yeatman, *Bureaucrats, Technocrats*.
31. Waters, *Globalisation*.
32. Brown et al., *Education Culture*, 8.

33. John Knight and Bob Lingard, "Ministerialisation and Politicisation: Changing Structures and Practices of Educational Policy Production," in *A National Approach to Schooling in Australia?* ed. Bob Lingard and Paige Porter (Canberra: Australian College of Education, 1997), 26–45.
34. Bob Lingard and Paige Porter, eds., *A National Approach to Schooling in Australia?* (Canberra: Australian College of Education, 1997), 26–45.
35. Allan Luke, "New Narratives of Human Capital: Recent Directions in Australian Educational Policy," *The Australian Educational Researcher* 24, no. 2 (1997): 1–21.
36. Stephen Ball, *Education Reform: A Critical and Post-structural Approach* (Buckingham, Eng.: Open University Press, 1994).
37. Roger Dale and Jenny Ozga, "Two Hemispheres—Both New Right? Education Reform in New Zealand and England and Wales" in *Schooling Reform in Hard Times*, ed. Bob Lingard, John Knight, and Paige Porter (London: The Falmer Press, 1993), 63–87. Terry Eagleton illustrates this admixture of the market and cultural restorationism in commenting on some British politicians, presumably Tories: "It is not unusual to find British politicians who support the commercialization of radio but are horrified by poems which don't rhyme." Terry Eagleton, *The Illusions of Postmodernism* (Oxford, Eng.: Blackwell, 1996), 132.
38. Appadurai, *Modernity at Large.*
39. Anthony Giddens, *Beyond Left and Right* (Stanford: Stanford University Press, 1994).
40. Zygmunt Bauman, *Postmodernity and its Discontents* (Cambridge, Eng.: Polity Press, 1997).
41. Nancy Fraser, "From Redistribution to Recognition: Dilemmas of Justice in a 'Post-Socialist' Society," *New Left Review* (July–Aug. 1995): 68–93.
42. McKenzie Wark, *The Virtual Republic: Australia's Culture Wars of the 1990s* (Sydney: Allen and Unwin, 1997).
43. Cameron McCarthy, *The Uses of Culture Education and the Limits of Ethnic Affiliation* (New York: Routledge, 1998).
44. Bob Lingard and Peter Douglas, *Men Engaging Feminisms: Pro-feminism, Backlashes and Schooling* (Buckingham, Eng.: Open University Press, 1999).
45. Allen Luke, Bob Lingard, Bill Green, and Barbara Comber, "The Abuses of Literacy: Educational Policy and the Construction of Crisis," in *Education Policy*, ed. James Marshall and Michael Peters (Oxford, Eng.: Edward Elgar, 1999).
46. *Beyond Left and Right*, the book by Anthony Giddens (Stanford: Stanford University Press, 1994), has been an influential source of third-way thinking in the United Kingdom. In many ways, however, it seems to represent a rather pallid version of old social democracy, inflected by environmental concerns. It is also important to recognize that the old Keynesian welfare state was a third way between the command economies of state socialism and North American market liberalism. See also a more recent book by Anthony Giddens, *The Third Way* (Cambridge, Eng.: Polity Press, 1998).
47. For example, Sandra Harding, *The "Racial" Economy of Science* (Bloomington: Indiana University Press, 1994); and Sandra Harding, *Is Science Multicultural? Postcolonialisms, Feminisms and Epistemologies* (Bloomington: Indiana University Press, 1998).

48. Pierre Bourdieu, *Practical Reason* (Cambridge, Eng.: Polity Press, 1998).
49. Anna Yeatman, *Postmodern Revisionings of the Political* (London: Routledge, 1994), 106.
50. Jean-François Lyotard, *The Postmodern Condition* (Manchester, Eng.: Manchester University Press, 1984).
51. The culture of performativity also helps produce a new form of governance in education, namely self-governance, a new form of governing apparently without government. [Compare R. A. W. Rhodes, *Understanding Governance Policy Networks, Governance, Reflexivity and Accountability* (Buckingham, Eng.: Open University Press, 1997); and Tom Popkewitz, "Rethinking Decentralisation and State/Civil Society Distinctions: The State as a Problematic of Governing," *Journal of Education Policy* 11, no. 1 (1996): 27–51.] There is an interesting and different analysis that could be developed here seeing governance as inclusive of the older notion of government and the Foucauldian concept of governmentality, with performativity then seen as a new form of governmentality contributing to new practices of governance.
52. Yeatman, *Postmodern Revisionings*, 110.
53. Yeatman, "Trends and Opportunities," 117.
54. Bob Lingard, James Ladwig, and Allen Luke, "School Effects in Postmodern Conditions," in *School Effectiveness for Whom? Challenges to the School Effectiveness and School Improvement Movements*, ed. Roger Slee, Gaby Weiner, and Sally Tomlinson (London: The Falmer Press, 1998), 84–100.
55. Bourdieu, *Practical Reason*, 39.
56. Ball, "Big Policies/Small World."
57. Michael Muetzelfeldt, "Democracy, Citizenship and the Problematics of Governing Production: The Australian Case," in *Labour, Unemployment and Democratic Rights*, ed. Ray Jureidini (Geelong, Australia: Centre for Citizenship and Human Rights, 1995), 44.
58. Deacon et al., *Global Social Policy*.
59. David Held, *Democracy and the Global Order: From the Modern State to Cosmopolitan Governance* (Cambridge, Eng.: Polity Press, 1995).
60. For example, David Halpin and Barry Troyna, "The Politics of Education Policy Borrowing," *Comparative Education* 31, no. 3 (1995): 303–10.
61. Giddens, *Beyond Left*.
62. Sklair, "Conceptualising."
63. Connie McNeeley and Yveite Cha, "Worldwide Educational Convergence through International Organisations: Avenues for Research," *Educational Policy Analysis Archives* 2, no. 14 (1994).
64. Waters, *Globalisation*, 113.
65. Yeatman, "Trends and Opportunities," 149.
66. Ibid., 146.
67. Ibid.
68. Deacon et al., *Global Social Policy*.
69. Held, *Democracy*.
70. Deacon et al., *Global Social Policy*, 2.
71. Ibid., 3.
72. Ibid., 5.

73. Ibid.
74. This section draws heavily on research and writing conducted with Fazal Rizvi, Miriam Henry, and Sandra Taylor. See, for example, Taylor et al., *Educational Policy*, 68–71; Taylor, "The OECD"; Miriam Henry and Sandra Taylor, "Globalisation and National Schooling Policy in Australia," in *A National Approach to Schooling in Australia?*, ed. Bob Lingard and Paige Porter (Canberra: Australian College of Education, 1997), 46–59; Bob Lingard and Fazal Rizvi, "Globalisation and the Fear of Homogenisation in Education," *Change: Transformations in Education* 1, no. 1 (1998): 62–71; Robert Lingard and Fazal Rizvi, "Globalisation, The OECD, and Australian Higher Education," in *Universities and Globalization: Critical Perspectives*, ed. Jan Currie and Janice Newson (Thousand Oaks, Calif.: Sage, 1998); and Miriam Henry, Bob Lingard, Fazal Rizvi, and Sandra Taylor, "Working With/Against Globalisation in Education," *Journal of Education Policy* 14, no. 1 (1999). Our forthcoming book, Miriam Henry, Bob Lingard, Fazal Rizvi, and Sandra Taylor, *The OECD, Globalisation and Education Policy Making* (Oxford, Eng.: Pergamon Press), deals with these issues in a more detailed and extended way.
75. George Papadopoulos, *Education 1960–1990: The OECD Perspective* (Paris: OECD, 1994), 11.
76. OECD, *OECD Brochure Outlining the Functions and Structure of the OECD* (Paris: OECD, undated), 10.
77. Ibid., 6.
78. Meng Hongwei, Zhou Yiqun, and Fang Yihua, eds., *School Based Indicators of Effectiveness: Experiences and Practices in APEC Countries* (The People's Republic of China: Guangxi Normal University Press, 1997).
79. Deacon et al., *Global Social Policy*, 70.
80. Papadopoulos, *Education*, 12.
81. Deacon et al., *Global Social Policy*.
82. Deacon et al., *Global Social Policy*, 72.
83. David Istance, "Education at the Chateau de la Muette," *Oxford Review of Education* 22, no. 1 (1996): 94.
84. Papadopoulos, *Education*, 203.
85. Sandra Taylor, "The OECD and the Politics of Education Policy-making: An Australian Case Study" (paper delivered at the Australian Sociological Association Conference, December, 1996).
86. Andreas Schleicher, "Developing Indicators on the Performance of Education Systems in an International Context: The OECD Education Indicators," in *School Based Indicators of Effectiveness: Experiences and Practices in APEC Countries*, ed. Meng Hongwei, Zhou Yiqun, and Fang Yihua (The People's Republic of China: Guangxi Normal University Press, 1997), 251–64.
87. OECD, *Governance in Transition: Public Management Reforms in OECD Countries* (Paris: OECD, 1995).
88. McNeeley and Cha, "Worldwide Educational Convergence."
89. Clive Archer, *Organising Europe: The Institutions of Integration*, 2d ed. (London: Edward Arnold, 1994).
90. Margaret Vickers, "Cross-National Exchange: The OECD and Australian Education Policy," *Knowledge and Policy* 7, no. 1 (1994): 25–47.

91. Robert Lingard and Fazal Rizvi, "Globalisation, The OECD, and Australian Higher Education."
92. Bob Catley, *Globalising Australian Capitalism* (Cambridge: Cambridge University Press, 1996), 205.
93. Sandra Taylor, Fazal Rizvi, Bob Lingard, and Miriam Henry, *Educational Policy and the Politics of Change* (London: Routledge, 1997), 61.
94. Ball, *Education Reform*; and Richard Bowe, Stephen Ball, and Anne Gold, *Reforming Education and Changing Schools: Case Studies in Policy Sociology* (London: Routledge, 1992).
95. Ball, *Education Reform*, 10.

Managerialism and Educational Policy in a Global Context: Foucault, Neoliberalism, and the Doctrine of Self-Management

Michael Peters, James Marshall, and Patrick Fitzsimons

New Managerialism and Governmentality

The restructuring of state education systems in many Western countries during the last two decades has involved a significant shift away from an emphasis on administration and policy to an emphasis on management. This "new managerialism" has drawn theoretically, on the one hand, on the model of corporate managerialism and private sector management styles, and, on the other, on public choice theory and new institutional economics (NIE), most notably agency theory and transaction cost analysis. This phenomenon needs to be viewed in the context of the rise of neoliberalism as the predominant ideology of globalization "which manifests itself in local contexts as set variations on the theme of managerialism as a technology for institutional organization not only in the private sector but also increasingly in the public sector."

These themes, their global import, and their associated technologies are explored in the following sections, titled "New Public Management," "New Managerialism and Neoliberalism," "New Managerialism, Education, and Self-Governance," and "The Doctrine of the Self-Managing School." Our approach to managerialism and educational policy in the global context is through an examination of the Foucauldian theme of governance and its application in the critical understanding of managerialism as an expression or technology of neoliberalism.

A specific constellation of these theories is sometimes called New Public Management (NPM), which has been influential in the United Kingdom, Australia, Canada, and New Zealand. These theories and models have been used both as the legitimating basis and instrumental means for redesigning state educational bureaucracies, educational institutions, and even the public policy process. Most important, there has been a decentralization of management control away from the center to the individual institution permitted by a new contractualism—often referred to as the doctrine of self-management—coupled with new accountability and funding structures. This shift has often been accompanied by a disaggregation of large state bureaucracies into autonomous agencies, a clarification of organizational objectives, and a separation between policy advice and policy implementation functions. The "new managerialism" has also involved a shift from input controls to quantifiable output measures and performance targets, along with an emphasis on short-term performance contracts, especially for chief executive officers (CEOs) and senior managers. In the interest of so-called productive efficiency, the provision of educational services has been made contestable; and in the interest of so-called allocative efficiency state education has been marketized and privatized.

Employing Michel Foucault's notion of governmentality,[1] we argue that the new managerialism functions as an emergent and increasingly rationalized and complex neoliberal technology of governance that operates at a number of levels: the individual ("the self-managing student" and teacher), the classroom ("classroom management techniques"), the academic program (with explicit promotion of the goals of self-management), and the school or educational institution (self-managing institutions). In this chapter we will focus upon the first and the last of these levels, that is, on the relations between individual and institutional self-management, understood in the literature as the doctrine of self-management and construed in this chapter as a form of neoliberal governmentality in Foucault's sense. This chapter charts and analyzes these changes in educational policy in a global context, emphasizing two caveats: first, we do not support a thesis of globalization as a merely convergent or unifying phenomenon; second, our chapter makes the distinction between theoretical management discourses and their embodiment in specific policy regimes in particular countries. In regard to both points, Pat O'Malley has pointed out problems of rationalization within the governmentality literature.[2] He suggests that mentalities of rule involve what he calls a "double moment of contingency" in the sense that genealogical investigations of policies or programs show "no smooth path of development or evolution"; rather, their formation is an utterly contingent and pragmatic affair driven by what is thought might work. Only over time does a process of systematization generate government rationalities, and O'Malley turns to Nikolas Rose to explain that neither Britain nor the United States "were underpinned by a coherent and elaborated political rationality that they sought to implement."[3] One of the principal difficulties concerns the tendency to treat second-order constructs, such as that proposed by Rose of "advanced liberalism," as real rationalities, thus fabricating a new universal in a form of totalizing analysis that Foucault and any self-respecting Foucauldian would reject. Such idealizations involve a premature closure of genealogy, and O'Malley wants to restore mentalities to "an active and authentic . . . place in governmentality research."[4] If we restore genealogy to its rightful place alongside rationalization, then we will be more able "to open up analysis to an examination of the present [and] to questions that disrupt our rationally formulated diagnoses."[5]

On the basis of this understanding we will first outline, at the level of discourse, two major elements or strands comprising the new managerialism: public choice theory and New Public Management. If there is little talk initially about education policy, then it is because one of the major tenets of new managerialism is that there is nothing distinctive about education; it can be conceptualized and managed like any other service or institution. Part of the success of the globalized new managerialism lies precisely in its claims for these generic aspects: its applicability to *all* spheres of administration and its homogenization of all technical or institutional problems as *management* problems. In the second section, we focus specifically on the doctrine of self-management within the particular site of New Zealand and examine the ways in which such a notion has been put in the service of the policy regime of Tomorrow's Schools—the implementation document for the educational reforms beginning in 1998. While focusing on the New Zealand context that we know best, we are fully aware that similar policies are on the rise in educational systems around the world. In the remainder of this introduction we introduce Foucault's notion of governmentality as a theoretical basis for understanding the rise of the managerialist discourse.

Foucault uses the term "governmentality" to mean the art of government and, historically, to signal the emergence of distinctive types of rule that became the basis for modern liberal politics.[6] His starting point for the examination of the problematic of government is a series of concepts: security, population, government. He maintains that there was an explosion of interest on the "art of government" in the sixteenth century motivated by diverse questions: the government of oneself (personal conduct); the government of souls (pastoral doctrine); and the government of children (problematic of pedagogy). Foucault says that the problematic of government can be located at the intersection of two competing tendencies: state centralization and a logic of dispersion. This is a problematic that poses questions of the *how* of government, rather than its legitimation, and seeks "to articulate a kind of rationality which was intrinsic to the art of government without subordinating it to the problematic of the prince and of his relationship to the principality of which he is lord and master."[7] Only in the late sixteenth and early seventeenth centuries did the art of government crystallize for the first time around the notion of "reason of state," understood in a positive sense whereby the state is governed according to rational principles that are seen to be intrinsic to it. In charting this establishment of the art of government Foucault thus details the introduction of "economy" into political practice (understood as "the correct manner of managing goods and wealth within the family"[8]). In line with this analysis, Foucault defines governmentality in terms of a specific form of government power based upon the "science" of political economy, which, over time, he maintains, has transformed the administrative state into one fully governmentalized and led to the formation of both governmental apparatuses and knowledges (or *savoirs*). In elaborating these themes Foucault concentrates his analytical energies on understanding the pluralized forms of government, its complexity, and its techniques. Our modernity, he says, is characterized by the "governmentalization" of the state. He is interested in the question of how power is exercised and, implicitly, he provides a critique of the contemporary tendencies to overvalue the problem of the state and to reduce it to a unity or singularity based upon a certain functionality. This substantive feature—the rejection of state-centered analyses—has emerged from the governmentality literature as it has become a more explicit problematic.

Foucault argues that an analysis of power relations should be conducted under five main headings, which we present here in abridged form:

- the systems of differentiations that permit one to act upon the actions of others—differentiations determined by law, traditions, economic conditions, and so forth—which give some prima facie position for power relationships to be brought into play;
- the types of objectives pursued intentionally by those who act upon the actions of others when power relations are brought into existence;
- the means of bringing power relations into play, by force, compliance, consent, surveillance, or economic reward;
- the forms of institutionalization. These may be a mixture of legal, traditional, or hierarchical structures, such as the family, the military, or the state; and
- the degree of rationalization that, depending upon the situation, endows, elaborates, and legitimates processes for the exercise of power.[9]

For Foucault's argument about the strategic reversibility of power relations to hold, he needs to develop a theory of governance that presupposes agency but requires and gains the cooperation of the subject.[10] He provides an account of technologies of self and their intersection with technologies of domination through the notion of governmentality. Foucault identifies four techniques that human beings employ to interpret, control, and turn themselves into subjects. These are technologies of domination, technologies of self, technologies of production, and technologies of sign systems.[11] Technologies of domination and technologies of self are the ones under consideration here, as their intersection produces what Foucault calls "governmentality."

In Foucault's terms, governmentality meant both governance of self and others. This would locate the self as the politically constituted subject of managerialism as a relevant domain of study. Foucault's research focuses on questions such as: Who can govern? What does governing mean? and Who is governed? The target of the analysis of governmentality is not

> "institutions," "theories," or "ideology," but "practices"—with the aim of grasping the conditions which make these acceptable at a given moment; the hypotheses being that these types of practice are not just governed by institutions, prescribed by ideologies, guided by pragmatic circumstances . . . but possess up to a point their own specific regularities, logic, strategy, self-evidence and "reason." It is a question of analyzing a regime of practices—practices being understood here as places where what is said and what is done, rules imposed and reasons given, the planned and the taken for granted meet and interconnect.[12]

Foucault asks "how" questions for the immanent conditions and constraints of practices. Governmentality is about critique, problematization, invention, imagination, and changing the shape of the thinkable. Governmentality is the relation between self and itself, interpersonal relationships involving some control and guidance, relations within social institutions and community. The notion of governmentality is, thus, counterposed to statist conceptions of power, which in Foucault's view erroneously dominate modern understandings of social relations. The theory of power surrounding the modern state is a problem: the state and sovereignty both rely on juridical conceptions of power as a negative or repressive force. The limited conception of power as an institutional and prohibitory phenomenon cannot adequately explain the range of power relations that permeate the body, sexuality, the family, kinship, and discourse. Certain forms of managerialism and governmentality share characteristics such as power relations, and to this extent are connected and overlap.

Foucault, in historicized Kantian terms, speaks of governmentality as implying the relationship of the self to itself (and to others), referring explicitly to the problem of ethical self-constitution and self-regulation. Governmentality is thus defined as the set of practices and strategies that individuals in their freedom use in controlling or governing themselves and others. Such an analytics of power bypasses the subject of law, or the legal concept of the subject, that is demanded by an analysis of power based upon the institution of political society. Foucault's point is that if you can conceive of the subject only as a subject of law, that is, as one that either has rights or not, then it is difficult to bring out the freedom of the subject and ethical self-constitution in games of freedom. In Foucault's account the relationship of the self to the self is a possible point of resistance to political power, and it is the historic role of critical philosophy to call into question all forms of domination and (deriving from the Socratic injunction) to "Make freedom your foundation, through mastery of yourself." "The task according to Foucault," write Barry et al., "was not to denounce the idea of liberty as a fiction, but to analyze the conditions within which the practice of freedom has been possible."[13]

Let us propose a quick summary: first, a neo-Foucauldian approach to the question of governance avoids interpreting liberalism as an ideology, political philosophy, or an economic theory, but rather reconfigures it as a form of governmentality with an emphasis on the question of how power is exercised. Second, such an approach makes central the notion of the self-limiting state, which in contrast to the administrative (or police) state, brings together in productive ways questions of ethics and technique, through the "responsibilization" of moral agents and the active reconstruction of the relation between government and self-government. Third, it proposes an investigation of neoliberalism as an intensification of an economy of moral regulation first developed by liberals and not merely or primarily as a political reaction to "big government" or the so-called bureaucratic welfare state of the postwar Keynesian settlement. Indeed, as Barry et al. point out, some who adopt this approach see welfarism as an aberrant episode that has little to do with liberalism per se.[14] Fourth, the approach enables an understanding of the distinctive features of neoliberalism. It understands neoliberalism in terms of its replacement of the natural and spontaneous order characteristic of Hayekian liberalism with "artificially arranged or contrived forms of the free, entrepreneurial and competitive conduct of economic-rational individuals."[15] Furthermore, it understands neoliberalism through the development of "a new relation between expertise and politics,"[16] especially in the realm of welfare, where an actuarial rationality and new forms of prudentialism manifest and constitute themselves discursively in the language of "purchaser-provider," audit, performance, and "risk management."[17] We see such language increasingly apparent in educational policy discourses as well.

New Public Management

The purpose of this section is an account of a particular form of managerialism referred to in the literature as New Public Management (NPM),[18] or simply as public management.[19] Jonathan Boston outlines the features of NPM as: an extensive use of written contracts and performance agreements; a reliance on short-term employment contracts; an emphasis on economic rewards and sanctions; a reduction in multiple accountability relationships; a minimizing of opportunities for ministerial discretion in the detailed operation of government agencies; the institutional separation of the funding agency from the provider; the separation of advisory, delivery, and regulatory functions; an introduction of accrual accounting; capital charging; a distinction between the state's ownership and purchasers' interests; a distinction between outcomes and outputs; an accrual-based appropriations system and an emphasis on contestable provision and contracting out for service.[20]

NPM has a history that can be traced at least to cameralist ideas. Hood says that such ideas underpinned the new administration of the eighteenth century.[21] Their common underlying features included: a "top-down" orientation; a shared view that thrift was the queen of virtues in public management; a predilection for particular forms of organization; an ascendancy built less on the production of conclusions drawn from "hard data" than on maxims followed by reasons and persuasive examples.[22] Hood suggests that most of these features are shared by today's equivalent to cameralism—the NPM.[23] NPM has gained political acceptance in at least three different countries: Australia, New Zealand, and the United Kingdom.[24] He says that all of these three variants of NPM share some general features. They include: the switch in emphasis from policy formulation to management and institutional design; from process controls to output controls; from integration to differentiation; from statism to subsidiarity.

Hood considers that the NPM is not sufficiently theorized and concludes with a discussion about several possible areas of concern, which are especially pertinent for educational policy.[25] The first concerns the change in public service ethics, loyalty to the service as a whole, and resilience to political crisis: political accountability involves much more than achieving measurable results. Another concern is about the limits of the NPM revolution. There seems to be no end to the individualizing and atomization process. Hood refers to the possibility of *selling* government administrative positions so that the purchaser could then invest in the successful discharge of their duties. Another concern is the problem of exactly what kind of public service the NPM revolution is aiming to produce. Should the really high salaries go to the public sector, or to the so-called private "wealth producing" sector? In the latter case, how then could the public sector attract the necessary talent—or would it be structured to produce the very mediocre performance that it was so criticized for in the past?

Similarly, Pollitt draws attention to a recently emerging analysis that sets limits on the practical usefulness managers can derive from any general theory of management.[26] This notion of limits is attributed to the idea that managerial skills differ considerably from other sorts of expertise in their limited standardization across industries, their susceptibility to change, their specificity to situations rather than problems, and their diffuse, varied knowledge base. Effective management will require more than mere knowledge of management theory. This suggests that to the extent that we see the same model of management spread across all situations, in the public sector, it will be appropriate to ask how realistic this is in terms of the very different requirements between the various public areas. Whitley argues, "Where judgment and discretion are involved in complex tasks which are highly context-dependent, skills are much more specific to particular situations and organizational fields."[27] This implies that management in education will be context-dependent.

As Pollitt notes, however, the managerial literature contains little reference to the welfare state, or to the characteristic modes of thought of its policymakers, administrators, and service providers.[28] He also notes that social needs, professional standards, deprivation, community, and equity have historically played little or no part in the development of managerialism. He says, "The transfer, during the last decade or two, of managerialism from private sector corporations to welfare-state services represents the injection of an ideological 'foreign body' into a sector previously characterized by quite different traditions of thought."[29] Similarly, Martin argues that the notion of public management developed so far does not differ adequately from private sector management.[30]

New Managerialism and Neoliberalism

As noted earlier, managerialism is one of the prime elements in a shift to a neoliberal educational policy discourse. Yeatman distinguishes the old collectivist notion of the social contract from a "new contractualism," which she says represents a neoliberal politicization of public management.[31] No longer are citizens presumed to be members of a political community, which it is the business of a particular form of governance to express. The old and presumed shared political process of the social contract disappears in favor of a disaggregated and individualized relationship to governance. Although the contract can be regarded as a source of legitimacy—on the basis of the social contract—the idea of contract as an instrument of government can also be invoked. As Hindess points out, while contract theory is commonly regarded as addressing questions of the legitimacy of government, it can be seen as the core of an autonomous rationality of government on three counts: first, it specifies the population to be governed as "autonomous" citizens; second, it identifies a rationality of government that depends on no external principles; and third, it tells us that individuals are to be governed on the basis of the presumed social contract.[32]

Yeatman provides an account of neoliberal governance structures. She says, "What is at stake . . . is not so much the ethos and practice of management as the culture and structure of governance."[33] By governance she means the "culture and structure of the relationship between what Max Weber called legitimate domination and those who are subject to it."[34] What Weber meant by legitimate domination was a form of domination justified by an authority structure that was in turn legitimated by legal-rational authority. But governance based on a management model is not in the main legitimated by Weber's notion of legal-rational authority, but by a form of legitimacy or rationality that depends upon efficiency in the market.

Neoliberalism is a substantive discourse of governance potent precisely because of its capacity to combine economics, the social, and politics on behalf of rational choice as a principle of legitimacy. Scott points out that governance arrangements can be classified into simple purchase-and-sale arrangements, bilateral arrangements for more complex relationships (as, for example, with joint ventures), trilateral arrangements where third parties are involved in processes such as arbitration, and vertical integration where the transaction costs are reduced by forming a firm.[35] He also claims that, while the institutional analysis of the public sector (for example, selecting governance structures that minimize transaction costs) is fundamentally concerned with the same issues as the private sector, the actual issues and concepts of the public sector are different from the private sector.[36] Whereas in the private sector firms may fail, the same cannot be allowed for government structures even under marketized conditions.

The contractual model is merely one of many devices that arrange the conditions of life to promote certain behaviors and limit others. There are other formal and informal means of governance. In this respect Hindess includes the design of buildings where individuals come under the regulatory gaze of others, the constitution of markets with economic rewards and sanctions, the design of welfare and taxation systems so as to encourage some behaviors and limit others, and macroeconomic management of the financial system.[37] Such "indirect legislation" makes instruments of government out of the independent activities of free agents. This emphasis on governance extends the idea of managerialism working through such conditions and supports our contention that managerialism is strongly associated with governmentality, within which individuals come to regulate their own behavior "autonomously" in the approved manner under these sorts of conditions.[38]

New Managerialism, Education, and Self-Governance

Foucault and, more recently, Nikolas Rose have shown us how the human sciences have been embroiled within systems of power whereby human subjectivity could be constituted and enter into the calculations of authorities. As Rose puts it:

> On the one hand, subjective features of human life can become elements within understandings of the economy, the organization, the prison, the school, the factory and the labor market. On the other, the human psyche itself has become a possible domain for systematic government in the pursuit of socio-political ends.

Rose looks at how government intervenes in the shaping of the private self to achieve its socio-political aims, not directly, because that would be an illegal invasion of privacy in a liberal democracy, but, instead, "by way of the persuasion inherent in its truths, the anxieties stimulated by its norms, and the attraction exercised by the images of life and self it offers us."[39]

It is not just that particular notions of the self are peddled in education along these lines but also that this notion of the self as an endless chooser and consumer of commodities (including education) permeates much of our social thought. There are a number of common "truths" permeating the economy; by treating everything as an economic commodity, they permeate education, health, social welfare, organizations, and the labor market.

Now we propose to consider how new managerialism becomes a form of self-governance. First we will argue that the self is constituted by such theories, not as being personally autonomous (in some version of the Enlightenment sense of personal autonomy, although it trades on such a notion), but as the autonomous chooser.[40] Second, we will argue that this level of self-governance is the fundamental level for governance, for it is at the basic metaphysical level of the individual where the linchpin of neoliberal thinking, practice, and theory is to be found.

A notion of a "free" autonomous chooser underlies neoliberal education. But just as the Enlightenment notion of personal autonomy did not provide freedom according to Foucault, neoliberal autonomous choosers, too, will not be free, because forms of rationality and the laws within which the free market will be required to operate and function will shape people as particular kinds of subjects so that they will choose in certain general ways. By choosing in these ways, we argue, they will not only be governed but also, more important, be *self*-governed. They will be self-governed because they believe that they are autonomous choosers. But this belief comes about through an effect, which is an extension of Foucault's notion of biopower, which we call "busnopower," a key element of governance and self-governance.[41]

Foucault had introduced the term "biopower" as follows:

> The disciplines of the body and the regulations of the population constituted the two poles around which the organization of power over

life was deployed. The setting up, in the course of the classical age, of this great bipolar technology—anatomic and biological, individualizing and specifying, directed towards the performances of the body, with attention to the processes of life—characterized a power whose highest function was perhaps no longer to kill, but to invest life through and through.[42]

Biopower carries with it a specifically anatomical and biological aspect and is inscribed on the body of individuals as members of a population, first so that their sexuality and individuality are constituted in certain ways but, second, so that this connects with issues of national policy. Thereby, according to Foucault, docile and healthy bodies can be inserted into the machinery of production. In this way populations can be adjusted in accordance with economic processes. Foucault discusses in considerable detail how the requisite techniques and technologies for the exercise of biopower were developed and applied as technologies of domination and technologies of the self. Technologies of domination act essentially on the body, classifying and objectifying individuals. They were developed in disciplinary blocks such as the prison, the hospital, and the school. Insofar as these objective classifications are adopted and accepted by individuals, so their selves are also constituted. The key to technologies of the self is the belief, now common in Western culture, that it is possible to reveal the truth about one's self. By telling the truth about one's sexuality, where the "deepest" truth is embedded in the discourse and discursive practices of sexuality, individuals become objects of knowledge both to themselves and to others. In telling the truth one knows oneself and is known to others in a process both therapeutic and controlling. Eventually, according to Foucault, we learn how to do these things to ourselves. Thus biopower is exercised upon the self and its effect is self-governance.

In the literature, and the new practices and processes of neoliberal education, there are stated to be, or there are assumptions of, fundamental principles of freedom and choice. Students and parents are seen as persons who are capable of deliberating upon alternatives, choosing between alternative educational programs according to individual needs, interests, and the qualities of programs. But, in addition, it seems to be presumed that it is part of the very nature of being human to make, and want to make, continuous consumer-style choices. The traditional liberal and Enlightenment notion of autonomy, however, and accompanying notions of needs and interests, presuppose that such choices are the chooser's own, that as choosers they are independent and that their needs and interests have not been imposed upon them in some manipulative way. But in the current educational environment, we believe, they *have* been imposed upon them by the structure of the free-market and the lawful extension to education of free market theories and practices.

Governmentality carries with it notions of leadership and husbandry, and policy from successive governments (such as in New Zealand) has carried strong overtones of both. (Rose sees this as an indirect invasion of the privacy of persons for sociopolitical ends.) It is not just that the individual should become an autonomous chooser but also that this connects with wider government policy and economic theory. The autonomous chooser becomes a unit in an enterprise and consumer-driven market totality.[43] These changed notions can and should be understood as involving changes in the forms that governmentality takes. But in providing leadership and husbandry successive governments in New Zealand have, at the same time, claimed to be providing a better form of security for those for whom access to educational services has been difficult, by targeting individuals who for whatever reason cannot afford to become skilled and qualified. They have not abandoned security, but rather reassessed it in terms of individualism and the autonomous chooser in particular. In so doing they are exercising a form of power that impinges on individuals both as individual living human beings and also as subjects of a population, for the new targeted individuals are not "normal" individuals, but deficient individuals. They are not responsible for such things as their own health, welfare, and education, and hence they are targeted as deficient (and delinquent in Foucault's sense).

This new form of power is not the biopower of Foucault introduced above. Biopower was directed at and through the body at the health and sexuality of the individual and, through that, at populations. This new form of power, which we are calling busnopower, is directed at the subjectivity of the person not through the body but through the mind, through forms of educational practice and pedagogy so that people come to accept certain "truths" about themselves. Through choices in education busnopower shapes the subjectivities of autonomous choosers. Education, embedded in the frameworks of busnopower and business-oriented forms of technocratic rationality, is the first educational step in the individualizing and totalizing functions of busnopower and of self-governance.[44]

But in producing and reproducing the form of human nature as autonomous choosers, busnopower also impinges upon the population as a whole, as individual consumer activity "improves" both society and the economy. Busnopower is directed not only at individuals, to turn them into autonomous choosers and consumers, but also at the population as a whole, by a total immersion in the enterprise culture of the social, the economy, and the new rationality of the state.[45] In the exercise of busnopower there can be seen then a merging of the economic, the social, and the activity of government. But this "improvement" has in part been manufactured by the laws that set up and govern the operation of the free market, including the privatization of what were formerly state-owned commercial enterprises—telecommunications, railways, airlines, and so on.

In New Zealand we note educational legislation that requires all education to have a vocational emphasis—hence any distinction between traditional views of liberal and vocational occupation (such as Dewey's discussion in *Democracy and Education*) becomes lost, and subsequently, any distinction between education and training becomes occluded. All choice in education has become then a mere choice between institutions, all offering an education that *must* have vocational implications. As a result, people see education as being only vocational, through the governance of their public choices and thereby the constitution of their understandings and their very selves. As in other cases of "free choice," the consumer can only choose from among alternatives whose characteristics they *do not* choose.

The "truths" of government are that we are free, that the free market is best for us. But liberal education, which could have provided a critique of such consumerist notions, may no longer be a choice for many within state-controlled education. When consumers purchase education, education becomes a contract between the buyer and the chooser, and, as we have seen above, when education becomes a contractual purchase it becomes nonpolitical. Thus the changes to policies in ministries of government, and the devolution of issues to schools, have essentially involved the depoliticization of education in the names of "choice" and "quality" (defined in terms of the occluded notions of busnopower and busnocratic rationality). Choice and quality after devolution are now negotiated at the contractual level between student (or parent) and provider. Choice on social issues at the noncontractual level has been occluded and depoliticized in this relation.

The Doctrine of the Self-Managing School

From a revised analysis of James Coleman's national database, John Chubb and Terry Moe develop two general arguments.[46] First, they argue that school organization is a function of a school's institutional environment. Second, they argue that student achievement is a function of school organization and the structure of school governance. The policy implications of these arguments prioritize school autonomy, and parent and student choice, rather than democratic control and bureaucracy. In fact, choice is seen as the panacea.[47]

In the context of recent reforms to the schooling system in New Zealand, Smelt argues that these elements—parental choice, delegation of powers to school level, parental voice at the school level, and contractual relations between the school level and the "client"—are "far from creating a voucher scheme or a fully decentralized or market driven system."[48] In this section of the chapter we are interested in examining Smelt's finding that "overall, there is considerable potential to develop the existing system further . . . as the optimal balance is unlikely to have been struck yet" in terms of the dynamics of self-management.[49] An important question arising is What is the nature of this further institutional development?

The doctrine of the self-managing school arises from the neoliberal policy environment that presents the self-manager as the neoliberal subject of managerialism. That subject is a rational, self-interested utility maximizer. The three key elements within this conception—rationality, individuality, and self-maximization—can be examined for the ways in which they function under neoliberal educational policy.

Rationality and individuality normally imply autonomy and hence capacity for choice. But an unproblematic belief in personal autonomy masks the very idea that choice is integral to neoliberal assumptions of rationality and desire (produced through marketization) underlying "freedom" to act. Because of its accent on an individual's power over his or her immediate environment, choice (an element of self-governance) is welcomed in organizations in the interests of maximizing resources, including human ones. Choice implies that the individual knows what he or she is choosing, and why. Such choice presupposes a free agent with thinking processes not coerced by historical or cultural circumstances. This view of reason was articulated by Descartes, who assumed that the "I" who does the thinking—"the thinking thing"—assumes itself to be fully conscious and hence fully self-knowable. It is not only knowable and autonomous but also coherent. The idea of another psychic territory in contradiction to consciousness is therefore unimaginable. Descartes's subject is a narrator who imagines that he or she speaks without simultaneously being spoken. In this view of the universe, we are spoken or speak ourselves into existence. This creates the illusion that, a priori, the individual is fully responsible for his or her thoughts and actions.

This is the idea of self-determining freedom: the idea that I am free when I decide for myself what concerns me, rather than being shaped by external influences. It is a standard of freedom that obviously goes beyond what has been called "negative liberty," where I am free to do what I want without interference by others because that is compatible with my being shaped and influenced by society and its laws of conformity. Self-determining freedom demands that I break the hold of all such external impositions, and decide for myself alone.[50] And, as Taylor points out, "self-determining freedom has been an idea of immense power in our political life . . . [and] has been one of the intellectual sources of modern totalitarianism."[51]

There are, however, inherent problems in this subject position. The choices that an individual makes, for example, may be based on a rational analysis, but desire may subvert rationality. The often contradictory positions that are evidenced in life may also mitigate against the Cartesian notion of rationality. In the sense that an individual is said to "know" what he or she is choosing, there are several practical implications: that the individual is well informed, that there is no distortion in the communication, that desire is not a subversive influence, that the person could choose otherwise, and so on. The picture of choice, however, is not so simple, and from this we begin to unravel the productive power of managerial approaches to education.

Foucault has continually argued that power is seldom exercised in overt observable ways. More often it is unobtrusive and embedded in the work process itself, or in the language through which it is defined. In educational organizations, to a large extent, power is exercised through a form of politics in which managers manage and mediate the meaning of organizational life in the context of policy. It is the policy environment that creates para-meters for the exercise of power that allows the production of certain con-texts in preference to others. Within this context, meaning is managed through a legal configuration of social relations, and while this meaning can be contested, it would be within an already defined scope. It would, for example, be difficult to critique notions of "efficiency," "quality," and "choice," which, within a managerialist model, are accepted as relatively unproblematic; the typical questions are more concerned with *degree* of quality, with "quality" being defined as minimum standards, rather than the attribution of value by the participants.

Similarly, the managerial language of "choice," "voice," "contractual-ism," and "delegation" are, according to Smelt, "the four instruments of reform."[52] The same language also informs the organizing principles of self-management in everyday life. The management by an individual of him- or herself and the immediate environment requires choices to be made, the ability to be heard ("voice"), the agreement with key perfor-mance indicators on a contractual basis, and the power to carry out dele-gated tasks. Caldwell and Spinks promulgated the doctrine of the self-managing school in the educational administration literature, which sub-sequently became the focus of programs in Australia, England, Wales, and New Zealand.[53] The model offers a collaborative management framework for schools where the notion of excellence is deemed equivalent to the additive effect of a series of managerial constructs: "quality," "effective-ness," "equity," "efficiency," and "social capital." A sample of the lan-guage is appropriate here to see its inherent idealism:

> The vision for a school is a mental image of a preferred future, a desirable and credible state of affairs which in some ways is better than is currently the case. The image may be as vague as a dream or as precise as a statement of objectives.[54]

Although Caldwell and Spinks provide an operational means for intro-ducing self-management as culture change in schools themselves, they do so with a functionalist bias devoid of any theoretical or political analysis of educational policy. They say, for example, "Decentralization is adminis-trative rather than political, with decisions at the local level being made within a framework of local, state, or national policies and guidelines."[55]

They also pursue the separation of policy development from policy implementation and argue for a generic form of professional management for policy implementation, which, they presume, can be applied to most possibilities. That application will convert substantive political questions into process issues for management, where problems can be more effectively dealt with since they "often arise because of a failure to clearly and/or appropriately specify responsibility for particular activities and programs."[56] Effective management is seen as the answer. In fact, as they say, "building a base of policies for a school is not as complex a task as is often suggested. Most policies can be quickly written by documenting the current approach in the format recommended for a policy."[57] They present a version of culture change that attempts to secure the consent of teachers and integrate it with otherwise unchanged managerial practices.

Relying solely on the market for public policy, however, is problematic. Hogan, for instance, points out that accepting a series of simplifying assumptions about the nature of economic (or social) action and the character of market processes leads Chubb and Moe to assert that parent choice and deregulated educational markets would increase "exchange efficiency" and "productive efficiency."[58] These economic exchanges, however, represent a "search for universally applicable hypotheses . . . which transcend institutional, systematic and historical variations and . . . are abstracted from social organizations and cultural patterns."[59] A market is simply not an allocative device: it is also a system for creating and measuring value, for producing and ordering preferences that in turn become embedded in culture. It is, therefore, a political device. By virtue of these ambient processes of cultural production, the market (in a circular logic) generates the very standards, including exchange efficiency, that neoclassical economists employ to evaluate market outcomes. Education, for example, is as much an investment in human capital formation, cultural property, social capital, and competitive advantage as it is a consumption choice about which school a child will attend.

Furthermore, since in many modern nations the state is the monopoly supplier of education, while at the same time setting conditions for its consumption, the capacity for autonomy or self-management among education providers as well as "consumers" is severely diminished. Both public and private sectors—in fact all of the "education market"—operate under the same conditions, under which legislation, standardized curriculum delivery, and systems of accreditation all combine to govern the state education funding regime.

Given these technologies of domination, any notion of a priori autonomy of the subject is questionable. The very interpretation of education as consumable represents the imposition of an individualizing, totalizing, economic, and instrumental narrative of education. And as Marshall points out in his critique of the neoliberal individual as the "autonomous chooser," this interpretation of education is rather myopic.[60] Autonomy, in everyday use, implies that there is some measure of "free" choice. As we have argued here, however, autonomy is problematic. As we see it, the notion of autonomy that underpins self-management in schools is actually produced by the types of changes suggested by Smelt and, as a result, will necessarily be of a certain limited kind.

Conclusion

Our argument has been that the restructuring of state education systems has involved an emphasis on a new managerialism, but that this has taken place within a general notion of governance of population. While the security of the state requires a general presupposition of agency, the achievement of the aims of new management requires the cooperation and support of these very same agents. This can be achieved through discourses such as those of self-management, the autonomous chooser, and the self-managing school. It is important for new management that the "truths" of these discourses be accepted by individuals, but this requires the intervention of the state into the public sector, so that individuals either accept them "rationally," or implicate themselves in their own governance. There are then two possible positions here.

On the one hand, neoliberal explanations for the insertion of managerialism into the public sector attribute to the manager a faculty of authority that is assumed to be a matter of birthright (or inherent ability), which is merely seeking a suitable territory within which to exercise itself. This explanation implies that neoliberal structures—including the autonomous constitution of the self—are rational and the individual is merely an ideologically driven technician. On the other hand, if the accounts of managerialism are simply descriptions of an individual functioning within a territory appropriated by the power of certain groups, we have a different issue for the self. In this latter case, the self requires an ethic that implicates it in its own governance. If the accounts of managerialism are acknowledged as maps that engender the territory within which self-managers can then manage, we have a different story yet again: a kind of semiotic image of a cartographer designing the chart. State-induced self-management can be characterized as a discourse-bound, neoliberal form of governmental discipline. Therefore, any belief in the appeal to a new level of freedom for the individual based upon providing more choices and opportunities within self-management as part of a reason of state is an illusion that operates to secure acceptance by the individual of his or her role in his or her own governance. The actual specifications for the freedom of the individual that are provided through managerialist forms of education, then, are nothing more than a moment in an individualizing and totalizing process, governmentality. Education, as we have seen, is one of the primary contexts in which this takes place.

Notes

1. Michel Foucault, "Governmentality," in *The Foucault Effect: Studies in Governmentality*, ed. Graham Burchell, Colin Gordon, and Peter Miller (Hemel Hempstead, Eng.: Harvester Wheatsheaf, 1991), 87–104.
2. Pat O'Malley, "Neo-liberalism, Advanced-liberalism and Neo-conservatism: Problems of Genealogy and Rationalisation in Governmentality" (paper delivered at the University of Auckland, New Zealand, 1998).
3. Nikolas Rose, *Governing the Soul: The Shaping of the Private Self* (London: Routledge, 1989), 3.
4. O'Malley, "Neo-liberalism," 6–7.
5. Ibid., 12.
6. Foucault, "Governmentality."
7. Ibid., 89.
8. Ibid., 92.
9. Michel Foucault, "Afterword: The Subject and Power," in *Michel Foucault: Beyond Structuralism and Hermeneutics*, ed. Hubert Dreyfus and Paul Rabinow (Chicago: The Harvester Press, 1982), 223.
10. Ibid., 221.
11. Michel Foucault, "Technologies of the Self," in *Technologies of the Self: A Seminar With Michel Foucault*, ed. Luther H. Martin, Huck Gutman, and Patrick H. Hutton (London: Tavistock, 1988), 18.
12. Michel Foucault, "Questions of Method," in *The Foucault Effect: Studies in Governmentality*, ed. Graham Burchell, Colin Gordon, and Peter Miller (Hemel Hempstead, Eng.: Harvester Wheatsheaf, 1991), 75.

13. Andrew Barry, Thomas Osborne, and Nikolas Rose, eds., *Foucault and Political Reason: Liberalism, Neo-liberalism and Rationalities of Government* (London: U.C.L. Press, 1996), 8.

14. Ibid.

15. Graham Burchell, "Liberal Government and Techniques of the Self," in *Foucault and Political Reason*, ed. Andrew Barry, Thomas Osborne, and Nikolas Rose (London: U.C.L. Press, 1996), 23.

16. Ibid.

17. Pat O'Malley, "Risk and Responsibility," in *Foucault and Political Reason: Liberalism, Neo-liberalism and Rationalities of Government*, ed. Andrew Barry, Thomas Osborne, and Nikolas Rose (London: U.C.L. Press, 1996), 189–208.

18. For example, Jonathon Boston, John Martin, June Pallot, and Pat Walsh, *Public Management: The New Zealand Model* (Melbourne, Australia: Oxford University Press, 1996); Jonathon Boston, "Origins and Destinations: New Zealand's Model of Public Management and the International Transfer of Ideas," in *New Ideas, Better Government*, ed. Patrick Weller and Glyn Davis (New South Wales, Austraila: Allen & Unwin, 1996), 107–31; Christopher Hood, "De-Sir Humphreyfrying the Westminster Model of Bureaucracy: A New Style of Governance?" *Governance: An International Journal of Policy and Administration* 3, no. 2 (1990): 205–14; Christopher Hood, "A Public Management For All Seasons?" *Public Administration* 69 (spring 1991): 3–19; Christopher Hood, "The New Public Management Model and its Conceptions of Performance Engineering," in *The Public Sector Challenge: Defining, Delivering and Reporting Performance* (Plaza Hotel, Wellington, New Zealand: New Zealand Society of Accountants Public Sector Convention, 1992), 35–50; Peter Aucoin, "Contraction, Managerialism and Decentralisation in Canadian Government," *Governance: An International Journal of Policy and Administration* 1, no. 2 (1988): 144–61; Peter Aucoin, "Administrative Reform in Public Management: Paradigms, Principles, Paradoxes and Pendulums," *Governance: An International Journal of Policy and Administration* 3, no. 2 (1990): 115–37; and Peter Aucoin, "Comment: Assessing Managerial Reforms," *Governance: An International Journal of Policy and Administration* 3, no. 2 (1990): 197–204.

19. Christopher Pollitt, *Managerialism and the Public Services: The Anglo-American Experience* (Oxford, Eng.: Basil Blackwell, 1990), 156.

20. Boston, "Origins and Destinations," 108.

21. Hood, "De-Sir Humphreyfrying," 205.

22. Ibid.

23. Compare Foucault, "Governmentality."

24. Hood, "De-Sir Humphreyfrying," 205.

25. Ibid., 214.

26. Pollitt, *Managerialism*, 25.

27. Ibid., 26.

28. Christopher Pollitt, ed., *Handbook of Public Services Management* (Oxford, Eng.: Blackwell, 1992), 11.

29. Ibid.

30. John Martin, "The Role of the State in Administration," in *Leap into the Dark: The Changing Role of the State in New Zealand since 1984*, ed. Andrew Sharp (Auckland, New Zealand: Auckland University Press, 1994), 41–67.

31. Anna Yeatman, "The New Contractualism: Management Reform or a New Approach to Governance?" in *New Ideas, Better Government*, ed. Patrick Weller and Glyn Davis (New South Wales, Australia: Allen & Unwin, 1996), 285.

32. Barry Hindess, "A Society Governed by Contract?" in *The New Contractualism?* ed. Glyn Davis, Barbara Sullivan, and Anna Yeatman (Melbourne, Australia: Macmillan, 1997), 18.

33. Yeatman, "The New Contractualism," 283.

34. Ibid., 282.

35. Scott, "The New Institutional," 155.

36. Ibid., 156.

37. Hindess, "A Society Governed," 20.

38. James Marshall, "The Autonomous Chooser and 'Reforms' in Education," *Studies in Philosophy and Education* 15, no. 1 (1996): 89–96.

39. Rose, *Governing the Soul*, 10.

40. Marshall, "The Autonomous Chooser."

41. James Marshall, "Foucault and Neoliberalism: Bio-power and Busno-power," in *Philosophy of Education*, ed. Alven Neiman (Urbana, Ill.: Philosophy of Education Society, 1995), 320–29.

42. Michel Foucault, *The History of Sexuality, Vol. 1,* (New York: Vintage, 1980), 139.

43. See Lyotard here on the concept of performativity. Jean-François Lyotard, "The Postmodern Condition: A Report on Knowledge," *Theory and History of Literature* 10 (Minneapolis: University of Minnesota Press, 1984).

44. For example, busnocratic rationality. See Marshall, "Foucault and Neoliberalism."

45. Lyotard, "The Postmodern Condition."

46. John Chubb and Terry Moe, *Politics, Markets and American Schools* (Washington, D.C.: The Brookings Institute, 1990).

47. Chubb and Moe, *Politics*, 112, 186, 217.

48. Simon Smelt, *Today's Schools: Governance and Quality* (Wellington, New Zealand.: Institute of Policy Studies, Victoria University of Wellington, 1998), ix.

49. Ibid., xii.

50. Charles Taylor, *The Ethics of Authenticity* (Cambridge, Mass: Harvard University Press, 1991), 27.

51. Ibid., 28.

52. Ibid., 46.

53. Brian Caldwell and Jim Spinks, *The Self-Managing School* (London: The Falmer Press, 1988).

54. Department of Education, *The Self-Managing School Workshop Manual* (Wellington, New Zealand: National Department of Education, 1989), 42.

55. Caldwell and Spinks, *The Self-Managing School*, vii.

56. Ibid., 187.
57. Ibid., 41.
58. David Hogan, "The Social Economy of Parent Choice and the Contract State," in *New Ideas, Better Government*, ed. Patrick Weller and Glyn Davis (New South Wales, Australia: Allen & Unwin, 1997), chap. 9.
59. Ibid., 125.
60. Marshall, "The Autonomous Chooser."

Globalization: A Useful Concept for Feminists Rethinking Theory and Strategies in Education?

Jill Blackmore

"Globalization," a much-used, ill-defined, and abstract term, has become the new regime of truth in the 1990s, imbued with its own rationality and self-fulfilling logic. Globalization is typically described as increased economic, cultural, environmental, and social interdependencies and new transnational financial and political formations arising out of the mobility of capital, labor, and information, with both homogenizing and differentiating tendencies. But does globalization describe some fundamental economic and social transformation in the late twentieth century? This chapter points to how feminist thinking about educational policy is being informed by the debates about globalization and, in turn, how feminists view "globalization." Feminists ask, How is globalization understood, who is pushing particular viewpoints and policies in response to globalization, why are they taken up, by whom, and with what equity effects?[1] Does the notion of globalization offer feminists something useful, theoretically or strategically?

The concept of globalization has been loosely, if not promiscuously, used in educational policy texts to justify the radical restructuring of state education systems since the mid-1980s in most Western, liberal capitalist, and increasingly many "developing" nation-states.[2] Nation-states are told that we are all now on a level (global) playing field and that we must adjust accordingly in order to be more efficient, productive, and flexible. Industry (now including education) must become more export-oriented; while unions and other "interest" groups (for example, women) must temper their demands for equality, otherwise the nation-state will lose its competitive global advantage. Education has, in most instances, been reshaped to become the arm of national economic policy, defined both as the problem (in failing to provide a multiskilled flexible workforce) and the solution (by upgrading skills and creating a source of national export earnings); and women are now seen as a wasted resource able to contribute to national productivity. Individuals, institutions, local communities, and nation-states are now expected to "measure up" against normative benchmarks of "international best practice."

In this context, the nature of educational policy and of policy production, its practical, symbolic, and transformative capacity, has also significantly changed.[3] Educational policy has been more closely linked to economic needs and productivity gains, and policy production has been more tightly controlled by the state, to the exclusion of other stakeholders (such as educators and feminists).[4] Many Western liberal states increasingly use policy and funding mechanisms designed at the center to steer from a distance more autonomous local units, yet maintain control and coordination of these subunits through strong accountability mechanisms of performance management and outcome-based evaluation. Educational policy, in such instances, has shifted emphasis from input and process to outcomes, from the liberal to the vocational, from education's intrinsic to its instrumental value, and from qualitative to quantitative measures of success. Structural adjustment policies prescribe cutting public expenditures for education, health, and welfare; reducing state funding away from program provision to program regulation with devolution; shifting responsibilities onto the "third sector" (families, community bodies, and charitable agencies); and depoliticizing the relationship between state and civil society and politicizing the public services by separating (1) policy and implementation, and (2) centralized, mandated policy and competition in provision. School systems have become aggregates of individual schools tightly controlled through national curriculum, national qualification systems, and national audit systems.[5] All these tendencies signal radical changes in the social relations of gender in education.

Yet gender is remarkably absent from mainstream discussions of globalization, just as it is from the policy texts on educational reform and restructuring. The focus of globalization is often upon the economic, political, cultural, and aesthetic dimensions, rather than the ecological, social, or ethical ones, and on the formation of new ethnic, race, and class, but not gender, identities.[6] Yet gender is central to both the processes of globalization and how one views globalization. One paradox highlighted by taking a feminist perspective on globalization is that while globalization discourses refer to fast-moving educational changes and fluid flows of money, people, ideas, images, and goods globally, there has also been a reassertion of the "new fundamentalism."[7] Feminists suggest that this is because globalization in many anglophone countries has been used to justify new Right ideologies of market liberalism and social conservatism wedded to a particularly limited vision of the individual as an autonomous, rational, self-maximizing chooser.[8] Economic orthodoxies of structural adjustment prescribing a small state, balanced budgets, free markets, deregulated finance and labor markets, and increased flexibility have framed educational solutions to globalization in the United States, United Kingdom, New Zealand, Australia, and Canada, and new democratic states such as South Africa. These new Right economic discourses restructuring economic relations in a postwelfare state tap into social prejudices and fears about race, gender, and class identities. Thus, paradoxically, "aspects of progressivism feature alongside re-invigorated traditionalism, and centers of innovation espouse traditional social values."[9] Women feel both the pain and the pleasure associated with seductive notions of choice, but they largely bear the responsibility as the competitive state withdraws from its social welfare obligations while reprivatizing women's productive labor.

Mainstream globalization theories have tended to either ignore gender or to view gender relations around a range of binaries: convergence/divergence, core/periphery, and "globalization from above" or "below."[10] Debates in educational management, for example, focus upon policy convergences around issues of devolution, self-managing schools and school effectiveness, and divergent local readings.[11] Feminist postcolonial theorists criticize core/periphery analyses for their assumption of a unilateral exploitative exchange of Third World nation-states by the West, how such binaries ignore how gender relations "take different forms in different social formations and even in different periods of development in capitalist societies," and how gender divisions are confused by race and class.[12] Privatization of education may improve class and race relations in the new South Africa, where privileged white populations had enjoyed state support under apartheid, but it may work to the detriment of girls due to long-held cultural attitudes about women.[13] Materialist feminists are troubled by top-down/bottom-up binaries that damn the global and idealize the local, as contradictory policies often emanate from the same international bodies and decentralization does not guarantee local democracy.[14] And policies change. Whereas modernization based on rapid expansion of mass education and women-friendly self-help programs during the 1980s rapidly improved girls' education participation rates in African, Asian, and Latin American states, structural adjustment policies in the 1990s advocating a weak state and strong market forces have reasserted male privilege in the market.[15]

Theoretically, therefore, globalization points to a range of contradictions for feminist theorists. Despite these complexities, feminist analyses of "globalization," and policy responses to globalization, suggest changing patterns in gender relations. The new international economic orthodoxy of structural adjustment, which focuses upon balanced national budgets and "export-oriented industrialization" based upon increasing female participation as semiskilled and unskilled labor, often means education is complicit in the production of the "docile and unskilled worker in foreign controlled enterprises."[16] Such policies continue to assume a gender-neutral postcolonial state and a gender-neutral education system, ignoring the historically constituted class/gender/race inequalities of past regimes. Regardless of structural variations in education (centralization or decentralization), the gendered division of labor persists, and has perhaps been exacerbated in particular anglophone states, with educational restructuring. Regardless of their educational achievement, women are still disadvantaged in the education market, and post-Fordist education workplaces tend not to be more democratic. Indeed, evidence suggests the remasculinization of the "hard" core by a largely Anglo-Saxon, male, and professional middle class in professional/managerial/technical high-wage positions, the arena of transnational masculinities,[17] and the further casualization of the "soft" periphery dominated by women, ethnic, and racial "minorities" at the local level.[18] This pattern of recentering of male power has occurred in more hierarchically managed *decentralized* systems with the reassertion of executive prerogative through restructuring in a type of structural backlash.[19] The backlash, fueled by the "hollowing out of the white professional male middle class," and following upon the job losses of blue-collar male trades with deindustrialization in the increasingly feminized service-oriented anglophone economies, has produced a discourse of crisis in masculinity, reverberating in schools across national boundaries: "What about the boys?"

Strategically, the gender implications are also contradictory. "Hollowing out of the state" theories warn of borderless states and the homogenization of cultural identity, putting national educational systems as well as cultural identities under threat from convergences to regional or global norms. Fear of universalization has led to local "hybridization" with the reassertion of national and regional identities around citizenship, and with some possibilities for greater inclusivity in notions of citizenship, nationhood, and community sensitive to feminist claims. But "end of state" theories also point to the restructuring of (1) internal structural and political relations within nation-states, (2) industrial relations, and (3) social and welfare policies, all of which signal the dismantling of the welfare state in many Western liberal democracies, a strategic concern for feminists.[20]

More optimistic accounts see a stronger world polity, the global network of international governmental and nongovernmental organizations, as possibly exerting positive pressure on individual states for progressive gender equity policies as symbolizing "modernization."[21] Regionally, the European Union has proactively created an equal opportunity infrastructure monitoring effects based on notions of a social market, corporatism, and human rights. Because workplace equity (and education) are seen to be central to European Union economic growth, the European Union has sometimes overridden regressive national legislation, countered more regressive New Right policy responses to globalization, or prescribed equity measures for "old democracies" such as the United Kingdom.[22] Yet the European Union's social policies are always subject to the economic test, as those equal opportunity policies seen to be economically detrimental are often under resourced and downgraded in priorities by individual member states. Significantly, social clauses dealing with equity or human rights have been absent in other regional agreements, such as NAFTA.

Overall, feminist discussions of globalization have focused upon the restructuring of *relations* between education, the market, the state, the family, and the individual, highlighting the assumptions of citizenship underpinning the reformation of relations between the civic and the civil, the public and the private.

Weak State, Strong State, or No State at All?

Globalization, with regard to the state, presents new problems and aggravates old ones for feminists. The old problems center around: (1) issues of women's dependency on the welfare state; (2) how feminists engage with, and make claims upon, the state; (3) the shifting boundary between public and private; and (4) how the state defines what constitutes disadvantage. Many feminists see the state being fundamentally altered due to globalization.[23] In particular, they see a shift from the welfare protectionist state of many anglophone nations to a more "competitive" state, which now mediates the excesses of the market, rather than actively regulating the market to promote equity. Gender equity has been dealt with quite differently depending upon the nature of the state. The Scandinavian model of universal social citizenship promoted economic independence of wo men; the Bismarckian model (in Germany and Austria) was based upon male models of full employment, which marginalized women; the Anglo-Saxon or residual model of welfare (in North America, the United Kingdom, and Australia) provided welfare only to those "in need"; and the Latin rim model (in Spain, Portugal, and South America) provided no guaranteed rights but relied heavily on women to provide "hidden welfare" through voluntary labor in the family.[24] Some models are more under threat than others.

The growth of many Western welfare states has been closely tied to strong public education systems and large, if bureaucratic, public service sectors that have been a source of employment (teaching), welfare (benefits), and support (child care) for women. While the welfare state tended to protect women and facilitate independence for men, globalization is seen to have weakened the social equity activities of the state as new regional political and economic formations impinge upon individual state sovereignty, reducing autonomy. Previously, the welfare state, positioned against the market, was the means by which feminist (and other social movements) made equity claims. Now, as the state's interests increasingly coincide with the market as the state becomes just another market player, state legitimacy is less dependent upon meeting social democratic claims. At the same time, the state has simultaneously increased control over educational policy while dismantling public education systems with the rise of self-management (for example, charter schools and self-governing schools) in market-oriented systems.

The above signals a shift in individual/state relations that requires feminists to rethink their strategies. Feminists have engaged with the state differently. Australian and Swedish "state feminism" proactively sought to use the state for feminist purposes by installing feminists to work from within the state for women. Feminists in the United States and the United Kingdom have been more suspicious of the state, and maintained strong nongovernmental lobbies, as in Canada.[25] In education, the state has been more critical for the success of gender equity policy in the more centralized state models of Scandinavia, Australia, and New Zealand than in more decentralized and voluntarist models, as in Canada, the United Kingdom, and the United States. For reasons described above, globalization puts the strategies of "state feminism" in particular at risk.[26]

Small state ideologies have also been fueled by, and inform, a backlash against women, multicultural, and Aboriginal or First Nation populations. Conservative governments in Australia, New Zealand, and Canada have dismantled equity infrastructures, marginalizing feminist capacities to work from within the state, and downplayed gender through liberal-market, ostensibly "gender-neutral" ideologies of procedural justice, administration, and individual merit.[27] Education has been redefined as a private, not a public good within the "user pays" and "market choice" models. To position education as an individual investment, as has "New Labor" in the "postwelfare" United Kingdom, ignores familial, cultural, and institutional practices that historically privilege investment in men's, but less so in women's, training and education.[28] These policies collectively have regressive gender equity effects and indicate a shift in values away from collective to competitive individualism by the corporate state, privatizing much of the business of state policymaking, withdrawing it "from public discussion or modes of accountability," and therefore making it less accessible to women's lobbies.[29] Equity, based upon moral and ethical principles of fairness and justice, is cast as too costly and ignored, as efficiency, an amoral notion, triumphs.

The specter of a weak state in social policy raises the issue about where feminists should make their appeals and how they should engage with new state forms. Women have worked with the state on the basis of its political unity in making claims for equal opportunity, antidiscrimination, and equal pay, with some success. Will the task of governance shift to subnational levels (the logic of devolution) or supranational and transnational institutions (the logic of globalization), in which the nation-state only plays a mediating role of management between these two levels (for example, in the International Labor Organization, the United Nations, and UNESCO)?[30] While feminists have criticized the paternalistic state, the state remains critical for gender equity. Certainly, nation-states are increasing their control over education as they lose control over national economic sovereignty. But the state is not less relevant or less powerful, as conservative ideologies would have us believe; it continues to regulate gender relations and mobilize particular gender identity formations. Feminists have yet to theorize adequately these more complex interstate and intrastate relations as nation-states become less self-determining.

Workplace Restructuring

Capital's reconfiguration during the 1980s was contingent upon workplace restructuring. While women teachers in many nations had benefited during the 1980s from progressive reforms including permanent part-time employment, family leave, and superannuation, the argument in the 1990s was that economic adaptability was incompatible with the centralized labor markets that had protected women workers. Labor market reform moved to deregulate, seeking productivity gains by making workforces more mobile and flexible. Industrial relations and employer-worker relations reform in previously centralized systems in Australia, New Zealand, and Sweden moved toward decentralized wage bargaining. While feminist unionists were seduced by possible gains recognizing women's traditional skills and redefining skill hierarchies in more democratic workplaces with multiskilling job redesign, flexible workplace arrangements, and training-based career paths, this optimism was relatively short lived. Underpinning the new work order were gender-neutral notions of generic, transportable competencies, assuming the human capital model of the white male worker.

Indeed, devolution to self-managing competitive educational institutions has been contingent upon the casualization (and feminization) of educational work across all education sectors at the same time that managerial prerogatives (usually male-dominated) have been asserted through greater regulation of work, conditions of employment, and worker discipline. Decentralized enterprise-based wage bargaining similarly favors highly unionized, usually male-dominated occupations, while feminized unions tend to negotiate away pay bonuses for flexibility in hours to undertake home duties.[31] Decentralized wage bargaining has, in Australia, New Zealand, and Sweden, reduced gender wage parity and stripped women of the few institutional mechanisms designed to counterbalance employers' superior economic and legal power.[32] Instead, local agreements extend working hours to increase employers' flexibility, consuming private time. Legislative protection in the labor market (antidiscrimination and affirmative action laws, and so forth), while weaker than industrial law, has also been weakened (for example, in repeal of affirmative action laws in California and Ontario). Flexibility discourses privilege employer, not worker, needs.[33]

The restructuring of industrial relations in the face of globalization gives impetus to debates over teacher professionalism. Flexibility debates put tenure up for negotiation as institutional flexibility in self-managing educational institutions is dependent upon casualized labor. Dynamic flexibility (multiskilling, quality assurance, and quality circles) has challenged teachers' professional control over their work as the managerial state imposes tighter regulatory frameworks (such as in new teacher registration bodies, standards councils, and competency frameworks) and teacher hierarchies (as in Advanced Skills Teachers) in the United Kingdom, Australia, New Zealand, and the United States.[34] Globalization thus threatens unionism, reduces real wages, and intensifies work in poorly resourced workplaces.[35] This restructuring of educational work has profound implications for women given their numerical dominance in teaching and underrepresentation in educational management.

Educational Governance

Devolution and corporate managerialism have been the key strategies of particular anglophone governments simultaneously to increase labor flexibility and reduce government expenditure by "faxing the crisis down the line" to more "autonomous" educational institutions while catering to "client" choice and diversity.[36] Welfare states with "big government" profiles have had more motive for radical administrative reforms than have small government states. Thus New Zealand, Australia, and the United Kingdom managerialized their public service; some decentralized systems became more centralized in some aspects for example, in the national curriculum of the United Kingdom. Devolution in many anglophone education systems has produced even stronger centralized controls through curriculum guidelines, financial management, accountability mechanisms, and weaker decentralization tendencies.[37]

Under centralized-decentralization, Fordist work practices coexist beside post-Fordist practices in educational institutions. Teachers, academics, and managers experience tendencies toward empowerment, enhancement of skills, and flexible modes of teaching while experiencing at the same time occupational intensification, fragmentation, and differentiation.[38] Teamwork operates, but within more hierarchical organizations privileging management over teaching and research. Any individual flexibility for teachers is undermined by the intensification of labor. The trend toward marketization and client-oriented education, strongest in the anglophone states, indicates that

> there has been something of a move away from the notion that the
> teaching profession should have a professional mandate to act on
> behalf of the state in the best interests of its citizens to a view that

teachers (and indeed other professions) need to be subjected to the rigors of the market and greater control and surveillance on the part of the re-formed state.[39]

Teaching, as a numerically "feminized" quasi-public-sector profession, is thus precariously positioned, located neither in the hierarchical bureaucratization model of the modern state or the marketized individualist provision model of private industry. Feminist critiques of this "hybrid" managerialism in education refer to the marginalization of equity discourses across all education sectors (community, schools, higher education, and vocational training) as efficiency discourses are privileged.[40] Furthermore, the management mind-set and reassertion of executive prerogative, now associated with new modes of hegemonic strategic or transnational masculinities, has excluded feminist policymakers.[41] Gender is also central to the conception/execution divide within the policy process, women being more likely to be excluded from policy production but included in policy implementation as change agents.[42] For example, in South Africa, the pre-1994 education policy production phase largely excluded feminists, but the post-1994 implementation phase meant that due to the "professionalization of curriculum policy making from the mid-1990s, academic feminist policy makers were able to open up a space for themselves."[43]

But there are new arenas in which feminists can engage at the regional and transnational level. In the European context, Pillinger talks about the feminization of policy parallel to the feminization (in part-time labor) of the labor market, due to the significant European Union investment in equal opportunity institutional infrastructure and nominal support for equity principles (such as the European Women's Lobby, European Network of Women, Information Office, and EO Unit), although such social policies still work within the limits of male-dominated "institutional" power.[44] While gender equity can be embedded into legislation and policies, such policies are often more symbolic and less about changing practice in ways that may reduce profit or threaten male dominance. In general, devolution of educational governance in conjunction with marketization has encouraged in many anglophone states more individual and competitive relationships between self-managing institutions but without the strong top-down imperatives, coordination, and monitoring requirements necessary to promote equity. Local institutions are left to select or reject equity policies depending upon their marketability.[45] In response, feminists in many states have sought to exploit the accountability and regulatory mechanisms of devolved educational systems and organizations to work for equity, by inserting equity into performance management outcomes and measures, although with limited success.

Markets

The emergence of education markets has been central to globalization and education reform in many anglophone states.[46] Policy texts advocating restructuring along market principles argue that education will be more efficient if based upon competitive market relations where individual choice is facilitated. Globalization in many nation-states marks a discursive shift in policy around what O'Neill refers to as the "construction of the individual as the rational market man . . . living in an enterprise culture."[47] Kari Delhi points out that political debates about marketization in schooling have largely been constructed around a binary between state and market, which are treated as fixed entities with intents and with coherent, systemic, and concrete identities.[48] But the market, as feminists have argued, does not operate either freely or efficiently and is not value neutral. Markets are abstractions premised upon normative models of how people should behave rather than how they do behave, often to the neglect of "the social and the personal" models that collapse when the experiences of women are factored in.[49] Human capital theory is premised upon the self-maximizing, autonomous, individual chooser and upon national productivity measures. These ignore child-rearing responsibilities, domestic labor, and the contribution of voluntary labor to national productivity. Likewise, structural adjustment policies simplistically position the public sector as bad and the private sector as good, quite the contrary to many women's experiences.[50] Yet the "managerial" state has historically actively created education markets through policy, regulations, contractual, and financial arrangements, such as provider-client relations under contractualist arrangements. It manages teacher labor markets, not just to provide a public education system but also increasingly to meet the needs of flexible specialization within a global market.[51]

Education labor markets are particularly gender segmented in terms of the division of labor, the images of leadership, and the gatekeeping criteria for recruitment, promotion, and definitions of merit. The articulation between education, certification, and the market works differently for men and women, given their different life cycles (which often include child rearing) and given cultural attitudes to paid employment for women. Women are not rewarded equally to men in the market for their comparable educational achievements. Markets are influenced by biases and prejudices about particular groups of workers, students, and clients. Globalization, despite the rhetoric of flexible markets and generic "gender-neutral" skills, has not reduced market segmentation premised upon class and race. Skilled and mobile educated women may experience more opportunities, but working-class black or migrant women are more likely to experience more exploitation, while at the same time the normative model of the white, skilled, mobile educated male worker limits all women's possibilities. The majority of women education workers are increasingly "locked into regional/local environments with restructured collective consumption and declining infrastructure," further reducing their occupational mobility.[52]

Yet the construction of the new post-Fordist work order and worker identity is contingent upon changing the social relations of gender. For example, the restructuring of higher education in many nation-states has selectively altered the access of women from lower socioeconomic status and mature-aged students to higher education and promoted the entrepreneurial academic leader (almost always male), because occupational mobility is mitigated by domestic responsibilities. Additionally, the commercialization and internationalization of education shifts resources to immediate useful outcomes and targets the strategic disciplines in universities: the applied sciences, and technology, where women are not concentrated, often resulting in the downsizing of education, social sciences, and humanities faculties where women are concentrated as academics and students.

Education markets also offer advantages and privileges to certain "skilled consumers" and bestow disadvantages on others as "some patterns of inequality are inherent with the mode of consumption itself," while others derive from the "political structuring of the market so as to achieve particular social and economic goals."[53] Education markets require the "normalizing" mechanisms of standardized national and international tests to facilitate individual choice and prove competitiveness—tests which rank students, teachers, schools, and even states against each other. Such modes of testing and assessment work against the range of inclusionary and formative assessment practices and pedagogies successfully promoted by gender equity reforms during the 1980s.

Finally, the fragmentation of anglophone and, increasingly, many "developing" state education systems toward "autonomous" self-managing schools in education markets serving discrete client groups removes individual schools from any sense of collective responsibility for all students or to the public. This has considerable social justice and citizenship implications. Devolved, marketized education systems already indicate an increased disparity between individual schools due to inequitable resourcing, and ghettoization based upon class, race, and ethnicity.[54] The gender effects in such scenarios are complex. Single-sex girls' schools may attract fee-paying middle-class patrons or meet the needs of particular religious groups. But the twin strategies of user pays and localization, as the new tenets of mass education systems, tend to undermine gender equality as cultural attitudes toward women lag behind economic and political changes. The local "market" can mobilize old prejudices ("woman are prone to get pregnant," "women are not competitive," "survival of the fittest") that mitigate against women, especially those without child care.[55] Even in institutional labor markets, women's achievements are not rewarded to the same extent as are men's, because employers are reluctant to pay for maternity benefits or leave.[56] Education markets, as with all markets, are premised upon inequality, upon winners and losers.

Family, Market, and State

Globalization leads feminists to frame the questions differently. In trying to understand parental responses to schooling and education, in particular around issues of markets, choice, and schooling, the question becomes, "How are socioeconomic and changing family contexts changing parents' perspectives and understandings as well as access to educational reforms and opportunities?"[57] Kari Delhi refers to how education policies foreground "parents in talk of decision making, stressing outcomes, standards, and accountability; encouraging partnerships with corporations" yet "locally grounded research shows that apparently general and universal terms such as 'parents' and 'choice' are attached with quite different and contested meanings over time and across geo-political space."[58]

In such discourses parents are often read as being a "unified constituency with coherent interests." Yet specific gender roles are played out as family, school, and work relations are being reconfigured, blurring home/school boundaries. In the case of the anglophone states, self-managing schools claim to lead to equal power sharing between parents as consumers and teachers and administrators as producers. Feminist studies indicate that there is a privatization of educational labor underway as, on the one hand, educational outworkers (predominantly women) working under more flexible delivery regimes, bring work home and as, on the other hand, women as parents increasingly contribute their voluntary labor to assist overworked teachers (also largely women) with larger classes and in underresourced schools, thus filling the gap left by state withdrawal of funds and support from public education. As educational labor and costs are increasingly privatized, capital begins to recolonize the family as a site of production as well as consumption. Many women reenter paid work to pay for children's education in private schooling.[59] And it is women who tend to be the most active choosers in the education market place since they tend to be most responsible for children's education:

> Mothers' experience of the processes of bringing up and educating their children are not all in harmony with the public policy discourse of their being free to choose. This official discourse is in itself contradictory and confusing, veering between classical and normative economics. Mothers make continual "choices" in a continual process of making "decisions" about how to live their lives—with men, with partners, with children, with friends and with parents. These "choices" are continually and contingently constrained by the diversity of contexts in which they find themselves, both moral and structural.[60]

At the same time, discourses of parental choice have a conservative twist. In England and Australia, the Right has been able to co-opt, marginalize, or denigrate progressivist and social-justice-oriented discourses of participatory decision making and local parent-teacher partnerships. The new school governing bodies, even when women are represented, are not more democratic and are more about implementing mandated government policies. Conservative governments have *dis*enfranchised well-established constituencies of parents represented by formal, more progressivist parent organizations by their exclusion from representation on school councils and policy making bodies. Community has thus been redefined as an aggregate of individual choosers.[61] The new Right in England, Canada, and increasingly in Australia has effectively mobilized discourses of dissatisfaction and anxiety among middle-class parents to focus upon standards and to spread blame onto particular families and particular groups of parents—usually single mother and non-Anglo-Saxon parents whose "deficiencies in parenting" are seen to drain limited educational resources in their demands for addressing difference and inequality.[62] Certainly, parents have also called upon discourses of choice to argue *against* racist, sexist, and classist education, as in the case of parent-teacher partnerships in some Canadian and Australian states and in former English Labor Education Associations.[63] But feminist work perceives an overall shift in responsibility from the state to a particularly narrow vision of the family, a vision which ignores the family as a site of violence, unequal power and work relations, and contested interests and needs. This convergence of economic and political ideologies has powerful gender effects.

Knowledge and Curriculum Production

Finally, the speed and proliferation of information flows resulting from new information technologies challenge both the definitions of what constitutes valued knowledge and progressive pedagogies. Information is now seen to be the key to power, and information-based industries informed by new technologies the key to economic reconstruction in the face of globalization. In education, this has led in part to greater flexibility in curriculum, certification, and assessment with the development of seamless pathways between education sectors, the workplace, and the home in order to promote lifelong learning in a range of sites focusing on "learning how to learn," and new modes of flexible learning. Paradoxically, however, there has also been a narrowing of curriculum to refocus upon the new "fundamentals" of literacy, numeracy, and technology, as well as increased standardization and universalization of curriculum and assessment as nation-states exert greater control through national curriculum frameworks.[64]

Again these moves are gender-inflected. The shift to work-related competencies in most anglophone states promotes traditional female skills or "the ability to communicate well, handle information, work in teams, solve new problems, apply knowledge and skills in different contexts, and to think conceptually and creatively" as critical to the flexible and adaptable worker while simultaneously vocationalizing the liberal curriculum through the introduction of "generic" employment-related competencies, the emphasis being upon the vocational, rather than the social, aspects of learning and upon competitive, rather than collaborative, social relations in the hidden curriculum of the market.[65] The vocationalization of education privileges "strategic" knowledges (those with immediate economic benefits to improve economic productivity) over "social" knowledge (such as the humanities or ethical and moral studies). The generic competencies have also been restricted to paid work to the neglect of family and household management skills, while the competency-based curriculum has challenged feminist pedagogical practices.[66] Globalization privileges those gender equity policies that have observable economic benefits; ironically, these gender equity policies have encouraged women to enter those nontraditional occupations most under threat from deindustrialization (such as the blue-collar trades). Meanwhile, the discourse of "user choice" privileges certain users over others. Equity is subordinated as the education sector renegotiates its position in the context of contradictory national imperatives of responsiveness, quality, accessibility, and efficiency. The managerial solution has been to replace regulation with quality assurance and group disadvantage with individual client choice. Given that equity practices were already weak even with strong regulatory policies, weak policies in a more deregulated framework will likely have even less impact.[67]

Interestingly, in the face of economic globalization, there has been a renewed emphasis on cultural identity and citizenship education. This emerges out of new Right attacks on the public in the United Kingdom, moves to republicanism in Australia, the fragmentation of nation-states in postcommunist Europe, political reunification in Germany, and ongoing disunity in the Balkans and Korea, alongside the emergence of new ecopolitical regions such as the European Union. While much of this is spurred on by jingoism, ethnic identity politics, and conservatism, for many on the Left, including feminists, "the concept of citizenship seemed to be offering an over-arching concept that could unite various people involved in work on social justice" in the face of the regressive tendencies of globalization.[68] Madeleine Arnot argues that globalization and recent new Right reforms have led feminists to ask, "What have we been doing with respect to democracy; how democratic has feminism been?"[69] Yeatman queries the inclusivity of past feminist claims upon the modernist state when she suggests that indigenous women were excluded in New Zealand and Australia, and thus have less investment and therefore less to lose than white women in the increasingly anachronistic culture of citizenship claims made on the postwar welfare state, claims which presupposed a culturally and racially homogenized national community.[70]

The new individualization of market-driven times has led feminists to rethink notions of the individual, the role of schooling in liberal democracies, and the relationship between citizenship, education, and the market. Certainly, the principles underlying the Keynesian Welfare state were moral as well as economic, embodying particular notions of the modern citizen and governmental roles in minimizing social inequality.[71] Feminism recognizes the different citizenship discourses in different countries, although they are affected by the same market forces of deindustrialization, corporate capitalism, and globalization. Citizenship, many feminists argue, provides new ways of thinking through the problematic of "education, gender, difference, restructuring of education, curricular issues, spatiality, embodiment, questions of knowledge, political issues" in the context of "different levels of marketization, competition, and the restructuring of the labor market, the Europeanization and globalization processes within national formations."[72] Globalization requires new understandings about citizenship vis-à-vis the nation-state in order to address the severe tensions between citizenship and the market, which pit materialism against spirituality, rationality against emotion, selfishness against altruism, atomism against solidarity, and wants against needs, along gender lines.[73] Does the rise of the market endanger the relationship between civil society and nationhood?

Globalization has destabilized, if not uprooted, modernist conceptualizations of citizenship that situated education as producing good citizens, even if they were embodied in the abstract individual (male) worker-citizen, which pseudo-included women. Does globalization mean feminists are forced to "consider what those autonomies now mean and what women want from citizenship? Do past classifications—the nature/culture split, the public-private spheres, the market and the citizen—have value any more?"[74]

Conclusion

Globalization does not necessarily mean the death of the state, or of particular imagined communities, including the women's movement. It is about the changing nature of state relations and relations between different communities (local, regional, and global); labor and capital relations; relations between the individual, state, and market, and between nation-states; and how education is positioned in these shifting relations. The issue for feminists is to understand better how these new formations and relationships are gendered and to consider how we need to "develop anti-imperialist curricula and transnational feminist practice."[75]

Economic globalization has imparted primacy to a market that is not gender-neutral, but which has the potential to reassert a new fundamentalism in gender relations and unreconstructed patriarchal masculinities. The issue for feminists is to consider how the market can create "possibility spaces" for women individually and collectively and how the contradictions between "individual interests, centralized political power on one hand, and the logic of the market on the other" can be exploited.[76] It is clear that while one can seek to change and engage with "the market," "the market" needs to be controlled politically. To this end, feminists need to reconsider how they may work strategically in the multiplicity of economic social and political arrangements. Can new regional blocs be pressured by a world polity that views gender equity policies as the mark of modernization? Strategies need to focus upon old as well as new political formations such as the European Union, voluntary as well as government organizations, and intranational bodies such as UNESCO to develop new strategies. Can the European Union, for example, provide "best practices" or a "model" of how to integrate gender equity provisions into restructuring for other regional blocs? The OECD report, *Shaping Structural Change*, argued that for any active society, compatibility between employment and family commitment must be ensured.[77] It is clear that whatever the nature of the state (whether socialist, postwelfare, postcommunist, or social democratic), an interventionist state is critical to maintain past benefits, and to achieve new ones to counter the destructive asocial formulation of the market, particularly in regard to education. Globalization is not some inevitable juggernaut, but conservatives have effectively diverted attention away from alternative policy responses in many instances.[78]

Theoretically, given the changing nature of the state, feminist theorizing of state/education relations needs to focus not only on threats to national sovereignty and local democracy but also on the relativities and relations between and within nation-states and how feminists may work simultaneously within and across local, national, and supranational levels. Despite structural and textual convergences, globalization requires feminists to rethink our conceptualization of social justice in ways that attend to difference and to fairness between differentially positioned groups in specific contexts. Feminists must develop a more powerful critique of the range of labor markets and their relationships to education and of market liberalism in general on its own terms. Finally, feminism as a political and theoretical force needs to recognize the capacity of new types of intranational and international networks of activism in relation to new forms of local, national, and international governance.

Notes

1. Jane K. Gibson-Graham, *The End of Capitalism (As We Knew It): A Feminist Critique of Political Economy* (London: Blackwell, 1996).
2. Elaine Unterhalter, "States, Households, and Markets in World Bank Discourses 1985–1995," *Discourse* 17, no. 3 (1996): 389–402.
3. Sandra Taylor, Miriam Henry, Bob Lingard, and Fazal Rizvi, *Policy and the Politics of Education* (Sydney: Allen and Unwin, 1997).
4. Taylor et al., *Policy;* and Unterhalter, "States, Households, and Markets."
5. Roger Dale and Susan Robertson, "Resiting the Nation, Reshaping the State: Globalisation Effects on Education Policy in New Zealand," in *Education Policy in the 1990s*, ed. Mark Olssen and Kay Morris (Wellington, New Zealand: Bridget Williams Press, 1996).
6. I. Grewal and C. Kaplan, eds., *Scattered Hegemonies: Postmodernity and Transnational Feminist Practices* (Minneapolis: University of Minnesota Press, 1994).
7. Anthony Giddens, *Beyond Left and Right: The Future of Radical Politics* (Cambridge, Eng.: Polity Press, 1995), 100.
8. Ann-Marie O'Neill, "Privatizing Public Policy: Privileging Market Man and Individualizing Equality Through Choice Within Education in Aotearoa/New Zealand," *Discourse* 17, no. 3 (1996): 403–16; and Janine Brodie, "New State Forms, New Political Spaces," in *State against Markets: The Limits of Globalisation*, ed. Robert Boyer and David Drache (New York: Routledge, 1996).
9. Sharon Gewirtz, Stephen Ball, and Richard Bowe, *Markets, Choice and Equity in Education* (Buckingham, Eng.: Open University Press, 1995), 137.
10. Richard Falk, "The Making of Global Citizenship," in *Global Visions: Beyond the New World Order*, ed. J. Brecher et al. (Montreal: Black Rose Books, 1993), 40.
11. Andy Green, *Education, Globalisation and the Nation State* (Routledge: London,

1997).

12. Emma Obasi, "Structural Adjustment and Gender Access to Education in Nigeria," *Gender and Education* 9, no. 2 (1997): 161–77. Also see Chandra Mohanty, "Cartographies of Struggle: Third World Women and the Politics of Feminism," in *Third World Feminism and the Politics of Feminism*, ed. Chandra T. Mohanty, Ann Russo, and Loudre Torres (Indianapolis: Indiana University Press, 1991).

13. Unterhalter, "States, Households and Markets," 389–402.

14. Lyn Davies, *Equity and Efficiency? School Management in an International Context* (London: The Falmer Press, 1990).

15. Rosemary Gordon, "Education, Policy and Gender in Zimbabwe," *Gender and Education* 6, no. 2 (1994): 131–39; and Nelly Stromquist, *Gender Dimensions in Education in Latin America* (Washington, D.C.: Interamer, General Secretariat of American States, 1996).

16. Gordon, "Education," 133.

17. Connell, "Men in the World."

18. Jill Blackmore, "The Level Playing Field? The Restructuring and Regendering of Educational Work," *International Review of Education* 43, no. 5–6 (1997): 1–23; and Stromquist, *Gender Dimensions*.

19. Jane Pillinger, *Feminising the Market* (Basingstoke, Eng.: MacMillan, 1992); Ann Edwards and Susan Magarey, eds.,*Women in a Restructuring Australia* (Sydney: Allen and Unwin, 1995); Jill Blackmore, *Troubling Women: Feminism, Leadership and Educational Change* (Buckingham, Eng.: Open University Press, 1999); and Bob Lingard and Peter Douglas, *Men Engaging Feminism: Pro-feminism, Backlashes and Schooling* (Buckingham, Eng.: Open University Press, 1999).

20. Jill Blackmore, "Globalisation, Localisation, and the Midwife State: Dilemmas for State Feminism," *Journal of Education Policy* 14, no. 1 (1999).

21. Karen Bradley and Francisco Ramirez, "World Polity and Gender Parity: Women's Share of Higher Education 1965–85," *Research in the Sociology of Education and Socialisation* 11 (1996): 63–91.

22. Jane Pillinger, *Feminising the Market* (Basingstoke, Eng.: MacMillan Press, 1992).

23. Anna Yeatman, "Women's Citizenship Claims, Labour Market Policy and Globalisation," *Australian Journal of Political Science* 27 (1992): 449–61.

24. M. Langan and I. Ostner, *Gender and Welfare: Towards a Comparative Framework*; and Ann Shola Orloff, "Gender and the Social Rights of Citizenship: The Comparative Analysis of Gender and Welfare States," *American Sociological Review* 58, no. 3 (1993): 303–28.

25. Marian Sawer, "Feminism and the State: Theory and Practice in Australia and Canada," *Australian-Canadian Studies* 12, no. 1 (1994): 49–68; and Linda Gordon, "The New Feminist Scholarship on the Welfare State," in *Women, the State, and Welfare*, ed. Linda Gordon (Madison: University of Wisconsin Press, 1990).

26. Nelly Stromquist, "Sex Equity Legislation in Education: The State as the Promoter of Women's Rights," *Review of Educational Research* 63, no. 4 (1992): 379–408; Stromquist, *Gender Dimensions*; and Blackmore, "Globalisation."

27. O'Neill, "Privatising Public Policy."

28. Sharon Gewirtz, "Post Welfarism and the Reconstruction of Teachers' Work in the U.K.," *Journal of Education Policy* 12, no. 4 (1997): 217–31.

29. Yeatman, "Women's Citizenship Claims," 452.
30. Yeatman, "Women's Citizenship Claims," 451.
31. Di Zetlin and Gillian Whitehouse, "Citizenship and Industrial Regulation: A Feminist Perspective" (paper delivered at the Culture and Citizenship Conference, Brisbane, Australia, 30 Sept.–2 Oct. 1996).
32. Prue Hyman, *Women and Economics: A New Zealand Feminist Perspective* (Wellington, New Zealand.: Bridget Williams Books, 1994).
33. Sylvia Walby, *Gender Transformations* (London: Routledge, 1997).
34. Pat Mahony and Ian Hextall, "Teaching in the Managerial State" (paper delivered at the AARE Conference, University of Queensland, Asutralia, Nov. 1997).
35. Susan Robertson and Harry Smaller, *Teacher Activism in the 1990s* (Toronto: James Lorimer, 1996).
36. Blackmore, "The Level Playing Field?"; and Geoff Whitty, Sally Power, and David Halpin, *Devolution and Choice in Education* (Hawthorn, Australia: ACER Press, 1998).
37. Whitty et al., *Devolution and Choice*; and Gewirtz et al., *Markets, Choice and Equity*.
38. Mahony and Hextall, "Teaching in the Managerial State."
39. Quoted in Mahony and Hextall, "Teaching in the Managerial State," 12.
40. Miriam Henry and Sandra Taylor, "Globalisation and National School Policy in Australia," in *A National Approach to Schooling in Australia*, ed. Bob Lingard and Paige Porter (Canberra: Australian College of Education, 1996).
41. Connell, "Men in the World."
42. Jill Blackmore, "Localization, Globalization and the Midwife State: Dilemmas for State Feminism," *Journal of Education Policy* (in press).
43. Elaine Unterhalter, "Unpacking the Gender of Global Curriculum in South Africa" (paper delivered at the Annual AERA Meeting, San Diego, April 1998), 4.
44. Pillinger, *Feminising the Market*.
45. Gewirtz, "Post Welfarism."
46. Jane Kenway and Debbie Epstein, "The Marketisation of School Education: Feminist Studies and Perspectives," *Discourse* 17, no. 3 (1996): 301–14.
47. O'Neill, "Privatising Public Policy," 412.
48. Kari Delhi, "Between 'Market' and 'State?' Engendering Education Change in the 1990s," *Discourse* 17, no. 3 (1996): 363–76.
49. Elaine Kuiper and Jolande Saps, *Out on the Margins: A Feminist Economics* (London: Routledge, 1995).
50. Hyman, *Women and Economics*.
51. Mahony and Hextall, "Teaching in the Managerial State."
52. Mahony and Hextall, "Teaching in the Managerial State," 45–46; and Ian Menter, Yolande Muschamp, Peter Nicholls, Jenny Ozga, and Andrew Pollard, *Work and Identity in the Primary School: A Post-Fordist Analysis* (Buckingham, Eng.: Open University Press, 1997).
53. Gewirtz, "Post Welfarism," 207.
54. Gewirtz et al., *Markets, Choice and Equity*; and Whitty et al., *Devolution and Choice*.
55. S. Rai, "Modernisation and Gender: Education and Employment in Post-Maoist China," *Gender and Education* 6, no. 2 (1994): 119–29.

56. Pillinger, *Feminising the Market.*
57. Miriam David, "Choice Within Constraints," *Gender and Education* 9, no. 4 (1996): 406.
58. Delhi, "Between 'Market' and 'State?'" 375.
59. Val Hey, "'A Game of Two Halves'—A Critique of Some Complicities: Between Hegemonic and Counter Hegemonic Discourses Concerning Marketisation and Education," *Discourse* 17, no. 3 (1996).
60. David, "Choice Within Constraints," 409.
61. Rosemary Deem, Kevin Brehony, and Sally Heath, *Active Citizenship and the Governing of Schools* (Buckingham, Eng.: Open University Press, 1995).
62. Delhi, "Between 'Market' and 'State?'"; and Hey, "'A Game of Two Halves.'"
63. Delhi, "Between 'Market' and 'State?'"
64. Unterhalter, "States, Households and Markets"; and Taylor et al., *Policy.*
65. Sally Power and Geoff Whitty, "Teaching New Subjects? The Hidden Curriculum of Marketised Education Systems" (unpublished paper, London Institute of Education, 1996).
66. Sandra Taylor and Miriam Henry, "Reframing Equity in the Training Reform Agenda: Implications for Social Change," *Australian Vocational Education Review* 3, no. 2 (1996): 46–55.
67. Ibid.
68. Madeleine Arnot and Tuula Gordon, "Gender, Citizenship and Marketization: A Dialogue between Madeleine Arnot and Tuula Gordon," *Discourse* 17, no. 3 (1996): 377–78.
69. Ibid., 379.
70. Yeatman, "Women's Citizenship Claims," 458.
71. Zetlin and Whitehouse, "Citizenship and Industrial Regulation."
72. Arnot and Gordon, "Gender," 386.
73. Ibid., 382.
74. Ibid., 386.
75. Mahony and Hextall, "Teaching in the Managerial State," xii.
76. Rai, "Modernisation and Gender," 128.
77. OECD, *Shaping Structural Change* (Paris: OECD, 1992).
78. Janine Brodie, "New State Forms, New Political Spaces," in *State against Markets: The Limits of Globalisation*, ed. Robert Boyer and David Drache (New York: Routledge, 1996).

Reform as the Social Administration of the Child: Globalization of Knowledge and Power

Thomas S. Popkewitz

This essay is about the study of educational reform. My concern here is with educational reforms as global practices that produce systems of inclusion and exclusion. But to get to that concern, I will move historically by focusing on reform as a political practice that, at least since the late nineteenth century in Western and colonial contexts, embodies efforts to administer change. But this administration is not one of organizing governmental policy to set directions and principles for educational practices, nor is it the designing of organizational practices that limit or permit individual success. The governing of schooling is the inscription of political rationalities in the sensitivities, dispositions, and awarenesses of individuals. My focus, then, is on the knowledge of reform as systems of reason that shape and fashion problem-solving activities of education. This governing is what Michel Foucault called "governmentality," a notion that gives attention to the connection of knowledge to power through the rules and standards of reason itself.[1]

I excavate this governing function of reform by exploring its modern shape as state administrative practices to bring people liberty and freedom. The freedom sought is not some absolute principle about individual or collective emancipation that exists outside of history, but rather is a "freedom" socially constructed within "boundaries of action." The social administration of freedom relates political rationalities with the boundaries of the inner qualities and characteristics of the *self*. To put this relation of social administration and freedom somewhat differently, there is no notion of freedom without some conception of history, culture, and society in which the individual is "made" capable of acting with some sense of responsibility and seeming autonomy. This essay is about reform as the constructions and changes of these boundaries through which freedom is socially administered.

The social administration of freedom, with its ironies, is a global phenomenon of modernity that crosses national boundaries and "colonial" and "postcolonial" contexts. The reform of the state and the individual are joined as a social project. Progress is produced, it is reasoned, not only through institutional change but also through changing the inner capabilities of the individual so that the person acts as a self-responsible and self-motivated citizen, what I will later call the governing of the soul.[2] The social administration of the soul is most deeply embodied in school pedagogy. One needs only to look at the educational systems of the former Soviet Union, the liberal democracies of Europe, or the nations of Latin America to grasp the relation of political rationalities, school reforms, and the strategies of governing and of governmentality. In this historical context I explore the problem of school reform and inclusion and exclusion. Pedagogy administers (develops and nurtures) the child's "soul."

This discussion about reform, then, moves against the grain. It does not assume schooling is a principled activity to measure specific programs against social goals, such as those of justice, equity, the democratic citizen, or a more adjusted and competent worker. In contrast, I place reform within a particular problematic. That problematic is of administering the governing of the individual's soul so that the individual can be governed at a distance through the principles by which an individual becomes self-motivated, self-actualized, and "empowered."

The State, Science, and the Projects of School Reform: Registers of Social Administration and Freedom

To consider the problem and problematic of reform, I turn first historically to the idea of reform that appears in Europe and North America in the nineteenth century. My turning to these contexts is to recognize a number of different historical conjunctures that make possible the scaffolding of ideas about the modern school, reform, and the social administration of individuality. My further concern is with the inscription of particular systems of reason that tie the historical practice of reform to the social administration to schooling and pedagogical knowledge. The particular concrete practices need to be accounted for as I move to current reform initiatives, viewed as global projects of change in education.

The State as a Governing Practice. The idea of social reform in Europe and North America is related to the construction of the modern conception of the state as a legal/administrative agency, brought into colonial contexts to provide an administrative apparatus for the colonization practices occurring globally.[3] The care of the state shifted from protecting its territorial boundaries to that of caring for its populations.[4]

The shear brute force of the sovereign and the church in governing was put into relation with new forms of exercising power associated with liberalism and democracy. The art of governing no longer condoned beating down the door and commanding obedience (although that is still possible). The state was to shape the individual who mastered change through the application of rationality and reason.[5] The good citizen, good family member, good worker, and good student entailed administrative practices to shape and fashion the citizen.[6] New forms of participation, interpretation, social management, and amelioration were constructed. Enlightenment beliefs about the citizen were based upon assumptions about political reflection, social administration, and scientific rationalities. The art of governing was practiced through the principles of "reason" and "reasonable people" that disciplined and produced action and participation. Governing was "at a distance" through the systems of knowledge that enacted principles for the individual to act as a self-responsible, self-motivated citizen, worker, family member, and so forth.

The state as the art of governing, what Michel Foucault calls "governmentality," is one way to think about the practices of reform that relate problems of globalization to the modern state. Throughout Europe, North America, and their colonies, a particular globalization occurred that was related to and complemented the administration of territories. The globalization was a mobilization of particular discourses about the state as a project to administer freedom. Certain and particular principles of participation and government were taken as universal principles for action. The American and French Revolutions, for example, embodied this universalism through notions about the "inalienable rights" of citizens. These discourses about the individual, however, seemed to posit a global notion of the citizen, but the universal principles were in fact particular Western bourgeois norms about a liberal political order. The discourses of social administration in its European contexts, however, were not only of European images and narratives but also inscribed the colonized "other" within the texts of the citizen.[7]

Social reform connected the two registers of social administration and freedom. The register of social administration embodied an assumption that proper planning would provide direction to the evolution of society. New institutions of welfare, culture, and economy were produced to function in the creation of a new, more liberal, and democratic society. Mass schooling was embedded in this movement to socially administer the growth, development, and evolution of society. The projects of reform embodied this problem of social administration and enabled social institutions to become responsive to changing issues of governing.

But the registers of social administration were not only about social evolution and development. The registers of social administration were woven into the register of freedom. Turn-of-the-century discourses about citizenship and individuality were based on liberal ideals about the autonomous, participating, and self-realized individual. Theories of action saw the locus of change in the actor who enacts cultural interests and produces a collective authority—a view of society and individuality that was different from previous notions of a transcendent entity, of a world fixed by placement by birth, and of humans as subject to fate or the gods.[8] Modern social science and pedagogy combined the two registers of administration and freedom through theories about child development and learning.

The Care of the "Soul." The joining of the registers of social administration and freedom in the practices of reform had certain effects. It inscribed the "soul" as the site of administration. No longer a religious "soul" to be saved in an afterlife, it was instead the object of social administration that focused on governing the inner dispositions, sensitivities, and awarenesses of the individual. The narratives of individual salvation were expressed now in the name of "freedom" and progress.

The quest for the soul derives from a specifically Western messianic tradition of redemption.[9] Previous church conceptions of revelation, however, are transferred to strategies that were to administer personal development, self-reflection, and the inner, self-guided moral growth of the individual.[10] These practices were to inscribe the dispositions, capabilities, and sensitivities of liberal democracy as the identity of the individual, replacing the religious sense of the soul with one associated with modernity and its rational, active capabilities of being. The practices of social administration as proper planning, it was thought, would produce a New Citizen/"New Man" [sic] who could perform competently in changing social, economic, political, and cultural contexts.

The construction of reform as joining the registers of social administration with those of the registers of freedom provides a way to revisit a seeming paradox of American schools. While the popular public (and academic) mythology of U.S. educational reform tends to define the United States as a decentralized system governed by local school districts and state governments, this is not so when the governing is examined at the discursive level of pedagogy and policy. The policies and sciences of social administration not only provide a cognitive knowledge for social planning but also discipline the capabilities, values, dispositions, and sensitivities through which individuals problematized their world and individuality.

Thus, at the very historical time when a philosophy and social theory conceptually split the state from civil society and the private, the two spheres were practically woven together through joining the registers of social administration and freedom. If the modern school is examined, for example, in this manner, the discourses of pedagogy had a particular shape.

The pedagogies were to rescue the child so that the child can become an adult who is self-disciplined, self-motivated, and a productive participant in the new collective social projects of the day. Thus, the struggles for the American curriculum that Kliebard historically traces in the years at the turn of the twentieth century,[11] for example, can also be understood as inscribing systems of governing that link the new problems of social administration with the knowledges of the child and schooling. From diverse standpoints in the United States, the discursive practices of the child-study movement of G. Stanley Hall, the pragmatism of John Dewey, and the social efficiency of David Snedden were projects that linked the registers of social administration with the registers of freedom.

But even in the formative years of schooling, the process of governing the child through schooling was a global process that linked institutional developments with discursive patterns. Hamilton's study of the construction of pedagogical discourses illustrates, for example, that the phenomenon of schooling crossed the national borders of Europe from the eighteenth century and, later, into at least North America.[12] Thus, while one can compare the different formal, local/federal governing mechanisms of U.S. schools with other, more centralized countries in terms of institutional planning, there are few differences in the knowledge systems and "reason" of schooling and pedagogy among nations.[13] The globalized qualities of schooling are embedded in the systems of reason that order and divide the capabilities of children, teaching, and teacher education.[14]

The social administration of the new citizen, however, did not develop through principled arguments tied to political philosophy, but came about instead as a pragmatic response to multiple historical trajectories that began prior to but moved into the nineteenth and twentieth centuries. The particular joining of the governing of the state with the governing of civil society (public/private) emerges in the seventeenth- and eighteenth-century European religious wars.[15] Distinct realms of "public" and "private," representing two distinct types of ethical comportment, were to pacify divided communities through the imposition of a politically binding conception of the public good. Hunter argues that the freedoms associated with liberal societies—religious toleration and freedom of worship—were produced as part of administrative state efforts to govern fratricidal communities, rather than being the expression of democratic institutions or popular resistance. A nonviolent tolerance and pragmatic sphere of political deliberation were created by forcefully separating the civic comportment of the citizen from the private persona of one's conscience and by subordinating spiritual absolutes to governmental objectives. Schooling was a mechanism used by the state to conceptualize and organize a massive and ongoing program of pacification, discipline, and training responsible for the political and social capacities of the modern citizen.[16]

Why have I stressed this idea of the social administration of freedom with the problem of studying reform? There is a paradox (and irony) in the twin registers that, I will argue, is still with us today. Reforms from the turn of the century and from today embody principles of the cosmopolitan subjectivities that can travel across multiple boundaries that form the worlds of business, politics, and culture. This cosmopolitan subjectivity makes possible the globalization that is given focus in the current literatures of world systems and internationalization.[17] But the principles that seem to travel globally are not universalistic but *particular* patterns of ordering and selecting that, I will argue later, produce new forms of exclusion as educational reforms relate to poverty, race, and gender.

Social Administration, Reform, and Governing the Soul: The Knowledge Practices of the Social Sciences

Reform is the administration of freedom embodied in professional, expert knowledge systems. This entails the particular rationalizations typically associated with bureaucracy but also with the systems of knowledge produced in the disciplines of the social sciences. The construction of global cultural and associational processes, of which schooling is the most prominent, as Meyer et al. argue, was made possible through worldwide "salvation stories." These stories posited a universal narrative about action initiated and carried out by actors inscribed in the theories of change. Professional knowledges "assimilated and developed the rationalized and universalistic knowledge that makes action and actorhood possible."[18] If I place the production of reform within this process of rationalization, reform inscribed a universalistic narrative about rational action and legitimated a collective authority through the production of expectations and entitlements of individuals who act as agents of their own interests.

These salvation stories in the social sciences were related to a radical assumption that human agency can produce its own improvement through a rational means of control. The new social sciences of the nineteenth century, for example, were to be in service of the democratic ideals through providing seemingly objective, nonevaluative descriptions to order and guide social planning. The authority of the expert, it was believed, was founded in evidence and dependent upon the rules of logic and reference to the empirical, rather than to the social status of the speaker or to the authority of God.

But this "rational" system of logic and planning constructed particular salvation stories. The linking of social reform, social policy, science, and progress embodied and revisioned an Enlightenment belief in the potential for reason in social betterment. Darwinism, for example, made possible the bringing of science into social policy and social planning. But the sciences were also to maintain a secularized notion of religion that made possible conceptualizing reform as a secular form of progress that focuses on the administration of the soul. Discourses of progress and salvation were merged in science. Frederick Taylor, who revolutionized the workplace worldwide through work-time studies of the labor process, thought of his labor-saving devices as emancipating the worker!

The discourses of psychology and sociology are examples of this joining of science, progress, and salvation. The social sciences, institutionalized in the late nineteenth century, replaced revelation with the administration of reflection in finding human progress. Religious confessional practices were transferred to the realm of personal self-reflection and self-criticism. American sociology, for example, maintained a millennial perspective.[19] The theories and methods of the Chicago School of Sociology did not grow out of any pure science, but rather from theology and social work. The research focused on issues of social control (in the sense of institutional planning) that were not only to improve the life situation of the poor[20] but also to remake the poor and immigrants who lived in the city in light of a millennial perspective.

The educational sciences also provided discursive practices that link school reform to the social administration of the child. The Progressive Education reform movements in the United States, for example, were part of intense social and political changes labeled "The Age of Reform."[21] The reorganization of schools was not only in the administration of teacher hiring, the organization of grades, the production of testing, and in teacher training programs. It brought the universalistic logic of social science into the practices of schooling. The narratives of the pedagogical practices of Progressive Education inscribed urban, middle-class professional knowledge in the visioning and revisioning of society and its individuals. The discourses of pedagogy made it possible to administer children's inner sense of "self" as earlier religious discourses had focused on the salvation of soul. Personal salvation and redemption were tied to personal development and "fulfillment," words that signaled religious motifs but placed them in secular discourses of psychology. Categories about attitudes, learning, and later, self-actualization and self-esteem signified religious motifs but placed them in secular discourses of science and rational progress.

Reform, then, can be understood historically as a governing practice. It joined the registers of social administration with the registers of freedom. The governing, however, was not only in giving direction to institutional planning and welfare functions of the state. The globalization of mass schooling, carried into the twentieth century, was a particular set of governing practices that inscribed the principles of "reason" to shape and fashion individual action and participation. While I have focused on this joining of registers of social administration and freedom in the United States, such changes were also embodied in the constructions of schooling and teaching found in other countries, such as Finland and Portugal,[22] and in Soviet pedagogies that spoke about "upbringing."[23] The universal narratives of salvation that are embodied in the school, as Meyer et al. have illustrated, have become a global phenomenon.[24]

Globalization/Regionalization and the Reconstituting of Education Practices

Current discussions of educational globalization and reform can be approached through focusing on the registers of social administration and the registers of freedom. One of the central educational motifs in discussions of educational reforms is that of "neoliberalism." At one level, neoliberalism is a salvation story. It brings economic thought into social policies through concepts about markets, privatization, client "choice," and the social "delivery" of welfare practices. It incorporated social theories related to the Chicago School of Economics into the policies of the Thatcher government in Britain and the Reagan administration in the United States. Its "life," however, is longer than that of a political party in power, as rhetorical constructions of neoliberalism underlie the current

Labour government in Britain and social democratic governments in northern Europe, as well as World Bank policies toward developing nations. While neoliberalism is not one set of policies, but multiple trajectories in terms of social welfare policy, it is argued from the Left that neoliberalism has led to the dismantling of the welfare state through incorporating a conservative economist logic.

While it is popular to label the changes of neoliberalism as a "conservative restoration" and as giving up the collective obligations of the welfare state, such analyses, I believe, are misplaced and mistaken. It is a mistake to accept the political and categorical distinctions produced in the political arena as the historical phenomena to be scrutinized. Such a strategy, I believe, is dangerous in the social sciences, as the very concepts of analysis (neoliberalism, markets, and so forth) "belong" to the phenomena that are in need of historical explanation. Taking neoliberalism as its category of analysis and critique embodies a particular liberal notion of time that is linear, continuous, and unidirectionally progressive, whether that notion of time is Lockean or Hegelian (dialectical). The discursive representation of time, according to some postcolonial theorists, for example, leaves unscrutinized a particular Western narrative of progress and enables the management and surveillance of the "Third World" in the guise of some notion of "development."[25] Discourses of and about neoliberalism reinscribe the state/civil society distinction, a distinction that itself is an effect of power I talked about earlier with the construction of the liberal welfare state itself. A consequence of such narratives and critiques of neoliberalism is that they legitimate each other through inserting salvation narratives that make action and actorhood possible.

While it is clear that the moral and political rhetoric of educational struggles has shifted through the languages of neoliberalism, analyses of neoliberalism (markets, choice, privatization) beg the question of the changes in the historical conditions through which power is constructed and deployed. What is called "neoliberalism" and the dismantling of the welfare state is more appropriately a reconstruction of governing practices that do not start with recent policies, but are part of more profound social, cultural, and economic changes that occurred well before Thatcher in Britain or Reagan in the United States.[26] This brings me back to a paradox in the registers of social administration and freedom in the practices of reform. If the modern school is a governing practice, then contemporary reform strategies need to be examined in relation to changes in its governing principles. This leads, I believe, to recognizing the shift from governing practices related to the formation of collective social projects to contemporary projects that focus on cultural identities.

National Imaginaries: Cultural Identities as the Political. Earlier, I talked about reform discourses as salvation narratives. One can think of contemporary reform narratives as a revisioning of previous collective social narratives of the turn of the century. In the past, national identity was articulated through single sets of ideas about citizenship, such as those found in turn -of-the-century notions of "Americanization." The operative metaphors of progress and redemption were derived from collective social norms, common roles, and fixed identities. The child-study movement, as well as competing curriculum theories, inscribed principles of progress and redemption in the discourses about the self-governing child of a liberal democracy. From the pragmatism of John Dewey to the social utility theories of David Snedden and the child-study movement of G. Stanley Hall, there was a concern with the "making" of a universal, "Americanized" citizen who would participate in the collective projects of the new society.

Today, the social, collective idea of a nation and citizenry is being confronted through pressures produced by minority groups, racial issues of equality, and changing migration and demographic patterns within nations. These struggles about the subject and subjectivities are cultural, rather than social. One can think of discussions about the literary canons in American universities and multicultural debates about the school curriculum as expressing larger social and political concerns about the cultural systems of representation through which national and global identities are constructed. The restructuring of teaching and teacher education in contemporary educational reforms can be understood as a revisioning of a new citizenry with the skills relevant to a global economy and, at the same time, as practices that can produce a more inclusionary and thus equal society.

The Production of Memory/Forgetting. The new salvation narratives about the images of the citizen and nation are related to the construction of national imaginaries and the production of memory and forgetting. A broad range of historical and anthropological scholarship has directed attention to how the discourses of public policy and the theories of the social sciences generate conceptions of personhood and identity. This literature has called attention to how there is no "natural" national community, but only communities that are dependent upon the discourses that form individuals into the seam of a collective narrative.[27] The formation of a nation as well as current national efforts to reform the school, from this perspective, are not merely expressive of national goals, but embody how people are to know, understand, and experience themselves as members of a community and as citizens of a nation.

Anderson has called this institution of an imaginary unity an "imagined community," one in which cultural representations are historically fabricated to produce a "nation-ness."[28] In particular, the language, narratives, and images of the field of education and its sciences are not recuperating national memories through the forms of constructed representation, but are producing new memories and forgetting. Huyssen argues, "The past is not simply there in memory but it must be articulated to become memory. Memory is *recherché* rather than recuperation."[29]

Recent historiography in the United States, for example, has examined how different writers and particular conceptions of history provided narratives through which a national identity was constructed.[30] The school has historically played a pivotal role in these constructions of national representations.[31] One can look at late-nineteenth-century American pedagogical theories, for example, as providing principles by which personal narratives are constructed through the cultural practice, by which personhood (identity) is defined.[32] To bring this construction of memory and forgetting into the jargon of contemporary U.S. politics: debates about the "traditional family," "back-to-basics," and conservative restorations have little to do with what the past was, but instead with constructing new sets of collective representations and principles for action and participation. These images and narratives of national identity exist only as part of present constructions, rather than as past realities.

This has important implications for how today's educational reforms are considered. The languages, narratives, and images of the new teacher and child that circulate within educational reforms produce ideas about the "participatory teacher," collaboration, "action research," the construction of knowledge, and decentralized school decision making, among others. These narratives and images seem global as they relate political and cultural discourses about the citizen to pedagogical practices. In this respect, the discourses of the educational sciences in teaching and teacher education can be viewed as not only about the learning and teaching of children who are to participate in the new social and economic conditions but also about shaping the personality and knowledge of the child who is to master the social and cultural changes that are occurring. Thus, the scientific discourses of school reform that circulate between nations and in international forums are more than ways to represent more efficient approaches to schooling; they embody images and principles of the citizen who is to participate and act within the different national systems.

In this sense, we can think of the construction of national imaginaries as not providing the missing conception of identity for groups that demand recognition, in contrast to recent debates about a multicultural curriculum in many countries. Rather, these new conceptions of identity are forged out of the relations constituted in the new cultural practices. As Huyssen reminds us, "Memory is not some natural generality of forgetting that could be contrasted with some form of more reliable representation. Memory is given in the structure of representation itself."[33]

Reforms produce a national imaginary. In Argentina, for example, they are related to recouping a sense of national commitment through producing new monuments and hero/heroines as the military government is replaced by a democratically elected government. There is a strong notion of reconciliation that has become inserted into public discourses to come to terms with the past of its military dictatorship. Alongside the discourse of reconciliation are debates about where and how to build monuments and museums that are to produce new memories and new readings of the past through the articulation of new heroes, all of which lead to new ways of thinking about national identities.[34] These discussions over national identities are expressed today in different terms. The discourses of reconciliation focus on cultural and collective memory, rather than on assumed identities of the nation, as dominated discussions in earlier periods. The European Union's educational policies, as well, are pursuing curriculum and school reforms in which a European identity is sought, an identity formed around the walls of the Maastricht Treaty that excludes a larger sense of Europe even as it seeks inclusion. In the United States, the national imaginary embodied in "the Americanization" of the immigrants, Native Americans, and former slaves of the turn of the century is being replaced today by new images of identity that are embodied in narratives contesting bilingual education, multiculturalism, and moral education.

If we view the construction of national imaginaries as "making/remaking" the principles of participation and citizenry, then we also have to consider that these imaginaries are not without cultural anxieties. Such constructions of memory entail a deconstitution of old images. The production of new memories by which people know, understand, and experience themselves must be dissociated from the old collective identities and reimagined with another collective narrative.[35] Older identities are estranged and one's "home" (identity) is no longer located where one thought it was.[36] The struggles over identity that now exist over minority rights and gender, for example, have produced new exclusions and taboo zones, as monolithic notions of identity clash with the convictions of identities that are heterogeneous. Current discussions in the United States about revising (re-visioning) the school curriculum, for example, can be understood as transforming the geopolitical imaginaries and notions of community.

Educational Sciences and the Reflexive Governing of Individuality. Central to the production of salvation narratives and national imaginaries are the contemporary social disciplines and the social/educational sciences. These social practices still maintain their position in the social administration of individuality. The "paradigm wars" between the "moderns"—the cultural and neo-Marxisms—and the variations of "postmodern" literary criticism, cultural theory, and feminism, are not merely wars about who is sanctioned to speak about discipline work. The struggles over the systems of reason in the social and educational disciplines are embedded in changing patterns of the social administration of freedom. These struggles are, borrowing from Anthony Giddens, part of the reflexive monitoring and governing mechanism of modern societies.[37]

This reflexive monitoring and governing embodies certain global discourses in the educational sciences. The discourses of social and educational policy and the social sciences can be viewed as providing the sanctioned images of the attitudes, dispositions, and capabilities of the "citizen" who is to contribute and participate in the processes of modernization. In contemporary national contexts, the narratives of reform can be thought of as forging narratives that instantiate a vision of the citizen and the nation. In Spain, these debates are related to struggles between national and autonomous regions; in Argentina they are expressed in discussions over human rights; and in the United States the discourses of multiculturalism have become a site of contestation over national memory and identity.[38]

In the current global restructuring of education, it is the deployment of "reasoning" through which the teacher and child construct capabilities and actions that perform governing practices. Reforms of teaching, pedagogy, and teacher education have made this "being," capability, or subjectivity the locale for intervention. The focus on capacity revisits turn-of-the-century concerns with the social administration of governing "the soul" as the doxa of work and school reform—the unquestioned belief and normative imperative of reform to remake the person. The sites of change are the cognitive and moral capabilities of the individual. In many countries, curriculum reforms are concerned less with the specific content of school subjects and more with making the child feel "at home" in a cosmopolitan identity that embodies a pragmatic flexibility and "problem-solving" disposition. In recent policy discourses, embedded in the rhetoric of neoliberalism (for example, of community health, community schools, and community-based welfare systems[39]), we see the predominant image of the local, constructivist agent.

Professional educational knowledge, as well, replaces the "social" with the new "local" culturally oriented researcher who speaks of "the personal knowledge of teachers," "the wisdom of teachers," and the relation of teachers to communities and parents. Whereas turn-of-the-century teacher education discourses sought to remove communal and ethnic influences in creating social collective identities, current discourses of teacher education reinsert the family and ethnicity into pedagogical practices as a way to administer social actions and participation.

Today's educational reforms reconstitute the image governing the child. The collective social identities and universal norms embodied in previous reforms are replaced with images of the local, communal, and flexible identity. Reforms inscribe a decentralized citizen who is active, self-motivated, participatory, and problem solving.[40] The teacher and the child are constructed as having multiple identities, oriented to collaboration, being part of a local "community," and having a flexible problem-solving disposition.

Such discussions alter the forms of representation and images through which culture and the temporality of life are constructed.[41] As older conceptions of one's "home" are juxtaposed with new images that are being imagined into existence, there are ambiguities and conflicts emerging in the new cultural territories.[42] As discussions about the "cultural wars" in the

United States indicate, these forms of representation contest the "home" in which one is to locate identity.[43] In part, one imagined unity is instituted against other possible unities.[44] The inscription of national imaginaries conjure away the appearance of disorder and disjuncture through the consolidating languages of solidarity and coherence.[45]

Why is this process of memory and forgetting through the production of knowledge important for contemporary social and educational analysis? The educational discourses of reform and research should be thought of not only as exhortations of change but also as constructions of a national memory that potentially embodies a deep reshaping of the images of social action and consciousness through which individuals are to participate. At the same time, the construction of national imaginaries produces cultural anxieties and "forgetting," as people's "home" is no longer where they think it is.

Hybridity and Power: Globalization/Regionalization. The national imaginaries embodied in the new school reforms maintain the registers of social administration and freedom through rationalized and universalistic knowledge about action and actors. This reflexive knowledge of reform is not a single discourse about progress and change of agents, but rather is a hybrid where global, national, and local images meet. That is, there is an overlay of global, national, and local practices in the knowledge produced, as in a weaving that has its own configurations and implications. This overlay or hybridity in thinking about educational reform, I argue below, enables a rethinking of the nineteenth-century binaries of state/society (civil society), centralization/decentralization, objective/subjective, and global/local that have guided the analyses of Left and liberal programs of reform.

Thinking about national imaginaries as hybrids is to consider the construction of educational reform as a problematic that moves from examining the nation or state as a legal/administrative entity that produces action, or as a suprastate entity such as the European Union, to understanding the discourses that circulate in reform efforts as a complex web of simultaneously global *and* local governing practices. The histories of colonization, for example, continually explore this relation as one that is not unidirectional or univocal, leading from the colonialist to the colonized, but as an overlay or scaffolding of different discourses that join the global and the local through complex patterns that are multiple and multidirectional.[46]

The idea of hybridity is underscored in the formation of political agendas for the new South Africa. Its politics embody fluid and pragmatic relations within a field of multiple power relations. The results are practices that are "a residue of Marxism, a spoonful of Chicago economics, a dash of West European social democracy, and much local spice. Like post-communists everywhere else."[47]

The concept of hybridization makes it possible to think of educational reforms as plural assumptions, orientations, and procedures in which the practices of reform are effected. This hybridity of discourses is evident within the national imaginary of European Union "unity." Current reforms give reference to Europe as a continent of diversity while also speaking of a European identity, but with that identity built inside the Union by the Maastricht Treaty—while at the same time there is a silence about those in Eastern Europe who are outside "the walls."[48] Educational reforms in Argentina can also be understood as embodying a complex scaffolding of techniques and knowledge that are not exerted through fixed strategies and hierarchical applications of power that move uncontested from the center nations of the world system to the peripheral and less powerful countries. Rather, Argentinean reforms embody processes of mediation and transformations of "the space of political rationalities to the modality of techniques and proposals that are used in particular locales."[49]

This hybridization can also be found in the modern construction of the school curriculum. The idea of curriculum, as Kliebard in the United States, Hamilton in Europe, and Dussel et al. in Argentina point out, is itself a hybrid that results from an alchemy of different traditions, disciplinary movements, and coalitions.[50] The "postcolonial" educational policies of Eastern Europe, Africa, and Latin America, as well, are mixtures that embody certain colonial discourses about European liberty with discourses that move in the interstices of the colonial and the colonized. In different contexts, the formulation and realization of policies entail plural assumptions, orientations, and strategies to effect reform.

Hybridity, however, is not merely a matter of hegemony and dominance by the powerful over the less powerful—a power that moves from the core nations to the periphery. Nor does it suggest that there is some non-European "voice" that exists in a pristine state to be deployed to counteract the colonialism of the European. To put the ideas of hybridization in a different context, while the rhetorical constructions of today's reforms speak of giving marginal groups "voice" in schools, there is no natural "voice." There are only mediated distinctions and divisions that are the historical effects of multiple discourses through which power is effected. The construction of "voice" is an effect of power and is never outside the power relations in which it is positioned.

As recent historical discussions of colonization illustrate, there are slippages and processes of translation of ideas from the colonial metropolis as discourses are rearticulated in different contexts from those in which they were originally produced.[51] At the same time, the metropole was itself reconstructed in a manner that is still relevant today. Europe, for example, was made by its imperial projects as much as the colonial encounters were shaped by conflicts within Europe itself.[52] The inclusions and exclusions through which nineteenth-century European nations refashioned notions of citizenship, sovereignty, and participation cannot be adequately understood without exploring the relation of European practices to Asian and African political movements as well as to European self-doubts about the moral claims of liberalism in the face of the colonial enterprises.

Hybridization, then, provides a way to consider the interrelation of processes of globalization and regionalization as constituted through fluid, multiple, and historically contingent patterns, rather than as hierarchical or linear, or produced by structural forces. At the same time, we need to recognize that the playing field in which these processes of change occur is not level. In one context, Latin American and African national reforms can be positioned in relation to international funding agencies and other centers such as Europe and North America. Furthermore, the ideas of history and the "public sphere" in many national movements assume a historicism, an agency, and a gendered quality that are themselves of European construction.[53] These double relations become important to the reading of contemporary literatures that focus on curriculum change.

The Indigenous Foreigner. At this point, I would like to explore the hybridity in national imaginaries of reform through the idea of the "indigenous foreigner." I use this concept to direct attention to a particular type of hero and heroic global discourses of change that are brought into specific sites of social administration through the construction of national imaginaries. I view the indigenous foreigner as particularly important in contemporary understandings of the relation of knowledge and power in educational reforms.

It is common in national policy and research for the heroes of progress to be foreigners who are immortalized in reform efforts. The names of foreign authors, for example, appear as signs of social, political, and educational progress in national debates. The turn-of-the-century American philosopher, John Dewey, and the Russian psychologist, Lev Vygotsky, for example, have become icons to explain the "new" principles of pedagogy in South Africa, Spain, the Scandinavian countries, and the United States, among others. In critical social theory traditions, the names of the German social theorist, Jürgen Habermas, the Brazilian Paulo Freire, and the French philosopher, Michel Foucault, among others, are inserted into national debates to provide principles for social change and, in some cases, educational planning. They seem to embody some special human values that are to be inscribed in national imaginaries.

While these heroes and heroines circulate as part of global discourses of reform, such heroes and heroines are also promoted in national debates in what appears to be a seamless movement between the global and the local. The invocation of the indigenous foreigner functions to bless the projects of reform with the images of new intentions and new concepts. The "saints" help to produce emancipatory projects. In many nations, the constructive pedagogy of the "problem-solving" teacher and child invoke the names of Dewey and Vygotsky, for example, in what appears to be a serial continuity of the past, present, and future.[54] From critical traditions, the German Frankfurt School's critical theories overlay with the Italian Gramsci's language of "hegemony," and with the Brazilian Catholic worker heritage of Freire's "critical consciousness" and "dialogics," to forge a discourse that promises universal liberation and empowerment.

If the discourses of reform and science are thought of as a form of storytelling, then the knowledge and competence embodied in the indigenous foreigner are part of the power relations embodied in the stories of global/regional relations. The importance of the indigenous foreigner, then, is not in the individuality of the person who is made the heroine, per se, but in the deployment of a hybrid mixture of discursive practices that orders the memory about progress and that divides "reason" from nonreason. National discourses of educational policy and research embody multiple historical trajectories as principles for governing action and producing participation. Furthermore, the discourse is of a professional cleric who holds a true universal knowledge about "how to do things" in the names of a populism: "the people," "voice," empowerment, democracy.

But when the narrative of the indigenous foreigner is examined closely, it is a discourse that is empty of history—an abstract, serial continuity, rather than a series of specific historical contingencies in which the discourses of education are produced. Dewey, Vygotsky, and Foucault are read not as writers whose ideas are produced in other, foreign fields of power relations, but as local "saints" who forge an apparent continuity and evolution in the governing systems. The empty history of these educational reforms has no social mooring to the interpretations and possibilities of action. In Latin American discourses about "action research" in teacher education and about decentralization and marketization of educational practices, for example, reforms emerge in relation to different ideological positions but coexist as part of the local efforts to modernize schools.[55] Action research, decentralization, and marketization, sometimes separately and sometimes within the same policy discussions of educational change, construct the new manifest destiny of the country through claims of economic prosperity, personal liberation, and social reconstruction. While these categories of reform and research reports in Latin America are mixtures of Spanish educational literature (which is itself one that is transmogrified from translations of British and American texts), the processes of importation and translation no longer appear as such. The national narratives circulate *as if* they were local and with no history except in the logic of the principles that the categories represent: the problem-solving child, the progressive curriculum, the professional teacher, the decentralized school.

The new registers of social administration of freedom (in current languages of emancipation, empowerment, or voice) weave specific cultural and psychological conditions into principles of, for example, "liberalism" so as to seem to be preconditions for the actualization of individual capacities.[56] The discourses of administration appear as universal categories that order the interpretations and possibilities of national practices—the paths that one must take toward salvation and emancipation. The national imaginaries of emancipation and empowerment in liberalism embody particular sets of bourgeois norms that have historically contradictory impulses that contain narratives of rights and democracy as well as the production of violence both within European nations and in colonies. These effects need to be continually interrogated, rather than assumed.

The indigenous foreigner is part of reform as the social administration of freedom. Yet studies by academics tend to restrict their focus primarily to the production of *ideas* within national boundaries. The history of the social sciences, for example, attends to how ideas are produced in response to national policy and a particular cultural milieu. The discussion of the European intellectual migrations prior to World War II focuses on the immigrants' contributions to the local economy of ideas.[57] This myopia is also exhibited in current social and cultural-studies discussions of the relation of postmodern theories to French intellectuals. Anglo-American critics identify this phenomenon as the "faddism" of French thought, without questioning how the indigenous foreigner has settled into national discourses as part of a process of both globalization and regionalization.

National Imaginaries and Social Inclusion/Exclusion

It is at this point that I can approach the initial problem posed in this chapter, that is, the relation of reform to the problem of social inclusion and exclusion. The contemporary shifts in the registers of social administration and registers of freedom to a cultural rather than a social politics signal, I believe, a movement to particular sets of practices in the qualifying and disqualifying of individuals for participation. In the search for collective social forms of participation and action, inclusion is taken as a moral principle to judge the effectiveness of policy. Studies of inclusion identify access to social practices and values, seeking to include others within power arrangements. Exclusion is something separate from inclusion; something that is a by-product of incorrect practices that can be corrected by, for example, better policies that give representation (or "voice") to the varied social interests. Research on policies related to school choice in Britain and the United States, for example, point to the uneven effects of efforts to increase parental options and involvement in the schools through school choice policies.[58] But the assumption of such critical studies is that school choice is the wrong set of policies by which to obtain the principle of inclusion, with inclusion as an absolute value by which to judge the effects of social practices.

The movement to a cultural politics signals a different problem of governing that embodies inclusion/exclusion through the generation of principles for action and participation. The assumption is that there is no inside without an outside, no inclusion without exclusion. If I return to the production of memory and forgetting in pedagogical practices, then the "memories" deployed to reason about the child embody normalizations about "being." That is, the discourses of pedagogy sanction the norms of the healthy capabilities and dispositions of the "self." The categories and distinctions of pedagogy tell what is to be valued and sought as successful—the habits and sensitivities of the successful child. But this memorialization of the childhood of the child forms a system that simultaneously excludes as it includes. To phrase this somewhat differently, whereas the social projects of saving the soul focused on systems of categorical inclusions and exclusions, such as that of identifying which groups are not fully participating, the current concerns with the active, self-motivated, and problem-solving child and teacher produce distinctions and divisions that include *and* exclude at the level of the reasoning "being."

Let me provide a recent example from a concert given by a group of Soweto children in South Africa. The children were from the poorest families in Soweto and learned to play classical European music through learning stringed instruments. The program demanded that the children not only learn to play but also to follow the rule of learning that included, according to the brochure, "regular attendance, discipline and commitment to the group. Active parental and community involvement" was also required. Notwithstanding the contradictions and tensions in this activity, what is important is that the "choice" of inclusion or "dropping out" was placed on the child, who disqualified him- or herself through "deciding" not to accept the commitments of the program.

This memorialization of "being," which functions as simultaneous systems of inclusion and exclusion, can be further illustrated in the American idea of "urban education" reforms.[59] Contemporary U.S. reforms in teaching and teacher education "draw" distinctions and divisions to differentiate urban children from those children who are not urban. The "urbanism" in educational discourses constructs a particular normalized space or "map." When the phrase "urban education" is used in the United States, it is embedded in a particular overlay of discourses that weaves together social, pedagogical, and psychological discourses. The particular set of distinctions is recognized as soon as one leaves the reforms of social administrations. In a different context, urbanness is tied to ideas of cosmopolitanism and modernity; urban education, in contrast, historically gives attention to those whose attitudes, norms, values, and behaviors are different from what is silently constructed as the norm and as normal. Thus, the signifier "urban" stood as a social practice that simultaneously noticed that something was absent in the urban child. But these absent qualities were presumed necessary in order to produce success, such as through pedagogical distinctions about the different learning styles of urban children, notions of low self-esteem, and conceptions of childhood "development." These distinctions and divisions about what is present yet absent in the being of the urban child makes it impossible for that child ever to be normal and "average."

Such divisions and normalizations of the urban child are at the level of the inner qualities, dispositions, and sensitivities that enable and disenable action. The lack of capabilities in the child and the parents to act properly (to provide books and reading time in the home, for example), to have positive self-esteem, or to participate in "appropriate" and "successful" interactions around school activities appears as the product of a natural and universal "reason" about learning. The distinctions of children's "problem-solving" capabilities are not universal, but rather are particular distinctions, "tastes" and "problem-solving" strategies that are historically bounded. The particular distinctions of pedagogy are produced by particular social actors within a social field whose dispositions and sensitivities are authorized as the reason for schooling.[60] What are taken as universal capabilities of problem solving in pedagogy inscribe divisions in a manner that makes the normalcies seem natural and unproblematic. It is at this level of inscription of dispositions and sensitivities that the inclusions/exclusions occur—that is, at the level of the child's "being."

At this level of knowledge of the self the problem of social inclusion and exclusion functions in pedagogical theories of the "normal" child and teacher in national reforms. In the context of global discourses of reform found in the practices of the World Bank, USAID, the European Union's Tacis, Swedish SIDA, and semiprivate international foundations, the discourses governing the construction of the capabilities and "being" of the modern citizen, the teacher, and the worker in "assisted" countries need to be excavated. While drawing the discourses of reform of the school and the child from particular social fields within the geopolitical and economic centers, the "donor" discourses enter into the "recipient" nations as hybrids that inscribe unequal power through sanctioning particular inclusions and exclusions. In South Africa, the minister of education talks about reform through an international discourse of performance-based education that obscures the particular material legacies (discursive and nondiscursive) of the system of apartheid.

To summarize: my concern with issues of inclusion and exclusion is to place them within a single continuum through which knowledge differentiates and divides. Analyses of inclusion have overlooked this continuum. Power, in the sense of the production of principles that exclude as they include, is located in the classifying and dividing practices at the level of the "being" of the child and teacher. My concern, then, with the problem of inclusion/exclusion is to provide a comparative strategy by which to understand global and national relations as hybrid systems of reasoning constituted in an unequal playing field, in the sense of the principles generated about the "being" of the child and teacher.

Notes toward a Conclusion

Current discussions and critiques of educational reform have treated its activities as principled arguments related to social progress. These arguments focus, at one level, on the global qualities of the educational system in the modernizing processes of the nation-state. It is possible to travel to Spain, Argentina, Sweden, or South Africa and hear talk that juxtaposes social goals with the practices of reforms that encourage action research in teacher education, school-community collaboration, and "giving voice" to subaltern groups. Typically, both advocates and critics of reform maintain a principled argument about the possibility of progress. Embodied in the discourses of reform is a commitment that the policies and sciences of education can serve to improve the school or to emancipate. The uses of such principled arguments have led to certain interpretative distinctions in contemporary reform that I have argued are historically misleading, such as the separation of the private and public; or the separation of the state and civil society that is embedded in discussions of neoliberalism; or the separation of the "European" from the "Non-European."

My concern in this chapter is to go against this grain. I want to historicize the systems of reason that are embodied in reform. I have argued that the merging of the registers of social administration with the registers of freedom has a certain irony: it does not produce freedom in an absolute sense, but revisions the individual through the governing of the soul. I have tried to locate present notions of reform in the production of national imaginaries whose systems of representation embody a collective memory and forgetting. By moving from the first decades of this century to today, I have considered how the construction of individuality involves shifting terrains of knowledge and power; these shifting terrains produce different sets of internments and enclosures as the discursive patterns move from collective social projects of the past to the cultural and "community" metaphors of present-day reforms.

My historical argument, however, was not only to interrogate the past but also to problematize the particular ways of reasoning about educational issues found in contemporary reforms. My argument centered on systems of reasoning as a focus of critical interrogation rather than to assume the existing categories and distinctions that circulate as the "reason" of change. Where most educational literature accepts the inscription of salvation stories, these stories need to be continually interrogated as governing practices that simultaneously produce systems of exclusion—spaces of internment and enclosures of "the other"—as they seem to open up social spaces. These systems of inclusion and exclusion are not necessarily found in categorical systems of representation (excluding groups by categories such as race or gender, for example), but in the principles generated by pedagogical and psychological theories of action and participation. My argument is that while the former focus is necessary, it is not sufficient in studies of reform and power.

In the discussion of inclusion/exclusion I have sought to focus on contemporary reforms that celebrate problem-solving, participatory, collaborating teachers and students, as producing rules of reason that function to qualify and disqualify individuals in terms of their capabilities for action and participation. The norms and distinctions that construct community inscribe divisions that situate particular teachers, children, and parents outside the bounds of "normal." My discussion of the urbanness of the child as a particular historical discourse of education illustrates how social spaces that intern and enclose children function through the knowledge applied. My introduction of the notions of hybridity and the indigenous foreigner provides a way to rethink systems of reason as effects of power through a historicizing of the discourses that organize policy and research about educational change.

The problem of globalization and reform, then, has two dimensions. There is a geographical concept of globalization that considers differences among national territories, such as those between the United States, Sweden, and Argentina. But globalization also relates to the systems of reason deployed in educational reform. This notion of globalization is concerned with how particular systems of ideas are deployed as universals and made to seem as "natural" dispositions of the teacher or child who is good, successful, competent, and growing "developmentally." This notion of globalization focuses on the ways in which the ideas of particular historical localities and social fields are consecrated through the emptying of history and thus are seen and acted upon as universal and appropriate to all. But the ideas that circulate as global about the child, school reform, and teaching are not global in the sense of being unfettered with particularistic values and social principles. The emptying of history in the knowledge of pedagogy and childhood in reform discourses produces a memory that functions to normalize and to produce systems of inclusion and exclusion when these universal ideas are brought back into particular social sites as principles of action and participation.

The lack of historicity as it relates to the construction of "reason" in educational policy and educational research is also its irony. The construction of memory and forgetting continually assumes that policy and research are guided by normative purposes without reflecting on how these normative constructions of purpose and fulfillment are the effects of power. What is forgotten is the relation of social scientific knowledge to the state in the social administration of freedom.[61] Also forgotten is the historical relation between policy and policing that emerged in the nineteenth century. And also forgotten is how discourses of redemption in the social and educational arenas are systems of reason that include and exclude.

Notes

1. Michel Foucault, *Discipline and Punish: The Birth of the Prison*, trans. Alan Sheridan (New York: Vintage Books, 1979).
2. See Nikolas Rose, *Governing the Soul* (New York: Routledge, Chapman & Hall, 1989).
3. Bertrand Badie and Pierre Birnbaum, *The Sociology of the State*, trans. Arthur Goldhammer (Chicago: University of Chicago Press, 1983).

4. See, for example, Abram de Swann, *In Care of the State: Health Care, Education, and Welfare in Europe and the USA in the Modern Era* (Cambridge, Eng.: Polity Press, 1988).

5. See, for example, Ian Hunter, *Rethinking the School: Subjectivity, Bureaucracy, Criticism* (New York: St. Martin's Press, 1994).

6. See, for example, Peter Wagner, *The Sociology of Modernity* (New York: Routledge, 1994).

7. Uday Mehta, "Liberal Strategies of Exclusion," in *Tensions of Empires, Colonial Cultures in a Bourgeois World*, ed. Frederick Cooper and Ann Stoler (Berkeley and Los Angeles: University of California Press, 1997), 59–86.

8. John Meyer, John Boli, George Thomas, and Francisco Ramirez, "World Society and the Nation-State," *American Journal of Sociology* 103, no. 1 (1997): 144–81.

9. While our contemporary idea of progress as a linear pattern of development is an invention of the Renaissance, the notions of development and progress are found in classical thought. The Greeks, for example, had a conception of the world that did not place people at the center. While there was a belief in development and growth, social improvement was not the basis of the organization of society—there was no notion of a philosophy of biological change or cultural improvement of humanity; each living thing had its own laws of cause, mechanism, and purpose; and each living thing had its own fixed succession of stages and purpose. With Christianity, the elements of resignation and fatalism of the classical attitude were altered to ones of hope and progress. Time becomes linear and nonreversible; and a dialectical movement from birth to crisis, crucifixion, and resurrection is introduced. There is also an idea of historical necessity. What happened in the past is believed not merely actual but necessary.

10. See Michel Foucault, "Technologies of the Self," in *Technologies of the Self: A Seminar with Michel Foucault*, ed. Luther Martin, Huck Gutman, and Patrick Hutton (Amherst: University of Massachusetts Press, 1985), 16–49; and Rose, *Governing the Soul*, for discussions about religious cosmologies and theories of social change. For discussions about evaluation, see Thomas S. Popkewitz, *Paradigm and Ideology in Educational Research, Social Functions of the Intellectual* (London and New York: The Falmer Press, 1984); and Thomas S. Popkewitz, *A Political Sociology of Educational Reform: Power/Knowledge in Teaching, Teacher Education, and Research* (New York: Teachers College Press, 1991). Religious systems of authority were also redefined, in part through the merging of the state and religion, and in part through changes in social cosmologies in which religion was to be seen. For a discussion of religion in modernity, see Peter Berger, *Pyramids of Sacrifice, Political Ethics, and Social Change* (Garden City, N.Y.: Anchor, 1976); and Thomas Luckmann, *The Invisible Religion: The Problem of Religion in Modern Society* (New York: Macmillan, 1967).

11. Herbert Kliebard, *Struggle for the American Curriculum* (London: Routledge and Kegan Paul, 1986).

12. David Hamilton, *Towards a Theory of Schooling* (London: The Falmer Press, 1989).

13. Thomas S. Popkewitz, "The Culture of Redemption and the Administration of Freedom in Educational Research," *The Review of Educational Research* 68, no. 1 (1998): 1–34; and Meyer et al., "World Society."

14. Thomas S. Popkewitz, "Rethinking Decentralization and the State/Civil Society Distinctions: The State as a Problematic of Governing," *Journal of Educational*

Policy 11 (1996): 27–51.

15. Hunter, *Rethinking the School.*
16. Ibid., 152–63.
17. Meyer et al., "World Society."
18. Ibid., 165.
19. Cecil Greek, *The Religious Roots of American Sociology* (New York: Garland, 1992).
20. Barry Franklin, "The First Crusade for Learning Disabilities: The Movement for the Education of Backward Children," in *The Formation of School Subjects: The Struggle for Creating an American Institution*, ed. Thomas S. Popkewitz (New York: The Falmer Press, 1987), 190–209.
21. Richard Hofstadter, *The Age of Reform, From Bryan to F.D.R.* (New York: Vintage, 1955).
22. See, for example, Hannu Simola, "Educational Science, the State, and Teachers: Forming the Corporate Regulation of Teacher Education in Finland," in *Changing Patterns of Power: Social Regulation and Teacher Education Reform*, ed. Thomas S. Popkewitz (Albany: SUNY Press, 1993), 161–210; and Antonio Nóvoa, "The Portuguese State and Teacher Education Reform: A Socio-Historical Perspective to Changing Patterns of Control," in *Changing Patterns of Power: Social Regulation and Teacher Education Reform*, ed. Thomas S. Popkewitz (Albany: SUNY Press, 1993).
23. Popkewitz, *Paradigm and Ideology.*
24. Meyer et al., "World Society."
25. See, for example, Dipesh Chakrabarty, "Provincializing Europe: Postcoloniality and the Critique of History," *Cultural Studies* 6 (1992): 337–57; and Akhil Gupta, "The Reincarnation of Souls and the Rebirth of Commodities: Representations of Time in 'East' And 'West,'" in *Remapping Memory, The Politics of TimeSpace*, ed. Johnathan Boyarin (Minneapolis: University of Minnesota Press, 1994), 161–84.
26. See Andrew Barry, Thomas Osborne, and Nikolas Rose, *Foucault and Political Reason: Liberalism, Neo-Liberalism, and Rationalities of Government* (Chicago: University of Chicago Press, 1996); Popkewitz, *A Political Sociology*; Thomas S. Popkewitz, "Dewey, Vigotsky, and the Social Administration of the Individual: Constructivist Pedagogy as Systems of Ideas in Historical Spaces," *American Educational Research Journal* 35, no. 4 (1998): 535–70; and Geoff Whitty, "Creating Quasi-Markets in Education," in *Review of Research in Education*, ed. Michael W. Apple (Washington, D.C.: American Educational Research Association, 1997), 3–48. At one level there is historical change through the breakdown of the Fordist compromise in postwar Europe and the United States, a compromise among workers, industrialists, and the state which produced a division of labor and mechanization in exchange for a favorable wage formula and the implementation of a state welfare system, as Fordism lost its efficiency with technologies and markets. The organization of work that we are now witnessing is in part a response to the lack of efficiency of Fordist mass production. But at a different level, there is a range of other challenges formed by social movements that emerged during these same decades from civil libertarians, feminists, radicals, socialists, sociologists, and others. The reorganized programs of government utilize and instrumentalize the multitude of experts of management, of family life, and of lifestyle who have proliferated at the points of intersection of sociopolitical aspirations and private desires for self-advancement.

[Nikolas Rose and Peter Miller, "Political Power beyond the State: Problematics of Government," *British Journal of Sociology* 43, no. 2 (1992): 201.]

27. See also Etienne Balibar and Immanuel Wallerstein, *Race, Nation, Class: Ambiguous Identities*, trans. Chris Turner (New York: Verso, 1991), 49; and Andreas Huyssen, *Twilight Memories: Marking Time in a Culture of Amnesia* (New York: Routledge, 1995).

28. Benedict Anderson, *Imagined Communities: Reflections on the Origin and Spread of Nationalism*, rev. ed. (London: Verso, 1991).

29. Huyssen, *Twilight Memories*, 3.

30. See Myra Jehlen, *American Incarnation: The Individual, the Nation, and the Continent* (Cambridge: Harvard University Press, 1986); Priscilla Wald, *Constituting Americans, Cultural Anxiety, and Narrative Form* (Durham, N.C.: Duke University, 1995); and José Rabasa, *Inventing A-m-e-r-i-c-a: Spanish Historiography and the Formation of Eurocentrism* (Norman: University of Oklahoma Press, 1993).

31. Meyer et al., "World Society."

32. See, for example, Thomas S. Popkewitz and Marie Brennan, eds., *Foucault's Challenge: Discourse, Knowledge, and Power in Education* (New York: Teachers College Press, 1998).

33. Huyssen, *Twilight Memories*, 11.

34. I appreciate the help of Inés Dussel in thinking about current changes in Argentina.

35. Balibar and Wallerstein, *Race, Nation, Class*.

36. Wald, *Constituting Americans*.

37. Anthony Giddens, *The Consequences of Modernity* (Stanford: Stanford University Press, 1990).

38. I use these examples in relation to a current research project concerned with the production of national imaginaries and the educational sciences in Spain, Argentina, Sweden, and the United States.

39. Nikolas Rose, "Expertise and the Government of Conduct," *Studies in Law, Politics and Society* 14 (1994): 359–97; and Nikolas Rose, "The Death of the Social? Refiguring the Territory of Government," *Economy and Society* 25, no. 3 (1996): 327–56.

40. For comparative discussions of child-centered, constructivist pedagogies, see Valerie Walkerdine, *The Mastery of Reason: Cognitive Development and the Production of Rationality* (London: Routledge, 1988); Kenneth Hultqvist, "A History of the Present on Children's Welfare in Sweden," in *Foucault's Challenge: Discourse, Knowledge, and Power in Education*, ed. Thomas S. Popkewitz and Marie Brennan (New York: Teachers College Press, 1998); and Hunter, *Rethinking the School*.

41. Popkewitz, "Dewey."

42. See, for example, Partha Chatterjee, *The Nation and its Fragments: Colonial and Postcolonial Histories* (Princeton: Princeton University Press, 1993); and Wald, *Constituting Americans*.

43. Thomas S. Popkewitz, *Struggling for the Soul: The Politics of Education and the Construction of the Teacher* (New York: Teachers College Press, 1998).

44. See, for example, Michael Shapiro, "Sovereign Anxieties" (paper delivered at the University of Turku Seminar: State Regulation, Citizenship, and Democracy, May 1996).

45. See, for example, Michael Shapiro, *Violent Cartographies: Mapping the Culture of War* (Minneapolis: University of Minnesota Press, 1997).
46. See, for example, Paul Gilroy, *The Black Atlantic: Modernity and Double Consciousness* (Cambridge: Harvard University, 1993); Robert Young, *Colonial Desire: Hybridity in Theory, Culture and Race* (London: Routledge, 1995); Anderson, *Imagined Communities*; Gayatri Chatrovorty Spivak, "The Politics of Translation," in *Destabilizing Theory: Contemporary Feminist Debates*, ed. Michele Barrett and Ann Phillips (Stanford: Stanford University Press, 1992), 77–200; and Pradeep A. Dhillon, "(Dis)locating Thoughts: Where Do the Birds go After the Last Sky?" in *Critical Theory and Educational Discourses: Essays in the Intersection of Philosophy, Social Theory and History*, ed. Thomas S. Popkewitz and Lynn Fendler (New York: Routledge, 1999), 191–220.
47. Thomas Ash, *True Confessions* (New York Review of Books, XLIV, 1997), 33.
48. See Nóvoa, "The Portuguese State."
49. Ines Dussel, Alejondra Birgin, and Guillermina Tiramonti, "Decentralization and Recentralization in the Argentine Educational Reform: Reshaping Educational Policies in the 90s," in *Educational Knowledge: Changing Relationships between the State, Civil Society, and the Educational Community*, ed. Thomas S. Popkewitz (New York: SUNY Press, in press).
50. Kliebard, *Struggle*; Hamilton, *Towards a Theory*; and Dussel et al., "Decentralization."
51. See, for example, Bart J. Moore-Gilbert, *Postcolonial Theory: Contexts, Practices, Politics* (New York: Verso, 1997).
52. Fredrick Cooper and Ann Stoler, *Tensions of Empire: Colonial Cultures in a Bourgeois World* (Berkeley and Los Angeles: University of California Press, 1997).
53. Gyan Prakash, "Subaltern Studies as Postcolonial Criticism," *The American Historical Review* 99 (1994): 1475–90. Also see Carole Pateman, *The Sexual Contract* (Stanford: Stanford University Press, 1988). The issue of globalization/ regionalization raised in this postcolonial literature is not to eliminate European Enlightenment ideas of bourgeois equality, citizen rights, and self-determination within the sovereign nation-state, but to challenge the historicism that projects the West as History. This argument is not relativistic, but rather documents how reason/science/universals of the Enlightenment are mobilized in historically and culturally specific practices in which the claims to empower are produced in circumstances that have also engendered violence.
54. Popkewitz, "Dewey."
55. See Dussel et al., "Decentralization."
56. For discussion of liberalism, see, for example, Metha, "Liberal Strategies."
57. See, for example, Louis Coser, *Refugee Scholars in America: The Impact and Their Experiences* (New Haven, Conn.: Yale University Press, 1984).
58. Whitty, "Creating Quasi-Markets."
59. Popkewitz, *Struggling for the Soul*.
60. See, for example, Pierre Bourdieu, *Distinction: A Social Critique of the Judgment of Taste* (Cambridge: Harvard University Press, 1984); and Pierre Bourdieu, *The State Nobility; Elite Schools in the Field of Power*, trans. L. Clough (Stanford: Stanford University Press, 1989/1996).
61. Wagner, *The Sociology*.

Globalizing Pedagogies: Power, Resentment, and the Re-Narration of Difference

Cameron McCarthy and Greg Dimitriades

Over the years, we have come to see multiculturalism as a set of propositions about identity, knowledge, power, and change in education; as a kind of normal science; and as a form of disciplinarity of difference in which the matter of alterity has been effectively displaced as a supplement. On the terms of its present trajectory, multiculturalism can be properly diagnosed as a discourse of power that attempts to manage the extraordinary tensions and contradictions existing in modern life that have invaded social institutions including the university and the school. At the heart of its achievement, multiculturalism has succeeded in freezing to the point of petrification its central object: "culture." Within the managerial language of the university, culture has become a useful discourse of containment, a narrow discourse of ascriptive property in which particular groups are granted their nationalist histories, their knowledges, and, alas, their experts. Cultural competence then becomes powerfully deployed to blunt the pain of resource scarcity and to inoculate the hegemonic knowledge paradigms in the university from the daylight of subjugated knowledges and practices.

It is wishful thinking on the part of university bureaucrats, however, to attempt to hold still or at bay the extraordinary social currents unleashed in popular life now bearing down upon the modern subjects that inhabit contemporary industrial societies. These currents can be located, in part, in the destabilizing political economy and cultural imperatives unleashed in the push and pull of globalization and localization. On the one hand, the tensions and contradictions of economic reorganization, downsizing, and instability in the labor market have spawned paranoia and uncertainty among the working and professional classes. On the other hand, culture and ideology ignite the false clarity of essential place, essential home, and the attendant practices of moral and social exclusionism. These dynamic forces have taken hold in the "body politic," so to speak. They reveal themselves at the level of the subject in terms of excesses of desire, unfulfilled appetites, incompleteness, and general insecurity, anger, violent passions, frustrations, and resentment. At the level of social institutions these tensions of unfulfillment must be understood as a problem of social integration of difference in a time of scarcity. The educational project then becomes a site of unbridled consumerism—shopping for futures in the context of what C. L. R. James calls "the struggle for happiness."[1]

For cultural critics like ourselves, a key place to read these dynamics is at the level of the popular. We therefore want to take the subject of diversity, knowledge, and power to a place that is normally considered outside the circuit of the education field itself, to the end point and margin of education, to the terrain of popular culture and its pedagogies of wish fulfillment and desire. Desire is understood here as a productive agency of lack, the excess rising below and above needs, the latent wish for totality and completeness in a context of containment, limits, and constraints—power disguised and raw.

In so doing, we want to shift attention from the multiculturalist complaint over current modes of teaching and curriculum, per se, to the broader issue of the cultural reproduction of difference and the coordination of racial identities, what Larry Grossberg calls the "organization of affect."[2] We want to look at the problem of diversity and difference in our time as a problem of social integration of modern individuals and groups into an increasingly bureaucratic, commodified, and deeply colonized and stratified life world. All of this raises the stakes for the practices of cultural reproduction and their role in identity formation, foregrounding the connections between the production and reproduction of popular cultural forms and the operation of power in daily life. Power is understood, here, as a modern force in the Foucauldian sense, inciting and producing certain possibilities, subject positions, relations, limits, and constraints. Power in this sense does not simply prohibit or repress. It is a force that is dispersed. It circulates. It is not outside relations. It produces relations. It is not simply a question of who or what exercises power, but rather how power is exercised in the concrete.[3]

Power is above all discursive—technologies and practices of "truth" that deeply inform how social individuals conduct themselves in relation to each other in the domain of the popular. This is the whole area that Michel Foucault calls "governmentality": the site at which state, industry/economy, and education meet the massive technologies of textual production and meaning construction associated with media and the popular arts. The locus of power struggles in the modern society is not now to be found pure and simple in the classic sites of state politics, labor-capital arm wrestling, or bulldozing actions of civil rights and union-based political actors and their detractors. Modern power struggles are quintessentially to be located in the deeply contested arena of the popular, the domain of struggles over social conduct, popular commitments, anxieties and desires, and, ultimately, the disciplining of populations.[4]

The cultural Marxist C. L. R. James similarly maintained that understanding popular culture was critical to understanding the play of power in modern life. In critical ways, as James insists in books such as *American Civilization*, one can get a better insight into the tensions and contradictions of contemporary society by observing and interpreting popular culture, rather than by analyzing canonical educational texts. James makes this argument in a radical way in his essay, "The Popular Arts and Modern Society":

> It is in the serious study of, above all, Charles Chaplin, Dick Tracy, Gasoline Alley, James Cagney, Edward G. Robinson, Rita Hayworth, Humphrey Bogart, genuinely popular novels like those of Frank Yerby (*Foxes of Harrow, The Golden Hawk, The Vixen, Pride's Castle*) . . . that you find the clearest ideological expression of the sentiments and deepest feelings of the American people and a great window into the future of America and the modern world. This insight is *not* to be found in the works of T. S. Eliot, of Hemingway, of Joyce, of famous directors like John Ford or Rene Clair.[5]

What James is pointing toward through this revisionary strategy is the fact that what we call popular culture is our modern art, a modern art deeply informed by and informative of the crises and tensions of cultural integration and reproduction in our time.

The tensions indexed in popular art forms have been inextricably complicated by global pressures working on and through popular media industries today. Multinational companies are consolidating at the point of distribution while proliferating at the point of production. Hence, consumers around the globe have a seemingly increasing array of "choices" about which products they will consume today, products which are being picked up and used in a variety of ways by many and differently situated audiences. However, these products are also being forged in the service of increasingly few, vertically integrated multinationals, thus exerting a key counterpressure to the above. The result, as Morley and Robins tell us, is a constant contest between homogeneity and heterogeneity in cultural texts and the kinds of identities they enable.[6] Social integration and reproduction have become, in turn, much more complex phenomena, ones that need to be explored and interrogated in multiple sites.

One of the principal crises of social integration in modern life is the crisis of race relations. We are defining racial antagonism in this chapter as an effect of the competition for scarce material and symbolic resources in which strategies of group affiliation and group exclusion play a critical role. This crisis of racial antagonism must be seen within the historical context of the contradictions of a global society and the rapid changes taking place in the material reality and fortunes of people, their environments, the institutional apparatuses that govern and affect their lives, their relations with each other, and their sense of location in the present and in the future. Rapid changes of this kind have meant rapid movement and collision of peoples and media images across the globe, disrupting the traditional isomorphism between self, place, and culture. Above all, as Arjun Appadurai has argued, these processes have necessitated a diremption of the central site of the work of the imagination from the ecclesiastic arena of high art and aesthetics to the banality of everyday practices and the wish fulfillment of the great masses of the people across the globe, from the United States to the Caribbean and beyond.[7]

These tensions, as one of us has argued elsewhere, must be foregrounded in any discussion of the resurgence of racial antagonism and the accompanying restlessness among the working and professional white middle classes.[8] In what follows, we try to understand these developments by reading patterns of recoding and renarration in public life as foregrounded in popular culture and policy discourses. Although we focus, by and large, on the United States, these issues are entirely imbricated in complex and disjunctive global processes. We direct attention in this area to the twin processes of racial simulation, or the constant fabrication of racial identity through the production of the pure space of racial origins, and resentment (the process of defining one's identity through the negation of the other). We look at the operation of these two processes in popular culture and education and we argue that they operate in tandem in the prosecution of the politics of racial exclusion in our times, informing key policy debates.

The Public Court of Racial Simulation

Highlighting the centrality of simulation and resentment foregrounds the fact that American middle-class youth and suburban adults "know" more about inner-city black and Latino youth through electronic mediation, particularly film and television (for example, the show *Cops*), than through personal or classroom interaction or even through textbooks. Yet, these processes are coconstitutive, as school textbooks, like academic books generally, have become part of a prurient culture industry with their high-density illustrations, their eclectic treatment of subject matter, and their touristic, normalizing discourses of surveillance of marginalized groups. In this sense, education (and multicultural education in particular) is articulated to popular culture in ways that implicate broader cultural imperatives.

The logics here are multiple and complex. Hence, critical pedagogues like Steinberg and Kincheloe are correct to note the ways in which popular texts and their complex pleasures and pedagogies are elided from dominant classroom culture today,[9] an insight underscored by an important body of work in cultural studies and education.[10] In this sense, school life is largely divorced from the realities of the popular. However, in another and equally important sense, schools are, in fact, entirely imbricated in the kinds of market logics and imperatives so intrinsic to popular culture. As Andy Green notes, for example, movements for "school choice" index the ways schools are accommodating, not contesting, dominant discourses of consumer capitalism.[11] These discourses are implicated at all levels of the educational process—from decisions about policy and administration to the situated realities of the classroom. As such, Ruth Vinz calls attention to the "shopping mall" approach to multicultural education so prevalent today, giving a most compelling (hypothetical) example:

> On Monday of a given week, students begin their unit on Native Americans. They learn that Native Americans lived in teepees, used tomahawks to scalp white folks, wore headdresses, and danced together around a fire before eating their meal of blue corn and buffalo meat. By Wednesday of the same week, literature is added as an important cultural artifact; therefore, one or two poems (sometimes including Longfellow's "Hiawatha") represent tribal life of the past and present. By Friday, students take a trip to The Museum of the American Indian with its unsurpassed collection of artifacts and carry home their own renditions of teepees, tomahawks, or headdresses that they made during their art period.[12]

The following week, she notes, students might continue their virtual tour of the globe, moving to, for example, Latin American cultures—that is, "During the second week, students study Latinos." As Vinz makes clear, dominant approaches to multicultural education evidence a kind of market logic, putting multiple and fabricated cultural products at the fingertips of students to consume in very superficial ways. This "we are the world" approach to education elides the complexity and tension of the emerging global reality, making it one more product for consumers to consume in simple and simply unproductive ways.

In this sense, educational institutions are always in synch with popular culture in terms of strategies of incorporation and mobilization of racial identities. Indeed, we live in a time when "pseudo-events" fomented in media-driven representations have usurped any relic of reality beyond that which is staged or performed, driving, it is crucial to note, incredibly deep and perhaps permanent wedges of difference between the world of the sub-urban dweller and his or her inner-city counterpart. Daniel Boorstin writes, "We have used our wealth, our literacy, our technology, and our progress, to create a thicket of unreality which stands between us and the facts of life."[13] These Durkheimian "facts of life"—notions of what, for example, black people are like, what Latinos are like—are invented and reinvented in the media, in popular magazines, in newspaper and in television, music, and popular film. As critics such as Len Masterman point out, by the end of his or her teenage years, the average student will have spent more time watching television than he or she would have spent in school.[14] In the United States, it is increasingly television and film that educate American youth about race. Here, again, popular culture and dominant educational imperatives are mutually articulated in complex ways.

Resentment, Identity Formation, and Popular Culture

In *On the Genealogy of Morals*, Friedrich Nietzsche conceptualized resent-ment as the specific practice of identity displacement in which the social actor consolidates his identity by a complete disavowal of the merits and existence of his social other.[15] A sense of self, thus, is only possible through an annihilation or emptying out of the other, whether discursively or mate-rially. These practices of ethnocentric consolidation and cultural excep-tionalism—evident on a global scale—now characterize much of the tug-of-war over educational reform and multiculturalism—and the stakes could not be any higher, for all parties involved.

Indeed, resentment has become perhaps *the* preeminent trope in which and through which "whiteness" is lived in the United States today. Whiteness is an unspoken norm, made pure and real only in relation to that which it is not. "Its fullness," as Michelle Fine and Lois Weis note, "inscribes, at one and the same time, its emptiness and presumed inno-cence."[16] Offering a key example, Fine and Weis explore in telling ethno-graphic detail the saliency of resentment for the white, working-class men of Jersey City, New Jersey, and Buffalo, New York, two cities ravaged by deindustrialization. As they note, these men, men who have lost the economic and cultural stability of the past, blame "ethnic others" for their condition. While the marginalized black men Fine and Weis interview (as part of the same research project) are more apt to offer critiques of "the system," white men ignore such considerations. Personal resentment reigns supreme. Larger structures, the structures that have traditionally supported and served them, are left uninterrogated and naturalized. Fine and Weis write:

> Assuming deserved dominance, [white working-class men] sense that their "rightful place" is being unraveled, by an economy which they argue privileges people of color over white men in the form of affirmative action, and by pressure from blacks and Latinos in their neighborhoods wherein they feel that their physical place is being compromised.[17]

Hence, resentment has become a key way to buck a growing and, for these men, painful tide of difference. This sense of resentment is reinforced and undergirded by several key discourses made available in popular culture and academic circles today, discourses that seek to manage the extraordinary complexities which so mark contemporary cultural life. These discourses have become most salient for white men, but they cannot be and have not been so contained. Rather, they proliferate in complex and contradictory ways, offering and enabling multiple effects for differently situated groups and individuals, both in the United States and globally. These discourses now dominate the public sphere and involve the critical process of the renarration of social identities in a time of ever-widening economic and cultural anxiety. We will limit our discussion to four such discourses.

First, we would like to call attention to *the discourse of origins* as revealed, for example, in the Eurocentric/Afrocentric debate over curriculum reform. Discourses of racial origins rely on the simulation of a pastoral sense of the past in which Europe and Africa are available to American racial combatants without the noise of their modern tensions, contradictions, and conflicts. For Eurocentric combatants such as William Bennett or George Will, Europe and America are a self-evident and transcendent cultural unity.[18] For Afrocentric combatants, Africa and the diaspora are one "solid identity," to use the language of Molefi Asante.[19] Proponents of

Eurocentrism and Afrocentrism are themselves proxies for larger impulses and desires for stability among the middle classes in American society in a time of constantly changing demographic and economic realities. The immigrants are coming! Jobs are slipping overseas into the Third World! Discourses of Eurocentrism and Afrocentrism travel in a time warp to an age when the gods stalked the earth.

These discourses of racial origins provide imaginary solutions to groups and individuals who refuse the radical hybridity that is the historically evolved reality of the United States and other major Western metropolitan societies. The dreaded line of difference is drawn around glittering objects of heritage and secured with the knot of ideological closure. The university itself has become a playground of the war of simulation. Contending paradigms of knowledge are embattled as combatants release the levers of atavism, holding their faces in their hands as the latest volley of absolutism circles in the air.

For example, Michael Steinberg tells the story of his first job (he was hired during the 1980s) as "the new European intellectual and cultural historian at a semi-small, semi-elite, semi-liberal arts college" in the Northeast.[20] As Steinberg notes, during a departmental meeting he unwittingly contradicted the hegemonic hiring practices of his new institution by "voting for the appointment to the history department of an African Americanist whose teaching load would include the standard course on the Civil War and Reconstruction." Several minutes after the meeting, one of the white academic elders of this northeastern college informed Steinberg that: (1) his function as a European intellectual was "to serve as the guardian of the intellectual and curricular tradition," (2) he should "resist at all costs the insidious slide from the party of scholarship to the party of ideology," and (3) if he "persisted in tipping the scales of the department from tradition to experimentation and from scholarship to ideology," he would be digging his own grave insofar as his own, "traditionally defined academic position would be the most likely to face elimination by a newly politicized institution."[21] Unwittingly, Steinberg had been thrown pell-mell into the war of position over origins in which the resources of the history department he had just entered were under the strain of the imperatives of difference.

A second resentment discourse at work in contemporary life and popular culture is *the discourse of nation*. This discourse is foregrounded in a spate of recent ads by multinational corporations such as IBM, United, American Airlines, MCI, and General Electric (GE). These ads both feed on and provide fictive solutions to the racial anxieties of the age. They effectively appropriate multicultural symbols and redeploy them in a broad project of coordinating and consolidating corporate citizenship and consumer affiliation.

The marriage of art and economy, as Stuart Ewen defines advertising in *All Consuming Images*, is now commingled with the exigencies of ethnic identity and nation.[22] One moment, the semiotic subject of advertising is a free American citizen abroad in the open seas sailing up and down the Atlantic or the translucent aquamarine waters of the Caribbean sea. In another, the free American citizen is transported to the pastoral life of the unspoiled, undulating landscape of medieval Europe. Both implicate a burgeoning consumer culture undergirded by the triumph of consumer capitalism on a global scale.

Hence, the GE "We Bring Good Things to Life" ad, in which GE is portrayed as a latter-day Joan of Arc fighting the good fight of American entrepreneurship overseas, bringing electricity to one Japanese town. In the ad, GE breaks through the cabalism of foreign language, bureaucracy, and unethical rules in Japan to procure the goal of the big sell. The American nation can rest in peace as the Japanese nation succumbs to superior United States technology.

Third, there is *the discourse of popular memory and popular history*. This discourse suffuses the nostalgic films of the last decade or so. Films such as *Dances with Wolves* (1990), *Bonfire of the Vanities* (1990), *Grand Canyon* (1993), *Falling Down* (1993), *Forrest Gump* (1994), *A Time to Kill* (1996), *The Fan* (1997), *Armageddon* (1998), and *Saving Private Ryan* (1998) foreground a white middle-class protagonist who appropriates the subject position of the persecuted social victim at the mercy of myriad forces—from "wild" black youth in Los Angeles (in *Grand Canyon*), to Asian store owners who do not speak English well (in *Falling Down*), to a black baseball player, living the too-good life in a moment of corporate downsizing (in *The Fan*). All hearken back to the "good old days" when the rules were few and exceedingly simple for now-persecuted white men.

Joel Schumaker's *A Time to Kill* is a particularly good example here, offering key pedagogical insights about social problems concerning difference from the perspective of the embattled white suburban dweller. The problem with difference is, in Schumaker's world, symptomatic of a crisis of feeling for white suburban middle classes—a crisis of feeling represented in blocked opportunity and wish fulfillment, overcrowding, loss of jobs, general insecurity, crime, and so forth. The contemporary world has spun out of order, and violence and resentment are the coping strategies of such actors.

In *A Time to Kill*, Schumaker presents us with the world of the "New South," Canton Mississippi, in which social divides are extreme and blacks and whites live such different lives they might as well be on separate planets. But this backwater of the South serves as a social laboratory to explore a burning concern of suburban America: retributive justice. When individuals break the law and commit acts of violent antisocial behavior, the upstanding folks in civil society are justified, the film argues, in seeking their expulsion or elimination. The film thus poses the rather provocative question: When is it respectable society's "Time to Kill?" Are there circumstances in which retribution and revenge and resentment are warranted? The makers of *A Time to Kill* say resoundingly, "Yes!" This answer is impervious to class or race or gender. As a technology of truth the film works to piece together a plurality of publics.

In order to make the case for retributive justice, Schumaker puts a black man at the epicenter of this white normative discourse—what Charles Murray calls "white popular wisdom."[23] What would you do if your ten-year-old daughter is brutally raped and battered, pissed on, and left for dead? You would want revenge. This is a role play that has been naturalized to mean white victim, black assailant—the Willy Horton shuffle. In *A Time to Kill*, however, the discourse is inverted: The righteously angry are a black worker and his family, as two redneck assailants brutally rape and nearly kill his daughter. Carl Lee, the black lumberyard worker, gets back at these two callous criminals by shooting them down on the day of their arraignment. One brutal act is answered by another. One is a crime, the other is righteous justice. Crime will not pay. In this revenge drama, the message of retributive justice is intended to override race and class lines. We are living in the time of an eye for an eye. The racial enemy is in our private garden. In the face of bureaucratic incompetence we have to take the law into our own hands.

These films are steeped in nostalgia, enmeshed in the project of rewriting history from the perspective of bourgeois anxieties and the feelings of resentment that often drive them. This project is realized perhaps most forcefully in the wildly successful *Forrest Gump*. A special-effects master-work, this film literally interpolates actor Tom Hanks into actual and recreated historical footage of key events in United States history, renar-rating the latter part of the twentieth century in ways that blur the line between fact and fiction. Here, the peripatetic Gump steals the spotlight from the Civil Rights movement, Vietnam War protest, the feminist move-ment, and so forth. Public history is overwhelmed by personal con-sumerism and wish fulfillment. "Life," after all, "is like a box of choco-lates. You never know what you're gonna get." You might get Newt Gingrich. But who cares? History will absolve the American consumer.

Finally, we wish to call attention to *the conversationalizing discourses of the media culture*. From the television and radio talk shows of Oprah Winfrey and Jenny Jones to the rap music of Tupac Shakur to pseudo-academic books like *The Bell Curve, The Hot Zone*, and *The Coming Plague*, to self-improvement texts like *Don't Sweat the Small Stuff . . . and It's All Small Stuff*, popular culture psychologizes and seemingly internal-izes complex social problems, managing the intense feelings of anxiety so much a part of contemporary cultural life. Television talk shows, for exam-ple, reduce complex social phenomena to mere personality conflicts between guests, encouraging them to air their differences before encourag-ing some kind of denouement or resolution. Histories of oppression are thus put aside as guests argue in and through the details of their private lives, mediated, as they often are, by so-called experts. Racial harmony becomes a relative's acceptance of a "biracial" child. Sexual parity is reduced to a spouse publicly rejecting an adulterous partner. Psychologistic explanations for social phenomena reign supreme and are supported by a burgeoning literature of self-improvement texts, which posit poor self-esteem as the preeminent societal ill today. These popular texts and media programs are pivotal in what Deborah Tannen calls "The Argument Culture," in which the private is the political, and politics is war by other means.[24]

Identities are thus being formed and reformed—"produced," following Edward Said—in this complex social moment, where the global "tide of difference" is being met by profound renarrations of history. It is precisely this kind of rearticulation and recoding that one of us has called *nonsyn-chrony*.[25] Here, we have tried to draw attention to how these complicated dynamics operate in debates over identity and curriculum reform, hegemonic cultural assertions in advertising, popular film, and in the conversa-tionalizing discourses of contemporary popular culture. Further, as we have shown, these discourses are imbricated in a global popular culture industry, one that has radically appropriated the new to consolidate the past. This is the triumph of a nostalgia of the present as "difference" comes under the normalizing logics and disciplinary imperatives of hegemonic power. Diversity, as such, can sell visits to theme parks as well as it can sell textbooks. Diversity can sell AT&T and MCI long distance calling cards as well as the new ethnic stalls in the ethereal hearths of the shopping mall. And sometimes, in the most earnest of ways, diversity lights up the whole world and makes it available to capitalism.

Educational Policy and the Pedagogy of Resentment

Importantly, and most disturbingly, we wish to note that this kind of diver-sity is also increasingly informing—indeed, producing in the Foucauldian sense—educational policy on both the Right and Left, as evidenced by sev-eral key debates now circulating in the public sphere. These debates have had very real material effects on the dispossessed, those quickly losing the (albeit meager) benefits of affirmative action (for example, California's Proposition 209), bilingual education (for example, California's Proposition 227—the so-called "English for the Children" initiative), and need-based financial aid. The idea of high-quality (public) education as the great poten-tial equalizer—a good in and of itself—is now being lost to the bitter resent-ments at the heart of contemporary culture, lost to petty market logics and the free-standing subject-positions so enabled by them. The pressures of globalization—for example, new patterns of immigration, the proliferation of media images, or the ravages of deindustrialization—have been met here and elsewhere by calls for the weakest kinds of self-serving "diversity." This diversity, as noted, is encouraged by a consumer capitalism that is entirely linked to the imperatives of resentment explored throughout. In a particu-larly stark example of this process, Martin Luther King Jr.'s revolutionary dream of the day when his "four little children will . . . live in a nation where they will not be judged by the color of their skin, but by the content of their character," has been appropriated by right-wing commentators like Shelby Steele to contest the advances of affirmative action.[26]

How the discourse of resentment has (explicitly) propelled the conservative agenda here is fairly obvious. A new and seemingly beleaguered middle class is looking to recapture its once unquestioned privilege by advocating "color blind" hiring and acceptance policies (in the case of affirmative action) while forging a seemingly unified—and, of course, white Anglo—cultural identity through restrictive language policies (in the case of bilingual education). Indeed, the consolidation of seamless and coherent subjects at the heart of contemporary cultural media flows (as explored above) has enabled and encouraged the overwhelming public support and passage of bills like California's Propositions 209 and 227 (in the case of the latter, by a 2 to 1 margin). These evidence the popular feelings of resentment that Fine and Weis so powerfully document among white working-class men in *The Unknown City*.[27]

Yet, these resentments run deep and operate on numerous levels here; hence, the tensions now erupting between African Americans and Latinos vis-à-vis many such bills. A recent *Time* magazine article entitled "The Next Big Divide?" explores burgeoning conflicts between African Americans and Latinos in Palo Alto over bilingual education, noting that these disputes

> arise in part from frustration over how to spend the dwindling pot of cash in low-income districts. But they also reflect a jostling for power, as blacks who labored hard to earn a place in central offices, on school boards and in classrooms confront a Latino population eager to grab a share of these positions.[28]

It has been suggested, in fact, that efforts to institute black "ebonics" as a second language in Oakland was prompted by competition for shrinking funds traditionally allotted to bilingual (Spanish) programs. Resentment, spawned by increasing competition for decreasing resources, is key to unraveling the complexities of these struggles, for, as Joel Schumaker tells us, its power transcends both race and class lines.

Perhaps more important, however, the discourse of resentment is also informing seemingly more liberal responses to these issues and bills as well. The importance of public education in equalizing the profound injustices of contemporary American society is increasingly downplayed in favor of discourses about self-interest and the rigid feelings of resentment that undergird them. Affirmative action, thus, is a good because education will keep dangerous minorities off of "our streets" by subjecting them to a life-time of "civilizing" education, crafting them into good subjects for global cultural capitalism. Further, the story goes, affirmative action really helps middle-class women more than blacks or Latinos, so it should—quite nat-urally—remain in place.

These discourses inform the debate on bilingual education, as well, a debate that has similarly collapsed liberal and conservative voices and opin-ions. Indeed, bilingual education, many argue, should be supported (only) because it will prepare young people for an increasingly polyglot global cul-tural economy, hence keeping immigrants and minorities off of public assis-tance, allowing them to compete in an increasingly diverse (in the sense developed above) global community. Cultural arguments are also elided from within these positions, for, as many so eagerly stress, bilingual educa-tion really helps immigrants learn English and become assimilated faster— a bottom-line supported by an ever-present spate of quantitative studies.

Market logics are all-pervasive here and are deeply informed by self-interest and resentment. These forces have shown themselves most clearly in recent decisions to provide less need-based financial aid for higher edu-cation to the poor, apportioning the savings to attract more "qualified" middle-class students.[29] Competition for the "best" students—seemingly without regard for race, class, and gender—has become a mantra for those wishing to further destroy educational access for the dispossessed. Indeed, why, many argue, should poor minorities take precious spots away from the more qualified wealthy? The resentment of the elite has now come full circle, especially and most ironically in this moment of unmatched eco-nomic wealth. As Jerome Karabel, professor of sociology at the University of California, Berkeley (the site of key roll-backs in affirmative action) comments, "College endowments are at historically unprecedented heights, ₊₀ the number of need-blind institutions should be increasing rather than decreasing."[30] As we all know, these are not lean, mean times for every-body. We also live in an era of unbridled wealth, won in large measure for the elite through, in part, divide-and-conquer strategies and the triumph of resentment and its ability to dictate public policy.

Conclusion

Resentment, in sum, is produced at the level of the popular, and at the level of the textual. Yet its implications run deep, across myriad contexts, especially in public policy, which is increasingly defined by the logics of resentment. Thus, those of us on the Left, those wishing to help keep the promise of public education a real one, must question the terms on which we fight these battles. We must question whether our responses will further reproduce a discourse with such devastating and wholly regressive implications. As Foucault reminds us, we must choose what discourses we want to engage in, the "games of truth" we want to play. Indeed, what will be our responses to the burgeoning trend of eliminating need-based financial aid policies? What game will we play? Toward what end?

Such questions are crucial and pressing, as this moment is replete with both possibility as well as danger. This period of intense globalization and multinational capital is witness to the ushering in of the multicultural age—an age in which the empire has struck back, and First World exploitation of the Third World has so depressed these areas that there has been a steady stream of immigrants from the periphery seeking better futures in the metropolitan centers. With the rapid growth of the indigenous minority population in the United States, there is now a formidable cultural presence of diversity in every sphere of cultural life. Clearly, as Appadurai reminds us, social reproduction and integration have been inextricably complicated by globalization and the new and unpredictable flows of peoples as well as money, technology, media images, and ideologies it has enabled.[31] All, he stresses, must be understood individually and in tandem if we are to understand the emerging cultural landscape and its imbrication in a multifaceted global reality.

Indeed, if this is an era of the "post," it is also an era of difference—and the challenge of this era of difference is the challenge of living in a world of incompleteness, discontinuity, and multiplicity. It requires generating a mythology of social interaction that goes beyond the model of resentment that seems so securely in place in these times. It means that we must take seriously the implications of the best intuition in the Nietzschean critique of resentment as the process of identity formation that thrives on the negation of the other—the dominant response from those facing a new and complex global and local reality. The challenge is to embrace a politics that calls on the moral resources of all who are opposed to the power block and its emerging global contours.

This age of difference thus poses new, though difficult, tactical and strategic challenges to critical and subaltern intellectuals as well as activists. A strategy that seeks to address these new challenges and openings must involve as a first condition a recognition that our differences of race, gender, and nation are merely the starting points for new solidarities and new alliances, not the terminal stations for depositing our agency and identities or the extinguishing of hope and possibility. Such a strategy might help us to understand better the issue of diversity in schooling and its linkages to the problems of social integration and public policy in modern life. Such a strategy might allow us to "produce" new discourses as well, especially and most importantly in this highly fraught and exceedingly fragile moment of historical complexity.

Notes

1. C. L. R. James, *American Civilization* (Oxford, Eng.: Blackwell, 1993), 166.
2. Lawrence Grossberg, *We Gotta Get Out of this Place: Popular Conservatism and Postmodern Culture* (New York: Routledge, 1992).
3. Stuart Hall, "Cultural Studies: Two Paradigms," *Media, Culture, and Society* 2 (1980): 57–72.
4. Toby Miller, *Technologies of Truth: Cultural Citizenship and the Popular Media* (Minneapolis: University of Minnesota Press, 1998).
5. James, *American Civilization*, 119.
6. David Morley and Kevin Robins, *Spaces of Identity: Global Media, Electronic Landscapes and Cultural Boundaries* (London: Routledge, 1995).
7. Arjun Appadurai, *Modernity at Large: Cultural Dimensions of Globalization* (Minneapolis: University of Minnesota Press, 1996).
8. Cameron McCarthy, *The Uses of Culture: Education and the Limits of Ethnic Affiliation* (New York: Routledge, 1998).
9. Shirley Steinberg and Joe Kincheloe, eds., *Kinderculture: The Corporate Construction of Youth* (Boulder: Westview Press, 1997).
10. See, for example, Henry Giroux, *Fugitive Cultures: Race, Violence, and Youth* (London: Routledge, 1996).
11. Andy Green, *Education, Globalization and the Nation-State* (London: Macmillan Press, 1997).
12. Ruth Vinz, "Learning from the Blues: Beyond Essentialist Readings of Cultural Texts," in *Sound Identities*, ed. Cameron McCarthy et al. (New York: Peter Lang, in press).
13. Daniel Boorstin, *The Image: A Guide to Pseudo-Events in America* (New York: Atheneum, 1975), 3.
14. Len Masterman, *Teaching the Media* (New York: Routledge, 1990).
15. Some commentators on Nietzsche associate resentment only with "slave morality." By this formulation, we are taken "back," genealogically, to "literal slaves" in

Greek society, who, being the most downtrodden, had only one sure implement of defense: the acerbic use of emotion and moral manipulation. However, we want to argue along with Robert Solomon that contemporary politics are "virtually defined by resentment." See Robert Solomon, "Nietzsche, Postmodernism, and Resentment: A Genealogical Hypothesis," in *Nietzsche as Postmodernist: Essays Pro and Con,* ed. C. Koelb (New York: SUNY Press, 1990), 278. This is a strain of resentment that is racially coded. It is a resentment that, in the words of Soloman, "elaborates an ideology of combative complacency [or what Grossberg, *We Gotta Get Out of This Place: Popular Conservatism and Postmodern Culture* (New York: Routledge, 278) calls "impassioned apathy"]—a leveling effect that declares society to be 'classless' even while maintaining powerful class structures and differences." Resentment in late-twentieth-century society is the project of disoriented white working and professional classes, confronted with the panoply of difference that marks the institutional and social environment in which modern subjects live in industrialized societies.

16. Michelle Fine and Lois Weis, *The Unknown City: Lives of Poor and Working-Class Young Adults* (Boston: Beacon Press, 1998), 156–57.
17. Ibid., 133.
18. William Bennett, *The Book of Virtues* (New York: Simon and Schuster, 1994); George Will, "Eurocentricity and the School Curriculum," *Baton Rouge Morning Advocate* 18 Dec. 1989, 3.
19. Molefi Asante, *Malcolm X as Cultural Hero and Other Afrocentric Essays* (Trenton, N.J.: Africa World Press, 1993).
20. Michael Steinberg, "Cultural History and Cultural Studies," in *Disciplinarity and Dissent in Cultural Studies*, ed. Cary Nelson and Delip P. Gaonkar (New York: Routledge, 1996), 103–29.
21. Ibid., 105.
22. Stuart Ewen, *All Consuming Images: The Politics of Style in Contemporary Culture* (New York: Basic Books, 1988).
23. Charles Murray, *Losing Ground: American Social Policy, 1950–1980* (New York: Basic Books, 1984).
24. Deborah Tannen, *The Argument Culture: Moving from Debate to Dialogue* (New York: Random House, 1998).
25. McCarthy, *The Uses of Culture.*
26. Shelby Steele, *Content of Our Character: A New Vision of Race in America* (New York: St. Martins Press, 1990).
27. Fine and Weis, *The Unknown City.*
28. Romesh Ratnesar, "The Next Big Divide?" *Time,* 1 Dec. 1997, 52.
29. Ethan Bronner, "Universities Giving Less Financial Aid on Basis of Need," *New York Times,* 21 June 1998, A1, A16.
30. Jerome Karabel, cited in Ethan Bronner, "Universities Giving Less Financial Aid on Basis of Need," *New York Times,* 21 June 1998, A16.
31. Appadurai, *Modernity at Large.*

International Education and the Production of Global Imagination[1]

Fazal Rizvi

For a country so proud of its postcolonial aspirations and so keen to parade its nationalism, Malaysia's approach to the contemporary processes of globalization is highly ambivalent. Nowhere is this ambivalence more evident than in the educational policies that the Malaysian government has recently pursued and in the desire of a large number of Malaysians to get an international education. The Malaysian government insists on the teaching of Malay culture and language in its own universities as a necessary force with which to bind the nation together; and yet it remains committed to an ideology of national development based on the principles of secular capitalism. Almost half of Malaysia's tertiary students attend a Western university abroad where they are exposed in a sustained way to cultural ideas that often conflict with "the Asian values" promoted so proudly by the Malaysian Prime Minister Dr. Mahathir. According to Marshallsay, more than sixty thousand Malaysian tertiary students are currently studying abroad.[2] True, some of these students go overseas because of the limited number of places available at home, but a larger proportion has a strong preference for an international education. How should their preference be interpreted? How do the students experience education in a different cultural site? And how does this experience affect the ways they think about their identity and imagine their future?

In this chapter, I want to discuss these issues of identity and education in relation to theories of globalization. If the current phase of globalization is largely characterized by increased cultural flows between nations, then how does international education contribute to the reconfiguration of cultural identities? How do cultures "travel"[3] within the contemporary epoch in which international education may be regarded as a manifestation of cultural globalization? If all identities are constituted within a system of social relations and representations, and require the reciprocal recognition of others, then how do identities firmly developed in one context become reshaped by another? If identities are dynamic, emergent forms of collective action, then how does international education affect the changing cultural landscape inhabited by the students? To what extent can the reconstituted landscape be viewed as contributing to the development of a global culture?

The discussion of these issues in this chapter is based on the data collected as part of a research project funded by the Australian Research Council on the manner in which Australian universities have during the past decade marketed education to Asia, and the ways in which international students experience higher education in Australia, positioning themselves as both students and consumers. The project involved in-depth interviews over a period of nine months with twenty-six Malaysian students living in Brisbane, enrolled at the University of Queensland, Queensland University of Technology, and Griffith University. Fourteen of these students were male, twelve were female, and fifteen were Malaysians of Chinese background. The data collected is a rich resource for exploring the diversity of views Malaysian students have in relation to the issues of identity and culture and for testing a range of theories about diaspora and cultural globalization.

Identity, Culture, and Globalization

Much of the recent literature on globalization views it as predominantly an economic phenomenon. In the popular media, "globalization" is a term often associated with the current expansion of neoliberal economic thinking and practices across the globe. It is suggestive of the increasing interdependence of regional and national economies and the spread of global trading agreements and relationships. George Soros's recent book on the current crisis facing the global economy is a good example of this definition of globalization.[4] But it is not only the economists who view globalization in such narrow terms, many of its critics too, like Hirst and Thompson,[5] focus largely on its economic dimensions. Capling, Considine, and Crozier, for example, argue that "globalisation refers to the emergence of a global economy which is characterized by uncontrollable market forces and new economic actors such as transnational corporations, international banks, and other financial institutions."[6] No mention is made here of the profound cultural changes that are now affecting every facet of life around the world.

While the emergence of a global economy is certainly one of its major characteristics, the focus on the economic is clearly inadequate for describing the complexities of globalization. It not possible to explain the move toward a global economy solely in economic terms, independent of its relationship to the issues of political and symbolic exchange. As Wiseman has suggested, an adequate understanding of the processes of globalization requires a more integrated approach, which illuminates the changing global economic relations in terms of the changing social, political, and cultural landscapes.[7] Waters's analysis is even more emphatic. He argues that the "globalisation of human society is contingent on the extent to which cultural arrangements are effective relative to economic and political arrangements."[8] Waters insists that the degree of globalization is greater in the cultural arena than in either economics or politics. This is so because increasingly global economic exchange is in symbolic commodities and human services rather than in raw materials. Whether Waters has overstated his case is of course an open question, but what is beyond doubt is that the contemporary phase of globalization cannot be adequately understood without reference to its cultural dimensions. Without an understanding of the increasing dominance of media and communication technologies, and of the increasing global movement of ideas, images, and people, we cannot fully appreciate the emergence of new cultural formations.

Globalization is of course not a wholly new phenomenon, although its current phase does seem different from its earlier forms in at least one important respect. As Pieterse and Parekh point out, in contrast to cultural imperialism, the era of globalization lacks "a single centre or a state-orchestrated character."[9] Contemporary cultural shifts are transforming social landscapes in a variety of uneven and chaotic ways.[10] New sociocultural spaces and processes are now emerging as the global begins to replace the nation-state as a major framework for social life. This is a framework in which global flows—in mediascapes, ethnocscapes, financescapes, and technoscapes—are coming to assume as much, perhaps even greater, importance than national institutions.[11] This position is in direct opposition to the view of theorists like Wallerstein, who typically subscribe to some sort of notion of a "world system" with a set of systemic properties.[12]

The cultural flows between nations are not, of course, detached from economic and political realities. As Ahmed and Donnan note, "Because of their origin some flows—mainly those in 'the West'—have more force than others and so reach a wider audience."[13] This observation has led some commentators to speak of globalization as another form of Westernization, sometimes referred to as "McDonaldization."[14] Others point to the emergence of a "global culture." But such a one-dimensional view overlooks the fact that Western cultural products may be received in different places in different ways and that they may become domesticated by being interpreted and incorporated within local traditions.[15] Also, in particular locations, enormous significance may be attached to some cultural products, while others are dismissed. According to Ahmed and Donnan, "Cultural flows do not necessarily map directly on to economic and political relationships, which means that the flow of cultural traffic can often be in many different directions simultaneously."[16] What typifies cultural globalization is a set of practices that are transcultural, emerging out of rapid flows of cultures across national boundaries, not only through global media and information technologies but also through the movement of people. The late twentieth century has witnessed massive movements of people from one state to another, for a range of purposes, including migration, tourism, business, and education.

With migration, the movement of people is often permanent. Migrants leave one place in search of another, often forced to assimilate into their new cultural milieu. In the globalization era, many people are constantly on the move, while others join communities, now typical of many parts of the globe, that had already become linguistically and culturally heterogeneous. Breckenbridge and Appadurai maintain that contemporary diaspora are less likely to have "stable points of origin, clear and final destinations and coherent group identities."[17] Such a dynamic cultural context has given rise to the so-called "third cultures" in which the stories of movement are best told under the signs of hybridity and cultural melange, rather than cultural adaptation. Hybridization differs from the earlier modernist requirement of assimilation because its cultural politics does not have a cultural "center of gravity."[18]

In contemporary nation-states, constituted through successive waves of migration, diasporas no longer constitute minority groups within an alien culture, but are increasingly posited as groups with experience in global cultural production, with political and economic connections making them well placed to take advantage of the new era. Cohen has argued that diasporic communities have skills in the cultural realm of ideas. They are able to link the cultural with the economic; "diasporas score by being able to interrogate the universal with the particular and by being able to use their cosmopolitanism to press the limits of the local."[19] And as Bhabha has pointed out, diasporic communities are not stranded minorities, but rather people who are able to interrogate the global through the local, with their lived experiences and insights into cultural production as this operates globally.[20] Their presence contributes to the creation of "in-between" cultural spaces not bounded by the dictates of geography.[21] They reconstitute localities by their mere presence.

This is of course a positive view of globalization. But the global movement of people also raises complex issues about identity and authenticity, not only for those who go abroad but also for those who remain behind. Those who go abroad have to deal with the vulnerability of having to redefine themselves in a world constantly on the move, diverse and fragmented, and in which cultural traces are difficult to identify. Globalization has not eradicated the problems of alienation, displacement, and uncertainty; it has simply redefined them in a context of deterritorialization. The diaspora has, moreover, raised issues of identity and cultural change at "home" too, among those faced with the fantasy if not the reality of moving.[22] With cultures becoming less bounded, those who do not move across national boundaries have to address nonetheless the task of cultural maintenance and renewal. As Harrenz points out, the detachment of culture from territory has unleashed a powerful force that affects us all, and not just those who are directly involved.[23]

Issues of identity are thus inextricably linked to the issues of diaspora and cultural globalization. Recent use in cultural studies of the metaphors of mobility, transculturation, and diaspora have highlighted

> the possibilities of hybrid identities which are not essentialist but can still empower people and communities by producing in them new capacities for action. The ethnic absolutism of the "root" metaphors, fixed in place is replaced by mobile "route" metaphors which can lay down a challenge to the fixed identities of "cultural insiderism."[24]

And as Hall has argued, "the notion that identity . . . [can] be told as two histories, one over here, one over there, never having spoken to one another, never having anything to do with one another . . . is simply not tenable any more in an increasingly globalised world."[25]

If this is so, then how do Malaysian students engaged in international education think about the issues of their identity? Why do they choose to get an education abroad? What values do they bring to an Australian university, and how are these subjected to the pressures of cultural change? In one sense, as cultural elites they can be expected to be the carriers of the values of secularization and cosmopolitization, but is this really the case? How does international education affect their ethnic and religious affiliations? How are their cultural and professional outlooks transformed by the experiences of international education? To what extent do these experiences serve to standardize expectations, desires, and aspirations creating new networks and practices of global cultural, political, and economic relations? In what follows, some of these issues of cultural globalization are examined through stories told by four Malaysian students approaching the final years of their tertiary studies in Australia. Before proceeding to this discussion, however, it may be useful to examine the ways in which

Malaysia is itself addressing issues of higher educational policy in the context of globalization.

Dilemmas of Educational Policy in Malaysia

Educational policy in Malaysia has always had to deal with a range of contradictory expectations. The origins of Malaysia's educational system lie in its colonial history. It is not hard to find traces of its cultural links to Britain, and even today Cambridge A-level examinations can be taken in Malaysia's elite schools. But the Malaysian education system also bears the distinctive marks of the country's postcolonial confidence. This is evident, perhaps in ways that are contradictory, in its nationalist sentiment, with its emphasis on the teaching of the Malay language and culture, and especially Islam, on the one hand, and its championing of the principles of global capitalism on the other. Until the economic crisis hit Southeast Asia in 1997, Malaysia consistently recorded rates of economic growth of around 10 percent and pursued policies of financial deregulation and corporate restructuring with a great deal of vigor. Educational policy in Malaysia occupies a place at the intersection of cultural traditionalism and economic globalism, raising a range of policy dilemmas. The government's response to these dilemmas has been consistently pragmatic; it has kept tight control over its own higher education system and yet has allowed, even encouraged, a large number of Malaysian students to go abroad in search of an education.

In recent years, such pragmatism has been sorely tested by the cultural changes brought about by globalization, on the one hand, and the emergence of a backlash Islamic fundamentalism on the other. In response, the Malaysian government has sought to restructure its major institutions, including education. In 1996, it overhauled its educational system through the publication of five key Education Acts, designed to ensure that Malaysia realized the goals set by the Prime Minister, Dr. Mahathir, in his *Vision 2020* statement. Dr. Mahathir wishes Malaysia to become an industrialized nation by the year 2020 within a policy framework that preserves its distinctive cultural traditions. The Malaysian leadership recognizes, however, the dangers posed to its national identity by the processes of globalization. To become an industrialized nation, it realizes it must become integrated within the global economy, but such an integration runs the risk of eroding its political and cultural sovereignty, and in particular the fragile consensus among its various ethnic groups. The government wishes to preserve the dominance of the Bumiputras (the term used to describe Muslim and indigenous people of Malaysia) through policies of affirmative action, while it claims to value the contribution that all ethnic groups are supposed to make to national unity and development. It wants education to play a major role in consolidating its nationhood. Its educational vision, as articulated in the new acts, therefore seeks to reconcile the competing demands of modernity and tradition, freedom and discipline, and educational equality and excellence. The Education Acts stress the need to find an appropriate balance between these social principles.

The 1996 Education Acts have not only addressed the issue of values but have also sought to grapple with the dilemmas of educational governance. The acts have recognized the importance of institutional choice and initiative and of letting local leadership assume responsibility for the management of curriculum, pedagogy, and resources. In seeking to corporatize Malaysia's public universities, they have effectively acknowledged that the educational bureaucracy had in the past constrained the development of Malaysian higher education and that greater devolution of responsibility would make public universities much more responsive to changing social and economic conditions and to the demands of the community. Yet the state has retained fairly tight control over the curriculum—for example, over language policy and over issues of funding and key appointments. The administrative policies prescribed by the acts thus sit uneasily with the rhetoric of institutional autonomy.

Dilemmas of educational governance are also reflected in the Malaysian government's 1996 Private Higher Education Institutions Act. This act permits the expansion of the private education sector in Malaysia that, by comparison with other ASEAN countries, was already fairly large. In addition to the large number of individuals who went overseas to study, private education in Malaysia had in the past taken the form of privately owned and managed colleges, many with twinning arrangements with overseas universities. The government now permits local private universities to be established and allows overseas universities to establish branch campuses in Malaysia. This extension of private education has clearly provided access to higher education within Malaysia for many students who had previously been forced to go overseas, but it also created an educational market in which there are major concerns about quality control, cultural relevance, and equality of opportunity.

The Malaysian government's attitude toward students who choose to go overseas for their higher education is one of ambivalence. Since it cannot provide sufficient places for the demand, international education is viewed as an attractive alternative. But the fact that a large amount of money simply flows out of Malaysia for the purposes of buying education is a matter of deep concern, as is the fear of Malaysian youth becoming enculturated in a Western country, embracing cultural and political ideas considered alien to Malaysian society. There is also the fear of students not wishing to return home. However, the government recognizes the major benefits of international education, as it strives to become an industrialized nation, with its economy integrated into the global economy. The students return to Malaysia with skills, professional competence, and international networks that the country feels it needs in its pursuit of the goals of *Vision 2020*. These sentiments are not lost on the Malaysian students studying in Australian universities. Most of them have a remarkably good understanding of the dilemmas of social life and public policy in Malaysia and also of the ways in which their education is linked to the broader processes of globalization.

Malaysian Students in Australia

The reasons given by the Malaysian students for their decision to go abroad to study are diverse and multiple. For students interviewed during our research, their primary objective was to obtain a well-recognized qualification that will enable them to secure a good job. The responses to the question as to where this job might be varied greatly. The status attached to an overseas qualification by Malaysian employers was cited as playing a major part in their decision. Others simply followed a family tradition. The lack of access to Malaysia's local universities was also mentioned as a reason, although in most cases the availability of a place would not have led to a preference to stay at home. According to Ahmad, a Muslim student completing the fourth year of his medical degree, he did not even entertain the possibility of an education at a Malaysian university. He and his parents had made up their minds for him to go overseas when he was ten years old. Britain was his first preference largely because of his familiarity with British cultural institutions as described in his school textbooks: "I had known about the castles and stuff, and wanted to see how people lived there. I didn't know much about Australia and was scared of the things that I had heard." However, since Australia was an English-speaking country, Ahmad was happy enough to accept the offer of a place at the University of Queensland.

In Malaysia, Ahmad had attended a school where the language of instruction was Malay. He had, as he said, "a good school-boy English," and while he expected to encounter difficulty with the English language in Australia, he nonetheless regarded the opportunity to improve his English as a major bonus: "English is the global language and even in Malaysia you cannot go very far unless you are a confident speaker of English. That is why the Malaysian government now realizes that it can't be anti-English like it was." Kakak, a medical student in her fifth year, also spoke passionately about the need for all Malaysians to improve their English. She felt that her "English was not very good still, but I cannot imagine learning medicine in Malay. So if I wanted to be a doctor English was very important." Kakak is a devout Muslim who received a Malaysian government scholarship to attend university in Australia. Why would the Malaysian government want its best students to go to a university overseas, we asked. Kakak's reply was intriguing: "I think the government is not confident about the quality of education at its own local universities, and they would like their students to have exposure to foreign things."

The term "exposure" appeared a great deal in the discourses of the Malaysian students. Exposure to things foreign—to different people and cultures, to different ideas and attitudes, and to different ways of learning and working—is a feature common in all our interviews. For example, Sylvia, a master's of business administration (MBA) student of Chinese background, who came to Australia via an undergraduate degree from the National University of Singapore, was most emphatic about the "need for exposure" to Western ideas. Presumably influenced by the ideological orientation of an MBA course, she talked a great deal about the requirements of a global economy. She had no doubt that an international education provided better preparation for working within the "global economy." According to Sylvia, "Like Singapore and other Asian countries, Malaysia has attracted massive amounts of investment from international corporations, so much so that its economic success is now tied to its ability to remain a player in the global economy. This will not happen unless there is an educated workforce which can perform on the international economic stage."

It is indeed true that most of the new jobs in Malaysia are now either in the service sector or in private sector management and, in particular, in those transnational corporations engaged in the business of exports and imports.[26] Employment in this sector requires particular kinds of skills, which the corporations feel are better able to be developed through an education in a Western university. Sylvia is convinced that "in the Malaysian job market overseas graduates have a definite advantage over the graduates from local universities who lack the exposure to other cultures, and other ways of doing things. The corporations feel that overseas graduates are able to speak English, which is the international language of commerce, but more than that, that they are more confident in being able to handle or deal with clients from Europe and North America." Clearly, the changing nature of the global economy is a significant factor in reshaping student preferences.

A large majority of Malaysian students in Australian universities are therefore enrolled in the faculties of management, commerce, or economics. In these faculties, students are taught a new seemingly universal organizational ideology based on some of the principles of Japanese business practices and their application in transnational corporations. For example, ideas about strategic management, just-in-time, total quality management, teamwork, managerial decentralization, and flexibility appear to have become central tenets of a "single idealisation of appropriate organisational behaviour."[27] Most management courses now appear committed to an education espousing this idealization. Malaysian students find it easier to obtain such an education in a Western rather than a local university, and as a result, many prefer to go overseas, even at the cost of the huge financial sacrifices made by their parents. With Malaysia's economy becoming increasingly globalized, international education is clearly attractive, especially for those students with a very utilitarian view of education.

The preference for an international education is also linked to the ethnic politics of educational provision within Malaysia. As Andersen suggests, one of the main factors that encourages non-Bumiputra students to go overseas for a tertiary education is the lack of places in local universities.[28] Many ethnic Chinese in particular feel that their sociocultural circumstances and the government's affirmative action policies leave them with little option. Educational opportunities for the Chinese in Malaysia are in part defined by the government's affirmative action policies that favor the Bumiputras. Some Chinese-Malaysians believe, moreover, that an internationally recognized degree would enhance their chances of emigration from Malaysia, should the political and economic circumstances become less attractive. Many Bumiputra students, on the other hand, attend overseas universities with the benefit of scholarships or loans provided by the government, providing them access to both specialized courses and high-quality courses in general.

As a result, nearly three-quarters of Malaysian students attending Australian universities are of Chinese background, almost twice the number that one would expect given the demographic composition of the country. What this statistic indicates is that the Malaysian educational system is structured along ethnic lines and that in Malaysia's public universities the politics of ethnic difference play a major part in determining not only access to education but also the ways students experience tertiary curriculum and pedagogy. Of course, ethnic politics affects not only education, it affects every aspect of economic and cultural life in Malaysia. As Oo Yu Hock points out, ethnicity is a most significant dimension of social life in Malaysia, from the ethnocentric articulation of its public policies to the constitution of its sociocultural environment.[29] Anyone who has visited Malaysia would agree that Malaysians invoke the idea of ethnicity freely in thinking about questions of identity, in organizing social relations, and in describing and explaining particular social acts.

How does the politics of ethnic difference at home inform the experiences that Malaysian students have in Australia? Many of the students of non-Bumiputra backgrounds we interviewed had an ambivalent attitude toward the consequences of their exclusion from Malaysia's public universities. While antagonistic toward and critical of affirmative action policies, most were pleased to be studying for a degree at an English-speaking university. Paradoxically, they feel their exclusion has brought them unexpected personal benefits, in terms of their prospects of obtaining a better job in the corporate sector. This is so because while Bahasa Malay, the language of instruction in local universities, may be useful to those who find employment in the public sector, the private sector, where most of the new attractive jobs are emerging, by and large prefers graduates who are able to speak English fluently and who have had exposure to a Western education. Most students interviewed maintained that one of the main reasons for wanting to study overseas was their perception that a Western degree is worth more in the emerging labor market, both within Malaysia and internationally. The expansion of market opportunities in Hong Kong, Singapore, Taiwan, and China has further strengthened the employment opportunities for Malaysians of Chinese background who are able to speak both English and Chinese, and who possess internationally recognized qualifications and experience of the world outside Malaysia. Sylvia used the phrase, "global imagination" to describe the benefits of her education in Australia: "I am not here merely to get an education but also to widen my horizons. I want to develop a global imagination."

Experiences of Diaspora

The idea of a global imagination is an interesting one. It suggests a range of critical insights about the contemporary processes of cultural globalization. The global imagination of which Sylvia spoke consisted mostly of a romantic vision of a world in which people around the world were connected with each other. It implies a cosmopolitanism in which irrational views of religious and ethnic difference did not prevail. She felt that the emerging market culture liberated the values and preferences that were once based on narrow parochialism: "I can see a time when everyone has access to a range of things which they can choose from. So if you like a particular kind of music or art, it is available. There is nothing stopping you from being a free spirit—go where you like and have what you like." Sylvia thus spoke enthusiastically about the potential of globalization. She was born in Sarawak, Malaysia, went to a university in Singapore, and was in Australia completing an MBA while continuing to work part-time for a Singapore company. She was unsure what she would do upon graduation, but returning home to Sarawak was highly unlikely.

Despite her cosmopolitan outlook, Sylvia insisted that she was still committed to her Chinese "roots" and that her current values were a mixture of Chinese and Western values. She dismissed the views of those who feared a loss of culture. She acknowledged the concern of many that the global movement of information and people, exacerbated by advances in new technologies, seriously threatened the integrity of national, regional, and specific ethnic identities, but she dismissed the claims that globalization could cause cultural disintegration and dissolution and could lead to cultural uniformity and homogeneity. On the contrary, Sylvia believed globalization could bring about greater pluralism of languages, dialects, and cultural practices: "My experience here in Australia has opened all kinds of new possibilities for me. I have made a lot of friends from all sorts of backgrounds, and I am learning about what it is like to live in another culture." Sylvia believed that her lecturers at the university did not always appreciate the cultural resources they had in their classes, "except my marketing professor; he has lived in many different parts of the world and he is always talking about whether a particular practice is relevant to a culture or not. He challenges us to think globally. I have learnt a lot from him about belonging to more than one place at the same time."

We asked Sylvia what she thought about Malaysian students in Australia, and whether ethnic differentiations in Malaysia lost their relevance in Australia: "Not at all. If anything they are stronger here. The Malay and Chinese students do not mix here like they do in Malaysia. The Chinese students discover that they have more in common with other students from Taiwan and Hong Kong and also Australian-Chinese." Sylvia added, "There is a lot of anger and resentment among Chinese students toward the Malays. Most of them have government scholarships, whereas Chinese parents have to make a lot of sacrifices to send their kids overseas." Ahmad, a Malay student, agreed that Chinese and Malay students do not mix on Australian campuses, but provided a different explanation: "Malay students are mostly shy and their English is not very good. Also, most of them do not like going to parties and things, and have to work much harder to pass." He thought that the view that Chinese students were resentful of the Malays was exaggerated.

Our interviews with Kakak provided a number of insights about the ways in which ethnic differentiations traveled from one country to another, finding new expressions in Australia. Kakak saw herself as a genuinely shy person, a "stay-at-home kind of person," as she put it. She came from a relatively poor background and never imagined that she could "make it this far." She was grateful to the Malaysian government for the generous scholarship that had enabled her to study in an Australian medical school. She felt a sense of deep loyalty toward her parents, her community, and her country. This sense of loyalty expressed itself in a range of ways. To begin with, she was incredibly hard-working, a serious student, and committed to working for the required ten years in a Malaysian rural area hospital once she graduated. Her network of friends were almost exclusively Muslims, not only from Malaysia but (significantly) from other parts of the world as well. She was part of a Muslim community that met every Friday for prayers and spent part of the weekend together. According to Kakak, "I think I have become a better Muslim since coming to Australia. I have had time to think about what Islam means to me, and my friends have helped me to understand how it is possible to be a Muslim in a Western country." Kakak insisted that "I am part of a global community. My friends come from Indonesia, South Africa, and Pakistan. Islam brings us together."

We asked Kakak whether, as a Muslim woman, she encountered any difficulties in her classes, or indeed within the broader Australian community. Kakak felt that in her course she was uncomfortable the first time she encountered male patients, and even a nude dead male body, but that she soon got over it and saw this as a normal part of her profession: "There are a lot of misconceptions about Muslim women in the West. But I can do anything as long as it is not anything immoral from the point of view of my religion." Kakak saw the Australian community as fairly tolerant: "I think there are only a few occasions when I have felt frightened. Once this group of drunken Australian men were calling out names and I think asking me to take my head cover off. I thought one of them would come over and grab it off me." Interestingly, a number of recent studies have emphasized that for many Muslim women living in the West the use of the head cover has become a politicized act whose meaning shifts depending on the articulation of the local with the global.[30] For Kakak, the head cover represented a way of coping with the challenges of living in Australia, and of emphasizing her Muslim identity. It was also a visible sign of her Islamic identity, which drew other Muslim women to her and by which she recognized them. This had the effect of forging a diasporic community of Muslim women regardless of where they were from.

Ahmad's attitude toward his Muslim background was in sharp contrast to that of Kakak. He felt that Islam no longer held any special significance for him: "Of course, I am a Muslim but I have also become very Westernized. My parents have noticed the difference and although they do not say this I know they disapprove. I can't see why you cannot be both

Muslim and Western." He added, "I used to go to the mosque in my first year, but then I got too busy, and felt I didn't want to hang around with Muslim students all the time." Ahmad was particularly upset with the pressure he felt he was put under to conform: "Muslim students, not only Malaysian Muslims but also Pakistanis, would come up to me and say why do I not go to the mosque any more. And that I was losing my culture and religion and stuff like that. I said you just want to control me, make sure that I do things that you want." Ahmad's story suggests some of the ways in which ethnic and religious identities are steered, disciplined, and monitored by diasporic communities in their various stages of formation. As Antoun has pointed out, in the context of a Western society, Muslim groups, besieged by their negative portrayal in the media and in the broader community at large, often resort to a range of surveillance measures to ensure that individuals maintain their faith.[31] As for Ahmad, he was happy to "live on the border" that has become so characteristic of the postmodern condition.

The story of Khai also reveals some of the ways in which international education is a site of diasporic experiences. Khai was born in Kuala Lumpur and came to Australia via senior schooling and two university courses in Taiwan. At the time of the interviews, he was undertaking his doctoral studies in sociology. His research was concerned with issues of Chinese ethnicity in Sarawak. Why did he go to Taiwan for studies? Khai explained, "I went to Taiwan because my parents had family links in Taiwan, and they felt that I would get a much better education in a Chinese-speaking country than in Malaysia where Malay language and culture are compulsory." Khai's family saw Taiwan as their home, a major reference point for defining its ethnicity. Yet, Khai's experiences in Taiwan demonstrated to him how different "Malaysian Chineseness" was, with its own distinctive cultural values and practices. In Australia, Khai had further developed his Chinese diasporic networks. He had a number of friends who were Australians of Chinese background born in a variety different countries. Khai believed that while the term "Chinese" did not represent a homogenous category, there was nonetheless a global network of Chinese people. He viewed international education in Australia as contributing to the consolidation of this network. He personally knew of an Indonesian student of Chinese background who "has established a business connection" with another student from Shanghai: "In my view, when we are in

Australia we work out new ways of being Chinese. We learn from each other, and help each other to cope with Australian education. In the process we become friends, which might last forever." Where was Khai planning to work upon graduation? "I would like to go back to Malaysia. My parents want me to. I think I can still do something there although my emotional attachment to Malaysia is not all that strong. But as a Chinese I am not sure I will find it easy to get a job there. I might go to the United States."

Education and Global Imagination

The stories of the four Malaysian students in Australia illustrate some complexities of the contemporary processes of globalization. Above all, they demonstrate that the fear of unbridled Westernization is misplaced. The suggestion that international education represents an accelerating trend toward Westernization is unfounded. True, the movement of students for education is largely unidirectional, but this does not imply that the international students soak up every cultural message they encounter in the West. Student identities can never be treated as self-evident: they are saturated with the experiences of colonial histories, local cultural diversity, and political complexity, on the one hand, and with the contemporary homogenizing experiences of "global media spaces" on the other.[32] Calhoun has argued:

> Identities are always rooted in part in ideals and moral aspirations that cannot fully realise. There is, therefore, a tension within us which can be both the locus of personal struggle and the source of an identity politics that aims not simply at the legitimation of falsely essential categorical identities but at living up to deeper social and moral values.[33]

And so it is with international education, which has clearly become a force that helps reshape student identities, their cultural tastes, and professional aspirations, but in ways that are neither uniform nor predictable. Students interpret their experiences in a variety of ways, and their global imagination is always a product of a range of factors, some of which are known to them, others of which are not.

It is just as well to remember that students from Asian countries like Malaysia had already been subjected to Western cultural pressures well before they came to Australia for education. The colonial history of education in Asia had already eroded many of the cultural traditions of learning in the region. Indeed, the very notion of bureaucratically organized mass education is a Western construct, which was imposed by Europe upon its Other. Schooling played a major part in the development of colonial imagination.[34] The curriculum offered in the colonies was strictly prescribed and monitored by the colonial authorities in Europe. The Cambridge examinations, it should be noted, are still popular in many parts of Asia. The colonial education did much to engender Western cultural tastes, aspirations, and values among the Asian elite. The nationalist movements in Asia viewed education as a major force for the decolonialization of the people they represented. The fear of many leaders of these movements with memories of freedom struggles is that, having gained a measure of cultural control, they now risk losing it again through the inducements of new technologies, cultural movements, and student mobility.

What the student stories do show, however, is that pressures toward homogenization witnessed under colonialism are different from the current forms of cultural globalization. Globalization is much more complex. It is not universally imposed by a colonial power upon the colonized, but rather is something that affects people and nations in a variety of different ways that are both asymmetrical and contingent. It has a commercial dimension that makes it sensitive to the needs of both markets and clients. It is sensitive to difference and preaches the need to respond to local needs. It has a culturally interactive disposition, even to the point of commodifying difference, constructing it so it can be sold in terms of a language of diversity and multiculturalism. As their stories suggest, the students do not feel any pressure to conform to Western norms.

At the same time, however, international education does appear to produce in students a global imagination in which the notions of mobility, tranculturalism, and diaspora are especially significant. Here I use the term imagination in ways similar to Appadurai. According to Appadurai, "There has been a shift in recent decades, building upon technological changes over the past century or so, in which imagination has become a collective social fact. This development, in turn, is the basis of the plurality of imagined worlds."[35] Imagination is the attempt to provide coherence between ideas and action, to provide a basis for the content of social relationships and the creation of categories with which to understand the world around us. What is imagined defines what we regard as normal. Thus viewed, imagination is not an attribute possessed by a few endowed individuals but, instead, denotes a collective sense of a group of people, a community that begins to imagine and feel things together. To Appadurai, this imagination, this collective sense of ourselves, characterizes contemporary diasporic spaces, resulting from the increased flows of ideas, people, and cultures. In the past, much of the work of imagination was mediated through the nation-state. But now imagination transcends national boundaries and emerges in a variety of ways.[36] And so it is that international education becomes a site for the creation of diasporic spaces. As the stories of Khai and Sylvia show, their global imagination is linked to their developing sense of identity as part of a Chinese diaspora, just as Ahmad is forced to consider issues of his religious affiliation within the broader context of a Muslim diasporic space.

Diasporic communities have, of course, always existed, but there is something new and distinctive about the flows of students in search of an international education. Unlike the immigrants or refugees of past generations who were forced by political, religious, and economic difficulties to migrate—the new diaspora of transnational and transcultural students move overseas temporarily, chasing economic, social, educational, and cultural opportunities. This new diaspora represents privileged elites for whom an international education plays a pivotal role in their identity formation. They, and other highly mobile groups like them, occupy powerful positions upon their return home and have considerable influence on policy and politics disproportionate to their actual numbers. As mobile groups, it is they who are able to imagine the nation and its links to the outside world in radically new ways. With formative international experiences, they are able to look at the world as dynamic and multicultural. This is so because they operate within a hybridized space and are equally comfortable in more than one cultural site. Their identity is intercultural with multiple cultural defining points. They typify a new global generation.

Notes

1. This research project, titled "Marketing Education to Asia," was funded by the Australian Research Council, whose support is gratefully acknowledged, as is the contribution of Don Alexander and especially Karen Dooley, who assisted with many of the interviews. The names used for the four students included in this essay are pseudonyms.
2. Zaniah Marshallsay, ed., *Challenges Facing Malaysian Education* (Melbourne: Monash Asia Institute, 1997), 2.
3. James Clifford, "Traveling Cultures," in *Cultural Studies*, ed. Lawrence Grossberg et al. (London: Routledge, 1992).
4. George Soros, *The Crisis of Global Capitalism* (Boston: Little, Brown, 1998).
5. Paul Hirst and John Thompson, *Globalisation in Question* (Cambridge, Eng.: Polity Press, 1995).
6. Ann Capling, Mark Considine, and Michael Crozier, *Australian Politics in the Global Era* (Melbourne: Addison-Wesley, 1998), 5.
7. John Wiseman, *The Global Nation: Australia's Response to Globalisation* (Melbourne: Cambrige University Press, 1998), 15.
8. Malcolm Waters, *Globalization* (London: Routledge, 1995), 9.
9. Jan Pietersen and Bikhu Parekh, eds., *The Decolonialisation of Imagination* (London: Zed Books, 1995), 14.
10. Zygmunt Bauman, *Globalization* (Cambridge, Eng.: Polity Press, 1998).
11. Arjun Appadurai, *Modernity at Large* (Minneapolis: University of Minnesota Press, 1996).
12. Imre Wallerstein, *The Politics of the World Economy*, 3d ed. (Cambridge: Cambridge University Press, 1991).
13. Akbar Ahmad and Hastings Donnan, eds., *Islam, Globalisation and Postmodernity* (London: Routledge, 1994), 3.
14. George Ritzer, *The McDonaldisation of Society* (Thousand Oaks, Calif.: Pine Oaks Press, 1993).
15. Rey Chow, *Writing Diaspora: Tactics of Intervention in Contemporary Cultural Studies* (Bloomington: Indiana University Press, 1993).
16. Ahmad and Donnan, *Islam*, 3.
17. Carol Brechenbridge and Arjun Appadurai, "On Moving Targets," *Public Culture* 2, no. 1 (1989): 1.
18. Pietersen and Parekh, *The Decolonialisation*, 15.
19. Robin Cohen, *Global Diaspora: An Introduction* (London: U.C.L. Press, 1997), 173.
20. Homi Bhabha, *The Location of Culture* (London: Routledge, 1994).
21. Joel Kahn, *Culture, Multiculture, Postculture* (London: Sage, 1995).
22. Gardner, quoted in Ahmed and Donnan, *Islam*, 6.
23. Urz Harrenz, "Cosmopolitans and Locals in World Culture," in *Global Culture: Nationalism, Globalisation and Modernity*, ed. M. Featherstone (London: Sage, 1990).
24. Stephen Pile and Nigel Thrift, *Mapping the Subject: Geographies of Cultural Transformation* (London: Routledge, 1995), 10.
25. Stuart Hall, "Old and New Identities, Old and New Ethnicities," in *Culture*,

Globalisation and the World System, ed. Anthony King (London: MacMillan, 1991), 48.

26. Harold Crouch, *Government and Society in Malaysia* (Sydney: Allen and Unwin, 1996).

27. Waters, *Globalization*, 81.

28. Curtis Andersen, *The End of an Era: Contemporary Trends in Malaysian Students Movement to Australia* (Adelaide, Australia: Asian Studies Discipline, Flinders University of South Australia Press, 1993).

29. Oo Yu Hock, *Ethnic Chameleon: Multiracial Politics in Malaysia* (Selangor, Malysia: Peelanduk Publications, 1991).

30. For example, Helen Watson, "Women and the Veil: Personal Responses to Global Processes," in *Islam, Globalisation and Postmodernity*, ed. Akbar Ahmad and Hastings Donnan (London: Routledge, 1994).

31. Richard Antoun, "Sojourners Abroad: Migration for Higher Education in a Post-peasant Muslim Society," in *Islam, Globalisation and Postmodernity*, ed. Akbar Ahmad and Hastings Donnan (London: Routledge, 1994).

32. David Morley and Kevin Robins, *Spaces of Identity* (London: Routledge, 1995).

33. Craig Calhoun, *Critical Social Theory* (Oxford, Eng.: Blackwell, 1995), 224.

34. Homi Bhabha, *Location of Cultures* (London: Routledge, 1995).

35. Appadurai, *Modernity*, 5.

36. Richard Wilson and Wanke Dissanayake, eds., *Global/Local: Cultural Production and the Transnational Imaginary* (Durham:, N.C.: Duke University Press, 1996).

Globalization, A Fading Citizenship

Juan-Ramón Capella

The Indefinite Globalization

Pier Paolo Pasolini says that the world always undergoes changes, but from time to time the change of the world produces an "end of the world."[1] There is one such change taking place now. We do not live in the world of Henry Ford, of mass workers, or of decolonization anymore, nor of course in the world of traditional society. A "great transformation," in the words of Polanyi,[2] has taken place, which is referred to as the beginning of a globalized society.

However, the uses of "globalization" are not uncontested, nor is this, whatever it is, the main element of this "great transformation." Nowadays globalization is still blurred and hard to define, as we shall see. Some of the uses of "globalization" mainly stress the planetary reach of the process of exchange of goods, the formation of gigantic multinational enterprises in the shape of networks of folded-up centers of production, or the virtual abolition of time because of the instantaneous quality of communications all over the planet. The concept of "globalization" forms the technological features of the contemporary world.[3] But is globalization fundamentally a by-product of technology? Why not then discuss the characteristics of the third industrial revolution? The lack of precision with which we sometimes talk about globalization, stressing the virtual abolition of time and distance as its main features, makes it difficult to critically and precisely regard this process of growing interconnection between societies.

Globalization has moved quickly in a few years. Limits to the flow of financial resources, goods, and services cease to exist or simply wane, and these flows are constant. This serves to show how much globalization depends on political factors. The globalization of communications is established in the sense of worldwide circulation as well as in the elimination of strongholds resilient to external social action. *Above all, "globalization" means interdependence.* Social action interweaves on a planetary scale and the consequences of human intervention turn out to be increasingly labyrinthine. A new structuration of space and distance, on the one hand, and time, on the other, is occurring. Some processes are now, paradoxically, *simultaneous* all over the planet, producing effects in many locations at once.

Nevertheless there are dark sides to this new interconnection: for instance, the global dimension of some environmental problems. Such is the case with the increasing destruction of the ozone layer in the Earth's atmosphere, acid rain, or the advance of deforestation and desertization. This globalization of ecological problems appears as the consequence of industrial technologies employed in an economy whose success depends on growth, on constant expansion.

If we call the increasing world interconnection of social relations "globalization," then it is necessary to include in that phenomenon both evident interconnections (for instance, the ones derived from communications technology) and less evident interconnections (such as those revealing certain aspects of the world environmental problem).

• • • •

Globalization is misshapen, or uneven, not uniform. The "world-system," to employ a term by Immanuel Wallerstein,[4] has a nucleus in the "North," composed of Japan, the European Union, and the United States, and the "South," or the periphery of scarcely developed countries. A new bipolarity has been generated.[5] The "North" includes semiperipheral surroundings that try to catch up with its standards of development, while the "South" has its own periphery, as it has sometimes been called an "external theater" of countries, which are not just dismal but atrociously and increasingly so.

Globalization affects various peoples around the planet in different ways. Regarded as a multinational network of financial markets it influences three or four "world centers": the United States, Europe, Japan, and Southeast Asia. In this aspect of globalization the rest of the planet appears as a black hole.[6] However, in this black hole, for the poor peasants of Asia, sub-Saharan Africa, and Latin America, other issues arise locally as well, influencing agricultural means and techniques, modified by episodes of the world markets or agro-industrial innovations, and dissolving traditional ways of life.[7]

Globalization is conspicuous in the hypermarket, in the big commercial surface of the "northern" metropolises, where agricultural produce does not know of seasons or origin anymore; where clothes of notorious makes, produced by enslaved children somewhere across the universe, lie available; and where, on the television sets on display, you can watch pictures of massacre or famine, or some sports show, all of it live.

Metropolitans live with the normality of this exclusion of others, which they cannot ignore even though they integrate it into their day-to-day routine. Globalization strains the crisis of society as such: it implies a hyper-socialization lived subjectively in the metropolises as a way to reject social life. The leading trend appears to be that contemporary metropolitans do not positively want the society they live in and individualistic and fundamentalist ideas than on gaining strength among them. A large majority of metropolitans neither want *another* society nor are they able to picture its possibility: they are privatized individuals, subjectively *dissociated* from the rest. However, globalization objectively composes a new economic and cultural universe; as an ultimate condition, it is a part of the processes generated by the third industrial revolution. The metropolitan destiny, the peripheral, and that of the poor are reciprocally interdependent.

In short, the current globalization is a tension-generating process, one from which a new world rises. It seems irreversible. This phenomenon, however, has become apparent during a phase of history characterized by: a general worldwide defeat of the classic emancipation movements, the workers' and peasants' movements, who see the breakthroughs of past decades vanish; the implantation of new liberation movements, such as feminism and antisexism; the end of the fall of the East-West polarity; and the end of the peasant culture as such in the metropolises of the "North."

Perhaps because of this, the social ocean is made far too rough by a large number of changes not necessarily interrelated, and it is not possible to predict accurately the basic features of globalization that are going to remain in the future. In this sense, the concept of "globalization" may be relatively indefinite.

We should analyze what globalization means to the intervention of human beings in the shaping of public policies, since, there too, essential changes are noticeable. However, the phenomenon of globalization seriously modifies the meaning of the expression "public policies." One wonders, more specifically, about the consequences of globalization for the *citizens*, the political subjects to whom the final determination of public policies is attributed, and for the foundations of modern political systems and institutions.

To that effect, I will analyze here, first, the conceptual features of citizenship in the modern era, its weaknesses and strengths and, second, the institutional features of contemporary power characteristic of globalization. From there, the conditions to form a provisional diagnosis will be offered.

Modern Citizenship: A Guide of Urgency

The citizenship of the moderns is not the citizenship of old. The citizenship of old was socially articulated not only as a privilege before the excluded but as a *quality* of the person. The Athenians were raised to be citizens.[8] They had a gymnastic education, since citizenship demanded the skill of a warrior capable of defending the city, and they were also educated at the agora, qualifying to discuss public affairs as business different from their own.

Modern citizenship, however, does not apparently demand an education

or qualifications in an explicit way. It does not appear as a personal quality. Neither is it, in principle, a privilege, at least during the modern era.
Our condition as citizens only exists in a special discursive sphere. It lies in
the political-legal universe. In other words, the symbolic meaning of the
modern citizen and his or her functions only appear in a universe constituted by typically modern political images.

An essential condition of that world of collective political images, its
basic hidden axiom, is the representation of all social relations as belonging to a distinct *sphere* (or "world"): the public sphere or the private
sphere.

In the modern political context the *private* sphere is the world of relations between particular human beings—a universe of relations which, as
a principle, are only relevant for those who take part in them, such as affec-
tive relations or business. This private sphere is the world of qualities and
particularities: thus, each person's religion, race, cultural qualifications,
and sexual orientation are the business of the private sphere. The *public*
sphere is the realm of common affairs in each modern society as such, in
the established society. It is, factually or potentially, the relevant sphere for
everyone.

This breakup of society into two spheres is typically modern and obviously occurs in the field of representation and the symbolic meanings acting upon those who live in modern societies. The feudal symbolic world
overlooks this distinction: feudal relations of hierarchy, for instance, are
not only both economic and, shall we say, political but also economic-
cultural-political in one indifferent block. Likewise, the feudal ruler is not
just the supreme political power: he is the *supreme power*, political, economic, and ideological-cultural all at once. By contrast, with modernity the
ruler only exists in the public sphere.[9] It is the ruler who must decide the
standards of public order in the private sphere (for example, banning drug
trafficking). The private sphere is subordinate to the public sphere at this
point: in the rules imposing "public order" upon the private sphere.

Modern citizenship is therefore made in a very peculiar manner. It is
mostly made just in the public sphere. In order to regard anyone as a citizen we must make a double intellectual operation. First, we have to deprive
them of all the attributions that characterize them as human. We have to
represent the individual deprived of sex, social class, race, community
roots, religion, personal qualities, wealth or poverty, and so forth, since all

these features are immaterial to citizenship.[10] Only when people become deprived of the features that characterize them in the private sphere is it possible to introduce them in the public sphere with the trappings of citizenship. These trappings are composed of the essential laws and rights: freedom of conscience, expression, reunion, association, demonstration; the right to live, to vote, to have property; the inviolability of the domicile; and the protection from arrest save in cases prescribed by the law.

Only by means of a double discursive operation, abstracting their qualities first and then attributing rights to them, can the people become equal and indiscernible in the public sphere. And so, as each vote is worth the same, each vote counts for one. Or, to put this point in a negative way: the citizen can be characterized by an absence of material qualities, whereas what characterizes citizenship is its rights.

It is worthwhile then to wonder what exactly those rights of citizenship are. It is not possible for someone to have a right if no one has a duty to match that right. The category "right," as Simone Weil sharply perceived, is not primary, but derived from the category of duty.[11] For instance, it is said that a person has the right to possess something; well then, in order for "having a right of property" to have content (that is, so that it is meaningfully relevant), it is imperative that the rest of society has a duty toward it—in this case, the *duty* not to interfere in what is protected by that person's right of property. That duty really exists if a public social institution, like the state, can be called to enforce it against those who do not observe the obligation not to interfere. The state's duty to intervene if it is necessary is the ultimate guarantee of any right on the formal-juridical plane.

There is no right whatsoever without the attached string of other peoples' and public institutions' duties, which amount to the "content" of the right. To speak about rights means to speak about sociopolitical relationships, but never between persons and things. The material relation between a person and a thing, for instance, between an inhabitant and a dwelling, is a relation different from the juridical ones that can be set in the constitution of a right upon that dwelling, such as being its owner, leaseholder, or a mere middle person without the title deed, which, in each case, implies different duties for others and for public institutions.[12]

One might now ask specifically about the content of the rights of citizenship. It is the same as asking who has the duties corresponding to those of citizenship. It is obvious that the duty of no interference corresponding to my right to life or freedom, and so forth, rests upon everybody else. But the state also has a duty, the duty to enforce rights against their transgressors. There are even basic rights of citizenship, like the right to vote, whose content is exclusively formed by the state's duties. And if we bear in mind the historic genesis of the modern rights of citizenship we shall notice immediately that they are *rights before the state*,[13] that is, that the duties corresponding to such rights are certain duties of the state.

It seems paradoxical that the essential content of the rights of citizenship should be the duties of an entity, the state, which is also obliged to enforce those rights. In this light, taking for granted the rights of citizenship seems extremely feeble. Juridically, nothing guarantees that a state, in certain situations of political or social tension, sticks to its duties. Whether it does so or not is a material question of sociopolitical power.

This paradox recalls the limited, or weak, foundation of modern democracy, based in real history on the *passion for autonomy and freedom* of some generations of the people, and on their loathing of the tyrannical exercise of political power.

● ● ● ●

Therefore the foundations of democracy are features of the real social world—features that are necessary so that the process of modern democratization will not enter a regressive phase. The foundations of democracy, elements of the political project of the real people, for whom autonomy and freedom become a passion, "in which its passion for autonomy and freedom crystallizes," have to be reproduced socially. In other words: this fragility of the democracy of the moderns shows that, in spite of appearances, education for autonomy and freedom is an implicit requirement of the project of political democracy crystallized in institutions.

But this is not the principal conclusion relevant to my analysis. It must also be seen that the condition of citizenship, as long as it is constituted of rights whose content originates in the duties of the state, has some material demands. On the one hand, there is a demand of *localization*. The rights, exercised before certain institutional entities, are guaranteed by magistrates and civil servants inside accurate institutional frames. The classics of modern political thought were clearly aware of the necessity of territorial localization of rights and power. On the other hand, there is a demand of *financing*. Asserting that citizenship needs to be financed economically may seem an economistic way to speak about it, a neoliberal absurdity, but this is not so. If citizenship consists of an ensemble of rights, and rights are guaranteed by institutions, those institutions' financing becomes a basic condition so that we can speak about rights at not merely an ideological level (although the ideological level is also real and has real functions, such as in education or propaganda). The institutions' financing is a requisite in order to be able to speak about rights and citizenship.

In another realm, citizenship demands essential requisites of *institutional legality*, that is, that public institutions work as such.[14] When this does not happen—for instance, in the "Vampire States," institutions completely or sufficiently patrimonialized by political elites for their own lucrative sake[15]—citizenship is just a ghostly entity. It also demands that its own survival is not generally questioned, as happens in some *not globalized* areas on the planet where people, among other shortcomings, even lack the capability of rebelling.

• • • •

There is a large amount of literature dealing with the universalism of modern citizenship rights. The universalism of rights is, at its very best, a programmatic intention.[16] The Bill of Rights did not give America's original natives their citizenship nor did the Men and Citizens' Bill of Rights free a single slave in the French colony of Haiti.

That the existence of citizenship should be so intensely dependent on institutions, as we pointed out before, can be explained by the fact that the modern stabilization of citizenship has been based on the citizen's juridical *rights* and not on his political *powers*. This deserves special consideration.

Historically, the people who have struggled to gain their autonomy and their freedom, whether they were American patriots rising against the British dominion, or French revolutionaries fighting against monarchic absolutism, had to get *power* before obtaining their *rights*. This historical process has the following order: first, significant sectors of the people obtain material power (which entails work, sacrifice, and organization); then, they gain institutional political power; and finally, they renounce significant sectors of material power in favor of the state, in exchange for their rights of citizenship. In all, the process neutralizes the struggling peoples' material power by turning it into rights—which ultimately means into the state's rights, leading to the absence of any *social powers* politically recognized outside those of the state's power. Modernity has given up building citizenship as *power*.

In substance, this is modern citizenship, upon which globalization, through substantial changes in the real systems of power, has its effects.

Vague Private Ruler and Open State

It seems necessary to begin a reflection upon contemporary power with an observation of a methodological kind. Until now the action of political power could be treated according to the physical metaphor of *causes*. As long as more complexity was introduced—because of the socialized nature of power in the modern state, functionally "split" between different pluripersonal institutions—it could credibly be said that certain social facts were *caused* by power itself. The cognitive efficacy of the metaphor of a (political) power agent, of a *causal* force set in motion by that agent's *will*, was taken for granted; it is not even unusual to find in political discourse derived metaphors like those of *correlation of political forces*, *square value of forces*, or *political distance*—metaphors borrowed from classical physics.

With globalization, understanding the phenomenon of general power (which we have been calling *public power*) ceases to be possible in such simple terms. If we want to conserve the idea of the determination of social life by entities bearing power we must resort to a more complex metaphor, such as the notion of a *force field*, from modern physics. That is, we must renounce the idea of a single causal agent and go on to speak about a realm wherein determinations are raised, even though these cannot be linearly attributed to a single generating agent, or even though, in any concrete situation, the determination of the generator gets obscured or is plainly impossible within the *field*. Here we are speaking about interrelated determinations.

On reconsidering the feudal, original concept of sovereignty as *indistinct* power, integrating what the moderns call distinct natures (political power, economic power, ideological power), the idea of a new sovereignty of a *pri-*

vate nature added to the power of the state will become admissible. Naturally, it compels us to question the axiom of modern political discourse, according to which the *private sphere* lacks public or political relevance. This is what must be rectified on the theoretical plane so as to conserve a minimal realism in the analysis of power.

Traditional political "theory"[17] comes to a crisis and loses its explanatory capability when it restricts itself to contemplating the powers of the state without admitting that there are external limitations in certain fields of action. These limits are imposed by the concentration and transnationalization of economic power, which was more fragmentary in the past. Globalization alters the "national" market, one of the foundations of the nation-state's power. Industrial capitalism, however, has not freed itself entirely from its original features, which make it regionally diverse: there are considerable differences between Japanese and American enterprises, or between American and European capitalisms, which result in distinctive productive, cultural, and social practices. For this reason, the features of the globalized world are still vague and nothing indicates that they could not change.

• • • •

"Political" power has modified its basic structure with globalization; for the first time since the birth of modernity it cannot be described in terms of simple sovereignty and legitimacy. The contemporary *force field* is constituted by the interrelation of a *vague suprastate private ruler* and—since the territorial basis of localization of power for determinate functions remains—an *open state* or *state associations* (such as the European Union), which are *permeable, open,* or *porous.*[18]

Likewise, it ceases to be true that the system of legitimation recognized in the accepted political version—in Western metropolises, the democratic-representative version—is the only operating one: the *force field* admits the simultaneous presence of various systems of legitimation. The existence of the new bipolar *force field* (on the one hand, a suprastate private ruler of vague character; on the other, an open state system), now falsifies all political discourse limited to the concept of the "ruler state." It falsifies it by making it ideological, in the sense of not giving a truthful representation of what happens in the world of experience.

There is indeed a new power imposing upon the state certain policies, especially in the configuration of the economic realm. This power has a suprastate character. On favoring monetarism, deregulation, free trading, unrestrained capital flow, and mass privatization, political representatives have enabled the transfer of fundamental decisions from the public sphere to the private sphere.

In the historical period of the interventionist state the transfer of large amounts of public financial resources to private companies (by means of programs of space exploration, military research, or programs of development) has already made these enterprises hugely powerful. The formation of the vague suprastate private ruler has been gradual. However, the vague suprastate private ruler is not a totally independent power. It acts in close relation with the *open states*, integrating a force field.

The power of the suprastate ruler, which is *private*, has effects of a *public* nature precisely because it determines the policies of the state. Not only is the *vague ruler* capable of imposing its political options on the state by penetrating the will of its institutions, but it also prevents carrying out certain policies decided by the institutions of the state when they happen to be inconsistent with suprastate policies.

The origin and nature of the *titular* of this suprastate ruling power is *private*, however (according to the distinction of *spheres* peculiar to the modern political version of society). This titular is neither a by-product of interstate agreements, nor an institution of international law, nor has it been established or legitimated by human beings' deliberate will. On the contrary: it is a power of objective nature, corresponding to the productive organization in the era of globalization. On the other hand, the power is vague: it is not concentrated in just a few hands or determinate headquarters.

The *suprastate private ruler* is constituted by the joint strategic power of big transnational companies and mostly, nowadays, of financial conglomerates. It imposes itself by organizations of diverse kind: conventional interstate ones, like the G-7 (a conference group of the most industrialized countries), which is essential for the regulation of world trade; institutions like the World Bank and the International Monetary Fund (both generated by the Bretton Woods agreements); the OECD; or the World Trade Organization. It also imposes itself through private law-making instances such as those set up so that large transnational economic groups can inter-relate, thanks to the new *lex mercatoria* resolved among them.

The suprastate private ruler has assumed the function of setting the general conditions necessary for the operation of transnational companies: to facilitate the flows of financial capital; to eliminate or graduate incompatibilities or frontiers of technology, politics, or customs and any type of barrier concerning the trade of goods and services; and to decide the realms of performance of the different economic groups. It has also assumed the general strategic orientation of a globalized economy. However, the decisions of suprastate ruling must still be orchestrated by auxiliary open powers of the state.

The suprastate private ruler marks the type and conditions of economic policy in each area of the globe, while simultaneously the conditions of the monetary system, and settles the main growth options and demands for the system of open states—states with limited sovereignty, relatively available for the new real sovereign. The states' corresponding public decisions range from economic and social policies themselves to decisions on military policy necessary for the preservation of the world's status quo. The open state (generally a nation-state), which originally assumed the explicit and manifest public power in a society,[19] must now implement policies marked by the vague ruler's supracommanding entity.

The enlarging of the state's bureaucratic apparatus and its political-administrative intervention into economic activity used to be seen as linked to the policies of the interventionist welfare state (prior to globalization); but, significantly, even as those politics disappeared or waned, and despite the new and imposed conditions of globalization, the state has not "withered away." Neither the state's bureaucratic apparatus nor its public intervention into social and economic affairs has disappeared or changed fundamentally, save for the privatization of public enterprises. An analysis of the functions of the open state explains these phenomena. The state's management and political-administrative intervention into economic activity keep up, just changing their sign. As a principle it can be said that where, formerly, the state was ready to enforce the duties imposed on business management, it now veils the privileges granted to it. As J. Petras writes, "Far from being opposed to the predominance of the state, multinational capital demands an 'activist state' that sets apart the *welfare state* in favor of globalization."[20]

The open or permeable state, undergoing a clear loss of ruling power, must continue to intervene in the economy with policies of deregulation and adjustment of regulations. It must give transnational enterprises juridical-political guarantees of autonomy, while simultaneously socializing the costs of labor in the realm of the public sphere. It must deregulate the labor market (eliminating entrepreneurial obligations in this area). It must create new economic spaces for private activity, and therefore is forced, first, to privatize the former public sector and, second, to exploit the public services in a measure compatible at once with social peace and the demands of the vague ruler.

Very significantly, it must create the conditions in which it is possible to directly privatize any social innovation, either produced in the private sphere or the public sphere. At the same time that the state must agree to provide transnational enterprises with financing, by now in competition with other states, so that the enterprises will establish segments of their productive network in the territory over which the state has ruling power, it must also invest in technological innovation susceptible to privatization—all of this without giving up its traditional functions, still compatible with economic globalization in some cases, and demanded by globalization in others. (For example, it has the burden of attending to those excluded from economic well-being; of securing a system of *circenses* as a way to escape from social tension; of repairing ecological damage; and, of course, of overseeing education and job training.)

The economic, fiscal, and labor policies of the open state are not the only ones modulated by the *force field* in which the state's institutions interact with the vague ruler. On the one hand there are environmental policies, whose importance seriously restrains the vague ruler. On the other hand, as noted previously, military policies play a very significant role. In other fields, like education, the demands on the open state made by the vague ruler are less urgent—that is, they allow the historical features of the ruled societies a larger scope of adaptation—although the public politics are strongly conditioned by the influence of the transnational companies of the cultural industry, whose impact on social conscience is nowadays superior to that of educational institutions themselves. Today the big products of the audiovisual industry—television series like *Dallas* or pop stars like *Madonna*, to point out instances that happen to be obsolete—end up being much more alive and influential in our collective conscience than the great historical creations of culture, from *Oedipus* to *Hamlet*, from *Quixote* to *The Passion According to St. Matthew*.

The limitation of the open state's ruling power creates a conflict within its legitimation system, which erodes the standard of democracy reached in each case. Also *open*, at least in the economic aspect, are those states whose legitimation system is not democratic, like those whose political authorities legitimate themselves through religious fundamentalism.

The open state ruled by a democratic-representative system is obviously based on "popular sovereignty." Since *this* sovereignty is hampered, the citizens themselves have their capability of decision making objectively limited. The central elements in the state pole of the system—the executive government, which is the state power par excellence, and the parliament—are subject to contradictory tensions: on one side, by demands from the vague suprastate ruler, who must reach the central decisive core of the state and be present in it; on the other, by the citizens' demands, until recently "sovereign," which may (and often do) contradict the former.

The crisis of public political representation—of parliamentary institutions in the first place—appears inevitable, even though the bureaucratization and oligarchization of the political party system contribute to that crisis, too. In certain ways political representation is doomed to lose all its legitimacy, and all its decisive capability, before the people. It reinforces a perverted self-fed logic: the trend toward depoliticization and passivity among the peoples who have tolerated the rise of a suprastate ruling power outside the democratic principles and institutions. Democratic politics, as a conscious and explicit activity of the collectivity concerned with the instauration of its institutions, tends to get obstructed.

• • • •

Both poles of the force field—the vague suprastate ruler and the open states—rely on different legitimation systems.

The nature of the suprastate ruler prevents it from taking over the legitimation systems adopted by the state's institutions. It cannot resort to legitimation systems of a communitarian type, such as those of nationalism or fundamentalism, for it is unable to present itself as a community since it is exclusive of the peoples as such. Nor can it present itself as a democratic power (not even in a debased conception of democracy as merely procedural), because it opposes the democratic powers in progress. It also cannot be legitimated for structural reasons: because it is vague, *not located*, and because it is manifested only spectrally, not *institutionally*, in the public sphere.

The legitimacy intended by the suprastate private ruler is that of *efficacy*. The strategic power of the great economic agents relies on a discourse of *technical-productive efficacy* that is beginning to be adopted not only by the public institutions but also by the dominated societies.[21]

This discourse of "productive" efficacy gains currency and gradually settles in the collective imagination of the "northern" peoples, as long as that discourse coexists with the representative institutions under which the vague ruler has arisen. The discourse of efficacy "with its patent truths of economic growth and progress" seems only natural to those persons who, instead of taking part as citizens, look on the political spectacle from their consumerist niche; it is fitting for those who lead "a very private life" and stick to their particular relationships, neglecting public affairs.[22] "Efficacy" is a "quality of the system," the *well-meaning tyrant* who is supposed to be providing a 2 or 3 percent annual income growth rate in the "northern" metropolises.

The transforming efficacy of industrialism, regarded as the capability to expand productive forces, cannot be denied. Still, in this light, "efficacy" is the name of a complex ensemble. This same efficacy, for example, is also responsible for the social and environmental catastrophes generated by the productivist expansion. Because of this complex mix of consequences, efficacy is not the *real* transforming capability that legitimates the vague ruler.

Instead, the legitimating effect of "efficacy" is as a Platonic ideal, rendered ideological by a belief in technoscientific transformation: a purged version of its perverted aspects, whether inadvertent or intrinsic.

The discourse of efficacy tries to present the right economic policy for the maximum expansion of big multinational enterprises and the maximum gain for financial capital as the only possible logic, the one logic of modernization. It presents the market as independent from its political conditions of existence, as the natural state of society. This discourse characterizes the suprastate ruler's projects as the only ones bearing rationality. That is why I. Ramonet has happily named it "only thought."[23] It is an exclusive discourse—that is, it does not give reasons, it does not converse with other logics. It is indeed a totalitarian discourse.

The discourse of "efficacy" expresses in fact the *law of the fittest*, not for individuals but socially/economically. It is the law of the big conglomerates, of economic agents capable of subordinating the smallest. One might call it the discourse of a partisan *ius natural*. It is, in fact, the same discourse addressed by the Athenians to the Melians, inhabitants of a little island that had the wrong idea of joining the enemies of Athens: "From now on—stated the Athenian ambassadors—the relations between us won't be ruled by convention, which is the law between equals, but by the Law of Nature." The Athenian ambassadors, on being asked by the Melians what that Law of Nature was like, answered, "You know it too well: It is the Law of Nature for the lamb to be devoured by the wolf."[24]

Toward a New Citizenship?

With the new power system of globalization, the realm of public policies that the citizen can determine through the state political systems decreases considerably. Politics in the sense of the assignment of general social goals or ends defines itself to an increasing degree in relation to a transnational private sphere. The classic institutions of *mediation*, the political parties, become organisms of national-state *accommodation* and leveling. These institutions determine which policies can be acceptable both for the vague ruler and for the citizens, eliminating or excluding the others.

The *location* of citizenship is the state, as a theoretical place of determination for public politics. Today its location is constituted by the open states, increasingly dependent upon the vague ruler for the definition of public policies.

Citizens can only act as such in public, through representative systems, in an increasingly residual way. The institutions must pretend not to hear their demands if they are to conduct the vague ruler's policies. Before the latter, rights of citizenship prove to be useless. The citizens exist in the public sphere and the vague ruler in the private sphere. The vague ruler is not to be found and citizens act through localization. The vague ruler shuns institutionalization, and the citizens require the institutions for legitimation.

The citizens as such cannot take part in the "private sphere," the realm where the "vague ruler" has been generated and resides. The *deregulation* imposed by this ruler on all of the open states entrusts negotiation, in the private sphere, between unequal particular subjects, over the most significant issues of social norms. Deregulation even goes as far as the public order of the private sphere. Yet, modernity has always considered the private sphere a realm immaterial to democratization, indeed, alien to it.

• • • •

A consequence of this fundamental change in the real political system is the increasing weakening of *the culture of citizenship*. The culture of citizenship is the kind of social ideology that, on the one hand, has raised social demands in the form of rights for almost two centuries, and that, on the other, has *demanded* these rights once they were recognized, acting upon and conserving them.

It must be attributed to the culture of citizenship that the chief programs of social change, from those aimed at the recognition of civil rights to those, later on, demanding the satisfaction of new social demands (of health, lodging, education—those called "rights of second generation") have been raised precisely in the form of *demands of rights*.

The existence of this culture of the people, which only settles after long periods of recognition by the state of citizens' rights, allows a distinction between societies where democratization has materialized to a certain degree, and those in which this process is restricted to a constitution or some merely nominal democratic institutions without real implantation in social life. The existence of *a culture of rights* enables isolated individuals to demand the restoration of their rights when they are disturbed, rather than forcing them to bend down before the disturbance and accept it. The so-called "culture of the mass worker"—which has attained the status of a "right of second generation"—consists of the extension of the culture of citizenship to the assisting social classes in several metropolitan societies.

One might observe that, with globalization, large populations all over the planet gain modernization without citizenship. So it is with the Chinese people. One might guess that, even if one day the Chinese conquer their rights of citizenship, they will lack the matching civic culture. It is still weak in Japan, a society still too close to its feudal past. In the "northern" metropolises, where representative democracy is supposed to be more established, a growing weakening of the "culture of citizenship" can be observed with the rise of globalization. The people are witnessing the loss of vitality in their citizenship.

The "culture of rights" does not count on tools to oppose the decisions of the new vague ruler. The vague ruler does not speak the language of rights, but rather the language of efficacy. It is clearly in the field of democratic culture where the citizens suffer their defeat.

• • • •

With globalization, opposed tendencies at the level of institutionalization take place. On the one hand, there is a boost in the barbarization of all social relations, which may result in new tyrannies and lasting social regressions. But, on the other hand, there is also still a weak tendency to a further implementation, despite structural inequalities, of the process of democratization. Should the first tendency impose itself, we would be facing a new world scene. As with the rise in Europe of a "universe of nation-states," a "universe of transnational companies" would appear globally—a universe whose institutional subjects would be multinational enterprises, manufacturers, or financial conglomerates (like pension funds) implanted over a worldwide network of huge metropolitan centers or territory-cities, advanced in the process of a third industrial revolution.[25] The public authorities in these "territorial metropolises" would be the instruments of the private ruler, maintaining the political conditions that favor commerce: deregulation, privatization of public companies, and socialization of private loss and costs.

The public agora, the headquarters of public opinion, which since the Enlightenment had been the intersubjective *locus* of modern democratization, is occupied at this stage by multimedia transnational enterprises that trivialize every signification. Discordant or critical voices are neither hushed by censorship nor excluded by conformist editors or news media; they simply get drowned, integrated in the general hullabaloo.

The needs of human beings lose autonomy. They become a variable, dependent on mass production. There is an entrepreneurial intervention in the object of desire. With the materialization of this tendency, the people, in turn, lose autonomy and freedom, since the origin of the needs they experience is increasingly alienated. The productive system assumes that consumers have feelings of deficiency, due to an industrial branch specifically devoted to the production of contents of consciousness. Nowadays this industry undertakes the process of determining social and cultural values.

In this prospect there will be no citizens or even persons, only replicants: the individuals would be homogenized by consuming categories, categories in turn determined by the demands of the productive system. The human being's life would become completely *private*, that is, lacking *general* aims. The demands of any residual universalism that might survive would be served by mass media through ritual acts, like sports championships or other spectacular events.

Thus, the world would be homogenized: through the absence of time, since life would be pure simultaneity; and through the absence of proper history, since the historical would be replaced with the "natural" and would make all experiences interchangeable or indifferent. This would mean leaving modernity behind without really emerging from it.

The other tendency noticeable in the contemporary globalized world is one leading growing sectors of the people to get interested directly or indirectly in occasional affairs of public character outside the traditional channels of political representation.

Generally speaking, single-issue movements of undeniable public value (such as, ecological, solidarity, pacifist, and urban organizations) attract a large number of persons in highly developed countries. Movements with their own "global" dimension remain: human rights campaigners; aid for the dismal scenes of the southern hemisphere; solidarity with immigrants of non-Western cultural roots; and so forth. And, once in a while, there is still a social outcry of a remarkable size over labor issues. In spite of the doubts raised by the single-issue movements about the capability of projecting the will of "northern" societies over the rest of the world, one cannot forget that the new social movements do represent a "spontaneous" novelty, that is, an imaginative creation of the people just at a time when traditional (or citizens') political intervention started to reach a crisis.

There are three kinds of possibilities of involvement for the human beings belonging to these relatively new movements: participation out of mere ideological empathy; participation by means of economic contributions (which actually implies an indirect participation, by means of representation, in financing the activity performed by others); or participation through the contribution of voluntary work, that is, direct participation. In all three cases—but very obviously in the third—a "culture of solidarity" is generated that bears certain resemblances in its potential to the culture of the unions in the nineteenth and early twentieth centuries.

This new unionism and, above all, the new political performances occurring within it, indirectly contribute to supporting the classic political form of representation, as strong collective demands are transmitted that oppose, in the public realm of the open state, the policies of the vague ruler or, at any rate, may be alien to its intentions.

There is a tendency toward a stable, voluntary public agora, different from the public sphere of the state (although related to it) as a realm for the performance of social movements. In this realm education for autonomy and freedom is of the utmost importance—the intergenerational transmission of fundamental ideas that modernity has not been able to settle and extend, even though modern societies are capable of inventing immanent and autonomous institutions dependent on the explicit will of the people.[26]

The essential question is whether the voluntary public agora will foster a "new citizenship" constructed from *powers*, seen as properties not of individual citizens, but of associative entities. The "citizenship based on powers" of solidarity movements that move in the public-voluntary realm may support and complete the limited "citizenship of rights." The novelty of this "citizenship based on powers" would consist of not delegating, that is, in not attributing only to the state the tutelage of the social needs recognized in public.

In any case, the division of the social world into public and private spheres, the foundation of the modern institutional organization and its corresponding political account, has been thrown into an accelerating crisis with the rise of globalization. What its fate will be remains to be seen.

Globalization, Citizenship, and Education

What are the implications of the development of this new power, the coupling of diffuse sovereignty and an open state, on the diverse facets of education? What are the effects of globalization?

The future is never linear, and there is always a possibility of contradictory tendencies. But if globalization is primarily conceived of as a result of the third industrial revolution, there is, from the organizational and technological point of view, the possibility of a substantial change in education, at least in the societies of the North. For example, the mere presence of computers in schools involves the possibility of bringing great quantities of previously inaccessible information to all areas and levels of education at very low costs.[27] They could eventually transform mass education, making it more efficient and increasing social mobility. However, computers and information technology are not readily available except in "developed" countries. In the educational sphere, this suggests that the abyss between the "center" and the "periphery" will, in the long run, become wider and more profound, and there does not seem to be a significant tendency in the opposite direction.

Furthermore, this new technological medium can contribute to making the traditional organization of education that is based on age groups disappear. It is well known that age-based grouping began with the work of De la Salle in the eighteenth century. This type of organization facilitated the standardization of the content of education and transformed the work of teachers from an individual to a collective endeavor. This standardization has configured the human landscape of the schools and universities as we know them and is the basis of the division of the active life of human beings into two successive periods: a "learning period" and a "productive period." However, the foundation of this division, which depends on a shared perception of a generally stable, salaried employment, is being destroyed by the organization of production in the age of globalization. Stable employment has experienced a clear retreat throughout the world, and new, flexible, precarious, part-time forms of employment are appearing. New generations only rarely think about stable employment. Part-time, unstable employment is more common, and thus productive life appears to be divided in discontinuous intervals of varying intensity.

In this new context, the division of time into successive periods of learning and production makes less and less sense. The opportunity for new learning periods surfaces, and there is a need for lifelong educational adaptation. Using age-based groups as the organizing principle for learning loses its raison d'être, while computers and information technology now offer the possibility of reorganizing teaching, at least at higher levels, on an individualized basis.

Nevertheless, the adoption of new organizational forms and means for education can also accommodate a reactionary variation. This could result in an educational system with various speeds that would adapt the different levels of education to the abilities of students. Obviously, a system that actually taught at various speeds would be the adaptation of educational institutions to the system of social classes, with the slow or low speed corresponding to the lower strata of the social structure.

It is beyond the scope of this discussion to determine which types of educational content are required by the changes caused by globalization. Ever since the first analyses about the impact of computers on the productive process, it has been claimed that there is a need for more training because tasks are increasingly specialized. This hypothesis seems inordinately general because, in the real labor market, there are too many overqualified persons. However, it is not unreasonable to suppose that the outlook for educational demands in the long run will be characterized by two features: increased education and the deficiency of any set of "required skills" because of their predisposition to change.

Yet this general tendency contrasts with the advancing marketization of culture, education, and even social values. The vague sovereign has obtained from the open state the surrender of educational institutions to the market. The third industrial revolution has not only destroyed the secular rural culture in developed countries, but it has also broken the barriers that relatively egalitarian systems still maintain as a minor antidote to the perpetuation of social inequalities. These are particularly visible in the societies of continental Europe where public educational institutions have functioned, until now, as one of the principal compensatory mechanisms to deal with social inequality. Whether or not it was designed as an exclusionary mechanism, public education has previously served as a type of "democratic reservoir" in developed societies. The commercialization of education increasingly minimizes the importance of public education, and annuls its democratizing function.

The commercialization of education can be considered from several points of view. The most obvious is the effective constitution of a market of "educational goods." This leads to a type of McDonaldization of education, which is as degrading for the training of individuals as fast food is hazardous to dietary habits. But this aspect is not, perhaps, the most important. More than anything, schools segregate. And the school market segregates. It does so externally (social segregation between central and peripheral schools) and internally (segregation according to levels of consumption within the school).

Globalization consists primarily in cultural change and in the decentering of power. The educational sphere is probably one of the areas in which the consequences of globalization are most seriously felt. Despite the inertia of the large institutional machinery of formal educational systems, which continue operating despite an internal crisis, traditional educational practices make less and less sense. And the logic of commercialization exerts pressure for changes in the relative importance of educators and mechanical media in the production of education.

In this context of increasing difficulties, the role of educational institutions and of educators recovers the social function that it has always had in moments of crisis. The preservation and strengthening of the declining culture of citizens greatly depends, as has been pointed out, on education for democracy. If the process of democratization involves the specification and institutionalization of preexisting social powers, converting them into explicit and defined powers that are questioned by the people requires a process of democratization that must first make the decentered power of the vague sovereign visible. It is only by doing so that the people can discern which power the new sovereign can maintain and which power must be given back to institutionalized political power.

Making the power of the vague sovereign explicit is by and large a task of democratic educational institutions. These institutions must also show the new generations the unjust and sexist consequences of the structures of patriarchy. These are matters that challenge the very basis of democratic educational discourse; this discourse cannot be "neutral," it must be explicitly antisexist and antisegregationist and cannot allow forbidden zones to democratic intervention.

The new democratic educational discourse will necessarily be a chorus, that is, a discourse with many voices reflecting the diversity of the sectors ignored by the globalizing discourse. From the point of view of a democratic citizenship based more on powers than on rights, the primary objective of this discourse is to teach to learn: to learn to conserve, to learn to cooperate, to learn to value solidarity and shared knowledge, to learn to innovate; and to join together to face new situations for which no educator will ever have the answer.

Translation: Eduardo Fuente Somohano

Notes

1. Pier Paolo Pasolini, *Scritti corsari* (Milan: Garzanti, 1976).
2. Karl Polanyi, *The Great Transformation* (New York, Farrar and Rinehart: 1944).
3. See Anthony Giddens, *Sociología* (Madrid: Alianza Ed., 1996), mostly chap. XVI; U. Beck, *¿Qué es la globalización?* (Barcelona: Paidós, 1998); and B. Amoroso, *Della globalizzazione* (La Meridiana: Molfeta, 1996).
4. Immanuel Wallerstein, *The Modern World-System* (New York: Academic Press, 1976).
5. See J.-Ch. Rufin, *L'Empire et les nouveaux barbares* (Paris: Ed. Lattès, 1991); and "Subcomandante Marcos," of the EZLN, "La 4é guerre mondiale a commencé," in *Le Monde Diplomatique* (Aug. 1997): 1, 4, 5.
6. The globalizing interrelation does not benefit the "South," which used to export raw materials but now exports mostly manufactured products. Most countries that specialize in agricultural or mineral primary products suffer the consequences of a drop in the value of their products. See B. Sutcliffe, "Nuevas formas de imperialismo en los años 80," in *Nuevas tendencias de la economía mundial hacia el 2000*, ed. C. Berzosa (Madrid: OIEPLA, 1990).
7. See Eric S. Grace, *Biotechnology Unzipped* (Washington, D.C.: John Henry Press, 1997).
8. W. Jaeger, *Paideia* (Mexico: FCE, 1957).
9. See L. Ferrajoli, *La sovranità nel mondo moderno* (Bari: Laterza, 1997); and my work "Una visita al concepto de soberanía," in *Los ciudadanos siervos* (Madrid: Trotta, 1993).
10. Obviously if someone lacks citizenship because of race, community roots, religion, and so on, it indicates that he or she is not inserted in modern political relations. Compare my work "Los ciudadanos siervos," in *Los ciudadanos siervos* (Madrid: Trotta, 1993).
11. Simone Weil, *L'enracinement* (Paris: Gallimard, 1949).
12. In American jurisprudence it is usual at this point to refer to W. N. Hohfled's work, *Fundamental Legal Conceptions* (New Haven, Conn.: Yale University Press, 1919). Hohfled's concepts cannot be made out if one does not perceive the multilaterality of juridical relations.
13. U. Cerroni, *La libertà dei moderni* (Bari: De Donato, 1968).
14. See John Locke, *Two Treatises of Government*, II, 136, 137.
15. J. H. Frimpong-Ansah, *The Vampire States in Africa: The Political Economy of Decline in Ghana* (London: J Curley Ed., 1991).
16. Jean Baudrillard, *Le paroxyste indifférent* (Paris: Ed. Grasset and Fasquelle, 1997). Baudrillard points out that globalization and universalism are rather exclusive; that globalization affects techniques, markets, and information, whereas universalism affects values.
17. Thus, for example, the works of Giovanni Sartori, *Democrazia* (Milano: Rizzoli, 1993); or R. A. Dahl, *La democracia y sus críticos* (1989), Spanish translation by L. Wolfson (Barcelona: Paidós, 1992), exemplify well the situation of political thought in the present crossroads: they both choose to ignore the problem of the state's sovereignty.
18. I have developed this subject in my works, "Democratización y neonaturalismo,"

in *Grandes Esperanzas: Ensayos de Análisis Político* (Madrid: Trotta, 1996); and *Fruta Prohibida* (Madrid: Trotta, 1997), especially chap. V.

19. For the concept of "explicit power," see Cornelius Castoriadis, *Les Carrefours du labyrinthe, IV: La montée de l'insignifiance* (Paris: Ed. du Seuil, 1996). Castoriadis's political philosophy is, next to Gramsci's, one of the most interesting of the twentieth century.
20. J. Petras, "El mito de la globalización," in *Ajoblanco*, no. 105 (1998).
21. See my work "Democratización y neonaturalismo," in *Grandes Esperanzas*, 161ff.
22. Such is the title of the novel by S. Freyn.
23. I. Ramonet, "El pensamiento unico," Spanish translation in *Mientras tanto* (Barcelona), no. 61 (1995): 17ff.
24. The episode is in Thucidides, *Peloponnesian Wars*, V, 84–113.
25. See Kenichi Ohmae, *The End of the Nation-State: The Rise of Regional Economics* (Chicago: McKinsey, 1995).
26. Cornelius Castoriadis, "Le délabrement de l'Occident," in *Les carrefours du labyrinthe, IV: La montée de l'insignifiance:* (Paris: Ed. du Seuil, 1996).
27. Sherry Turkle, *Life on the Screen: Identity in the Age of Internet* (New York: Simon & Schuster, 1995)

Multiculturalism and Educational Policy in a Global Context (European Perspectives)

Stephen R. Stoer and Luiza Cortesão[1]

To write on the theme of "Multiculturalism and Educational Policy in a Global Context" from a European perspective in the late 1990s is to write almost inevitably on what has been termed the "construction of Europe" as a supranational entity. Increasingly over recent years, it has been with reference to what counts as Europe and how European citizenship should be defined (in addition to the birth of the *information society*) that the impact of globalization has been most strongly felt. How has educational policy been affected by this impact? Is there a European dimension to educational policy, or is it still the preserve of nation-states making up

Europe? What is the contribution of education to European construction? How can education participate in the development of cultural bilingualism and transethnic identity formation?

Taking as a point of reference a series of articles published by the *European Journal of Intercultural Studies* (of the International Association of Intercultural Education, centered in the Netherlands),[2] we attempt in this article to respond to the questions raised above. Our analysis is not limited by any means to the data and arguments presented in these articles, but this selection does assure that our basis for analysis is in some sense representative of recent debate in Europe on the theme that is here presented.

In the first part of the chapter, we will refer to the debate that has developed around the notion of the European dimension in education. We will show how this notion inevitably intersects with the question of European citizenship. We will also establish the link that has developed between the latter and intercultural education. In the second part of the chapter, we will consider the obstacles involved in the elaboration and implementation of a European educational policy, particularly during an epoch of globalization. We will develop the notion of "benign Europeanization" to show the power of the status quo in resisting change. In the third and final part of the chapter, we will look for counter hegemonic tendencies that challenge such resistance, possibly opening the door for the development of a more critical intercultural dimension in European education.

European Citizenship and the European Dimension in Education

Étienne Balibar writes of Europe as an area of the intersection between several world spaces, rather than as an autonomous unit: "Euro-American"; "Euro-Mediterranean"; "Euro-Eastern," and so on.[3] What constitutes Europe is a major question at the center not only of the present construction of the supranational entity called the "European Union" but also of the very definition of what makes up "European identity."

Inevitably, as Balibar and many others have emphasized,[4] the "construction of Europe" is an historical problem of which migrations (both away from and toward Europe[5]) and racism are a part. The deep roots of racial discrimination in Europe can be found in colonialism and antisemitism, both of which attained maximum expression (and violence) through, on the one hand, the slave trade and, on the other, the Holocaust. The reemergence of right-wing extremism and nationalism, racism, and xenophobia in Europe is indeed based, to a large extent, on Europe's heritage. As we shall see below, the repercussions of this heritage are pervasive and difficult to control, working often in subtle ways to thwart their own demise.[6]

Rather than exporting a political model throughout the world, as it did for several centuries, Europe has been itself in recent years undergoing a process of the crystallization of all the problems associated with globalization. "The challenge of European citizenship," as it has been called,[7] is one of the solutions that has been offered, not so much in order to "resolve" such problems but more in order to "manage" them within the scope of possibilities available in a universe that is more than skeptical of "final solutions."

As we shall argue in more detail below, "The challenge of European citizenship" (brought to light in the Maastricht Treaty of 1992) is a crucial component of the contextualization of the problematic of multiculturalism and educational policy in Europe. Indeed, as in the construction of the nation-state, mass schooling is conceived as one of the crucial institutions in the development of this process. The name that has been given to this "challenge" in the field of education is the "European Dimension in Education" and includes the setting up of the European Dimension in Education Unit in Brussels.[8]

It is not by chance that "The Challenge of European Citizenship" arises in the final two decades of the twentieth century. The globalization process, including the advent of the "information society" and the crises of Fordism and the Welfare State, have made urgent what Carneiro calls the "renegotiation of the social contract" established at the beginning of the post–World War II era:

> The starting point in the 50s and 60s was that industrial society was untouchable; that the nation-state—that extraordinary invention that sustained democratic governance, based on principles of cultural homogeneity and assimilation—was to endure forever.[9]

New forms of governance require new forms of citizenship:

> The operative proposal with regard to citizenship is intercultural edu-

cation. It is the recognition, once and for all, of the move from culture to multiculture. It is the definitive affirmation that our society is no longer compatible with cultural homogeneity or with assimilationist dreams, and that the education system itself will have to recognize in diversity an enormous source of wealth—the internal diversity of Europe and the additional diversity of Europe as it welcomes into its midst populations from other continents.[10]

These weighty and portentous words of Carneiro[11] clash with the reality of Europe's heritage.[12] As Balibar has pointed out, already some individuals are de facto citizens of Europe, while others are mere subjects (permanent citizens-in-development) within the European space. "But whereas the former are citizens of a nonexistent state, the latter cannot in practice be kept in an absolutely rightless position unless it comes to forms of organized violence."[13] Who will exercise this violence?

In principle, the state has the monopoly over organized violence. Thus, as Balibar reminds us:

> In essence, modern racism is never simply a "relationship to the Other" based upon a perversion of cultural or sociological difference; it is a relationship to the Other mediated by the intervention of the state. . . . The modern state, for instance, opens the door to "clandestine" circulation of the foreign labour force, and at the same time represses it.[14]

In the absence of a "'European' law-governed state," each individual nation-state exercises violence, eventually in the name of the nonexistent European state. In the absence of both, other entities may take charge of exercising violence (such as, for example, the "mafias" that have become powerful in many Eastern European states). Balibar asks, How can one democratize a "nonstate?" Which, in turn, raises anew the question of the (non)existence of a European law-governed state. In fact, the "European state" appears in Europe as neither national nor supranational; rather it is ambiguous, conceived as "the state institution of a market"[15] and, therefore, without a genuinely social dimension.

As is well known, what is now the European Union has always functioned in the first place in terms of economic interests. The American political scientist Philippe Schmitter has pointed out, "It was easier to achieve agreement on economic questions than on political ones."[16] However, with the expansion of the European Union, free movement within it, and especially the policy of a single currency, there has grown the conviction that the European Union project

> cannot continue to define itself primarily in economic terms, as an organization of economic interests and consumers. Instead, the E.U. must be reimagined as constituting a cultural unit as well, where a sense of shared identity and citizenship can thrive.[17]

The development of "Europe's" social and cultural dimensions, however, depends directly on the development of its political dimension. The creation of a political base for the democratic functioning of Europe does not necessarily involve the creation of a European state in the same terms that one thinks of the nation-state.

> The first thing (one needs) to discuss is European citizenship—which has to do with the development of a set of individual rights and obligations relative to Europe that are distinct from those that exist at the national level. . . . It is necessary to recognize that, in Europe, people are not just citizens; they are "citizens of countries." And these countries have different sizes, different cultures, whose special characteristics people don't want to lose. . . . What I propose is a principle of proportional proportionality (that recognizes these differences). It is based on the square-root of the population: basically, each ten percent of Luxembourguese should be equal to each ten percent of Germans, or French, etc. If this formula is applied, for example, to the European Parliament, one obtains, curiously, something very close to the division which today exists and which is not based on any pre-established principle.[18]

In other words, difference has to be built into the very construction of European citizenship and European democratic governance. This is to a certain extent foreseen, as Nóvoa reminds us, in Jacques Delors's concept of "géometrie variable," where new forms of participation develop on the basis of the liaison between the supranational and the local.[19] The underdeveloped nature of both Europe's political and social dimensions has obvious repercussions in the attempts to develop its educational dimension, some of which will be discussed below.

Many theorists, including those of modernization, have shown that mass schooling has been crucial to the production of the nation-state.[20] However, in manufacturing "citizens," schooling also produces what Balibar terms "fictive ethnicities." These are made up of the mere "subjects" permanently in development, referred to above, which in the context of Europe are minority subjects without the political rights of citizens.[21] They are inherent to the production of the nation-state because the preservation and affirmation of national identity depend on contrasts with, and differences from, the "other" for their own construction. One of the questions we want to raise in this article is whether these "fictive ethnicities," at another level, do not also threaten the European dimension in education, at least as far as it has been developed up to now.

The European dimension in education, in addition to promoting the legal status of educational diplomas and certification in general, involves above all conceptualizing and developing Europe as a system of cultural representation, as what Hall terms, in characterizing the nation-state, a "symbolic community," able to generate a sense of identity and allegiance.[22] Thus, one comes to know what it means to be "European"; "Europeanness" comes to be represented as a set of meanings selected from European cultures. The way this latter process takes place is conditioned by the impact of globalization on the time-space coordinates that largely determine how identity—European identity—is located and represented. The pluralizing impact of globalization on identities, and on narratives that tell the story, for example, of European culture, makes the construction of Europe as a system of cultural representation a complex task, working at different levels from the local via the regional to the national, supranational, and global. Identities are less fixed, more fragmented, and suffer simultaneously processes of (de/re)territorialization. The possible effects of such processes are referred to, quite often, in rather coarse and unsophisticated language,[23] in E.U. documents such as the *White Paper on Education and Training: Teaching and Learning Towards the Learning Society*:

> However, one should be aware of the fact that to promote the European dimension of education and training has become, more so than in the past, a need for reasons of effectiveness, as a reaction against globalization and the risk of the dilution of European society.

> In order to preserve its diversity, the wealth of its traditions and its structures, Europe is going to become, even more so with future expansion, a pertinent level of intervention through the necessary cooperation in these fields between the European Union and its Member States.[24]

With regard to the nation-states that make up "Europe," Hall has called attention to what he terms "the myth of cultural homogeneity" within the nation-state:

> Instead of thinking of national cultures as unified, we should think of them as constituting a *discursive device* which represents difference as unity or identity. They are cross-cut by deep internal divisions and differences, and "unified" only through the exercise of different forms of cultural power. . . . *Modern nations are all cultural hybrids.*[25]

A major source of such cultural power has, of course, been mass education systems whose job has been to promote homogeneity by removing difference from the system on the basis of the principle of equality of educational opportunity. Once access has been guaranteed to all, difference must be denied to assure that progress through the system is based on the evaluation of each individual's cognitive competence. For those with less competence, or with "delayed" (in the sense of "late" developing) competence, the system offers compensatory education, in other words, larger quantities of more of the same thing.

What appears to be at stake, then, in the developing of the European dimension in education is, on the one hand, the "creation of a cultural community," of an "aide in the process of identity formation,"[26] and, on the other, the constitution of a new *discursive device* where unity is seen as diversity, where identity is seen as being both hybrid and unitary. The vehicle for such development is, as Carneiro emphasized above, inter/multicultural education.

The effects of the globalization process in Europe are particularly clear in the domain of education. Education, in the 1960s, in many European countries, developed at the level of official discourse on the basis of social-democratic values and was, therefore, expected to contribute to improving social justice. With the advent of globalization, education came to be seen as responsible for problems arising within the economic sphere of a society experiencing late modernity. It was therefore obliged to readjust its contribution to development on the basis of such values as efficiency and competitiveness.[27] The promotion of these values was far easier to articulate on the basis of a conception of selective monocultural education than on questions based on giving value and visibility to, and eventually empowering, minority groups increasingly present within the European space.

The grave problems that emerge in all education systems arising from a school that remains unchanged when challenged by increasing diversity have forced policymakers, at least at the level of rhetoric, to place such diversity on the agenda. These problems are related to others inherent to a disorganized capitalism. One sees in European education a tension between the need to contribute to competitiveness and the emergence (at least at the level of discourse, but also with regard to some official measures that have been taken) of situations that tend to reinforce the democratic character of schooling. The development of this democratic character is based, primarily, on giving attention to the diversity present in the school.

Developing the European Dimension in Education through Inter/Multicultural Education

> The European dimension is a confusing term. The subject of policies by both the European Commission (Resolution 88/c, 177/02[28]) and the Council of Europe (1993), its translation into national curricula in European countries shows it to be a term capable of wide interpretation, or even neglect, as in the case of the national curriculum for England and Wales. . . . A conflict exists between the resolutions which tend to emphasize cultural diversity and mutual understanding, and the inherent ethnocentrism of many of the national curricula (Flouris, 1995).[29]

This plea of anguish by Ritchie underlines what Hansen has referred to as a lack of "any real formal harmonizing powers in the field of education" by the European Union.[30] It may also go even deeper and be symptomatic of a more profound malaise that has to do with the particular understanding of European culture and identity on which Europe is trying to construct itself. This is, in fact, recognized by Ritchie when she refers to a "Europe defined more through exclusion than inclusion," where the definition of Europe and who is European is based on "ethno-cultural determinations," thus excluding, for example, both Turks and Asians for not being "European peoples."[31] Coulby and Jones, as multiculturalists, refer to this phenomenon, interestingly, as "bland self-satisfied Europeanization,"[32] what we would term "benign Europeanization," incapable of taking into account "the actualities of European diversity" and incapable of teaching young people that "plural identities are the reality for most Europeans, despite the desire of many individual European states and their education systems to deny this."[33] Thus, "Benign Europeanization," in Hansen's words, "thwarts a constructive discussion of how an inclusive trans-ethnic identity formation could be envisioned in the E.U. of today."[34]

Hansen's analysis of recent European policy documents underlines the "exclusiveness" of culture as it is defined in the European dimension in education. He argues that instead of "embracing cultural differences and multiple identities," the E.U. documents tend to "adhere to some of the key components of the nationalist discourse (they) seek to evade":

> The E.U.'s . . . articulation of "our common culture" also bears like-ness to the nation-state's in the sense that it unavoidably comes to masquerade as class neutral, as just an upright expression of what "we" have in common, and therefore something which seemingly should enthuse and be equally meaningful among school children and students from dissimilar social backgrounds.[35]

A telling example of such articulation occurs in the "Common Position" on the support for minority languages within the European Union, adopted by the European Commission in 1994, where "only those minority languages—such as Frisian, Breton, Sorbian, etc.—which are deemed 'indigenous to the European Union' are included."[36] Thus, a clear separation is established between "indigenous" (European) minority languages and "immigrant" minority languages.

Hansen's conclusion that "the articulation of the European dimension of education has been moving via an ethno-cultural direction, where, accordingly, the main purpose of education becomes to convey a collective iden-tity which bases itself on a transnational dissemination of uncritical and historically dubious versions of European traditions, heritage and civiliza-tion,"[37] confirms, at least as far as educational policy is concerned, that developing Europe as a system of cultural representation, as a "symbolic community," via the European dimension in education, during an epoch dominated by the forces of globalization and taking into account Europe's heritage, is not only, as foreseen above, a complex but also an inevitably conflictual process. Indeed, cultural power is now promoted to recognize diversity, but only when not endangering unity—a unity that, though socially constructed, is unproblematized and taken for granted, based on what Giddens terms "frozen tradition."[38] In other words, "benign Europeanization" aims at neither upsetting the status quo nor at challeng-ing the economic priorities of established political power.

"Benign Europeanization" is perhaps most aptly contextualized by what Bullivant has termed "The Pluralist Dilemma in Education":

> The dilemma can be stated in a nutshell: selections for the curriculum that encourage children from ethnic backgrounds to learn about their cultural heritage, languages, histories, customs and other aspects of their life-styles have little bearing on their equality of educational opportunity and life-chances. These are influenced more by struc-tural, social class, economic, political and racist factors operating in the wider pluralist society, and by the control exercised by its domi-nant groups over access to social rewards and economic resources.[39]

The culture of the "pluralist dilemma" is termed by Bullivant as "fos-silized culture," a culture more or less imposed on its recipients and frozen in time. It is also a conception of culture reduced to ethnicity. Perhaps para-doxically, "fossilized culture" is promoted by teachers and educators as a form of resistance to a more interactive conception of culture in the name of the principle of equality of educational opportunity. Teachers have no wish to discriminate, they say, against, for example, migrant groups by labeling them as "different."[40] Micheline Rey argues:

> It is true that intercultural education is difficult to put into practice, and that it is encountering a great deal of resistance from educational institutions that are tributaries of our societies, still wanting to be homogeneous and monocultural.[41]

Allemann-Ghionda reinforces this argument in the following terms:

> What seems to be lacking is an in-depth transformation of the education systems from a basically monolingual and monocultural approach to a structural openness through the plurality of languages and cultures, supported by an institutionalised legislative basis. . . . The whole issue of academic achievement of migrant children is poorly documented in most Western European immigration countries. . . . Poor documentation concerns not only statistics, but especially qualitative data. Above all, there seems to be little research that explicitly makes such connections and questions the effectiveness of various forms of intercultural education, as far as better academic achievement is concerned.[42]

Finally, Bell quotes from a research study, carried out by the OECD Center for Education Research and Innovation (CERI) in 1989, of multicultural education policies in Sweden, Finland, the United Kingdom, Ireland, Italy, the former Yugoslavia, Spain, Australia, New Zealand, the United States, and Canada:

> It is to be feared that in spite of the validity of the principles of schooling adapted to cultural and linguistic pluralism, multicultural education programmes will in practice remain dominated by educational and cultural traditions sufficiently resistant to keep them in subjection.[43]

To a large extent the ethno-cultural articulation of the European dimension in education feeds off the homogeneous and monocultural dominance that is still so strongly felt in European societies and their educational institutions. In this sense, it is a kind of "inverted multiculturalism"[44] that promotes likenesses as a form of difference and thus inevitably produces the "fictive ethnicity" against which such likeness can be constructed. It is against such dominance that both critical intercultural and multicultural education have developed. It is worth quoting at length Micheline Rey on the nature of this movement and on the distinction that she draws between inter- and multicultural education:

> The intercultural movement is essentially Anglo-Saxon. It is related

to several decades of efforts by North America and Great Britain to recognise ethnic minorities. In public opinion, however, these were groups on the fringe of society. This movement has been criticized, on the one hand, for its tendency to juxtapose, to isolate and to congeal the "ethnic" community in its identity and marginality. One fears the resurgence of the essentialist culturalism of the 19th century, which perceived culture as something static, rather than as a construction, or better yet, something under construction, transforming itself through social interaction. On the other hand, the multicultural approach tended to attribute problems due to social inequality and the imbalance of power to cultural variables. When the intercultural perspective was introduced in different Anglo-Saxon regions, especially in Great Britain, it inherited some of the culturalist and multiculturalist polemic. However, the intercultural approach questions that model (or its caricature as depicted by its detractors), adds a dimension of integration, recognises the power structure and insists explicitly on interaction. We have to recognise that practical applications do not always reflect their intentions and that intercultural education has not always been able to avoid the traps of marginalisation. Warnings remain justified, no matter which terms are used.

All argument aside, it is useful to keep alive all of these terms, handed down to us from different traditions, but we need to keep their meanings clear and distinct. One could assume that "multicultural" (some people use the word "polycultural"—"multi" in Latin, "poly" in Greek = many) or "pluricultural" ("plures" in Latin = several) implies a sense of status quo. Interaction is not being excluded but is not a part of the concept, as is the case with "intercultural," which strives to describe and promote a dynamic or a process.[45]

It is interesting to juxtapose this passage by Rey with another by Bhikhu Parekh:

> What is, perhaps clumsily, called multi-cultural education is ultimately nothing more than this. It is essentially an attempt to release a child from the confines of the ethnocentric straitjacket and to awaken him to the existence of other cultures, societies and ways of life and thought. It is intended to de-condition the child as much as possible in order that he can go out into the world as free from biases and prejudices as possible and able and willing to explore its rich diversity. Multi-cultural

education is therefore an education in freedom—freedom *from* inherited biases and narrow feelings and sentiments, as well as freedom *to* explore other cultures and perspectives and make one's own choices in full awareness of available and practicable alternatives.[46]

The "multi-cultural education" of Parekh is, for all intents and purposes, an education for living within a multicultural society. Rather than being in opposition to Rey's intercultural education, it obviously complements the emphasis on interaction, dynamics, and process so importantly present in the former, although there are those who oppose one or the other position on the basis, mainly, of how culture is defined. There has been for some time a strong debate between the so-called "enlightenment thinkers" and "romantics" along the lines of the structure/agency distinction, with the former emphasizing culture as a complex system that structures subjective experience, as a cognitive system encoded in collective representations.[47] The anthropologist Melford Spiro, for example, states, "When cultural propositions are learned by social actors, they become personal thoughts and, like emotions, are private; they are now 'located in the mind.'"[48] On the other hand, "romantic" thinkers such as Richard Schweder put the emphasis on culture as a social practice and on the view

> that the conceptual underpinnings of a social order are (ultimately) nonrational and that many of the customary practices of a society— from table manners . . . and dress codes . . . to child training practices and techniques of punishment . . . —are symbolic expressions of those nonrational choices. . . . The whole thrust of romantic thinking is to defend the coequality of fundamentally different "frames" of understanding. The concept of nonrationality, the idea of the "arbitrary" frees some portion of man's mind from the universal dictates of logic and science.[49]

It is important to emphasize, in light of these two different positions, what Boaventura Sousa Santos has termed as the need "to transcend the debate on universalism and cultural relativism":

> The debate is an inherently false debate, whose polar concepts are both and equally detrimental to an emancipatory conception of human rights. All cultures are relative, but cultural relativism, as a

philosophical posture, is wrong. All cultures aspire genuinely to ultimate, universal concerns and values, but cultural universalism, as a
philosophical posture, is wrong. Against universalism, we must
develop cross-cultural dialogues on isomorphic concerns. Against relativism, we must develop cross-cultural procedural criteria to distinguish progressive politics from regressive politics, empowerment
from disempowerment, emancipation from regulation.[50]

According to the same author, neither universalism nor relativism must
be argued for, but rather *cosmopolitanism*, that is to say, the globalization
of moral and political concerns with and struggles against social oppression and human suffering.

Intercultural Education for a Multicultural Society: The European Dimension in Education, Cultural Bilingualism, and "Inclusive Trans-Ethnic Identity Formation"[51]

European educational policy, such as it is, is caught up in the ambiguity of
desiring, on the one hand, to promote the European dimension in education, that is, to take decisions in what Nóvoa sets out as five big areas—
"Professional Training"; "Higher Education"; "Cooperation and
Exchange"; "Information and Assessment"; and the "European
Curriculum"[52]—and in considering, on the other hand, that "education is,
by definition, the space for the construction of national identity,"[53] and
that, therefore, there should be as little intervention in education by the
European Union as possible. Accordingly, "there is no uniform model of
intercultural education in the E.U.,"[54] and E.U. directives set out more
principles and guidelines for possible educational strategies, rather than a
clear project with concrete proposals. The problem with this ambiguity, in
addition to diluting the content of the European dimension,[55] is that, as
Nóvoa has pointed out so well, it not only makes possible but even reinforces two major "perversions" with respect to the development of educational policy in Europe. The first perversion is the "overdetermination of
education by the economic context and the world of work";[56] the second
is "the setting up within the European Union . . . of a *primitive* educational
policy which tries to become invisible and which denies itself the means of
democratic regulation and control."[57]

These perversions make it difficult, if not impossible, for the European dimension in education to provide the spaces and the dynamic within education necessary for what Gundara terms "the negotiation of the complexity of our societies,"[58] for what Cortesão calls "the development of cultural bilingualism where respect for and maintenance of indigenous culture coexist with the acquisition of knowledges and competencies of other cultures that range from language skills to the knowledge of norms and regulations,"[59] or for what Hansen refers to as a "constructive discussion of how an inclusive trans-ethnic identity formation could be envisioned in the E.U. of today."[60]

The creation of these spaces and dynamics depends upon a challenge to dichotomies such as homo/heterogeneous and mono/multicultural. Citizenship is a promise of the project of modernity, but as the events of 1968 (particularly with regard to Europe and Paris in May of that year) demonstrated so well,[61] gray, nondescript citizenship can also be seen as a serious obstacle to the fulfillment of modernity's promises. European citizenship, potentially, is about taking citizenship one step further, in the sense that, as we have seen above, its very construction depends on combating a formal citizenship that is incapable of taking subjectivities into account. It is also about *not* producing fictive ethnicities in the manner of the nation-state.

When teachers say that by recognizing difference they discriminate, what they are really saying is that social relations are power relations. In fact, diversity has been seen by modernity as chaos, as the "other" that needs organizing and civilizing. As we have seen, mass schooling has been the main vehicle for this homogenizing process. By passing through it, one gains the citizenship of a nation-state, but equally one not only assimilates the dominant culture but also is socialized into its power hierarchy. With the advent of postmodernity, the West has tried to give up its function of organizing diversity in one of two ways: either by entering into a process of mea culpa, which has often led to an extreme form of cultural relativism typical of certain currents of postmodernism; or by challenging the idea of diversity as chaos, even as it has been conceived by relativist Western discourse. With this latter position, the difficult, hard, "ugly" side of diversity is confronted and what has been termed the "new racism," based on cultural particularisms, is taken on for what it is.[62] Thus, instead of letting diversity escape through one's fingers, instead of treating diversity as a symbol of "chicness" and of assuming arrogance with regard to that diversity that is offensive, one confronts the incommensurability of cultures and one combats the soft, nice interpretation of difference that Bullivant designates as "benign multiculturalism."

Santos has proposed "diatopic hermeneutics" as a procedure for approaching incommensurability:

> Diatopic hermeneutics is based on the idea that the *topoi* of a given culture, no matter how strong they may be, are as incomplete as the culture to which they belong. Such incompleteness is not visible from inside the culture, due to the fact that its desire to be total leads it to take the part for the whole. The objective of diatopic hermeneutics is not, therefore, to achieve completeness—which is admittedly unattainable—but, on the contrary, to raise mutual incompleteness to maximum awareness by way of a dialogue that is carried out, so to speak, with one foot in one culture and the other in another. In this resides its dia-topic character.[63]

In these terms, as Santos has argued, human rights themselves are "incomplete." Pinxten, in the same vein, declares, "Human Rights are an idealization of consensual values and rights, as they were thought out and amended during the last century within the European middle classes."[64]

A concern with diversity and its incommensurability does not imply a rejection of modernity and its promises. To suggest that modernity is incomplete does not signify that one is antimodern. On the contrary, it is to recognize the following:

> What today has changed is the firm refusal, on the part of a large number of scholars and many other persons, to accept that alternative value systems are marginalized, a fact which has been reinforced by the (re)discovery that there are substantial irrationalities encrusted within modern rational thought. Consequently, the question which now confronts us is to know how to seriously face in our social sciences a whole range of different ways of living, without losing from sight the notion that there exists the possibility to know and to understand value systems which, in fact, can be, or may become, common to all humanity.[65]

It is on this basis that a new discursive device may develop where unity coexists with diversity.

Conclusion

As a result of globalization, the nation-state is no longer the only space of decision making in the field of education, although it continues to be the main one. The European dimension in education constitutes a challenge to nation-state decision making in education, but so far it appears to be a challenge that, in a sense, refuses to take itself seriously. For if, as Hall claims, "modern nations are all cultural hybrids," what is the European Union as a supranational organization? Certainly, a cultural hybrid par excellence! Yet it appears to develop against this "hybridity," setting itself up on the basis of a discourse of unity *without* diversity. Thus, it is accused of being exclusive and of failing to free itself from the heritage which the nation-states that make it up proudly promoted through their crusades to make the world one: a "false universalism," as has been demonstrated by Archer.[66]

The creation of a cultural community (to repeat Hansen's words), of an "aide in the process of identity formation," and the constitution of a new discursive device where unity is structured as diversity and where identity is hybrid, are the challenges that the European dimension in education must take up, if it wishes to be more than an "enigma."[67] Intercultural education is, indeed, the "operative proposal," as long as it adds, in Rey's words, "a dimension of integration, recognises the power structure and insists explicitly on interaction."[68]

Notes

1. Researchers of the Centro de Investigação e Intervenção Educativas of the Faculty of Psychology and Educational Sciences, University of Oporto, Portugal. The authors wish to thank the Instituto de Inovação Educacional (IIE, Lisbon) and the Programme Praxis XXI (of the Fundação para a Ciência e Tecnologia) for the funding of the project "Multiculturalismo e Educação intercultural em Portugal e na União Europeia" within the scope of which this article was produced.
2. Articles are cited from *European Journal of Intercultural Studies* 5, no. 1 (1994); through *European Journal of Intercultural Studies* 9, no. 1 (1998).

3. Étienne Balibar, "Es gibt keinen staat in Europa: Racism and Politics in Europe Today," *New Left Review* 186 (1991): 5–19.
4. See, for example, Michel Wieviorka, *Racisme et modernité* (Paris: La Découverte, 1992).
5. Giovani Campani and Jagdish S. Gundara ["Overview of Intercultural Policies within the European Union," *European Journal of Intercultural Studies* 5, no. 1 (1994): 3–8] refer to the southern countries of Europe as "new zones of immigration." These authors argue further that there has occurred a dilution of the concept of countries of emigration and others of immigration to the extent that the distinction no longer makes much sense.
6. The relatively recent Treaty of Schengen, for example, makes it both easier to move about within the European Union—that is, circulation between nation-state members is enhanced—and more difficult to gain entry into it (thus promoting the image of a "fortress Europe" aimed at keeping the "other" out).
7. Roberto Carneiro, "Construção da Europa: Contributos e limites das Políticas Educativas," in *Política Educativa, Construção da Europa e Identidade Nacional*, ed. Conselho Nacional de Educação (Lisbon: Conselho Nacional de Educação, 1997).
8. Raymond Ryba ["Toward a European Dimension in Education: Intention and Reality in European Community Policy and Practice," *Comparative Education Review* 36, no. 1 (1992): 10–24] argues that "formally, the notion of developing a European dimension in education first appears as part of the European Community's policy in the context of (the Community's first 'Action Programme on Education')," which dates from 1976. It was, however, only in 1988 that the "Resolution on Enhancing the European Dimension in Education" was published (see Resolution 88/c177/02 published in the *Official Journal of the European Communities* 1988, 6 June, no. C 177/5—compare Ryba, "Toward a European Dimension," 13). The first article on education of the Maastricht Treaty (1992) refers directly to the European dimension in education, and in 1993 the Commission of the European Communities published the *Green Paper on the European Dimension of Education*.
9. Roberto Carneiro, "Construção da Europa: Contributos e Limites das Políticas Educativas," *Política Educativa, Construção da Europa e Identidade Nacional* (Lisbon: Conselho Nacional de Educação, 1997), 78.
10. Ibid., 80.
11. Roberto Carneiro was for several years representative of the Portuguese government at UNESCO. From August 1987 to the end of October 1991 he was minister of education of the XI Constitutional Government in Portugal led by Cavaco Silva of the PSD (center-right).
12. Carneiro's words also draw our attention to a major difference of perception between the United States and Europe with regard to multiculturalism. As David Coulby ["Intercultural Education in the United States of America and Europe: Some Parallels and Convergences in Research and Policy," *European Journal of Intercultural Studies* 8, no. 1 (1997): 100–1] has argued, although "the literature (on multiculturalism and education) in the U.S. is wider, deeper and more substantial, it is in its consideration of the idea of the nation that the discussion on intercultural education in the U.S. is at its weakest." In many European countries, "the question

of nationality cannot be rendered invisible in educational institutions. . . . Nationality represents a category which educational discourse cannot afford to ignore. If it does it will render current conflict invisible and present an anodyne 'civic culture' version of often bloody historical conflicts."

13. Balibar, "Es gibt keinen," 19.

14. Ibid., 15–16.

15. Ibid., 17.

16. Philippe Schmitter, "Na Europa, só há cidadãos de países," *Público*, 15 Dec. 1996.

17. Peo Hansen, "Schooling a European Identity: Ethno-cultural Exclusion and Nationalist Resonance within the EU Policy of 'The European Dimension in Education,'" *European Journal of Intercultural Studies* 9, no. 1 (1998): 7.

18. Schmitter, "Na Europa."

19. António Nóvoa, "L'Europe et L'Éducation: Élements d'Analyse Socio-Historique des Politiques Éducatives Européennes," in *Challenges to European Education: Cultural Values, National Identities and Global Responsibilities*, ed. Thyge Winther-Jensen (Sonderdruck, Germany: Peter Lang, 1996), 66.

20. For an excellent summary of this process in Europe, see Nóvoa, "L'Europe et L'Éducation."

21. Here the Portuguese case is interesting, for the Portuguese tend to be simultaneously "citizens" and "subjects" within the same European space. See Stephen R. Stoer and Luiza Cortesão, "Critical Inter/multicultural Education and the Process of Transnationalisation: A View from the Semiperiphery," *Journal of Education Policy* 10, no. 4 (1995): 273–384.

22. Stuart Hall, "The Question of Cultural Identity," in *Modernity and its Futures*, ed. S. Hall, D. Held, and T. McGrew (Cambridge, Eng.: Polity Press in association with Blackwell Publishers and the Open University, 1992), 292.

23. Nóvoa, "L'Europe et L'Éducation," refers to Habermas's preoccupation (1992) with the deficit of participation of Europe's citizens in the construction of "Europe" and the predominance of a supranational bureaucracy, insufficiently accountable, making important decisions. The principle of subsidiarity, adopted by the European Union, which states that decisions must be taken at the appropriate level (local, national, supranational), aims at assuring a proper distribution of powers. Participation, however, can only be promoted by a construction based on inclusion and not exclusion, as seems to be the case (see below).

24. Commission of the European Communities, *White Paper on Education and Training: Teaching and Learning Towards the Learning Society*, COM (95) 590 final, Brussels, 29 Nov. 1995, 53.

25. Hall, "The Question," 297.

26. Hansen, "Schooling," 7.

27. Compare John Elliot, "Living with Ambiguity and Contradiction: The Challenges for Educational Research in Positioning itself for the 21st Century" (paper delivered at the European Conference on Educational Research, Slovenia, Sept. 1998).

28. This resolution calls on the education systems of member states to "strengthen young people's sense of European identity" and "make them aware of the advantages the Community represents . . . and improve their knowledge of the Community and its member states in their historical, cultural, economic, and social aspects." Jill Ritchie, "Europe and the European Dimension in a Multicultural

Context," *European Journal of Intercultural Studies* 8, no. 3 (1997): 294.
29. Ritchie, "Europe and the European Dimension," 291.
30. Hansen, "Schooling," 7.
31. Ritchie, "Europe and the European Dimension," 291.
32. David Coulby and Crispin Jones, "Post-modernity, Education and European Identities," *Comparative Education* 32, no. 2 (1996): 183.
33. Ibid., 178.
34. Hansen, "Schooling," 8.
35. Ibid., 16.
36. Ibid., 18.
37. Ibid., 19.
38. Ulrich Beck, Anthony Giddens, and Scott Lash, *Reflexive Modernization—Politics, Tradition and Aesthetics in the Modern Social Order* (Cambridge, Eng.: Polity Press, 1994).
39. Brian M. Bullivan, "Towards Radical Multiculturalism: Resolving Tensions in Curriculum and Educational Planning," in *Pluralism: Cultural Maintenance and Evolution*, ed. B. M. Bullivant (Clevedon, Avon, Eng.: Multilingual Matters, 1984), 42.
40. Christina Allemann-Ghionda, "Managing Cultural and Linguistic Plurality in West-European Education: Obstacles, Patterns and Innovations," *European Journal of Intercultural Studies* 6, no. 2 (1995): 41–51.
41. Micheline Rey, "Between Memory and History—A Word about Intercultural Education," *European Journal of Intercultural Studies* 7, no. 1 (1996): 7.
42. Allemann-Ghionda, "Managing Cultural and Linguistic Plurality," 42.
43. Cited in G. H. Bell, "Intercultural Pedagogy and the European Dimension in Education," *European Journal of Intercultural Studies* 5, no. 2 (1994): 26.
44. Luiza Cortesão and Stephen R. Stoer ["A Interculturalidade e a Educação Escolar: Dispositivos Pedagógicos e a Construção da Ponte entre Culturas," *Inovação* 9, no. 1–2 (1995): 35–52] develop this notion with regard to the efforts made by Salazar's *Estado Novo* (in 1961) to make invisible the "colonial empire" through the setting up of Portugal's so-called "overseas provinces." As a result, all inhabitants of these provinces became, practically overnight, Portuguese citizens in the name of a "united and indivisible Portugal." This exercise in administrative mass assimilation, contrary to that which was expected, had the effect, in the medium term, of contributing to heightening tensions within Portugal's colonies.
45. Rey, "Between Memory and History," 10, n. 3.
46. Bhikhu Parekh, "The Concept of Multi-Cultural Education," in *Multicultural Education: The Interminable Debate*, ed. S. Modgil, G. Verma, K. Mallick and C. Modgil (London: The Falmer Press, 1988), 26.
47. Professor Staf Callewaert of the Department of Education, Philosophy, and Rhetoric of the University of Copenhagen, introduced this debate into education in Portugal.
48. Melford E. Spiro, "Some Reflections on Cultural Determinism and Relativism with Special Reference to Emotion and Reason," in *Culture Theory: Essays on Mind, Self and Emotion*, ed. R. A. Shweder and R. A. LeVine (Cambridge, Eng.: Cambridge University Press, 1984), 325; see also Pierre Bourdieu, "Systems of Education and Systems of Thought," in *Knowledge and Control, New Directions*

for the Sociology of Education, ed. M. F. D. Young (London: Collier-Macmillan, 1967), 189–207.

49. Richard A. Shweder, "Anthropology's Romantic Rebellion against the Enlightenment, or There's More to Thinking than Reason and Evidence," in *Culture Theory: Essays on Mind, Self and Emotion*, ed. R. A. Shweder and R. A. LeVine (Cambridge, Eng.: Cambridge University Press, 1984), 46–48.; see also S. P. Mohanty, "Us and Them: On the Philosophical Bases of Political Criticism," *Yale Journal of Criticism* 2, no. 2 (1989): 1–31.

50. Boaventura Sousa Santos, "Por uma Concepção Multicultural de Direitos Humanos," *Revista Crítica de Ciências Sociais*, 48 (1997): 21.

51. This expression comes from Peo Hansen, "Schooling a European Identity: Ethno-cultural Exclusion and Nationalist Resonance within the E.U. Policy of 'The European Dimension of Education,'" *European Journal of Intercultural Studies* 9, no. 1 (1998): 8.

52. Nóvoa, "L'Europe et L'Éducation," 55–60.

53. Ibid., 46.; see also Stoer and Cortesão, "Critical Inter/multicultural Education."

54. Campani and Gundara, "Overview of Intercultural Policies," 8.

55. Bell identifies what he terms the "core" of the European dimension in education, that is, a commitment to citizenship and human rights curricula, on the one hand, and the development of international understanding based on tolerance on the other. This "core" is then developed through the *content* of teaching about Europe and the *process* of becoming a European citizen. To aid this process the Council of Europe report "Action to Combat Intolerance and Xenophobia" sets forth key themes specifying an ideal educational enterprise which:
   - takes account of contradictory messages of society and of the political environment;
   - makes young people capable of interpreting and judging a state's conduct toward people and communities;
   - is not afraid of current events;
   - can overcome pupil reticence and teacher reluctance to confront controversial issues; and
   - accepts that human rights teaching pervades all subjects. (cited in Bell, "Intercultural Pedagogy," 26)

   In addition, Bell suggests a need to focus on primary education, and to develop action-research and the evaluation of implementation strategies.

56. Nóvoa, "L'Europe et L'Éducation," 51.

57. Ibid., 51–52.

58. Jagdish S. Gindara, "Socially Diverse Polis: Social and School Exclusion," *European Journal of Intercultural Studies* 7, no. 1 (1996): 22.

59. Luiza Cortesão, "Reflexões críticas sobre a educação de crianças ciganas," in *O Povo Cigano: Cidadãos na Sombra*, ed. L. Cortesão and F. Pinto (Oporto: Edições Afrontamento, 1995), 27–36. In fact, cultural bilingualism is the attempt to concil-iate what Santos calls "a logic based on *roots* with another based on *options*": "The logic of roots is thinking about all that is profound, permanent, unique and singu-lar, all that gives security and consistency; the logic of options is thinking about that which is variable, ephemerous, replaceable, possible and indeterminable on the basis of roots." Boaventura Sousa Santos, "A queda do *Angelus Novus* : Para além da equação moderna entre raízes e opções," *Revista Crítica de Ciências Sociais* 45 (1996): 9.

60. Hansen, "Schooling," 8.

61. Immanuel Wallerstein, *Geopolitics and Geoculture* (Cambridge, Eng.: Cambridge University Press, 1991).

62. A good example is the exploration of the limits of difference in recent films such as Milos Forman's *Larry Flynt*, Mike Figgis's *Leaving Las Vegas*, Mathieu Kassovitz's *La Haine*, and Mike Leigh's *Secrets and Lies*.

63. Santos, "Por uma Concepção," 23.

64. Rik Pinxten, "IN and ICE as a Means to Promote a 'New Personhood' in Europe," *European Journal of Intercultural Studies* 8, no. 2 (1997): 156.

65. Immanuel Wallerstein, ed., *Para Abrir as Ciências Sociais, Relatório da Comissão Gulbenkian sobre a reestruturação das Ciências Sociais* (Lisbon: Publicações Europa-America, 1996), 122–23.

66. Margaret Archer, "Sociology for One World: Unity and Diversity," *International Sociology* 6, no. 2 (1990): 131–47.

67. Raymond Ryba, "Unity in Diversity: The Enigma of the European Dimension in Education," *Oxford Review of Education* 21, no. 1 (1995): 25–36.

68. Rey, "Between Memory and History," 10, n. 3.

A Situated Perspective
on Cultural Globalization

Allan Luke and Carmen Luke

In 1993, the Office of Royal Literature in Thailand commissioned a team of business leaders, journalists, and academics to debate and officially define "globalization."[1] After a vigorous two-year exchange between advocates and opponents of globalization, between economic and cultural positions, the Office of Royal Literature decreed the new word and definition into the Thai Royal Dictionary. Robertson and Khondker describe the outcome:

> The official translation of this word (globalization) is *logapiwatanam* which combines the Thai "world" with

the word *apiwatana*, meaning "to spread, to reach, to win over." This official meaning, which is not readily accepted by those committed to a unidimensional economic meaning . . . means "the expansion of the world, spread around the world, and change and effect all over the world.[2]

This chapter is a situated account of cultural globalization. We provide an alternative reading of dominant discourses on globalization that, we will argue, are based on a Euro-American authored "capitolocentrism."[3] That perspective accounts for the effects of globalization in determinist, causal, and unidirectional terms: north to south, west to east. Our discussion here of the impact of globalization on social, cultural, and educational change in Southeast Asia, and Thailand in particular, makes a simple point. We maintain that only through situated, local, and self-critical analyses can we begin to see the two-way, mutually constitutive dynamics of local-global flows of knowledge, power, and capital, of systematic as well as unsystematic and uneven "effects," and of local histories that always embed "the new" in existing and generative material-economic and cultural conditions. Our intent is not to refute accounts of the hegemonic effects of fast capitalist consumption and production, but rather to offer a counterpoint by arguing that homogenizing effects are always rearticulated in social fields where they are subject to local and regional force and power.

We begin with a narrative of our exchanges with Thai educators, explicated with links along the way to contemporary and historical "situational logics."[4] These situational logics serve as maps that, we hope, will represent the multiple embeddings of cultural, historical, economic, and social change that frame and punctuate the uses and effects of globalization. These same logics shaped our encounters "from afar" with the Thai educators and social scientists who had invited us to address collaboratively the educational issues of "New Times."[5]

Next, we situate our local narratives within the context of regional and Thai social, economic, cultural, and educational change. Here we provide a localized critique in order to reappraise global claims and assumptions about the efficacy of McCulture: the allegedly tenacious grip of Western hegemony over hapless "victim" nations and cultures. The final section of the paper concludes with an argument for the urgency of tempering the pull of grand narrativizing, of totalizing the other yet once again from the perspectivism of a Western "us" and "them" epistemology that, in effect, globalizes the discourses of globalization, and globalizes claims about the effects and processes of globalization. We locate this counterargument in a discussion of competing discourses about the role of education in "development."

Our perspective, analysis, and "take" on globalization is itself local and localized. As Australians, we are part of the region, although geographically on its southeastern periphery. Only ocean separates this continent from the Antarctic; East Timor and Papua New Guinea are our nearest northern neighbors, and Fiji, our eastern neighbor. Australia and New Zealand consider themselves as part of the intellectual and geopolitical West, yet our relatively isolated location on the globe in the "far south" and "far east" situates us very much on the geopolitical and cultural margins.

"Australia" historically was invented by England as a white diaspora at the edges of the empire, forcibly superimposed on Aboriginal and Torres Strait Islander lands and cultures, and often treated by the empire in little more benign terms than our Asian counterparts. In the past decade, Australia has deliberately attempted to redefine and realign itself as part of Asia, unsuccessfully seeking membership in the ASEAN economic/political bloc. Australia is not ethnically or culturally Asian, but we are a nation-state of some 17 million people with an Anglo-Celtic majority in the midst of a complex Asian diaspora.[6] For our northern/Western readers, then, our localized account can be read as a commentary on the margins from a margin, albeit a materially privileged one. In a region where Singapore and Hong Kong are financial and information centers, Sydney, Melbourne, and certainly Perth and Brisbane must work very hard to represent themselves as world cities worthy of participation in global capital and information flows.

Yet questions of cultural globalization are at least in part questions of optics and standpoints. All of these peripheries—Asian, Australian, and others—consider their histories and futures very much at the center. Neither existentially, economically, nor politically are these histories and futures taken by locals, including cosmopolitan locals, as mere footnotes in an inexorable or unproblematic process of globalization and homogenization driven by New York or London, Tokyo or Beijing. In this regard, while we and our Thai colleagues could be accused of a local myopia, it is equally problematic to generate a "far-sighted" perspective solely on the basis of one's myopia, as is often done through what we will here term the *inside-out theorizing* of the West.

We turn now to a narrative description of the micropolitics of a little habitat—the overlapping complexities and concurrent relations of local site, community, nation, and region. If all the recent lessons about the fundamental importance of situated analyses of the microcapillaries of power, of strands of histories within histories, of archaeologies of discursive sites, have failed—then we risk reverting to a new kind of Western intellectual colonization: a pathological ethnocentrism of inside-out theorizing, doomed to grand narrativizing and, this time, on an even grander scale. Globalization: the mother of all metanarratives. Our aim in this chapter, then, is to provide one case as a cautionary note against the polemics of globalization as "a brakeless train wreaking havoc."[7]

Postcolonial Agents and Market Relations

For the past three years we have been working closely with teacher educators and social scientists in two areas of Thailand: in the Eastern Seaboard Industrial Region outside of Bangkok, and in the northern provinces of Chiang Mai and Chiang Rai. The latter province straddles the Mekong River adjacent to China, Myanmar, and Laos in what is popularized in media folklore as the "Golden Triangle," home of the opium trade. But for regional economic planners and the local population alike, it is seen as a geographical nexus that has long connected these countries through cultural and spiritual events and histories. The Triangle—in reality a quadrangle of four countries—has been the ground of indigenous empires and border conflicts that stretch back across four centuries. Since the 1980s, it has been projected in regional development plans as an economic corridor that—with the overthrow of the military government in Myanmar, opening of borders with China, and better bridge systems to Laos—would join Thailand's extensive exporting, transportation, and telecommunications infrastructure with new labor and consumer markets. It is also viewed as a prime corridor into southern China for European and North American tourists, who can already take a short flight to the ancient Chinese walled city of Kunming which, during the last millennial era of high colonialism, was a favored gateway for French missionaries, traders, and soldiers.

Our work has been to assist in research projects and doctoral training at several of the Rajabhat Institutes, regional colleges that offer vocational, undergraduate, and postgraduate degrees, and whose royal mandate is community development. We were invited to participate after institute delegations surveyed and visited numerous Australian, British, United States, and Canadian institutions looking for what they considered appropriate collaborators—quite literally shopping on a globalized educational marketplace. In Australia, successive economic rationalist governments have pushed for the replacement of state funding of universities with "revenue-substitution" strategies based on increasing domestic fees and a burgeoning educational export industry focused principally on Asia. The educational export industry is one of the fastest growing sectors of the Australian economy.

When we began our work in 1997 we had an interesting dialogue with one of our Australian colleagues who was also about to embark on teaching in Southeast Asia. He warned about the need to avoid "exploiting the Thais," urging us to apply critical pedagogical principles to the development of our curriculum in ways that might lead toward more "emancipatory" and "empowering" outcomes. There was something both idealistic and naïve about his view. It presupposed a particular historical set of subject/object relations at work between us and the Thais, with our potential power as cultural imperialists taken for granted. It was not so much that he was "wrong" about the situation per se, for the dangers he warned of certainly factored into our negotiations and subsequent exchanges. But his understanding was a product of a particular historical era, material and political contexts that Freire, Fanon, and others had so accurately described two and three decades earlier.

Prevailing neo-Marxist and postcolonialist theorizations of center/margin relationships were historically produced to explain the postwar decolonization and sites of genocide and economic exploitation.[8] Such analyses remain relevant in many contexts, particularly those still making the transitions from agrarian to industrial economies, and, obviously, those still engaged in throwing off neocolonial or repressive governments. Yet for us the sobering prospect was that the relationships and spaces we were venturing into were the products of a very different context and epoch. Many of the axioms derived from what we would term *point-of-decolonization analyses* did not seem to hold in these new, unprecedented conditions and shifting "flows of power" and "power of flows."[9] Consider, for example, the ideological positions favored by historical figures like Mahatir and Suharto in the face of the recent crisis. They, too, tended to recite colonizer/colonized, center/margin dualisms that simplified responsibility for the economic situation, and ignored or concealed intranational, transnational, and regional dynamics of class, culture, generational, and corporate alliances.

For us the issue was not principally whether and how we were positioned as the "exploiters" or "colonizers" from the West. Indeed, the Thai delegation had contracted with us to deliver a specific curriculum product on *their* terms. Thais, Malays, Indonesians, Chinese, and others shopped for educational partners in a marketplace where supply outstripped demand, and, no doubt, they could select partners from a diversity of institutional types, histories, and, indeed, ideologies. This was the new globalized marketplace of culture, knowledge, and power, a field of new exchange relations, new commodities, and different flows of economic and cultural capital. There was no central determination of its key players, nodal points, or consequences "in the first instance."

We were on new ground. New questions emerged about which intranational and regional social fields we would be playing in, which institutions, which agencies, which class and cultural interests within the "contracting" nation-state would be using us, to what particular ideological agendas and ends, in what configurations of power, around which nodal points, and in whose interests. In this way, as the educrats, bureaucrats, and aidcrats in newly and rapidly industrializing countries have long known, the exchange of flows in postmodern conditions (as against earlier colonial conditions) has long been a case of "the tail wagging the dog."

Thai Encounters: A Narrative

During one of our first meals with the local educators in Chiang Mai and Chiang Rai, our partners in a joint training program, we had an animated discussion about what "New Times" meant to northern Thailand. They spoke at length about the unprecedented educational problems facing Thailand: government schools had a poor track record in promoting the success of the indigenous "Hill Tribes"—the Karen, Hmong, Ha, and other indigenous peoples whose tribal homelands straddled the borders between these nation states. These children tended to fail in schools and have difficulty with Thai literacy, despite high-profile pedagogy and cultural maintenance projects sponsored by the Thai Royal Family.

Additionally, teachers had to deal with migrant children from Myanmar and Laos who "didn't speak proper Thai," and whose parents and families lived in extreme poverty. Some were refugees housed in camps, others guest workers in bottom-end labor markets such as rice production, construction, and fishing. Not coincidentally, migrants, refugees, and guest workers were the first to be blamed by the national press for taking "Thai jobs" at the onset of the 1997 economic crisis and subsequent IMF intervention. At the other end of the socioeconomic spectrum, educators said they felt unprepared for the first generation of Thai youth—the children of the emergent middle class—who were impatient with traditional Thai and Buddhist values and seemed to be more preoccupied with MTV, video games, Michael Jordan, the Spice Girls, and hanging out in shopping malls. New times, we were told, had generated new educational problems and new identities.

In response, Thai federal government policy pushed for the hallmarks of educational modernity: extended compulsory education, standardized and commodified curriculum, increased retention rates, privatization of the tertiary sector, all based on a strong human capital rationale. The anachronisms, riddles, and shortcomings of hierarchical and patriarchal educational administration, traditional rote curriculum, "chalk and talk" pedagogy, and formal examinations seemed more glaring than ever. Moreover, many of the imported Western technocratic solutions on offer since the Vietnam War[10]—from psychologically based approaches to instruction, to counseling and testing, to commodified curriculum packages, to educational managerialism—did not appear to be solving these dilemmas.

But new conditions also had generated new alliances and partnerships in pursuit of solving complex problems—including ours—ones that did not necessarily entail the superimposition of technocratic, progressivist, or neoliberal educational solutions on local and indigenous contexts. In fact, the break in the financing of many government-funded projects caused by the economic crisis generated a host of ambivalent effects, enabling a space for the critique of scenarios for the importation, expansion, and exploitation of capital. It triggered a search for more cost-effective, local solutions to social and economic problems.[11] The army was enlisted in the cultivation of foodstuffs and the development of market gardens on military bases. Newspapers ran feature articles on self-sustaining Buddhist temple communities and the king appeared on national television with a traditional, native drum to extol the virtues of traditional culture as a productive resource in the face of the crisis. One of our colleagues explained to us how the crisis had encouraged some local communities to reexamine the use of traditional medicines, along with community and spiritual ethics of care, in the treatment of HIV-positive patients. This in a context where Western medical treatment and prevention campaigns were proving extremely costly and ineffective.

Standing from afar, many of the axioms and claims of the literature on globalization clearly are at work in northern Thailand, with rapid growth, large-scale capital investment (and disinvestment) in the tourist infrastructure, and cross-border trade and population movement all leading to deleterious effects: urban crowding and pollution in Chiang Mai, one of Thailand's most beautiful and historic cities; and industrialization and tourism that have disrupted agricultural productivity and community lifestyles. In some areas, it appears that community development is being addressed through a grocery list of modernization.

At the same time, globalization has generated new kinds of identity, new forms of intercultural communication and new forms of community. On the Myanmar-Thai border, kids wear Chicago Bulls hats back to front, pirated copies of Hong Kong videos and CDs are on offer, and Thai-made Toyota pickup trucks rule the road. We take these also as signs of cultural globalization. They include the emergence of "world kids" in the context of a new middle-class based on Western models of consumption and desire,[12] the same phenomena which place indigenous cultures and local cultures "at risk." The apparent similarities to the issues confronting Australian education are striking: immigration and population movement; unruly forms of identity; youth with cultural knowledge and technological multiliteracies that exceed those of their teachers; and consumer and media cultures overtaking more traditionally oriented rural, indigenous, and isolated communities.

Yet there is more than meets the Western eye to globalization in Asia. It is analytically tempting and rhetorically powerful to describe the practices and consequences of globalization principally around the metaphor of the Golden Arches.[13] The signs and wrappers of American McCulture have spread to cosmopolitan areas like Chiang Mai and Chiang Rai, which have become meccas for European and North American ecotourists. Certainly, an emergent middle-class youth culture is reconstructing itself around images and texts that are Thai appropriations of Western rock and popular culture. Yet such a position risks flattening out, one-dimensionalizing, the complex processes of globalization. These processes are not simply uncritical reproductions of Western cultures. Rather, their formation flows out of (1) a hybridization and reappropriation of Western cultures; and (2) long-standing incorporations and appropriations of other Asian and regional cultures.

Consider, for example, Thai folk, pop, and rock music. None of these are carbon copies of the genres of the Western music industry. Indeed, there is evidence that Thai popular music, like rock on the Indian subcontinent, has taken on a substantial life of its own, not only shaping youth culture but providing a space for innovative forms of social comment and cultural expression. The most popular songs include ballads that emulate Thai traditional folk music. Arguing against both dominant ideology and resistance theses common among Western cultural studies of music/pop culture, Siriyuvasak claims that Thai pop music is "the product of a complex articulation between Thai folk music and Western pop/rock."[14]

We visited one popular folk/rock club in Phitsanulok, a northern city off the tourist trail—where a visibly "countercultural" crowd, dressed like North American hippies, bikers, and alternatives, played music that blended Dylanesque folk with traditional Thai folksongs, which themselves owe a great deal to Chinese music. The instrumentation was a mix of Western folk instruments and traditional Thai instruments. Yet no English-language songs were played. Here the blending of both traditional Thai music and Western countercultures was used as a local generational and cultural nationalist statement against new middle-class values and, ironically, crass Westernization. Several kilometers down the road at a Thai-owned five-star hotel was a house band playing note-perfect copies of easy listening classics for European expats and tourists. In this community, we saw both a hybrid mode of critique side by side with a simple economy of musical importation and reproduction.

Hybridity, then, is not an invention of postmodernism, globalization, and postcolonial theory. Rather it is a social and cultural formation born out of complex and intersecting histories that often predate direct contact with the industrial and imperial West. Given their histories as blendings of indigenous/Chinese/Khmer cultures, northern and central Thai cultures are already hybrids, products of hundreds of years of complex cultural change and exchange. In fact, many Thai intellectuals argue that it is this capacity to absorb, hybridize, and appropriate that has enabled Thailand to survive war without colonization and, indeed, will enable it to give a particular slant to globalization.[15]

Population mobility is a further hallmark of globalization theories. Travel, displacement, and "border crossing" are often cited as indicative aspects of globalization, with population movements across national borders in search of work and improved quality of life. In Southeast Asia such movement predates late-twenty-first-century globalization and late-nineteenth-century industrialization. In the case of Thailand,

> central Siam in the nineteenth century was accustomed to a polyethnic population long before the term "multiculturalism" was invented . . . [and] the massive numbers of Chinese who migrated to Siam, beginning in the eighteenth century via the junk trade . . . has been a key to Thailand's post–World War II economic expansion.[16]

Chinese migration, in fact, is integral to the historical development of almost all Southeast Asian nations before, during, and after various regimes of colonization, including Laos, Cambodia, Vietnam, Indonesia, the Philippines, and peninsular Malaysia, including what would in the 1960s become the independent nation-state of Singapore. Interestingly, most Western explanations of globalization do not take into consideration the constitutive role of diasporic Chinese in the economic and cultural formation of countries in Asia and the Pacific, a pattern that has shaped Asian and Pacific nation states, economies, and cultures for centuries.[17]

Since the early 1980s, during the economic "takeoff" decades that saw the emergence of the Asian "Tiger" and "Cub" economies, countries like Thailand, Malaysia, and Singapore built their economic success stories using migrant labor from Myanmar, Indonesia, Laos, and Bangladesh. Before the 1997 crash, migrant guest workers filled the jobs that Thais were no longer willing to do: working on construction sites and in factories, on fishing boats, and loading and processing rice.[18] Likewise, the subsumption of indigenous and migrant cultures by a dominant central Thai culture—based on Chinese/Buddhist principles—has been an ongoing process that dates back to the 1920s and 1930s. Then, "racist" and "assimilationist" policies[19] sought to ward off any racial conflict that might emerge out of a potentially dangerous "threefold social division: Thai peasants tilled the land; Thai bureaucrats ran the government; Chinese merchants and labourers ran the urban economy."[20]

Another hallmark of globalization is the assumption of Western "capitalocentrism." Yet flows of power, capital, and control do not necessarily begin from or end in the West. In 1986, for example, Vietnam introduced economic liberalization (*doi moi*), and two years later

> the [Thai] prime minister proposed to "turn battlefields into market-places," to stop treating Indochina as an enemy, and start treating it as an economic opportunity. Thai businessmen immediately become lyrical about *suvannaphum* (golden land), an old fantasy of Southeast Asia as a land of prosperity focused on Siam.[21]

And this is the point: Asian capitalisms, economic power, and regional control within their own local social and economic fields are as pervasive and distinctive in their characteristic configurations and aspirations, hybrid values, identities, and practices as Western capitalisms. The Thais "eagerly seized the opportunities presented by the age of globalization,"[22] envisioning "Siam" as the center, as the focus of regional prosperity based on a platform of global investments, human capital development, and export production.

In 1994 for instance, Thai overseas investment (principally into ASEAN countries, Myanmar, China, and Hong Kong) was two-thirds of inflow of foreign investment. Thai hotel chains (for instance, Dusit Tani) bought into the U.S. market; Thai telecommunications and media expansion moved into India and China; and in the late 1980s diversification carved inroads into petrochemicals and oil refining, utilities, manufacturing, retail, and real estate—much of it in China and brokered through Hong Kong. In their "postboom" retrospective, Phongpaichit and Baker note that globalization in Thailand was seen as a huge opportunity to get on the Asian Tiger bandwagon. Given the lack of political and government restrictions on a growing private sector, one which had already seen profound growth during the previous four decades, and "because this private sector was oriented outwards,

[it] responded nimbly to the new opportunities of the globalizing decade."[23]

This, then, is not a victim narrative, not a story of economic brute force exerted by Wall Street, Ford, or News Corporation. From this particular vantage point, from this particular "optic," globalization has been about regional, national, and inter-Asian agency and capital, class, and cultural interests, as much as it could be said to be about an extension of American or Western hegemony.

We would add that there is a substantial debate over whether indeed the "subaltern" has become a Western intellectual construct.[24] It is certainly not a concept of identity that many East Asian cultures readily adopt or identify with. Nor do many feel particularly "contaminated" or "disrupted" in the sense described by Robertson and Kohndker. No Western product, cultural symbolism, or social practice maps onto *blank slate* indigenous or national cultures. Rather such forces dovetail in unpredictable and unsystematic ways into local histories and relations. Globalization, then, is neither a story of rapacious Western multinationals nor hapless Eastern victims. Clearly, fast capitalism must contend with *local prehistories of other forms of economic activity*, other kinds of regional and local exploitation, other fields of class struggle and cultural domination.

Globalization and Development: Inside-Out Theorizing

It should hardly be surprising that much of the theorizing about globalization has come from the West. In this regard, discussions of cultural globalization have tended to be forms of "inside-out" theorizing—that is, versions of the impact of the extension and articulation of the economic formations and cultural practices of dominant economies and cultures upon regional, diasporic, emergent, and, simply, smaller and less influential economies and cultures. As a result, there is the risk that such intellectual work on globalization risks reproducing the very forms of academic writing and discourse that the Western academy and, more specifically, the Anglo-American disciplines are so proficient at: theorizing the other, and therefore extending an ostensibly benign intellectual surveillance onto the other, and of theorizing the effects of us on "them."

Thus far, our focus has been on the cultural politics of the local. We have attempted to show, by reference to one local site, the complexity of the multidirectional traffic of "flows," of homogenizing and heterogenizing forces that are mutually implicated in the dynamics of so-called globalization. In this next section we turn briefly to some of the theoretical issues implicated in what several scholars have identified as the globalization of discourses of globalization.[25] The term globalization has rapidly gained theoretical prominence and intellectual cachet in the last decade, often used to characterize or indeed supplant the equally slippery and catchall term "postmodernism." Whereas postmodernism is now widely accepted to characterize both a philosophical standpoint and a shift in cultural and economic activity and social relations, globalization is less a philosophical position. Yet it shares two analytic features with postmodernism, namely a focus on the economic and cultural.

The most widely accepted definition of globalization is that it is a feature of late capitalism, or *the* condition of postmodernity, and, more important, that it is characterized by the emergence of a world system driven in large part by a global capitalist economy. This "capitalocentric" epistemology, this focus on the economic as the principal force driving cultural, social, and educational change on a global scale, fails to recognize that "economic activity always takes place and is embedded in a culturally constructed context."[26] Such economic determinism drags culture along as a causal outcome, not as a context or broader social field of cultural circuits of signification, identities, and power relations.

Robertson, Waters, and Appadurai all argue against simplistic economic-driven models of globalization.[27] Waters, for instance, takes a more culturalist position and defines globalization more along the lines of a global change in consciousness about changing global conditions—whether local contributions and/or solutions to global (environmental) problems,[28] the global drift to the information and electronic age,[29] or trends toward mega-alliances in corporate or nation-state management (the European Union, ASEAN, NAFTA, or Daimler Chrysler). As Waters sees it, globalization is

> a social process in which the constraints of geography on social and cultural arrangements recede and in which people become increasingly aware that they are receding. . . . A globalized culture is chaotic rather than orderly . . . it is not centralized nor unified . . . the meanings of its components are *relativized* into one another but it is not unified or centralized [emphasis added].[30]

The core feature of an economic conceptualization of globalization is that the forces and flows of capital sweeping the world and sucking up difference and diversity originate principally in "the West." That is to say, there is a sense that globalization is isomorphic with a kind of high-tech, multimediated economic and cultural imperialism that in an earlier age might have been termed "Westernization"—read Americanization—or else a postmodern mutation of colonialism. In that regard, globalization, like its parent term "postmodernism," has pejorative connotations in the sense that the metaphors and images associated with global markets and capital, and a global sweep eradicating or at least normalizing diversity and difference, paint a picture of a monstrous grotesque of Godzilla-like proportions voraciously gobbling up labor, markets, cultures, and traditions,[31] bringing NICs[32] and aspiring NICs to heel. In short, it is generally used to signify a terrifying compression of the world—"a brakeless train wreaking havoc,"[33] a shrinking if not an elimination of time and space and an erosion of "the local."

What has long counterbalanced this negative appropriation of globalization is its conceptual opposition to the beleaguered local, whether at the level of nation-states, communities, cultural "traditions," or identities. This fundamental polarity between local and global, macro and micro, is at the heart of much current debate about globalization in the social sciences.[34] Here the local is cast in a victim narrative, robbed of agency, stripped of authenticity, and reduced to nothing more than a hapless consumption machine. Robertson and Khondker, quite rightly we believe, have picked up a connection between proponents of the "globalization-equals-Western-hegemony" equation and an historically shaped and culturally located intellectual position: namely, the intellectual defense team of the subaltern. They write:

> This perspective centers on the proclamation that the West enjoys what is often called a hegemonic position in the world as a whole. In a certain sense, then, it is in the interests of those who maintain that they are representing subaltern or oppressed groups to cast the West as very dominant and thus to conceive of globalization as a form of westernisation or as imperialism or colonialism in a new guise. In this perspective many non-Western societies are regarded as *victims with-*

out agency and "globalization" becomes simply the pejorative symbol of all things that are allegedly contaminating or disrupting these societies.[35]

We would add that the "subaltern" is a Western intellectual construct and is not an identity Asian cultures identify with; nor do they feel particularly "contaminated" or disrupted. Here we find relevant Featherstone's comment about what the characteristic local response has been to the "self-appointed guardians in the West": "Don't other me."[36] As we noted earlier, many countries in the region currently undergoing economic and political/social upheaval are using elements of globalization (such as, the "new" financial sector accountability and corporate transparency, and the new global visibility via media and telecommunications) to challenge "internal" problems. Indonesia and Malaysia are currently witnessing pro-democracy *reformasi* social movements that challenge long-standing *internal* political and economic structures and processes.

At the same time, there is a not homogeneous "West" or "East," or indeed a singular academic, intellectual, or corporate voice on cultural globalization. In what follows, we explore two aspects of current discourses on globalization and development: (1) the diversity of agents of globalization; and (2) the diversity of competing, often divergent, discourses of globalization.

First, there is the issue of the very agents and objects of globalization. The irrefutable fact is that the United States has the world's largest economy and, via the world language of English, its intellectual industries, scientific and military systems, and mass media and publishing exert substantial control over dominant modes of representation and communication. Yet there are other varied agents and objects of globalization acting upon and deployed from the smaller regional countries and economies, including, obviously Japan, and, increasingly China—but also Canada, the United Kingdom, Australia, New Zealand, and others. The extension of these forces into newly industrializing economies does not necessarily have the selfsame ideological or cultural effects as that of American companies and NGOs.[37] Simply, globalization and, even more specifically, Westernization do not necessarily mean Americanization.

Second, there is an increasing complexity and diversity within governmental, academic, and corporate discourses of globalization. That diversity is evident in academic scholarship where disciplinary differences and differences of position within disciplines abound. Corporate and governmental discourses on globalization usually promote an agenda to legitimate economic expansionism and development. These include the official statements, annual reports, and trend analyses by multinationals, investment banks, and trusts, and also by transnational bodies such as the World Bank, the Asia Development Bank, the EEU, and others. Yet these do *not* necessarily read as discourses of exploitation and rapacious development, but have deliberately incorporated discourses on the prevention and amelioration of the negative social, cultural, and environmental effects of rapid and unplanned development.[38] In such accounts the problems with economic globalization are increasingly recognized and are said to lie with unplanned, unmonitored, and unregulated development. In the field of education, likewise, the developments of NGOs and transnational forms of governance range from basic education, rural access, informal education, women's programs, indigenous education and literacy, nutrition, and special education, to school restructuring and decentralization planning.[39]

Our point here is not to condemn or support the politics of aid, which have been roundly critiqued in 1970s dependency theory.[40] We wish to point out that NGOs, nation-state aid programs, and corporations alike are moving rapidly into heteroglossic discourses. This is particularly the case in educational planning and projects. Basic education projects in Laos, Vietnam, and elsewhere, or advanced educational aid/trade relations with Thailand, Malaysia, and China function, inter alia, to develop Western-sympathetic human capital for economic "takeoff" or consolidation. In the wake of the crisis, educational aid projects in Indonesia shifted from specialized kinds of curriculum or program enhancement (for example, special education, teacher education, or higher education expertise) to basic nutritional programs for school children. Malaysia scaled down ambitious information technology planning for schools, and refocused on basic education issues. In these and other instances, NGOs and government aid agencies have taken a dual role in the processes of globalization: both setting out enabling conditions for the cooperative development and extension of capital into new labor and consumer markets, *and* mopping up or ameliorating the negative effects of these same processes.

Competing discourses deployed by governments and corporations in the processes and practices of globalization necessarily are increasingly complex and heteroglossic, achieving both/and effects that are often ambiguous. The ambiguity of both/and effects is epitomized in market-driven versions of "democracy" that are redefining governmentality and economics in the region, setting out new conditions for the expansion and exploitation of capital, but also enabling ameliorative and progressive reforms. Without exception in the rapidly developing countries of Southeast Asia such reforms target education as a cornerstone of whatever vision of political, social, or economic change governments and corporate sectors decide upon. Educational policy, therefore, can be seen as a flashpoint—a nodal point—of competing discourses, all focused on issues of knowledge (curriculum), power (access/equity), and the human subject (teacher/student/citizen).

We have attempted here to describe and analyze but a few facets of the complexity of cultural globalization, but in a way this also suggests an alternative, situated perspective—that is, one that neither takes the privileged position of the center and presupposes the efficacy of that center, nor romanticizes heroic agency or the material, cultural, and social effects at the level of the local. The lenses through which we have come to understand the push-pull dynamics of local-global circuits, or what is now often referred to as the "glocal"[41] have been shaped by our varied experiences along these concentric hinterlands of Australia and southeast Asia that are both/and: center and margin. And it is our locale and location that have molded our analysis of and engagement with the "little habitats"—the communities, the schools, the colleges—where aspects of globalization seep in at different rates, in different colors, contours, and guises. We will now trace out a last contour and "color in" what a pedagogy and curriculum, purpose-built for problematizing globalization and New Times, can look like. More specifically, we will examine the context of one project problematizing the Thai tertiary education sector, in one locale, in post-IMF times.

A Postscript: On Educational Heterodoxies

We return to the dinner. After our Thai hosts had finished describing the problems for which they were seeking solutions, they outlined some potential areas for research and training. We were somewhat surprised when one department head asked us, "What do you know about performance indicators, quality assurance, school-based management?" The policy response of the Thai government to New Times had been to adapt aspects of a technocratic, neoliberal educational agenda. This included an increased focus on assessment, comparative analysis of school, college, and university outcome measures, partial privatization and increased marketization of postsecondary education, and the "devolution" of management to local regions and schools. In 1997, the Thai Ministry of University Affairs established a formal body to establish quality assurance mechanisms for evaluating and comparatively ranking universities; similar moves were underway in Indonesia.

If the principal premise of our argument here holds—that the effects of globalization unfold locally, regionally, and nationally in uneven and not always centrally predictable ways—then any educational solutions by definition would have to entail amalgams and blendings, requiring the on-the-ground generation of heterodoxic strategies. Many Asian countries have turned to emulate economic rationalist approaches to education, such as those prototyped in Britain, New Zealand, and, more recently, Australia. Not surprisingly, these policies complement IMF fiscal programs that call not only for increased financial transparency but also the reform of key state institutions to simulate corporate bureaucracies and to enter into direct competition with each other and with emergent private-sector providers of services and goods. As it has in the West, this has set the conditions for tighter "one-line" budgets, downsizing of staff, casualization and work intensification, intrasystem competition between educational institutions, and increased reliance on nonrecurrent, self-generated funding.[42] All of the Rajabhat Institutes we have worked with have been enabled by recent legislation to independently set fee levels and to establish businesses to subsidize their educational operations. These enterprises range from stores, restaurants, and hotels, to craft and manufacturing activities, cleaning and catering services, and water-bottling facilities. Following the 1997 crisis, these educational "reforms" were accelerated, with the universities and Rajabhat Institutes absorbing funding cuts of between 25 and 50 percent. Hence, the tendency across Asia has been for central governments to attempt to emulate Western systems' responses to decreased funding, new curriculum demands, and changing student populations.

In turning to us to contribute to educational exchange and development, our Thai colleagues put us in a profoundly difficult situation. For we knew that (1) such reforms had not generated the kinds of productive results promised in Australian contexts and elsewhere and had exacerbated inequality;[43] and (2) that the *local* and *regional* impacts of economic and cultural globalization would be best addressed by locally driven curriculum development, instructional innovation, and institutional reorganization.

Yet there is already evidence that, like the other aspects of globalization we have discussed here, the Asian implementation of technocratic and neoliberal educational policies has been idiosyncratic and heteroglossic. For instance, school-based management and decentralization is taken in the West as an archetypal Thatcherite move toward devolution, disinvestment, and "steering from a distance"[44] via indirect control mechanisms (such as quality assurance, performance indicators, and corporate systems of accountability). Yet even this most overtly ideological of educational policy moves becomes a hybrid when transposed to other national, regional, and local contexts. In the Philippines, the agenda for educational "devolution" is linked closely with overall policy moves toward reform of a hierarchical and bureaucratized system, reforms that include moves to "indigenize" the curriculum by bringing in more community, local, and ethnic content, to find alternatives to rigid standardized-testing-based approaches to instruction and assessment, and to introduce vernacular and minority languages as media of instruction.[45] In the case of Thailand, the attempt to move to school-based management and devolution is concurrent with moves to extend universal compulsory education beyond grade six into secondary schools, and to develop programs for dealing with cultural diversity and special education needs. There are, as we have argued here, complex local histories, political economies, and material conditions enabling and disabling these developments. Here particular policy discourses and practices that are affiliated with, for example, neoliberal market orientations in the West reappear in differing configurations, with different ideological collocations, in what appear to Western eyes to be unexpected juxtapositions with progressivist, classical liberal, and even radical educational alternatives.

It would seem, then, that even direct attempts to import and reproduce the most problematic of Western educational strategies are processes fraught with local inflections and adaptations. Policymakers are confronted with, for better and worse, an implementation nightmare. Hence, in analyses and development of local educational policy responses to cultural globalization, we side with Robertson's observation that:

It is not a question of *either* homogenisation or heterogenisation but rather of the ways in which both of these two tendencies have become features of life across much of the late 20th-century world. In this perspective the problem becomes that of spelling out the ways in which homogenising and heterogenising tendencies are mutually implicative.[46]

There is little doubt that the patterns of rapid development are straining and buckling the coping capacities of traditional, postwar, and in some instances postcolonial institutions of government and the civic state. In many countries in Southeast Asia, the schooling and higher education systems—complex blends of inter-Asian, secular and nonsecular, colonialist and postcolonialist remnants, many redesigned under the auspices of postwar Western and East Bloc intellectual and material aid during the cold war—do not seem well equipped to deal with New Times. At the same time, many of the educational, social, or cultural problems ostensibly produced by globalization have little or nothing to do with an irresistible, hegemonic, Americanized "world" culture at the service of multinationals. As breathtaking as the scope and rapidity of these developments may appear, they have "other" complex histories.

What is to be done locally? We were in a difficult pedagogical situation, where the uncritical transfer of these normative models—whether managerialist models of educational governance, technocratic models of pedagogy, *or* radical models of critical literacy, feminist pedagogy, and so forth— would have been extremely problematic. If there is an activity that epitomizes the Western logos and high modernity, then it is indeed critical literacy. And attempts to teach Thai students to "be critical," in the contexts of an emergent but at times tenuous move toward an "open" public sphere for debate and dissension, and in the face of long-standing Confucian and Buddhist traditions of reverence of pedagogic authority, generated as many questions as they might have addressed.

Finally, after many more meals with our Thai colleagues, we had collaboratively built a curriculum that was about the identification and solution of local, regional, and national educational problems through the development of hybrid models of institutional development and community-based research. The foundational content of that curriculum was the study of cultural and economic globalization and the principal theme of all of our studies was "New Times." We have begun each of our programs by reviewing and distributing key Western work on globalization, much of it cited here. But instead of treating these texts as accurate analytic and descriptive tools, we have tabled them with a simple pedagogical framework, stating, "This is how the 'West' is theorizing 'you,'" and then moving toward the critique of those positions, reworking those texts with students' local analyses of the actual discourses, practices, and effects of globalization on Thai life. Moving from world to local representations, we have also discussed local media reports on the economic crisis asking, "How is the 'reality' of the crisis constructed by Thai people for other Thais? What isn't said? Whose interests do these competing accounts serve?"

This chapter is, at least in part, a snapshot of the kinds of problem-solving pedagogical and conceptual work that we have been able to construct, from "the ground up," with our colleagues and students in the past three years. It is a work in progress, a kind of knowledge formation where meanings and analytic vocabularies have been exchanged and mobilized locally by our Thai colleagues: college and university teachers and researchers—mobile phone toting, "wired" global citizens, but local agents in and of their communities.

Notes

1. Craig Reynolds, "Globalization and Cultural Nationalism in Modern Thailand," in *Southeast Asian identities*, ed. Joel Kahn (Singapore: Institute of Southeast Asian Studies, 1998), 126.
2. Roland Robertson and Habib Khondker, "Discourses of Globalisation: Preliminary Considerations," *International Sociology* 13, no. 1 (1998): 35.
3. J. Katherine Gibson-Graham, "Re-placing Class in Economic Geographies: Possibilities for a New Class Politics," in *Geographies of Economies*, ed. Roger Lee and Jane Wills (London: Arnold, 1997), 87–97.
4. J. Iain Prattis, "Alternative Views of Economy in Economic Anthropology," in *Beyond the New Economic Anthropology*, ed. John R. Clammer (London: Macmillan, 1987), 11.
5. Stuart Hall, "The Meaning of New Times," in *Stuart Hall: Critical Dialogues*, ed., David Morley and Kuan-Hsing Chen (London: Routledge, 1996), 223–37.
6. Carmen Luke and Allan Luke, "Theorising Interracial Families and Hybrid Identity: An Australian Perspective," *Educational Theory*, in press.
7. David Harvey, *The Condition of Postmodernity* (Cambridge, Eng.: Polity Press, 1989), 8.

8. Bart Moore-Gilbert, *Postcolonial Theory* (London: Verso, 1997).

9. Manuel Castells, *The Informational City* (Oxford, Eng.: Blackwell, 1989), 171.

10. It is notable that during and following the Vietnam War, Thailand, as a U.S. client state, benefited through educational scholarships and aid programs. Many of Thailand's current university administrators and educational researchers were trained in American universities in the 1970s and early 1980s on U.S. and Thai government scholarships. The shift toward working with Australian, Canadian, and U.K. institutions has only occurred with the marketization of education in the 1980s and 1990s, and the availability, before the 1997 crash, of Thai private and government funds to support study abroad. In 1998, the government placed a moratorium on all overseas travel of government-employed educators and researchers.

11. When we first began working in Thailand and Malaysia in 1996, we would often query our hosts about the apparently uncritical embrace of rapid development with disastrous ecological and social effects. One response that we repeatedly heard was something like "capital only comes around once." Ironically, the economic crisis has generated some skepticism toward technocratic panaceas. The Malaysian government, for example, has been forced to scale down and delay its ambitious multimillion dollar plans for "smart schools" with computerized school administration and computer-assisted instruction.

12. Compare Kevin Hewison, "Emerging Social Forces in Thailand," in *The New Rich in Asia*, ed. Richard Robison and David Goodman (London: Routledge, 1996), 137–62.

13. James Watson, *Golden Arches East* (Stanford: Stanford University Press, 1997).

14. Ubonrat Siriyuvasak, "Thai Pop Music and Cultural Negotiation in Everyday Politics," in *Trajectories: Inter-Asia Cultural Studies*, ed. Kuan-Hsing Chen (London: Routledge, 1998), 206.

15. Reynolds, "Globalization."

16. Reynolds, "Globalization," 121.

17. For example, Aihwa Ong, "Flexible Citizenship among Chinese Cosmopolitans," in *Cosmopolitics: Thinking and Feeling Beyond the Nation*, ed. Pheng Cheah and Bruce Robbins (Bloomington: Indiana University Press, 1996), 135–62.

18. Pasuk Phongpaichit and Chris Baker, *Thailand's Boom* (Sydney: Allen and Unwin, 1996).

19. Reynolds, "Globalization," 121.

20. Phongpaichit and Baker, *Thailand's Boom*, 15.

21. Ibid., 49.

22. Ibid., 53.

23. Ibid., 54.

24. Dipesh Chakrabarty, "Reconstructing Liberalism: Notes towards a Conversation between Area Studies and Diasporic Studies," *Public Culture* 10, no. 3 (1998): 457–81.

25. For example, Roger Lee and Jane Wills, eds., *Geographies of Economies* (London: Arnold, 1997); Reynolds, "Globalization"; and Robertson and Khondker, "Discourses of Globalisation."

26. Philip Crang, "Introduction: Cultural Turns and the (Re)Constitution of Economic Geography," in *Geographies of Economies*, ed. Roger Lee and Jane Wills (London: Arnold, 1997), 10.

27. Roland Robertson, *Globalization* (London: Sage, 1992); Malcolm Waters, *Globalization* (New York: Routledge, 1995); and Arjun Appadurai, "Disjuncture

and Difference in the Global Cultural Economy," in *Global Culture*, ed. Mike Featherstone (London: Sage, 1990), 295–310.

28. Allan Mazur, "Global Environmental Change in the News: 1987–90 vs. 1992–96," *International Sociology* 13, no. 4 (1998): 457–72.
29. Manuel Castells, *The Rise of the Network Society* (London: Blackwell, 1997).
30. Waters, *Globalization*, 125.
31. Timothy Luke, "New World Order or Neo-World Orders: Power, Politics and Ideology Informationalising Glocalities," in *Global Modernities*, ed Mike Featherstone, Scott Lash, and Roland Robertson (London: Sage, 1995), 91–107.
32. Newly Industrialized Country.
33. Harvey, *The Condition*, 8.
34. Compare Waters, *Globalization*; Robertson, *Globalization*; Immanuel Wallerstein, *The Modern World-System II* (New York: Academic, 1980); I. Wallerstein, *Geopolitics and Geoculture* (Cambridge, Eng.: Cambridge University Press, 1991); Mike Featherstone, "Global and Local Cultures," in *Mapping the Futures: Local Cultures, Global Change*, ed. Jon Bird, Barry Curtis, Tim Putnam, George Robertson, and Lisa Tickner (New York: Routledge, 1993), 169–88; and Mike Featherstone, Scott Lash, and Roland Robertson, eds., *Global Modernities* (London: Sage, 1995).
35. Roland Robertson and Habib Khondker, "Discourses of Globalisation: Preliminary Considerations," *International Sociology* 13, no. 1 (1998): 32.
36. Mike Featherstone, "Global and Local Cultures," in *Mapping the Futures*, ed. Jon Bird, Barry Curtis, Tim Putnam, George Robertson, and Lisa Tickner (London: Routledge, 1995), 186.
37. Non-Governmental Organization.
38. For example, Asia Development Bank, *Handbook for Incorporation of Social Dimensions in Projects* (Manila: Asia Development Bank, Office of Environment and Social Development, 1994).
39. For example, Motilal Sharma, *Revitalizing Teacher Education: A Multi-Mode Approach for Quality and Equitable Access for Female Teachers* (Manila: Asia Development Bank, Agriculture and Social Sectors Department, 1991).
40. Colin Leys, *The Rise and Fall of Development Theory* (Bloomington and Nairobi: Indiana University Press and East African Educational Publishers, 1996).
41. Roland Robertson, "Glocalization: Time-Space and Homogeneity-Heterogeneity," in *Global Modernities*, ed. Mike Featherstone, Scott Lash, and Roland Robertson (London: Sage, 1995), 25–44.
42. Similar moves were recently part of Jiang Zemin's 1998 Chinese civil service reforms that have led to the 50-percent-phased-in downsizing of administrative staff in ministries of education, the emergence of a marketplace for private educational institutions, and the introduction of student fees.
43. Allan Luke, "New Narratives of Human Capital," in *Major Writings in Sociology of Education*, ed. Stephen Ball (London: Routledge, in press).
44. Robert Lingard, "Educational Policy Making in a Postmodern State," *Australian Educational Researcher* 23, no. 1 (1996): 65–91.
45. Personal communication, Dr. Andrew Gonzalez, FSC, Secretary, Department of Education, Culture and Sports, Manila, 15 Oct. 1998.
46. Robertson, "Glocalization," 27.

Globalization and New Social Movements: Lessons for Critical Theory and Pedagogy

Douglas Kellner

There is no doubt about it, "globalization" is the buzzword of the decade. Journalists, politicians, business executives, academics, and others are using the word to signify that something profound is happening, that the world is changing, that a new world economic, political, and cultural order is emerging. Yet the term is used in so many different contexts, by so many different people, for so many different purposes, that it is difficult to ascertain what is at stake in the globalization problematic, what function the term serves, and what effects it has for contemporary theory, politics, and critical pedagogy.

A wide and diverse range of social theorists are arguing that today's world is organized by expanding globalization, which is strengthening the dominance of a world capitalist economic system, supplanting the primacy of the nation-state by transnational corporations and organizations, and eroding local cultures and traditions through a global culture.[1] Marxists, Weberians, world systems theorists, structuralists and functionalists, post-structuralists, and many other contemporary theorists are converging on the position that globalization is a distinguishing trend of the present moment. Moreover, advocates of a postmodern break in history argue that developments in transnational capitalism are producing a novel historical configuration of post-Fordism, or postmodernism, as an emergent cultural logic of capitalism and global culture.[2] In major modern and postmodern social theories, globalization is taken as a salient feature of our times.

Yet the conceptions of globalization deployed, the purposes for which the concept is used, and the evaluations of the structures and processes described by the concept vary wildly. For some, globalization entails the Westernization of the world,[3] while for others it involves a cover for the ascendancy of capitalism.[4] Some see globalization as generating increasing homogeneity, while others see it producing diversity and heterogeneity through increased hybridization. For business, globalization is a strategy for increasing corporate profits and power; for government it is often deployed to promote an increase in state power, while many nongovernment social organizations see globalization as a lever to produce positive social goods like environmental action, democratization, or empowering of disempowered groups through new technologies and media.[5] Some theorists equate globalization with modernity,[6] while others claim that the "global age" follows and is distinctly different from the "modern age."[7] For many theorists, we live in an age in which globalization is *the* defining concept,[8] while others find claims for the novelty and centrality of globalization exaggerated.[9]

Yet the ubiquity of the term globalization suggests that it is part of a reconfiguring and rethinking of contemporary social theory and politics that is caught up in some of the central debates and conflicts of the present age. It is certainly arguable that during the past decades the world has been undergoing the most significant period of technological innovation and global restructuring since the first decades of the twentieth century. Part of the "great transformation" to a new stage of techno-capitalism has involved a fundamental restructuring and reorganization of the world economy, polity, and culture for which the term globalization serves as a codeword.[10] It is bound up with debates over post-Fordism, postmodernism, and a series of other "posts" that themselves signify a fundamental rupture with the past. It is thus centrally involved in debates over the defining features and changes of the present era.

In this article, I will sort out some of the dominant uses of the term globalization and discuss its challenges for critical pedagogy and radical democratic politics. I propose the need for a critical theory of globalization that overcomes the one-sidedness and ideological biases that permeate most conceptions of this all-embracing and complex phenomenon, while inquiring into how globalization has affected social movements, democratization, and critical pedagogy. To the "globalization from above" of corporate capitalism and the capitalist state, I will defend a notion of "globalization from below" in which oppositional individuals and social movements resist globalization and use its institutions and instruments to further democratization and social justice.[11] While on one level globalization significantly increases the power of big corporations and big government, it can also empower groups and individuals who were previously left out of the democratic dialogue and terrain of political struggle. Such potentially positive effects of globalization include increased access to education for individuals excluded from entry to culture and knowledge and the possibility of oppositional individuals and groups to participate in global culture and politics through gaining access to global communication and media networks and to circulate local struggles and oppositional ideas through these media. The role of new technologies in social movements, political struggle, and everyday life forces critical pedagogy to rethink education and literacy in a new globalized and high-tech era, and forces social movements to reconsider their political strategies and goals.

Theorizing Globalization Critically

Talking cogently about globalization requires, first, that we sort out the different uses and meanings of the term and try to specify what processes it is used to describe. In a sense, there is no such thing as "globalization" per se. Rather, the term is used as a cover concept for a heterogeneity of processes that need to be spelled out and articulated. The term is neither innocent nor neutral in many of its uses and often serves to replace older critical discourses like "imperialism," but also ideological conceptions of "modernization." As a replacement for imperialism, it could displace focus on domination of newly developing countries by the overdeveloped ones, or of national and local economies by transnational corporations. Moreover, it could serve as a cover to neutralize the horrors of colonialism and its aftermath and could be part of a discourse of neoimperialism that serves to obscure the continuing exploitation of much of the world by a few superpowers and giant transnational corporations, thus cloaking some of the more oppressive and destructive aspects of contemporary development.

Yet as a replacement term for modernization it can also rob this previously legitimating ideology of the implications that the processes connected with globalization are necessarily bringing improvement to the lives of people in developed and highly industrialized countries. Modernization discourse presented such things as industrialization and globalization as part of an inexorable trajectory of progress and modernity that is not to be—or that simply cannot be—contested or challenged. Compared to the discourses of imperialism (negative, critical) and modernization (positive, legitimating), the discourse of globalization is on the surface neutral. It thus displaces discourses of modernization (good) and imperialism (bad), covering over their evaluative components with a seemingly unbiased term. And yet the term globalization is also bound up with highly ideological discourses of the present age being used by some to represent an entirely positive process of economic and social progress, technological innovation, more diverse products and services, a cornucopia of information and growing cultural freedom, and a higher standard of living. Proglobalization boosters include champions of the market economy, which with the triumph of Thatcherism-Reaganism in the 1980s became a dominant ideology; Bill Gates[12] and avatars of the "information superhighway" and new technologies; and other political and economic elites, supported by their academic promoters and sociological theorists who exaggerate the inexorable and irresistible trajectory of globalization while covering over its more troubling aspects.

For its critics, however, globalization is bringing about the devastating destruction of local traditions, the continued subordination of poorer nations and regions by richer ones, environmental destruction, and a homogenization of culture and everyday life.[13] These critics include

Marxists, liberals, and multiculturalists who stress the threat to national sovereignty, local traditions, and participatory democracy through global forces; environmentalists who fear the destructive ecological effects of unchecked globalization; and conservatives who see globalization as a threat to national and local cultures and the sanctity of tradition.

The already highly complex articulations of the discourse of globalization are rendered more complicated because globalization is not only a replacement term for imperialism and modernization but also is caught up in the modernity/postmodernity debates as well. Some theorists are claiming that globalization is replacing concepts like modernity and postmodernity as the central thematic of contemporary theorizing,[14] although others have assimilated the discourse, variously, to both the modernity and postmodernity problematics. For some, globalization thus constitutes a continuation of the problematic of modernization and modernity, while for others it signifies something new and different and is bound up with the postmodern turn, or an altogether novel and as yet untheorized global condition.[15] Yet here, too, totally different valorizations of the modern, postmodern, and globalization process are possible. For some theorists, globalization is seen as a process of standardization in which a globalized media and consumer culture circulates the earth, creating sameness and homogeneity everywhere, thus bringing to light the bland and boring universality and massification of the modern project. Postmodernists champion, by contrast, the local, diversity, difference, and heterogeneity, and sometimes claim that globalization itself produces hybridity and multiplicity, arguing that global culture makes possible unique appropriations and developments all over the world with new forms of hybrid syntheses of the global and the local, thus proliferating difference and heterogeneity.[16] Postmodernists also argue that every local context involves its own appropriation and reworking of global products and signifiers, thus producing more variety and diversity.

The term globalization is thus a theoretical construct that is itself contested and open for various meanings and inflections. It can be described positively or negatively—or, as I shall suggest, multivalently—to describe highly complex and multidimensional processes in the economy, polity, culture, and everyday life. In order to theorize globalization adequately, it must be seen as a complex and multidimensional phenomenon that involves different levels, flows, tensions, and conflicts. Thus, transdisciplinary social theory is necessary to capture its contours, dynamics, trajectories, problems, and possible futures. In particular, globalization involves crucial economic, political, and cultural dimensions. A critical theory of globalization must theorize each of these levels, how they are interconnected, and how individuals and social movements and groups can intervene to engage critically the different aspects of globalization and reconstruct or inflect its dynamics and forms to serve the interests of democratization, human well-being, environmental preservation, and other positive values. This provides critical pedagogy with new challenges for both understanding and transforming the world.

A critical theory of globalization attempts to specify the interconnections and interdependencies between different levels such as the economic, political, cultural and psychological, as well as between different flows of products, ideas and information, people, and technology. Critical theory describes the mediations between different phenomena, the systemic structure that organizes phenomena and processes into a social system, and the relative autonomy of the parts, such that there are both connections and disjunctions between, say, the economy and culture. Concerned to relate theory to practice, critical theory also attempts to delineate the positive potentials for greater freedom and democratization, as well as the dangers of greater domination, oppression, and destruction.[17] Grounded in historical vision, critical theory stresses the continuities and discontinuities between past, present, and future, and the possibility of constructive political action and individual and group practice, grounded in hopeful potentials in the current constellation of forces and possibilities.[18]

While a critical theory of globalization analyzes both how globalization creates forces of domination and resistance and seeks and valorizes strategies of resistance to the oppressive and exploitative aspects of globalization, it avoids one-sided discourses on globalization that are purely denunciatory, and attempts to describe both the positive potentials that globalization opens as well as its forces of domination. In the following discussion, I therefore want to argue against all one-dimensional and partial positions that see globalization either as a necessary and positive vehicle of progress and diversity, or as a force of insipid homogenization and virulent destruction and domination. Both of these positions are obviously one-sided and so, as in many cases where we encounter oversimplified either/or binary positions, we should move to a higher level to develop a critical and dialectical theory of globalization that articulates both its progressive and regressive features, as well as its fundamental ambivalence that mixes old and new, homogenization and heterogeneity, innovation and destruction, and globalization from above opposed to globalization from below.

The term globalization is thus often used as a code word that stands for a tremendous diversity of issues and problems and that serves as a front for a variety of theoretical and political positions. While it can serve as a legitimating ideology to cover over and sanitize ugly realities, a critical globalization theory can inflect the discourse to point precisely to these phenomena and can elucidate a series of contemporary problems and conflicts. In view of the different concepts and functions of globalization discourse, it is important to note that the concept is a theoretical construct that varies according to the assumptions and commitments of the theory in question. Seeing the term globalization as a construct helps rob it of its force of nature, as a sign of an inexorable triumph of market forces and the hegemony of capital, or, as the extreme Right fears, of a rapidly encroaching world government. While the term can both describe and legitimate capitalist transnationalism and supranational government institutions, a critical theory of globalization does not buy into ideological valorizations, and does affirm difference, resistance, and democratic self-determination against forms of global domination and subordination.

Resisting Globalization

The spread of global culture has momentous effects that produce new challenges for education and the polity. Culture had been the particularizing, localizing force that distinguished societies and people from each other. Culture provided forms of local identities, practices, and modes of everyday life that could serve as a bulwark against the invasion of ideas, identities, and forms of life extraneous to the specific local region in question. Education in turn transmits the skills and materials that enable individuals to participate in their culture in a creative way. Certainly, culture is an especially complex and contested terrain today as global cultures permeate local ones and new configurations emerge that synthesize both poles, providing contradictory forces of colonization *and* resistance, global homogenization *and* new local hybrid forms and identities.

It is indeed impossible to resist or ignore globalization, which is influencing every aspect of life. Globalization involves the dissemination of new technologies that have tremendous impact on the economy, polity, society, culture, education, and individual experience. Time-space compression produced by new media and communications technologies are overcoming previous boundaries of space and time, creating a global cultural village and dramatic penetration of global forces into every realm of life in every region of the world.[19] New technologies in the labor process displace living labor, make possible more flexible production, and create new labor markets, with some areas undergoing deindustrialization (for example the "rust belt" of the Midwest in the United States), while production itself becomes increasingly transnational.[20] The new technologies also create new industries, such as the computer and information industry, and allow transnational media and information to traverse the planet instantaneously.[21] This process has led some to celebrate a new global information superhighway and others to attack the new wave of media and cultural imperialism.

The global flow of culture and rapid spread of new technologies have enormous consequences for education. On the one hand, globalization might entail the imposition of corporate management structures and imperatives on educational institutions, further colonizing education by business forces. It might lead to increased commodification of education and rendering quality education only accessible to elites who can afford it. The globalization of education might involve the privileging of Western, and particularly English-language, culture in the entire world, as English is emerging as the preferred language of the Internet.

On the other hand, there is utopian potential in the new technologies as well as the possibility for increased domination and the accumulation of capital. While the first generation of computers were large mainframe systems controlled by big government and big business, the current generation of "personal computers" creates a more decentralized situation in which more individuals own their own computers and use them for their own projects and goals. In relation to education, this means the possibility of opening opportunities for research and communication not previously available to students or teachers who did not have access to major research libraries or institutions. The Internet makes accessible more information and knowledge to more people than any previous institution in history, although it has its problems and limitations. Moreover, the Internet enables individuals to participate in discussions and to circulate their ideas and work in ways that were previously closed off to individuals who were not connected to the mainstream media of information and communication.

Thus, there are great possibilities for expanded and democratized education within new technologies and the Internet. But while it would be a mistake simply to demonize and dismiss globalization or the new technologies out of hand, it would be equally wrong to celebrate such things uncritically. For example, in relation to education, there are also the dangers that new technologies will be used to downsize teachers and will be part of a reorganization of universities along corporate lines. In a globalized economy and culture, "reforms" in one sector or region often spread rapidly to others, frequently without adequate debate and discussion, so that U.S.-inspired business models might be imposed upon a wide range of institutions throughout the entire world. It is also still an open question to what extent new technologies will solve the problems of education and what new problems their widespread implementation will produce.

In any case, the dramatic transformations of the economy and culture require in turn a rethinking of education. The new technologies require new literacies and pedagogy that will enable students and citizens to function in a high-tech economy and rapidly changing society and polity.[22] Critical pedagogy has traditionally endeavored to empower individuals to control democratically their own lives and society. In an increasingly globalized world, then, it must engage the new global forces, the new technologies and changing social and cultural conditions, and the new forms of political struggle in an effort to rethink education in the light of contemporary conditions. This involves empowering individuals to both understand and resist globalization.

To a large extent, globalization represents the triumph of the economy over politics and culture, in which once relatively autonomous spheres are controlled by economic elites and forces. From this perspective, globalization represents the hegemony of capital over all other domains of life and constitutes an even higher level of capitalist domination than that described by Marx. In this regard, the concept of globalization can be disempowering, leading to cynicism and hopelessness, evoking a sense that inexorable market forces cannot be regulated and controlled by the state, or that the economy cannot be shaped and directed by the people, thus undermining democracy and countervailing powers to the hegemony of capital.[23]

There are plenty of things to denounce and attack in the present era, but so far the principal critical voices against globalization have been mostly denunciatory and dispiriting, promoting a gloom-and-doom discourse on globalization that sees it as an unmitigated disaster for both progressive social forces and the people of the world. A critical theory of globalization, however, recognizes the multidimensional, complex, and contradictory reality of globalization, while seeking and promoting conceptions and practices of resistance and struggle that attempt to counter the most destructive aspects of global forces, or that inflect globalization for democratic and locally empowering ends. Very few progressives have attempted to theorize globalization from below, to detect how globalization can be used to foster a progressive social agenda, and to encourage the project of using globalization to promote emancipation and democratization.[24]

The present conjuncture, I would suggest, is marked by a conflict between growing centralization and organization of power and wealth in the hands of the few, contrasted with opposing processes exhibiting a fragmentation of power that is more plural, multiple, and open to contestation than was previously the case. As the following analysis will suggest, both tendencies are observable, and it is up to individuals and groups to find openings for resistance. Thus, rather than just denouncing globalization, or engaging in celebration and legitimation, a critical theory of globalization reproaches those aspects that are oppressive, while seizing upon opportunities to fight domination and exploitation and to promote democratization, justice, and a progressive reconstruction of education and society.

Against capitalist globalization from above, there has been a significant eruption of forces and subcultures of resistance that have attempted to preserve specific forms of culture and society against globalization and homogenization, thus exhibiting resistance and globalization from below. Most dramatically, peasant and guerrilla movements in Latin America, labor unions, students, and environmentalists throughout the world, and a variety of other groups and movements have resisted capitalist globalization and attacks on previous rights and benefits.[25] Several dozen people's organizations from around the world have protested World Trade Organization policies and a backlash against globalization is visible everywhere. Politicians who once championed trade agreements like GATT and NAFTA are now often quiet about these arrangements, and at the 1996 annual Davos World Economic Forum its founder and managing director published a warning entitled, "Start Taking the Backlash Against

Globalization Seriously." Reports surfaced that major representatives of the capitalist system are expressing fear that capitalism is getting too mean and predatory, that it needs a kinder and gentler state to ensure order and harmony, and that the welfare state may make a comeback.[26] One should take such reports with a proverbial grain of salt, but they express fissures and openings in the system for critical discourse and intervention.

On the terrain of everyday life, new youth subcultures of resistance are visible throughout the world, as are alternative subcultures of women, gays and lesbians, blacks and ethnic minorities, and other groups that have resisted incorporation into the hegemonic mainstream culture. British cultural studies has accordingly explored both mainstream hegemonic cultures and oppositional subcultures since the 1970s. It has focused on articulations of class, race, gender, sexual preference, ethnicity, region, and nation in its explorations of concrete cultural configurations and phenomena.[27] More recently, cultural studies has also taken on a global focus, analyzing how transnational forces intervene in concrete situations and how cultural mediations can inflect the influence of such global configurations.

Indeed, a wide range of theorists have argued that the proliferation of difference and the shift to more local discourses and practices define the contemporary scene, and that theory and politics should shift from the level of globalization and its often totalizing macrotheories in order to focus on the local, the specific, the particular, the heterogeneous, and the microlevel of everyday experience. A wide range of theories associated with poststructuralism, postmodernism, feminism, and multiculturalism focuses on difference, otherness, marginality, the personal, the particular, and the concrete over more general theory and politics that aim at more global or universal conditions.[28]

It can be argued that such dichotomies as those between the global and the local express contradictions and tensions between crucial constitutive forces of the present moment and that it is therefore a mistake to reject focus on one side in favor of exclusive concern with the other.[29] Our challenge is to think through the relationships between the global and the local by observing how global forces influence and even structure an increasing number of local situations. One should also see how local forces mediate the global, inflecting global forces to diverse ends and conditions and producing unique configurations of the local and the global as the matrix for thought and action in the contemporary world.

Globalization from Below, New Technologies, and Social Movements

Globalization is thus necessarily complex and challenging to both our theories and politics. But many people these days operate with binary concepts of the global and the local and promote one or the other side of the equation as the solution to the world's problems. For globalists, globalization is the solution and underdevelopment, backwardness, and provincialism are the problems. For localists, globalization is the problem and localization is the solution. But, less simplistically, it is the *mix* that matters, and whether global or local solutions are most salient depends on the conditions in the distinctive context that one is addressing and the specific solutions and policies being proposed. In a complex, globalized world, there is no easy formula to solve the intransigent problems of the present era, yet there are so many problems on so many levels that it should not be difficult for people of imagination and good will to find opportunities for intervention in a variety of areas.

Fortunately, there are numerous projects that illustrate the concept of globalization from below. It is important to note how many of these oppositional organizations resisting globalization are employing the methods of critical pedagogy developed by Paulo Freire and others.[30] The more progressive organizations of our time are rejecting the hierarchical and authoritarian models associated with political organizations of the past and are implementing more radical democratic principles. As Bella Mody puts it, alternative cultural institutions and political movements in the Third World use "community" and "popular communication" (that is, communicating with the people): "Their process is Freirean reflection and action, their direction is horizontal, their leadership is internal, and their end is an equitable economic and social whole in which the individual is an active subject."[31]

Since new technologies are dramatically transforming every sphere of life, key challenges for critical theory involve how to analyze this great transformation and how to devise strategies to make productive use of the new technologies. Obviously, radical critiques of dehumanizing, exploitative, and oppressive uses of new technologies in the workplace, schooling, public sphere, and everyday life are more necessary than ever, but so are strategies that use new technologies to rebuild our cities, schools, economy, and society. I want to focus, therefore, in the remainder of this chapter on how new technologies can be used for increasing democratization and empowering individuals.

Grasping the progressive potential of advanced communication technologies, Frantz Fanon described the central role of the radio in the Algerian Revolution,[32] and Lenin highlighted the importance of film in promoting communist ideology after the revolution. In addition, audiotapes were used to promote the revolution in Iran and to circulate alternative information by political movements throughout the world.[33] The Tiananmen Square democracy movement in China and various groups struggling against the remnants of Stalinism in the former communist bloc used computer bulletin boards and networks, as well as other forms of communications, to disseminate information concerning their struggles.

It is now clear that computers and new technologies are essential to work, politics, education, and social life and that people who want to participate in the public and cultural life of the future will need to have computer access and literacy. Moreover, although there is the threat and real danger that the computerization of society will increase the current inequalities and inequities in the configurations of class, race, and gender power, a democratized public sphere might provide opportunities to overcome these inequities. There are indeed by now copious examples of how the Internet and cyber-democracy have been used in oppositional political movements. A large number of insurgent intellectuals are already making use of these new technologies and public spheres in their political projects. The peasants and guerrilla armies struggling in Chiapas, Mexico, from the beginning used computer databases, pirate radio, and other forms of media to circulate their struggles and ideas. Every manifesto, text, and bulletin produced by the Zapatista Army of National Liberation, which occupied land in the southern Mexican state of Chiapas in 1994, was immediately circulated through the world via computer networks.[34] In January 1995, when the Mexican government moved against the Zapatistas, computer networks were used to inform and mobilize individuals and groups throughout the world to support their struggles against repressive state action. There were many demonstrations in support of the rebels throughout the world; prominent journalists, human rights observers, and delegations traveled to Chiapas in solidarity and to report on the uprising; and the Mexican and U.S. governments were bombarded with messages arguing for negotiations, rather than repression. The Mexican government accordingly did not pursue their usual policy of harsh repression of dissident groups, and as of this writing in spring 1999, they have continued to negotiate with the insurgents, although there was an assassination of perceived Zapatista forces by local death squads in early 1998—which once again triggered significant Internet-generated pressures on the Mexican government to prosecute the perpetrators.

Moreover, opponents involved in anti-NAFTA struggles made extensive use of new communications technology.[35] Such multinational networking failed to stop NAFTA, but it created alliances useful for the struggles of the future. As Nick Witheford notes:

> The anti-NAFTA coalitions, while mobilizing a depth of opposition entirely unexpected by capital, failed in their immediate objectives. But the transcontinental dialogues which emerged checked—though by no means eliminated—the chauvinist element in North American opposition to free trade. The movement created a powerful pedagogical crucible for cross-sectoral and cross-border organizing. And it opened pathways for future connections, including electronic ones, which were later effectively mobilized by the Zapatista uprising and in continuing initiatives against maquilladora exploitation.[36]

Thus, using new technologies to link information and practice is neither extraneous to political battles nor merely utopian. Even if material gains are not won, often the information circulated or alliances formed can be of use. For example, two British activists were sued by the fast-food chain McDonald's for distributing leaflets denouncing the corporation's low wages, advertising practices, involvement in deforestation, harvesting of animals, and promotion of junk food and an unhealthy diet. The activists counterattacked, organized a McLibel campaign, assembled a McSpotlight website with a tremendous amount of information criticizing the corporation, and assembled experts to testify and confirm their criticisms. The five-year civil trial, which ended ambiguously in July 1997, created unprecedented bad publicity for McDonald's and was circulated throughout the world via Internet websites, mailing lists, and discussion groups. The McLibel group claims that their website was accessed more than twelve million times and the *Guardian* reported that the site "claimed to be the most comprehensive source of information on a multinational corporation ever assembled."[37]

Many labor organizations are also beginning to make use of the new technologies. Mike Cooley has written of how computer systems can re-skill, rather than de-skill workers,[38] while Shoshana Zuboff has discussed the ways in which high tech can be used to "informate" workplaces, rather than automate them, expanding workers' knowledge and control over operations, rather than reducing and eliminating it.[39] Jesse Drew has extensively interviewed representatives of major U.S. labor organizations to see how they are making use of new communication technologies and how these instruments help them with their struggles. Many of his union activists indicated how useful e-mail, faxes, websites, and the Internet have been to their struggles and, in particular, indicated how such techno-politics helped organize demonstrations or strikes in favor of striking English or Australian dockworkers, as when U.S. longshoremen organized strikes to boycott ships carrying material loaded by scab workers.[40] Techno-politics thus helps labor create global alliances in order to combat increasingly transnational corporations.

On the whole, labor organizations note that computer networks are useful for coordinating and distributing information, but cannot replace print media (which are more accessible to many of its members), face-to-face meetings, and traditional forms of political struggle.[41] Thus, the challenge is to articulate one's communications politics with actual political movements and struggles so that cyber-struggle is an arm of political battle, rather than its replacement or substitute. The most efficacious Internet struggles have indeed intersected with real struggles encompassing campaigns to free political prisoners, boycotts of corporate products, strikes, and even revolutionary struggles, as noted above.

Hence, to capital's globalization from above, cyber-activists have been attempting to carry out globalization from below, developing networks of solidarity and circulating struggle throughout the planet. To the capitalist international of transnational corporate globalization, a Fifth International, to use Waterman's phrase,[42] of computer-mediated activism is emerging, one that is qualitatively different from the party-based socialist and communist internationals. Such networking links labor, feminist, ecological, peace, and other oppositional groups, providing the basis for a new politics of alliance and solidarity to overcome the limitations of postmodern identity politics.[43]

Moreover, a series of struggles around gender, sex, and race are also mediated by new communications technologies. Many feminists have now established websites, mailing lists, and other forms of cyber-communication to circulate their struggles. Younger women, sometimes deploying the concept of "riot grrrls," have created electronically mediated 'zines, web sites, and discussion groups to promote their ideas and to discuss their problems and struggles.[44] African-American women, Latinas, and other groups of women, too, have been developing web sites and discussion lists to advance their interests. And AIDS activists are employing new technologies to disseminate and discuss medical information and to activate their constituencies for courses of political action and struggle.

Likewise, African-American insurgent intellectuals have made use of broadcast and computer technologies to promote their struggles. John Fiske has described some African-American radio projects in the "techno-struggles" of the present age and the central role of the media in recent struggles around race and gender.[45] African-American "knowledge warriors" are using radio, computer networks, and other media to circulate their ideas and "counterknowledge" on a variety of issues, contesting the mainstream and offering alternative views and politics. Likewise, activists in communities of color—like Oakland, Harlem, and Los Angeles—are setting up community computer and media centers to teach the skills necessary to survive the onslaught of the media-ization of culture and computerization of society to people in their communities.

Indeed, a variety of local activists have been using the Internet to criticize local government, to oppose corporate policies, and to organize people around specific issues. These efforts range from developing websites to oppose local policies, such as an attempt to transform a military airport into a civilian one in El Toro, California, to gadflies who expose corruption in local government, to citizen groups who use the Internet to inform, recruit, and organize individuals to become active in various political movements and struggles.[46] Thus, new communications technologies enable ordinary citizens and activists to become political actors and communicators, to produce and disseminate information, and to participate in debates and struggles, thus helping to realize Gramsci's dictum that anyone could be a political intellectual.

Obviously, right-wing and reactionary groups can and have used the Internet to promote their political agendas as well. In a short time, one can easily access an exotic witch's brew of ultraright websites maintained by the Ku Klux Klan and a myriad of neo-Nazi groups including Aryan Nation and various patriot militia groups. Internet discussion lists also promote these views and the ultraright is extremely active on many computer forums, as well as on radio programs and stations, public access television shows, fax campaigns, video, and even rock music productions. These groups are hardly harmless, having promoted terrorism of various sorts extending from church burnings to the bombings of public buildings. Adopting quasi-Leninist discourse and tactics for ultraright causes, these extremist groups have been successful in recruiting working-class members devastated by the developments of global capitalism, which have resulted in widespread unemployment for traditional forms of industrial, agricultural, and unskilled labor.[47]

The Internet is thus a contested terrain, used by Left, Right, and Center to promote their own agendas and interests. The political battles of the future may well be fought in the streets, factories, parliaments, and other sites of past struggle, but politics is already mediated by broadcast, computer, and information technologies and will increasingly be so in the future. Those interested in the politics and culture of the future should therefore be clear on the important role of the new public spheres and intervene accordingly, while critical pedagogues have the responsibility of teaching students the skills that will enable them to participate in the politics and struggles of the present and future.

Globalization and Critical Pedagogy: Concluding Remarks

In light of the neoliberal projects to dismantle the welfare state, colonize the public sphere, and control globalization, it is up to citizens and activists to create new public spheres, politics, and pedagogies to use the new technologies to discuss what kinds of society we want, and to oppose the society we do not want. This involves, minimally, demands for more education, health care, welfare, and benefits from the state and a struggle to create a more democratic and egalitarian society. But one cannot expect that generous corporations and a beneficent state are going to make available to citizens the bounties and benefits of the globalized new information economy. Rather, it is up to individuals and groups to promote democratization and progressive social change.

Thus, in opposition to the globalization from above of corporate capitalism, I would advocate a globalization from below, which supports individuals and groups in struggle using the new technologies to create a more egalitarian and democratic society. Of course, the new technologies might exacerbate existing inequalities in the current class, gender, race, and regional configurations of power and give the major corporate forces powerful new tools to advance their interests. In this situation, it is up to the people, to us, to devise strategies to use the new technologies to promote democratization and social justice. For as the new technologies become ever more central to every domain of everyday life, developing an oppositional techno-politics in the new public spheres will become more and more important,[48] and it will be ever more important to rethink education in light of the technological revolution.

Consequently, critical pedagogy needs to develop new educational strategies to counter globalization from above, to empower individuals to understand and act effectively in a globalized world, and to struggle for social justice. This requires teaching new literacies such as media and computer literacy,[49] as well as helping to empower students and citizens to deploy new technologies for progressive purposes. Globalization and new technologies *are* dominant forces of the future, and it is up to critical theorists and activists to illuminate their nature and effects, to demonstrate the threats to democracy and freedom, and to seize opportunities for progressive education and democratization.

The project of transforming education will take different forms in different contexts. In the overdeveloped countries, individuals must be empowered to work and act in a high-tech information economy and thus must learn skills of media and computer literacy in order to survive in the new social environment. Traditional skills of knowledge and critique must also be fostered so that students can name the system, describe and grasp the changes occurring and the defining features of the new global order, and learn to engage in critical and oppositional practice in the interests of democratization and progressive transformation. This requires gaining a vision of how life can be, of alternatives to the present order, and of the necessity of struggle and organization to realize progressive goals. Languages of knowledge and critique must thus be supplemented by the discourse of hope and praxis.

It is interesting that one of the godfathers of critical pedagogy, Paulo Freire, was positive toward media and new technologies, seeing technologies as potential tools for empowering citizens, as well as instruments of domination in the hands of ruling elites. Freire wrote, "Technical and scientific training need not be inimical to humanistic education as long as science and technology in the revolutionary society are at the service of permanent liberation, of humanization."[50] Many critical pedagogues, however, are technophobes, seeing new technologies solely as instruments of domination. In a world inexorably undergoing processes of globalization and technological transformation, one cannot, however, in good conscience advocate a policy of clean hands and purity, distancing oneself from technology and globalization, but must intervene in the processes of economic and technological revolution, attempting to deflect these forces for progressive ends and developing new pedagogies to advance the project of human liberation and well-being.

Notes

1. Attempts to chart the globalization of capital, decline of the nation-state, and rise of a new global culture include the essays in Mike Featherstone, ed., *Global Culture: Nationalism, Globalization and Modernity* (London: Sage, 1990); Anthony Giddens, *Consequences of Modernity* (Cambridge, Eng., and Palo Alto: Polity and Stanford University Press, 1990); Roland Robertson, *Globalization* (London: Sage, 1991); Anthony D. King, ed., *Culture, Globalization and the World-System: Contemporary Conditions for the Representation of Identity* (Binghamton: SUNY Art Dept., 1991); Jon Bird et al., eds., *Mapping the Futures: Local Cultures, Global Change* (London and New York: Routledge, 1993); Paul Gilroy, *The Black Atlantic: Modernity and Double Consciousness* (Cambridge: Harvard University Press, 1993); Giovanni Arrighi, *The Long Twentieth Century* (London and New York: Verso, 1994); Scott Lash and John Urry, *Economies of Signs and Space* (London: Sage, 1994); Inderpal Grewal and Caren Kaplan, eds., *Scattered Hegemonies: Postmodernity and Transnational Feminist Practices* (Minneapolis: University of Minnesota Press, 1994); McKenzie Wark, *Virtual Geography: Living With Global Media Events* (Bloomington and Indianapolis: Indiana University Press, 1994); Mike Featherstone, Scott Lash, and Roland Robertson, eds., *Global Modernities* (London: Sage, 1995); Barrie Axford, *The Global System* (Cambridge, Eng.: Polity Press, 1995); David Held, *Democracy and the Global Order* (Cambridge, Eng., and Palo Alto: Polity Press and Stanford University Press, 1995); Malcolm Waters, *Globalization* (London: Routledge, 1995); Paul Hirst and Grahame Thompson, *Globalization in Question* (Cambridge, Eng.: Polity Press, 1996); Martin Albrow, *The Global Age* (Cambridge, Eng.: Polity Press, 1996); Jerry Mander and Edward Goldsmith, *The Case against the Global Economy* (San Francisco: Sierra Club Books, 1996); Ann Cvetkovich and Douglas Kellner, *Articulating the Global and the Local: Globalization and Cultural Studies* (Boulder: Westview Press, 1997); Linda Weiss, "Globalization and the Myth of the Powerless State," *New Left Review 225*

(1997): 3–27; Linda Weiss, *The Myth of the Powerless State: Governing the Economy in a Global Era* (Cambridge, Eng.: Polity Press:, 1998); and Roland Axtmann, ed., *Globalization in European Context* (London: Cassells, 1998). I will draw on these and other studies during the course of this article. I am, however, especially indebted to work with Ann Cvetkovich on a book, *Articulating the Global and the Local: Globalization and Cultural Studies*, and to work with Steven Best on *The Postmodern Turn* and our forthcoming *The Postmodern Adventure* (New York: Guilford Press).

2. David Harvey, *The Condition of Postmodernity* (Cambridge, Eng.: Blackwell, 1989); Edward Soja, *Postmodern Geographies* (London: Verso, 1989); Edward Soja, *ThirdSpace* (Cambridge and Oxford, Eng.: Blackwell, 1996); Fredric Jameson, *Postmodernism, or the Cultural Logic of Late Capitalism* (Durham, N.C.: Duke University Press, 1991); and Mark Gottdiener, *Postmodern Semiotics* (Oxford, Eng.: Blackwell, 1995).

3. Serge Latouche, *The Westernization of the World* (Cambridge, Eng.: Polity Press, 1996).

4. Marjorie Ferguson, "The Mythology about Globalization," *European Journal of Communication* 7, (1992): 69–93.

5. Web site searches on globalization that I did during 1997 and 1998 indicated that the concept of globalization turned up in most major corporate web sites, as well as many state and local governmental sites, political action group and social movement sites, and a plethora of academic sites, with many of the latter indicating globalization research projects, suggesting that the concept provides cultural capital and economic awards for academics as well as for business and government.

6. For example, Anthony Giddens, *Consequences of Modernity* (Cambridge, Eng., and Palo Alto: Polity and Stanford University Press, 1990); and Ulrich Beck, *The Risk Society* (London: Sage, 1992).

7. Martin Albrow, *The Global Age* (Cambridge, Eng.: Polity Press, 1996).

8. Barrie Axford, *The Global System* (Cambridge, Eng..: Polity Press, 1995); and Albrow, *The Global Age.*

9. Paul Hirst and Grahame Thompson, *Globalization in Question* (Cambridge, Eng.: Polity Press, 1996); Linda Weiss, *The Myth of the Powerless State: Governing the Economy in a Global Era* (Cambridge, Eng.: Polity Press, 1998).

10. Karl Polyani, *The Great Transformation* (Boston: Beacon Press, 1944/1957).

11. Richard Falk, "The Making of Global Citizenship," in *Global Visions: Beyond the New World Order*, ed. J. Brecher, J. B. Childs, and J. Cutler (Montreal: Black Rose Books, 1993), 39–50.

12. Bill Gates, *The Road Ahead* (New York: Viking, 1995).

13. See the studies in Jerry Mander and Edward Goldsmith, *The Case against the Global Economy.*

14. Mike Featherstone, Scott Lash, and Roland Robertson, eds., *Global Modernities* (London: Sage, 1995); Malcolm Waters, *Globalization* (London: Routledge, 1995); and Albrow, *The Global Age.*

15. On postmodern theory, see Steven Best and Douglas Kellner, *Postmodern Theory: Critical Interrogations* (London and New York: MacMillan and Guilford, 1991); and on the postmodern turn, see Steven Best and Douglas Kellner, *The Postmodern Turn* (New York: Guilford Press, 1997); and Best and Kellner, *The Postmodern Adventure.*

16. Stuart Hall, "The Local and the Global: Globalization and Ethnicity," and "Old and New Identities, Old and New Ethnicities," in King, *Culture*, 19–40 and 41–68.

17. Douglas Kellner, *Critical Theory, Marxism and Modernity* (Cambridge, Eng., and Baltimore: Polity Press and Johns Hopkins University Press, 1989).

18. Steven Best, *The Politics of Historical Vision* (New York: Guilford Press, 1995).

19. McKenzie Wark, *Virtual Geography: Living With Global Media Events* (Bloomington and Indianapolis: Indiana University Press, 1994).

20. David Harvey, *The Condition of Postmodernity* (Cambridge, Eng.: Blackwell, 1989).

21. David Morley and Kevin Robbins, *Spaces of Identity* (London and New York: Routledge, 1995).

22. Douglas Kellner, "Multiple Literacies and Critical Pedagogy in a Multicultural Society," *Educational Theory* 48, no. 1 (1998): 103–22.

23. See Paul Hirst and Grahame Thompson, *Globalization in Question* (Cambridge, Eng.: Polity Press, 1996).

24. An exception is found in the pages of the March/April 1998 issue of *Mother Jones* in which editor Jeffrey Klein and writer Walter Russell Mead call for a critical engagement of progressives with globalization. They project an optimistic scenario in which declines in national deficits, increases in economic growth, and an expanding tax base combined with tax reform could generate revenues that could be employed for progressive social programs, environmental preservation and restoration, and emancipatory social transformation. Seeing globalization as inexorable, Klein argues, "The choice is between pessimism and reaction or optimism and engagement." While I agree with the need for critical engagement with globalization, I would argue, however, that there is plenty to be both optimistic and pessimistic about, and that critical social theory should be both more negative and critical and more militant and activist than ever before in the face of contradictory tendencies in the present moment. For while a dramatic restructuring of global capitalism provides new possibilities and spaces for intervention, as I argue in this study, there are also new possibilities for domination and destruction. Thus, a critical theory of globalization is dialectical in the classical sense that sees the negative and positive possibilities and criticizes and attempts to overcome the negative while pursuing positive normative goals and vision.

25. On resistance to globalization by labor, see Kim Moody, "Towards an International Social-Movement Unionism," *New Left Review* 225 (1997): 52–72; on resistance by environmentalists and other social movements, see the studies in Mander and Goldsmith, *The Case*, while I provide examples below from several domains.

26. See the article in *New York Times,* 7 Feb. 1996, A:15.

27. See the studies in Stuart Hall and Tony Jefferson, eds., *Resistance through Rituals: Youth Subcultures in Post-War Britain* (London: Unwin Hyman, 1976); Dick Hebdige, *Subculture: The Meaning of Style* (London and New York: Metheun, 1979); Lawrence Grossberg, Cary Nelson, and Paula Treichler, eds., *Cultural Studies* (London and New York: Routledge, 1992); Simon During, ed., *The Cultural Studies Reader* (London and New York: Routledge, 1993); and Douglas Kellner, *Media Culture* (London and New York: Routledge, 1995).

28. Such positions are associated with the postmodern theories of Foucault, Lyotard, and Rorty, and have been taken up by a wide range of feminists, multiculturalists,

and others. On these theorists and postmodern politics, see Steven Best and Douglas Kellner, *Postmodern Theory: Critical Interrogations* (London and New York: MacMillan and Guilford, 1991); and Steven Best and Douglas Kellner, *The Postmodern Turn* (New York: Guilford Press, 1997).

29. Ann Cvetkovich and Douglas Kellner, *Articulating the Global and the Local: Globalization and Cultural Studies* (Boulder: Westview Press, 1997).

30. Paulo Freire, *Pedagogy of the Oppressed* (New York: Herder and Herder, 1972).

31. Bella Mody, *Designing Messages for Development Communication: An Audience Participation-Based Research* (Newbury Park, Calif.: Sage, 1991), 29. Cees Hamelink, *Trends in World Communication: On Disempowerment and Self-empowerment* (Penang, Malaysia: Southbound, 1994) also indicates how Freire's concepts are evident in alternative media activity within labor movements and new social movements, thus creating a "voice" for those previously left out of cultural and political communication and debate and indicating as well how such activity helps produce active subjects and (political) consciousness (Freire's *conscientização*).

32. Frantz Fanon, *For a Dying Colonialism* (New York: Grove Press, 1967).

33. See John Downing, *Radical Media* (Boston: South End Press, 1984).

34. See Harry Cleaver, "The Chiapas Uprising," *Studies in Political Economy* 44 (1994): 141–57; the documents collected in Zapatistas Collective, *Zapatistas: Document of the New Mexican Revolution* (New York: Autonomedia, 1994); and Manuel Castells, *The Power of Identity* (Oxford, Eng.: Blackwell, 1997).

35. See Joseph Brenner, "Internationalist Labor Communication by Computer Network: The United States, Mexico and Nafta" (unpublished paper, 1994); and Howard Fredericks, "North American NGO Networking Against NAFTA: The Use of Computer Communications in Cross-Border Coalition Building" (XVII International Congress of the Latin American Studies Association, 1994).

36. Nick Dyer-Witheford, *Cyber-Marx: Cycles and Circuits of Struggle in High-Technology Capitalism* (Chicago: University of Illinois Press, in press).

37. February 22, 1996; see www.mcspotlight.org. On the trial and its aftermath, see John Vidal, *McLibel: Burger Culture on Trial* (New York: The New Press, 1997).

38. Mike Cooley, *Architect or Bee? The Human Price of Technology* (London: Hogarth, 1987)

39. Shoshana Zuboff, *In the Age of the Smart Machine: The Future of Work and Power* (New York: Basic Books, 1988).

40. Jesse Drew, "Global Communications in the Post-Industrial Age: A Study of the Communications Strategies of U.S. Labor Organizations" (Ph.D. diss., University of Texas, 1998).

41. For an overview of the use of electronic communication technology by labor, see the studies by Kim Moody, *An Injury to One* (London: Verso, 1988); Moody, "Towards an International"; Peter Waterman, "Communicating Labor Internationalism: A Review of Relevant Literature and Resources," *Communications: European Journal of Communications* 15, no. 1–2 (1990): 85–103; Peter Waterman, "International Labour Communication by Computer: The Fifth International?" *Working Paper Series* 129 (The Hague: Institute of Social Studies, 1992); Jeremy Brecher and Tim Costello, *Global Village or Global Pillage: Economic Reconstruction from Bottom Up* (Boston: South End Press, 1994); and Drew, "Global Communications." Labor projects using the new technologies

include the U.S.-based Labornet, the European Geonet, the Canadian Solinet, the Mexican La Neta, the South African WorkNet, the Asia Labour Monitor Resource Centre, Mujer a Mujer, representing Latina women's groups, and the Third World Network, while PeaceNet in the United States is devoted to a variety of progressive peace and justice issues.

42. Peter Waterman, "International Labour."
43. On the latter, see Steven Best and Douglas Kellner, *Postmodern Theory: Critical Interrogations* (London and New York: MacMillan and Guilford, 1991); Steven Best and Douglas Kellner, *The Postmodern Turn* (New York: Guilford Press, 1997); and Steven Best and Douglas Kellner, *The Postmodern Adventure* (New York: Guilford Press, in press).
44. Mary Celeste Kearney, "'Don't Need You.' Rethinking Identity Politics and Separatism from a Grrrl Perspective," in *Youth Culture: Identity in a Postmodern World*, ed. Jonathan Epstein (Malden, Mass: Blackwell, 1998), 148–88.
45. John Fiske, *Media Matters* (Minneapolis: University of Minnesota Press, 1994).
46. See "Invasion of the Gadflies in Cyberspace," *Los Angeles Times*, 18 May 1998; and Manuel Castells, *The Power of Identity* (Oxford: Blackwell, 1997), chap. 2–4.
47. See discussion in Best and Kellner, *The Postmodern Adventure*.
48. See Douglas Kellner, *Media Culture* (London and New York: Routledge, 1995); Douglas Kellner, "Intellectuals and New Technologies," *Media, Culture, and Society* 17 (1995): 427–48; and Douglas Kellner, "Intellectuals, the New Public Spheres and Techno-Politics," *New Political Science* 41–42 (Fall 1997): 169–88.
49. Kellner, "Multiple Literacies."
50. Freire, *Pedagogy*, 157. Freire also stated, "It is not the media themselves which I criticize, but the way they are used" (136). Moreover, he argued for the importance of teaching media literacy to empower individuals against manipulation and oppression, and for using the most appropriate media to help teach the subject matter in question (114–16).

Does the Internet Constitute a Global Educational Community?

Nicholas C. Burbules

The Great Community

"Community" is one of the keywords of American education.[1] Partly out of a nostalgic memory of a time when most
schools were intimately involved with other local institutions
of civil society (families, churches, and so on), and partly out
of a principled decentralization of educational policy from
the national level to the state and from the state to the city
and district levels, American educational policy and practice
continually invoke this term to conjure support for schools
and to foster a sense of collective responsibility for what
happens in them. For example:

The move away from the dominant ethic of bureaucracy and competitive individualism and toward more democratic values of support, diversity, and community is most possible within a political climate of shared responsibility and trust. Projects aiming to create learning communities, therefore, attend to establishing new political relations among teachers, administrators, parents, students, and community members.[2]

Today, phrases like "community control," "community standards," "learning communities," and "communities of practice" are widely used in education, expressing the underlying, unquestioned idea that schools should be communities of some sort and should be closely integrated with larger communities of which they are a part.

This nostalgic vision of community rests upon a recollection, also, of a time when affiliation was based upon proximity, relative homogeneity, and familiarity: the community of a small town, a neighborhood, an extended family.[3] We see this nostalgia quite clearly, for example, in the influential ideas of John Dewey, who recalled the town hall meetings and small-town bonhomie of his childhood in rural New England while seeking to reconstruct a vision of community that could sustain the modern urban contexts of schooling that he was analyzing in his later career.[4] For Dewey, the challenge was to reconceive "community" in contexts where proximity, homogeneity, and familiarity no longer held; he called this vision the "Great Community," and for him it underlaid the conception of citizenship within the modern nation-state. His remembrance of, and faith in, the virtues of a local, face-to-face community carried over to his vision of democracy, as in *Democracy and Education*, where he argued that citizens are simultaneously part of two sorts of communities, those based upon like-mindedness, to which members hold one sort of allegiance, and those based upon broader civic obligations and a sense of common interest, to which members hold a different sort of allegiance. In one of the most memorable passages of his book, he argued that it is how democracies manage communication within *and* across these groups—two values that are by necessity often in tension with one another—that the vitality and self-governance of a democratic public can be maintained. Dewey (famously) notes in this context the related roots of the terms "community," "communication," and what is held in "common."[5] Hence even as he acknowledged the pluralism of modern urban contexts, his vision of community rested upon the idea of recognizing (or creating) elements of commonality that could sustain a sense of "community." At its broadest level—the Great Community—this meant a politically constituted public that rested not only upon "conjoint activity" but also on the recognition of consequences of collective actions and decisions that were of import to all, of common concern to all.[6]

As noted, Dewey understood that this collective sense of community was often in tension with local senses of community and that citizens often had to balance split loyalties between their affiliations based upon (as I have put it) proximity, homogeneity, and familiarity, and those based upon a more rational calculation of the long-term, aggregated consequences of personal and local decisions, the shared interests of a larger community. We see this sort of conflict today, for example, between local groups, often motivated by religious sentiment, who want to exclude from "their" schools curriculum content that brings students in contact with cultures and values that exist within the larger society. From the standpoint of the larger society, students should be prepared to think about, consider, and in many cases learn to tolerate such diversity, but from the standpoint of the local group, these alternatives maybe repugnant to their own values. Dewey recognized such tensions, but seemed to believe that they were generally reconcilable, partly because of his faith in the force of reason to persuade citizens of their larger obligations and interconnectedness and partly because he believed in the mythic force of the ideal of the nation and of the democratic public sphere.

Hannah Arendt had a very different and, I would say, more agnostic vision of this problem.[7] For Arendt, the public space is fundamentally identified with plurality, not with commonality, and the political constitution of public decision making often will not rest upon identifying real or perceived similarities or commonalities of interest, but upon reaching provisional conclusions that contending groups agree to accept. Such outcomes of political deliberation may rest upon some rational assessment of common interest or common purpose (Dewey's vision), or they may rest upon quite different considerations, each group for their own reasons, but balanced against one another in a compact acceptable to all. If this is a vision of "community," it is one much more attenuated and provisional than the idea of the Great Community. Yet another situation is one in which even this level of agreement may not obtain and in which the only ground for coexistence within a pluralistic context is one of tolerance, despite unreconciled difference.

This is the view, for example, of Iris Marion Young, one of the foremost critics of the ideal of "community" as it has come to us from liberal democratic theorists such as Dewey. Young writes:

> The ideal of community . . . expresses a desire for the fusion of subjects with one another which in practice operates to exclude those with whom the group does not identify. The ideal of community denies and represses social difference, the fact that the polity cannot be thought of as a unity in which all participants share a common experience and common values. In its privileging of face-to-face relations, moreover, the ideal of community denies difference in the form of the temporal and spatial distancing that characterizes social process. As an alternative to the ideal of community, I develop . . . an ideal of city life as a vision of social relations affirming group difference. As a normative ideal, city life instantiates social relations of difference without exclusion. Different groups dwell in the city alongside one another, of necessity interacting in city spaces . . . . [D]ifferent groups . . . dwell together in the city without forming a community.[8]

From this standpoint, we must always ask *who* is seeking to foster a sense of community, among which groups, and for what purposes? Who is being included within this community, and who is being left out?

The ideal of community has been similarly questioned, particularly in the context of the formation of the modern nation-state, by Benedict Anderson, who argues that communities, particularly at the national level, are always *imagined* (or to use alternative language, "constructed" or "constituted"), not givens.[9] This analysis is especially important as a corrective to visions of community (or nationhood) as something naturalized or based on essential similarities (as in defined communities of ethnicity or race). "Community" is imagined, or constituted, then, in specific historical conditions and against a background of political interests. The analysis of Young, or Anderson, belies the connotations of "community" as something based solely on warm feelings of affiliations, and, it views such ascriptions as something experienced by various "others," excluded or marginalized by communities, as a judgment or a threat—indeed, as something often meant precisely *as* a judgment or a threat. Hence, it is important not to read Anderson's use of the term "imagined" as meaning something merely made up and ephemeral. Even "imagined" communities are "real" in their effects on people.

The dichotomy of real or imagined obscures the actual dynamics of belief and action, which motivate and reinforce one another: believing that something is true makes people act and treat one another in certain ways; these actions and influences can come to create realities that (retrospectively) confirm and support those beliefs. This may be nowhere more clear than in the case of communities, where imagining certain affinities reinforces and is reinforced by ways of speaking and acting together and by practices of inclusion and exclusion that reify the imagined borders. Thus, communities that may be formed initially merely on grounds of efficacy or convenience, can over time take on stronger and stronger feelings of affiliation and commonality, even when (previously) these would not have been thought to exist. Conversely, commonalities (of character or interest, for example) that one might argue "really" exist may in fact *exacerbate* conflicts and heighten the feelings of competition and opposition between groups. According to this line of argument, then, commonality and difference are not the sole driving conditions of the politics of community, and identified communities may exist along multiple dimensions and forms, often based more in who they are excluding as "other," than in what binds them together.

This, in turn, raises a fundamental question that always needs to be posed in the face of ascriptions of community: What are the conditions under which this "community" is being secured?

With this background in place, I can turn now to the issue animating this essay: the idea that the Internet is becoming a sort of community (or "virtual community") itself and, because it is becoming the primary medium for the transmission of communication, information, culture, and goods and services around the world, that it is becoming a kind of "global community." What do these notions mean: "virtual community" or "global community"? And how do these emergent, imagined communities affect our understandings of educational policies and practices? I hope that this essay can provide a helpful way of thinking about these issues.

The Conditions of Community

The idea of community, as discussed in the previous section, rests between two sets of values: on the one hand, the idea that cooperation and shared responsibility provide the best context for human effectiveness in accomplishing social goals; and on the other, the idea that close ties of affiliation are beneficial and supportive, if not necessary, for the living of a good life. This makes the notion of "community" uniquely flexible in being able to appeal to both pragmatic, ends-oriented ways of thinking, as well as those based more on warm personal ties and strong group identification. It is, in short, an *ideology*. To call it ideological is simply to point out the way it operates within these different discourses, unifying and motivating social reform agendas that arise from quite different premises and intentions. The very vagueness and open-endedness of the term allows it to be used in these different ways, but always wrapped up in what Raymond Williams calls a "warmly persuasive" mood; as Williams says (not having Young's work before him), nobody has anything bad to say about the value of "community."[10] I believe this faith can be seen especially, though not uniquely, in contemporary discourses about American education, across the entire political spectrum.[11]

But today, the developments of post-Foucauldian theory cause us to ask a different, more skeptical set of questions about this ideal. We are more aware of how ascriptions of community, either as a description of a state of affairs or as an ideal to work toward, are based not in natural commonalities, but rather in mediated relations that are politically constituted in specific historical conditions and spaces. The existence of a "community" is not a given, therefore, but a claim, a proposal, that is bounded by a set of conditions and practices that have given rise to it. Hence it is a very different perspective on community to ask, *under what conditions* is it thought to obtain? A corollary question, in light of Young's concerns, is to examine the dynamics of exclusion, as well as those of inclusion, necessary to the formation of any particular community—to appreciate that there can never be, so to speak, a "Great Community." The very conditions that include some, exclude others (sometimes inadvertently, though often quite intentionally).

In this section I want to explore three sets of conditions that are part of the dynamic of creating and identifying a community: mediating conditions, political conditions, and conditions of space and place. I will then use these three sets of conditions to examine the sorts of communities the on-line environment seems to be fostering, and their meaning as educational communities.

Mediating Conditions of Community. All human interactions are mediated, even apparently "direct" face-to-face interactions. As Erving Goffman's work explores, even the most *immediate* social interactions are in fact still *mediated* by a variety of performances, gestures, and rituals that do as much to keep the participants opaque to one another as to facilitate some degree of understanding and cooperation. It is a myth to imagine that the more immediate interactions are always the most honest, open, and intimate ones. In other contexts, these mediating conditions may be more visible to people, but this does not in itself grant them more import or influence.

One type of mediating condition is the medium of interaction itself: through face-to-face conversation, different types of writing, or telephone or some other distance medium (including the Internet itself, which I will discuss later). It is important to see, I think, that these are not *degrees* of mediation, or contrasts between mediated and unmediated (face-to-face) interaction, but rather alternative forms of mediation, each of which works in its own distinctive ways to disclose and conceal—which is what media do, and what they are often explicitly designed to do. Any medium acts as a type of frame, highlighting certain elements of interaction and making them more visible while at the same time serving to block out elements that fall outside the frame. Some media have costs associated with them, sometimes quite material and economic costs, sometimes psychic ones (such as the risks of making one's self "public"); these costs have differential effects on persons. In comparing media, it is important, then, to contrast their distinctive inclusions and exclusions, not to attempt to rank them on a single, simple scale from more to less revealing. Social interactions, as in a purported community, take on particular features because of the media through which they take place.

Overlapping with these questions of media are the forms of communication available to social actors. Dewey was, I think, correct about this: the kind of community one strives to foster, and the kinds of communication that are encouraged and made possible among its members, are intimately (and dialectically) related issues. As in the case of media, I think there is a tendency in much social theory to want prescriptively to define and sort different forms of communication, to rank them along some continuum of desirability, rather than to see them as multiple forms, each with characteristic purposes and effects. Dialogue, for example, is often taken as the paragon of social discourse (especially in education): from Socrates to Freire to Habermas, there is a belief that the pursuit of a certain type of interactive discussion and debate makes for the optimal mode of publicly adjudicating common concerns. In the strongest versions of this faith, dialogue is even seen as self-correcting, in the sense that the only legitimate response to breakdowns or conflicts within a dialogue is more of the same.[12] It is, again, a far different starting point of analysis to regard forms of communication, like media (and often in close relation to them), as elements of interaction that reveal and conceal; that frame what is and what is not open to discussion; that encourage certain types of interaction (certain forms of community, if you will) and discourage others; and hence that have effects of inclusion and exclusion affecting different prospective participants differently. These issues, which I cannot review in detail here, include a broad range of factors including the language in which communication happens; the way in which parties to communication are positioned in relation to one another, what Elizabeth Ellsworth calls the "modes of address";[13] the roles of questioner and answerer (who gets to ask questions, and what sorts of questions get asked); and so on. None of these forms of communication are by nature more universal or more inclusive than others; each will be experienced by certain people as awkward, alienating, or silencing—and this too will give the community built around them a particular set of boundaries and omissions.

A third set of mediating factors is a variety of social practices that govern the ways in which social participants act toward each other and act together for concerted purposes. Obviously, these factors are closely related to the first two, and they are similarly multiple in kind. I want to focus on one set of such practices here—identity practices—because they are of special relevance to the topic of this chapter. "Identity practices" refer to the many individual and interactive moves that social actors make as a way of forming, expressing, and defending their identities (plural), in response to and in relation to one another. Sometimes these identity practices are relatively personal, private, even internal to people's thoughts and feelings; sometimes they are collective, public, and negotiated in conscious relation to (and sometimes in opposition to) the practices of others. They are, moreover, frequently dynamic, as people play out changing identities over time; and they are frequently multiple, as people play out more than one dimension of identity and work out the frictions of conflicted alternative identities they endeavor to maintain at the same time.

Political Conditions of Community. In addition to what I have been calling mediating conditions (media, forms of communication, and social practices), which shape and constrain the possibilities of community, there are those broader political (and historical) conditions that precede and overarch the choices and activities of participants, also shaping and constraining the possibilities of community. I would argue that these political factors are rarely determinative in any simple sense and that these conditions (like all the others I am exploring here) take on a differing significance depending on persons' and groups' responses to them. Nevertheless, they are not simply matters of personal choice, and they are factors that must be responded to, even if the response is one of resistance. In short, community rests upon ascriptions and sentiments of affiliation; some of these we choose, and some we do not choose. For we are born into certain communities (nation, family, or religion, for example), and while we can act in various ways toward them, even rejecting them, *that we must deal with them* we do not choose. Not all communities are purely voluntary.

I return here to the contrast between Dewey and Arendt. Both recognized that any public space fundamentally presents actors with the condition of difference, and that a central challenge to forming a democratic public is in dealing constructively with this condition. For Dewey, and progressive liberal theorists since him, difference is conceived primarily as diversity, as a condition with the potential for disagreement and conflict, but also as a condition with the potential for fruitful engagement precisely because of that difference. Indeed, for such theorists, democratic vitality (even down to the very practical level of generating alternative possible solutions to common problems) *requires* such differences, to insure that the broadest possible range of views is heard and that the broadest possible range of social actions, and their possible consequences, is given consideration. Hence the fundamental weight given in liberal societies to such ideals as free speech and tolerance.

For Arendt, difference is also a condition of public spaces, and it also poses a deep challenge to democracy. But it is a different sort of challenge.

For Arendt, difference is conceived as *plurality*, not a range of alternatives that can be simply articulated, compared, judged, negotiated, or combined in some set of social compacts or compromises (so that those who are different become, in certain respects at least, less different over time); it is, rather, an ongoing condition, in which even compacts and compromises, when they can be achieved, might retain fundamentally different meaning and significance for their participants—and in which many issues of fundamental importance may never be bridgeable at all.

Dewey clearly understood that broader democratic affiliations could not usually be based on the same elements of proximity, homogeneity, and familiarity that characterized local communities (and that they would often be in direct tension with them). But from this latter, Arendtian perspective, the conditions of proximity, homogeneity, and familiarity are actually *incompatible* with community within the public sphere. Once one leaves the realm of the private (where the conditions of proximity, homogeneity, and familiarity are more taken for granted, as in relations with immediate family members), any attempt to recreate those values in a public space leads to (what is for Arendt) a distortion of publicness, a third space that she calls the "social." In the social there is an immersion of distinct identity for the sake of belonging, an inappropriate and unhealthy (in her view) transferring of the virtues of the private onto the public sphere, and so a construction of proximity, homogeneity, and familiarity on the basis of a desire for conformity and avoidance of deep conflict in the face of plurality. This social sphere is not the true public sphere, and it retains none of the virtues of public engagement (the possibilities of personal growth and change through encounters with the strange, the difficult, and the challenging). It is a relatively safe space, where "safety" is conceived as the minimization of risk to identity and private affiliations. In this sense the "social" is antithetical to the possibilities of democracy.

Space and Place as Conditions of Community. A central theme in Arendt's view of public and private spheres is her analysis of the distinctive *spaces* that characterize and accommodate each mode of interaction—an analysis which she draws from ancient Greek concepts of the agora, or public square, and the household, or domicile (and argues, as just noted, for the gradual emergence of a third, social space).[14] Here I want to go beyond this idea that the public and private can be characterized in terms of distinctive (and discrete) spaces, to talk more broadly about how spatial arrangements and spatial practices constitute our very ideas of publicness and privacy. As in the case of previous conditions, these spatial arrangements and practices can be viewed as ways of shaping and constraining the possibilities of community.

The first question here is how a *space* becomes a *place*. "Place," and a sense of being in a place, develops from a sense of familiarity and recognizability: one has been here (or in places like it) before.[15] This sense may not be pleasurable: the recognition of danger is also a characteristic of certain places. At the other extreme, a home or homeland is a place where memory, familiarity, and the rhythms of daily life bring a sense of belonging or, for dispersed persons, a nostalgia for return to that place. Hence, place can be a condition for the formation and maintenance of communities (communities of family, neighborhood, or nation). Both public and private spaces are *places* when persons recognize where they are and know how to act there: the familiarity of the space and the familiarity of the activities characteristic of it create and support one another. We know where we are when we know what we are supposed to do, and vice versa.

People also sometimes transform spaces into places by acting within and upon them to make them their own (what Norberg-Schulz calls a "lived space"). Mapping is an example of trying to turn a space into a place.[16] Another example is the adaptation of a space to the patterns of daily use (and not only the adaptation of use to space). For example, many college campuses lay out a pattern of sidewalks, designed in advance, to connect various buildings, only to find that the grassy areas in between are often worn down by new paths that the residents of campus actually use in getting from building to building. Apparently (friends tell me), some campuses have learned to follow a different strategy, letting people use the campus for a while, looking to see where the pathways of use are, then laying sidewalks down there. The formation of *trails*, artifacts of personal use, convenience, and sense making, is another way in which people make spaces into their own places.[17]

The encompassing term for the transformation of space to place is *architecture*. It is crucial to see that architecture is not fundamentally about building boxes to keep the rain off one's head; it is about configuring spaces that both anticipate and direct activity. Residents of an architectural space adapt their activities to fit the space, and adapt the space to fit their activities—the relation is always both ways—and it is in this reciprocal adaptation that a space becomes a place. The "architecture" is not only the initial design or building, but the transformation of it over time; in this sense, people always help build the buildings they occupy, and the buildings are not fully finished until they have been used for a while (in one sense, then, they are never "finished"). In part, of course, this may mean quite literal rebuilding: tearing down walls, moving doors, adding rooms, and so on. But at a more subtle level, it is the pattern of daily choices and activities that reconfigure an architectural design: where people sit, move furniture, try to become comfortable.[18]

Theorizing these dynamics, I think it can be suggested that architecture is a way of anticipating and directing activity along a number of dimensions, including:

- movement/stasis;
- interaction/isolation;
- publicity/privacy;
- visibility/hiddeness; and
- enclosure/exclusion.

Again, however, the dialectical character of architecture should not be viewed in only one way: architecture anticipates and directs these activities, but the pattern of these activities also transforms and reshapes the architecture. Henri Lefebvre calls these activities "spatial practices," the activities through which spaces are experienced, perceived, and imagined.[19] In living their daily lives, people seek out spaces and reshape them according to the patterns of their needs and desires, although it is also true that these needs and desires are reshaped by the spaces available to them.

It is, then, one step further along this argument to consider architecture as the design of spaces generally: public spaces, private spaces, textual spaces (the layout and size of a newspaper, for example, agricultural spaces, educational spaces (classroom arrangements, for example), and on-line spaces. The design of such environments shapes, intentionally or inadvertently, the conditions for activity and interaction within them: conditions for the formation and development of communities. The five dimensions listed above can be seen as the polarities along which specific communities develop their character. Communities are manifestations of the places in which they settle (while the places change also to fit the community).

The Conditions of On-line Communities

With this framework in mind, it is possible now to turn to a set of specific issues about the ways in which, and the conditions under which, on-line communities are being formed. There is nothing natural about such communities; they are as "imagined" (and as "real") as any communities are. But they are formed under conditions that shape and constrain the kinds of communities they can become. I will explore these issues under the same three headings as before: mediating conditions, political conditions, and spatial/architectural conditions. Numerous features of the on-line environment constitute the conditions for community within it, and these conditions (including the condition of globalization, one of its most significant, overarching characteristics) shape and constrain the educational possibilities within and across these communities.[20]

Mediating Conditions of On-line Communities. The Internet is, of course, itself a medium; in fact, it comprises numerous media, all operating over the network of wires and computers that constitute it: HTML pages (the World Wide Web), e-mail, file sharing and transfer, listserves or other asynchronous discussion groups, IRC, or real-time "chat", teleconferencing and videoconferencing, among others. While each of these media has distinctive characteristics (some are text-based, others allow for voice or video transmission; some are synchronous, others are asynchronous; and so on), there are some general characteristics that typify the on-line medium.

The Internet has both facilitative and inhibitive effects on the formation of communities within it. On the one hand, the Internet has become a medium where collaboration happens and where people can create networks of distributed intelligence. This point is crucial because it means seeing the Internet as more than a repository for, or a means for the dissemination of, "information" (its usual characterization), and more than simply a medium of communication. It is also an environment that instantiates collaboration, in which participants can compose themselves as working groups, and where the identity of a working group *as* a group takes hold. There are many, many illustrations of this. For example, the pattern of hyperlinks within a topic area often tacitly define a group by the ways in which Web pages link to common sources, including one another or, alternatively, through the intentional choice by the members of certain interest groups to link all their pages to one another—what are conventionally called "Web rings." Listserves and chat rooms also attract and affiliate like-minded persons in a common conversation, although they are frequent sites of "flame wars" because these sites of association, given the common concerns of their members, can become sites of high-stakes disagreement. Modern developments of "Intranets," sometimes hermetically sealed off from the rest of the Internet by "firewalls," are designed to foster collaboration and information-sharing within organizations, while keeping these resources away from "outsiders"; these enforced communities are especially strict where matters of commercial interest, so-called "intellectual property," or secrecy are regarded as paramount values.

At the same time, the Internet can interfere with the formation of community, in part for the very same reasons already discussed. Some communities are not interested in encountering other perspectives and groups; it is easier to stay off-line entirely and seek other forms of affiliation. Some individuals and groups are put more at risk than others by the dangers of harassment, insult, or unwanted attention. Given the multiple lines of affiliation and community that the Internet makes possible, some communities may tend to "drown out" others. Perhaps most strikingly, the formation of strong on-line communities can sometimes interfere with the vitality of proximate, face-to-face communities off-line. Here, as in so many other respects, what the Internet gives with one hand it takes away with another; it is neither an unalloyed good nor an encroaching danger—it continually presents users with inseparable elements of both.

In short, the distinct media that the Internet comprises shape, and are shaped by, groups that use them for their distinctive purposes; it is not just a set of individuals connected to other individuals, but an environment, a space, in which existing groups work and interact with each other, and in which other groups, with no awareness of themselves as groups, come to constitute themselves as such. Newsgroups, operating via Usenet, are an early example of this; Web rings, discussed above, are another. On-line environments originally based on the "Dungeons and Dragons" game (MUDs, MOOs, MUVEs, and similar spaces) provide a stage upon which actors, often with fictional or imaginary personae, can explore rooms or mazes and interact with each other. More recently, service providers such as Geocities, Tripod, and now Excite and Yahoo, have begun promoting Web environments literally called "communities" (or sometimes "clubs"), for users with like-minded areas of interest. Geocities is a typical example, offering sites organized as thematic "neighborhoods," usually named for actual place names, which subscribers can join. These communities have codes of appropriate conduct, such as allowable or banned content for Web pages, and administrators who have responsibility for surveying the pages within their community and regulating who can and cannot be part of it. (There is an obvious parallel here with "gated communities," neighborhoods that erect actual barriers to entry, police and restrict who can enter their area, and which often have strict codes for the appropriate standards of houses, yards, and activities within them.)

The astonishing growth of these sectors of the Internet belies the idea that it is just a communications network; it is a space in which people come together and interact. For many users, these so-called "virtual" environments are more vital, exciting, and important to them than other areas of activity for their lives, as indicated by the amount of time they spend within them. The communities are centrally and intimately tied up with areas of interest and concern (collectors, joke tellers, sports fans, pet owners, and so on) that are often of fundamental centrality to the sense of self and enjoyment that these participants have in living. They are of special importance to older users, or those in outlying, rural regions, who rely on these media of community to relate to others whom they could never encounter otherwise. And, of course, they are the only media through which these sorts of communities can be formed on a truly global scale.

What I am trying to highlight here is that these media are distinctive (and hence so are the communities they help foster): some rely on explicit self-identification, others on imagined personae (often called "avatars"); some are openly accessible to new participants, others are decidedly not; some are highly regulated, restricting what can and cannot be shared or done within them, others more unregulated; and where regulation occurs, some involve strict top-down management, others more consensual, group-communicated norms. The media of on-line community facilitate not only the formation of communities but also communities of a particular type, composition, and character—by implication, they discourage the formation of communities of a different type, composition, and character.

A second set of mediating conditions are the forms of on-line communication: the use of language, text, voice, graphics, and other modes through which people relate. Up until recently, of course, the Internet was almost entirely a text-based medium. Now it is becoming more routine to transmit graphics, sound, and video; and increasingly the Internet is being used for direct audio or video conferencing. These forms, in turn, have direct effects on the kinds of verbal interaction they support and encourage (the important differences, for example, between dialogues that are synchronous and those that are asynchronous; or those that involve written text only, and those that include voice or video transmission). On the horizon are technologies that will allow some degree of tactile contact and interaction. It seems that whenever critics identify a barrier that makes on-line interaction "not like real interaction," new developments begin to blur that distinction. Rilke identified the five senses (sight, sound, touch, smell, and taste) as representing five levels or degrees of intimacy. On-line interaction seems to be steadily moving along that scale.

Nevertheless, text remains today the primary medium of on-line interaction. This category comprises not only the text of individual messages sent back and forth (for example, over e-mail) but also the form of new types of publications (newsletters, articles, zines, or other underground or samizdat publications[21]). Here too, writing and publication become conditions of community: both through the *processes* of collaboratively writing and composing publications, and through the *networks* of distribution through which they are shared. It is not new that communities of interest (from professional or academic groups, to political groups, to informal hobbyists) may sponsor newsletters or circulars that serve their members and help attract new members. But it is a new phenomenon when these materials can be continually adapted, revised, and added to in the processes of circulation themselves. The text or publication becomes a medium of actual community building, and not just a mode of communication within it.[22]

Finally, it is impossible to address these issues without noting the English-centric nature of most on-line communication. Language too is a mediating condition: as with these other media, it shapes and constrains who can participate in an on-line community (and who cannot), and how they participate. While there are vast areas of the Internet where people interact in their native languages, structural features, including the nature of HTML code, the software applications through which users access the Internet and conduct searches within it, and the prevalence of advertising, all mean that English-speaking users are privileged to have access to more resources and more avenues for interaction than any other users. Moreover, English is not just a condition of access to a great deal of on-line resources and interaction; participation in on-line interaction means that users who are not fluent English speakers will be exposed to this language on a regular basis and have many opportunities to practice it—the Internet becomes a medium for teaching the language and promulgating its spread. Indeed, many nonnative speakers of English will find it easier to use English in on-line contexts, where they can type their comments as deliberately as they need to, revise what they have written, and receive feedback on the meaningfulness and efficacy of what they have said. This is a kind of linguistic imperialism; but the irony is that the Internet would not be the Internet, and would not have the enormous potential (as well as the enormous dangers) that it has, without a common, or at least predominant, language within it.

The third set of mediating conditions of community comprise the characteristic practices of on-line work and interaction, of which there are many. Earlier I focused on the issue of identity practices, and these are clearly a central issue in on-line communities. There are myriad ways of "being on-line" (or, for that matter, types of "online beings").[23] On the one hand, humans who participate online adopt a variety of strategies of self-representation: some are fairly literal (using their birth names, informative signature files, descriptive return e-mail addresses, and so on, as descriptors to others of who they are); others are highly imaginary (made-up names, fictitious Web pages, avatars that represent them in MUDs and MOOs, etc.). It is a mistake, however, to draw the line too sharply between the literal and the imaginary, as if there were nothing performative or imaginary even in ordinary face-to-face interactions, or as if a person is not in some sense "really" representing who they are even when they create an imaginary persona to stand in for them.

On the other hand, once people begin to "be" on-line, there is an intrinsic sense in which their identity changes precisely because they are using this technology: what they do; what they like and care about; how they spend their time; and who they know are all changed from that moment on—and when these activities themselves involve on-line interactions and experiences, there comes an inevitable fusion between the "off-line" and "on-line" dimensions of their being. They become, in Donna Haraway's famous formulation, "cyborgs."[24]

On-line communities influence and are influenced by these multiple personae (especially because persons can be part of many on-line communities at the same time, as they are members of other communities). In the on-line environment, even more so than in other environments, one chooses, or not, to disclose aspects of one's personhood, or to disclose it in particular ways. This process is not entirely open to conscious control (one always reveals more or less than one intends, even in pretending), but to an extent "being on-line" means the continual selection and filtering of self-information through the portals of available media. Particular communities invite or discourage certain kinds of disclosure and participation; and they utterly ban others. Hence, in a very clear sense, here as elsewhere, choosing a community means in part choosing who one is; and changing communities, or exploring new communities, is a process of exploring or experimenting with new selves.

Therefore, it is an oversimplification, I believe, to draw a clear line between on-line and off-line activities, or on-line and off-line identities. The assumption that face-to-face interaction is more honest or direct than on-line interaction is belied by participants who say that they experience quite the opposite. The idea that a person is more "real" or more themselves when they are acting in one context than in another elides a number of much deeper issues about performativity and the ways in which *all* social interactions are mediated; and the belief that some communities are "real" and others "virtual" ignores what is "virtual" (imagined) about all communities and what is "real" even about on-line communities—as real as any community can be. Howard Rheingold writes about "virtual communities":

> People in virtual communities use words on screens to exchange pleasantries and argue, engage in intellectual discourse, conduct commerce, exchange knowledge, share emotional support, make plans, brainstorm, gossip, feud, fall in love, find friends and lose them, play games, flirt, create a little high art and a lot of idle talk. People in virtual communities do just about everything people do in real life, but we leave our bodies behind.[25]

I take this as an unintended argument for dropping easy distinctions like "real" versus "virtual" community in the first place. I tend to prefer the term "actual" to blur the real/virtual distinction. Actual communities have *specific* characteristics that reflect the conditions, here the mediating conditions, under which they are formed and develop. A great deal can be said about these specific characteristics: but distinctions like real/virtual do not carry that analysis very far, and they obscure deeper processes at work.

I hope it is clear now what the idea of "conditions of community" does for analysis. In on-line environments, communities of a remarkable range and vitality are being formed, are growing, and are developing new ways of using the Internet (and its constantly changing capabilities) to give their own identity *as* communities new form and significance. At the same time, however, this is not happening on neutral ground or with a blank slate: the conditions of on-line community tend to drive communities into particular forms or patterns; and although they adapt resources to their own purposes, however flexibly, they are still using resources not of their own design and control. Moreover, the very conditions that have the benefits of facilitating (certain kinds of) communities also, and inevitably, have the effect of ignoring, or even excluding, other actual or prospective communities that never come into existence because they do not have the privileges taken for granted by others. And, finally, there are on-line communities that are quite consciously exclusive of others, in part defined *by* their desire to exclude others: as in the "safe" neighborhoods of Geocities where members are reassured that they will not have to encounter dangerous or distasteful "intruders" into their gated community. Later, I will return to these issues in exploring how these conditions shape and constrain the possibilities of *educational* communities.

Political Conditions of On-line Communities. There is a dangerous misconception that because the Internet is a relatively unregulated and decentralized medium it is politically neutral. I think it should be clear from the analysis up until now that there are political and moral dimensions throughout the activities of people working and interacting on-line: for example, in the ways in which many communities are self-policing, identifying and enforcing explicit and implicit standards about what is and is not permitted among their members. The Internet, because it links together participants from many parts of the world and from many political, value, or religious systems, is being imagined as just another liberal pluralist space. A recent television advertisement proclaimed the Internet as a place where age, gender, and race at first do not matter. This appears to be true, since you can only tell these things about a person on the Internet if he or she chooses to disclose them. But this appearance obscures important issues: whether or not people choose to represent their identities, these remain present in the ways they think, act, and express themselves on-line (sometimes these qualities may be more apparent to others than the actors think). Moreover, these factors are always present in influencing the question of who is and is not even present in on-line environments; fundamental questions of access are strongly influenced by location and identity (especially for people in countries with little or no telecommunications infrastructure). Pretending that nationality, class, gender, or disability do not matter online, when in fact they do, is one more imaginary about the type of "community" that the Internet represents itself to be.

On the contrary, says David Shenk:

> Cyberspace is Republican. . . . Cyberspace is not politically neutral.
> It favors the political ideals of libertarian, free-market Republicans:
> a highly decentralized, deregulated society with little common discourse and minimal public infrastructure.[26]

Indeed, one might say, it is the very posture of imagining itself to be apolitical that reveals the Internet's deepest political tendencies.

As noted in previous examples, often the very things that make the Internet most appealing and useful also make it dangerous and difficult to cope with. Because the Internet is a broadly inclusive space, it continually brings one up against content, and perspectives, that are silly and pointless at best, repugnant and deeply hurtful at worst. Many families worry about this, especially where their children are concerned. Hence we see more and more attempts to carve out within this untamed frontier safe spaces that reestablish the traditional grounds of community: proximity, homogeneity, and familiarity. I compared this earlier with the rise of gated communities in some neighborhoods. Similarly, many communities insist upon filtering software for computers in schools and libraries, or in homes. Many Web rings and "portals" involve creating archives of resources that have been screened and approved for general access, including children. Participants run the risk of encountering "inappropriate" material if they venture outside of that protected space.

Here then we encounter another paradox. Because the Internet is a global network, it provides enormous opportunities for "tourism": travel to distant locales, encounters with the new, the strange, and the exciting; sampling cultural products from a variety of traditions. It allows one to jump outside of familiar communities, to explore new communities, and perhaps to become part of them. It contains the virtue of what Arendt called "plurality," taking one outside the realm of the proximate, the homogeneous, the familiar. But one consequence of plurality is the encounter with what is not only incompatible with one's proximate, homogeneous, and familiar communities but what is actually antithetical to them (sometimes it is what the community itself was formed to avoid). So it becomes like the person who moves to a large city because of the variety of ethnic restaurants, but who never leaves the house to sample them because he or she is afraid of "those people" on the streets.

Finally, there is one important way in which the Internet is becoming truly unbounded, and that is in its capacities as a commercial environment. Because the Internet has the capabilities of near-instantaneous communication and transfer of information, it has become enormously important to global business and financial transactions, and it is increasingly colonized by commercial Web sites, "junk" e-mail, and ubiquitous advertisements. The globalization of the Internet makes it a valuable medium both for the promotion of products, and for their purchase. And this commercialization, in turn, becomes a condition of community as well.

So we see, for example, growing calls for "smart communities," a term used to refer to wiring entire cities together, and into the broader Internet. There are countless uses and benefits that might come from such developments (including educational benefits), but it is clear that the primary purpose behind undertaking such investments is to promote more local and on-line commerce. To take an early example, when cities first began creating Web pages to attract visitors and to provide information for their citizens, 80 percent of them featured business-related resources, far more than any other category (fewer than half featured education-related resources).[27] In fact, the question today is no longer, Will the Internet become a commercialized entity? It is, rather, What sorts of economy will it support:

profit-making only, or gift economies that promote the open sharing of resources, ideas, and information without regard for commercial gain? These conditions will, in turn, change the sorts of communities that come to exist on-line and which people will be part of them—including, one might predict, on-line communities that members will have to pay to join (this is already true for subscribers to some on-line publications and services, which are communities of sorts).

Increasingly, the avenues of access to the Internet, and the communities within it, require travelling through pathways that are commercialized: service providers that are linked with large telecommunications or cable corporations, or—within the Web—through portals that are controlled by private services (such as Excite) and packed with advertisements. These conditions not only shape the possibilities of community, but in significant ways limit it:

> The creators' vision was that the Web would encourage connections among diverse sites and collaboration among distrubuted communities, not draw a growing mass audience into ever-fewer high-traffic sites. . . . The real conflict is not between commerce and community. It is between the traditional architecture of commerce (hierarchical systems of well-capitalized sources, distributors, and customers) and the traditional architecture of community (networks of one-to-one and few-to-few connections that create a sense of belonging and shared values.)[28]

Finally, the commercialization of the Internet also means a blurring between legitimate and illegitimate commercial ventures, especially on a global scale. Already the lack of regulation on the Internet has given impetus to child pornography, betting, bank fraud, counterfeiting, drug trafficking, and black marketeering by mafias all over the world. One of the chief problems in coming to grips with these activities is that, while they are illegal in some places, they are not illegal in others (or, even if illegal, unprosecutable). But when all places are linked together via this medium, the problem of one can become the problem of all. This returns us again to the conditions of on-line community: some of these will be labeled "criminal communities" by certain authorities, who have little or no jurisdiction over them. Yet by the same token, entirely legitimate and legal communities in other contexts (certain religious communities who use the on-line medium, for example), will be banned from others. Now, I am not arguing the equivalence of all these different sorts of communities, although in some cases a "mafia" from one standpoint will be someone else's "business network"; a devout religious community will be someone else's "fanatics"; gambling activities that are utterly banned by certain communities will be state-sponsored sources of revenue for others. What this shows is not that no moral distinctions can be drawn, but rather that the Internet is a medium in which few if any overarching moral standards exist and that the composition of the Internet as an unregulated amalgam of communities, each having its own powerful moral codes, may be an ineffective environment for these moral differences to be adjudicated. This makes it all the more ironic that the primary overarching ethos of the Internet seems to be a commercial sensibility, which, if it takes hold, will have an even more difficult time in delimiting legitimate from illegitimate business activity.

Space and Place as Conditions of On-line Communities. Where are you when you are on-line? What does it mean to be with others who are also on-line? Is it possible to have a community "at a distance," and what sort of *place* can support such a community? In this section, as in the previous two, I want to return to the general ways that space and place are conditions of community and then reexamine what these mean in the context of the on-line environment and experience.

The term "cyberspace," which started with William Gibson's book *Neuromancer*, has become part of our standard vocabulary for talking about the Internet. But what makes cyberspace a cyber*place*? Part of this process is users' becoming familiar with this environment, learning to recognize some of its features. The standardization of user interfaces, the similar design of Web browsers, the common basic elements of the pages they download, and other features of the on-line environment allow users with some degree of experience to adapt fairly quickly to new spaces they encounter there. They know their way around. However, these spaces are less amenable to the other main dimension of the space/place relation, namely, being able to customize and adapt spaces to one's own preferences and habits. The structure and contents of Web sites, the links between resources, and so on, are determined by the authors/designers of these spaces, and are not subject to modification by the casual user (as things stand now). This gives many users of the Internet the feeling of wandering through paths and spaces of others' making, in search of useful and interesting things, which are available only by assimilating to patterns, connections, and search strategies that fit the existing design and software demands. This makes cyberspace more space-like and less place-like, as it is experienced by many users. There are few ways to leave permanent "trails" that mark the pathways one prefers to follow.

The architecture of on-line space, like the architecture of buildings and other spaces, anticipates and directs personal activity along several dimensions I introduced earlier: these include movement/stasis; interaction/isolation; publicity/privacy; visibility/hiddeness; and enclosure/exclusion. In my view, these should not be viewed as "metaphorical" notions within cyberspace: movement, visibility, privacy, exclusion, and so on, have perfectly literal and direct application to activities and situations on-line. What is important to see here is the extent to which one's experiences along these various dimensions are only partly a matter of choice; it is also determined by elements of the design itself, which one does not choose (one can, for example, refuse to accept "cookies" from Web sites visited, but one cannot refuse to have one's visit recorded by a site). The degree to which one can make choices within these dimensions is a central factor in the extent to which this environment takes on the character of a place where one can live, act, and interact with some measure of confidence and security. And, in this respect, as in others, different people will experience these features in drastically different ways.

Here is what is different about being on-line: in other spaces, or places, the characteristics of the environment are to some extent independent of the means used to represent them; but with the Internet these two levels are utterly intertwined.[29] Paths of movement (for example, hypertext links) are also connections of meaning-making. "Being on-line" is both a place and a process: Samira Kawash offers an ingenious analysis of this condition in the uses of the "@" sign, for example in e-mail addresses. Although people colloquially now use "@" to abbreviate locations or time ("meet Jo @ café" or "meet Phil @ 2:00"). Kawash argues that the @ of being on-line (of being @ a particular e-mail address, for example), is a different sort of positioning, one that is not analogical to being "at" other locations; rather, it is distinctively a state of being on-line and only makes sense in that context:

"On line" is a metaphor denoting a complex network of electrical signals that translate inputs to my keyboard into computer operations in some remote elsewhere. "On line" is thus less a place than it is a mechanism of translation or transportation.[30]

Thus, the sort of place that "on-line" denotes is not a container, like a room or building or square that people occupy (or can leave), separate from the thing contained. Being on-line is itself a way of being defined by the place where one is. *That* being can't be in any other place. So when one is "@" a particular place (or time[31]) on-line, this is not the same as being "at" a place (or time) in ordinary life.

And lest one assume that it is different only because, as Howard Rheingold said when we go on-line "we leave our bodies behind," there are good reasons to think that a kinesthetic sense of movement and location persists even when users are moving through on-line spaces.[32]

Paul Virilio has even gone so far as to challenge the idea that on-line activity and interaction involve action "at a distance."[33] When a user can, with his or her hand in a data glove or prosthetic manipulator, "reach" or "touch" or "pick up" an object through a robotic arm or sensor; when users can observe remote locations (even other planetary surfaces) through video cameras that bring their perception into spaces they could never reach otherwise; when almost instantaneous communication, including voice and video, can be achieved between persons regardless of their location on the planet, something begins to happen to the very ideas of action, perception, and communication. In one way it makes sense to call them action, perception, and communication *at a distance*, but aren't they *always* "at a distance" (some distance)? In one way it makes sense to say that these examples involve action, perception, and communication that is *mediated* by something (here, technology), but aren't they *always* "mediated" by some processes, filters of interpretation, and social conventions? What does "at a distance" mean as a crucial, ontological difference? Not very much, Virilio suggests.

If one accepts this line of argument, then it is only a step further to suggest that the very ideas of identity, materiality, spatiality, and temporality are becoming increasingly interdependent. If I, wearing a data glove, can pick up an object in a far-off location and detect its weight and temperature, *where* do those sensations occur, *when* did they occur, *to whom* did they occur? Am *I* having the experience, or is it the glove, or is it the computer that tabulates the data and converts it into electrical impulses that my hand interprets as heat? Being on-line is always a state of being in-between, of being neither (simply) here nor there; mediation is not something that stands between the user and something else to which one is relating (an object, a Web page, or another user)—it *is* the relation, without which, strictly speaking, the parties to an on-line event do not exist.[34]

In fact, Virilio suggests that the term "globalization" be replaced by "virtualization," because globalization depends on a revolution in the speed of travel or transmission across global distances, converging on the speed of the electron itself, or the speed of light. The media of action, perception, and communication collapse the distance/time equation into a point of instantaneity. The danger of the term "virtual" here, however, remains troubling. If the virtual environment is an art museum, have you "really" seen the paintings or not? I visited the Louvre several years ago and had to stand in a crowd to see the *Mona Lisa*, sheltered in a protective glass case with a surface that reflected back the faces of the people standing in line to see it (and in some cases, to videotape it). Did I see the *real* painting? Would I have seen it just as well, or better, through a high-quality graphic that I could have downloaded on-line? Similarly, is a virtual conversation with someone, mediated by a two-way video link, less "real" than a face-to-face conversation? What if people happen to be more honest in video links than face-to-face—which interaction is more "real" then?

Does the Internet Constitute a Global Educational Community?

By way of concluding, I would propose two sets of answers to the above question. First, the Internet as a whole cannot be a community; it is too disparate, too diffuse, too inclusive. To call it a "community" would be to stretch the word beyond any useful sense or meaning. It might be better to call the Internet a "*meta*community," in both senses that prefix often denotes: an overarching congregation of communities, and a set of conditions that make communities possible, as a space in which communities happen. This chapter has presented an exploration of some of these conditions, and the kinds of communities they make possible, conditions that shape and constrain the possibilities of educational community, as in any other space.

One of the chief conditions of this space is its global character: that it makes worldwide, nearly instantaneous communication and interaction possible; that it has become an almost indispensable medium for commercial and financial transactions; that it brings cultures and societies of enormous variety into immediate contact. The Internet is thus both one of the chief manifestations of globalization and one of its primary causes. The condition of globalization, furthermore, is one of the things that gives online communities their characteristic qualities and their characteristic concerns. The scope of who can be part of a community is opened up; but the threat of "intruders" who do not share the community's values is opened up also. Communities can be formed around the values of diversity and inclusivity; but when they do this they struggle with maintaining the fabric of cohesion that gives them their sense of themselves as *communities*. Disparate communities can coexist side by side, as in Young's vision of the modern cityscape; but because the barriers between on-line groups are always provisional and semipermeable, incursions across these boundaries (whether intentional or not) will always occur. The Internet is a prime example of what Arendt called the condition of plurality in public spaces; this is a condition whose possibilities and problems can never be entirely settled or "solved," but which need to be struggled with almost continuously, and in continually new and imaginative ways. For Arendt, it is the necessity of learning to deal with plurality and to forge meaningful and effective social goods under such conditions, that gives the political endeavor its capacity to educate and reeducate us as citizens.[35] As I have discussed, many individuals, groups, and nations keep seeking ways to mitigate against the condition of plurality, in the Internet as in the other public and private spaces they inhabit (gated communities, government-imposed censorship, and so on). In this, they are resisting the possibilities of educational challenges to their belief and value systems. Ironically, perhaps, the very possibilities that a global Internet offers make such restrictions seem so desperate and self-defeating.

As one notes the affinity of commonality, community, and communication, one might also note the affinity of the polis, politics, and the police. The Internet is a kind of polis, a city-state or cluster of city-states that must continually struggle with their plurality, their frictions in contact with one another, and the limits of their own capacities of self-governability. The politics of the Internet revolve fundamentally around these same elements: struggles over centralizing and decentralizing tendencies (or, in other words, how and whether the Internet can police itself); struggles over the desire to maintain zones of "safety," usually interpreted around the traditional values of community (proximity, homogeneity, and familiarity); and struggles over the kinds of economy that this polis will maintain—gift economies based on sharing nonscarce resources, or economies based on restricting access and charging for services.

These shifting determinations and self-understandings about the Internet and the types of communities that constitute it are already being locked in by how certain structural decisions concerning the Internet are negotiated today: for example, by whether one will only be able to access the Internet through one company's Web applications; by how much of the Internet will be commercialized and accessible by fee only; by explicit moves of government censorship (or the more tacit form of censorship established by making certain resources scarce and expensive); by decisions about where Internet services will be accessible, and by whom, and at what cost; by technical standards that affect the design, operation, and language requirements of Internet resources; and so on. By and large, it must be noted, most of these decisions are being made with almost no public input; I suspect that most users of the Internet do not know about them, who is making them, or the consequences at stake.

Such decisions are fraught with educational importance, because educational institutions, at all levels from primary to higher education, are trying to establish themselves as communities in and of the Internet. Choices that have implications for the kinds of communities the Internet will comprise, and how it will privilege some and disadvantage others (inadvertently perhaps, but as a direct consequence of decisions that do not seem to be directly about access or fairness), are being made continually in those educational institutions and outside them. Such activities are neither new nor unique to the on-line environment itself. But the ways in which imaginaries become real, and the ways in which "virtual" communities become as or more important to users than any other sorts of communities that they have access to, need to be understood as having increased importance as more and more learning opportunities will *require* access to and participation within the on-line environment. These issues have to be viewed in terms of their implications for both local and global, both on-line and face-to-face, both "virtual" and "real" educational communities.

My second set of comments pertain to the multiple *kinds* of community the Internet can support. A chief feature of the Internet, as a space that I have called a metacommunity, is that many communities can coexist within it. While the conditions of community explored throughout this essay do constrain some of these options (the Internet is not a neutral medium, by any means), they remain to a large extent flexible enough to allow alternative communities, alternative *places*, to be formed within it. I have suggested the importance of analyzing the specific features of educational communities in architectural terms, considering the ways in which these spaces shape and constrain participants' experiences along the dimensions of movement/stasis; interaction/isolation; publicity/privacy; visibility/hiddeness; and enclosure/exclusion.

Moreover, in this context, as in others, people will belong to multiple communities at the same time; the Internet is not unique in this regard, but it does make these possibilities in many respects easier because of the variety of communities formed within it, and because of the number of communities formed outside the Internet, communities which nevertheless maintain some degree of identity and visibility within it. The number and variety of these prospective communities, of course, is also an expression of the Internet's global character.

These multiple communities will have varying degrees of intensity and centrality to the lives of people who join them on-line. Alaina Kanfer offers the useful distinction of "thin" and "thick" communities, in terms of the number and variety of associations shared among members within a group.[36] Another useful set of distinctions is offered by Michael Fielding, who (not referring to on-line interactions specifically) differentiates patterns of interaction as: coexistence, collaboration, collegiality, and community.[37] These four types vary according to the degrees of freedom, task-orientation, equality, and intensity of relation among groups working together. Coexistence is high in freedom but low in relationship, task orientation, and equality. Collaboration is high in task orientation but low in relationship, freedom, and equality. Collegiality is high in relationship, task orientation, and equality, but low in freedom. Community is high in relationship, freedom, and equality, but low in task orientation. So, from this perspective, many on-line communities might be (according to Fielding's categories) better understood as instances of collegiality, or collaboration, than community. It matters little whether one calls these all different kinds of community, or some "community," strictly speaking, and others by some other name. What is important is to understand that people are drawn together by quite different purposes and are held together by quite different threads. Encompassing terms like "community" can make groups whose inner dynamics and intentions are quite different from one another appear similar from the outside. Furthermore, some communities develop out of choices made by participants to affiliate with one another; others are structured as spaces that others can either join or not (on terms not of their choosing). Educational communities, in particular, more often partake of the latter form, and this has direct effects on who will and will not be able to benefit from them.

It should be clear, also, that distinctions like Kanfer's and Fielding's can be very useful in understanding the range of interactions that can support different educational purposes. Thinking that schools or classrooms must be "learning communities," for example, may obscure the significantly different ways in which effective teaching and learning can happen. Interactions like coexistence, collaboration, collegiality, and community may each support quite different, but equally valuable, educational goals. It is especially important to add here that these different forms of interaction may be to varying degrees comfortable or acceptable to prospective participants in these educational opportunities. If categories like "learning community" are understood in too homogeneous a manner, then participants with different learning styles or different appetites for affiliation may be left out of them. Here, once again, the traditional associations of community with proximity, homogeneity, and familiarity can be an impediment to forming *actual* communities—including on-line communities, which I believe will become of even greater importance to the educational opportunities of learners of all ages, across all parts of the world.[38]

Notes

1 . The term "keyword" comes from Raymond Williams, *Keywords: A Vocabulary of Culture and Society* (New York: Oxford University Press, 1983). Here is what Williams says about "community": "Community can be the warmly persuasive word to describe an existing set of relationships, or the warmly persuasive word to describe an alternative set of relationships. What is most important, perhaps, is that unlike all other terms of social organization (state, nation, society, etc.) it seems never to be used unfavourably, and never to be given any positive opposing or distinguishing term" (76).

2. Jeannie Oakes, "Technical and Political Dimensions of Creating New Educational Communities," in *Creating New Educational Communities: The Ninety-fourth Yearbook of the National Society for the Study of Education*, ed. Jeannie Oakes and Karen Hunter Quartz (Chicago: University of Chicago Press, 1993), 8. For an excellent review of the literature on "learning communities," see also Katerine Bielaczyc and Allan Collins, "Learning Communities in Classrooms: A Reconceptualization of Educational Practice," in C. M. Reigeluth, ed. *Instructional Design Theories and Models, Vol. 2* (Mahwah, N.J.: Erlbaum, forthcoming).

3. Peter Magolda and Kathleen Knight Abowitz call this the idea of community as a "tribe." See "Communities and Tribes in Residential Living," *Teachers College Record* 99, no. 2 (1997): 266–310.

4. See John Dewey, *The Public and Its Problems* (New York: Henry Holt, 1972) and *Democracy and Education* (New York: Macmillan, 1916).

5. John Dewey, *Democracy and Education*, 5–7, 95–96.

6. John Dewey, *The Public and Its Problems*, 148–52.

7. Hannah Arendt, *The Human Condition* (Chicago: University of Chicago Press, 1958).

8. Iris Marion Young, *Justice and the Politics of Difference* (Princeton, N.J.: Princeton University Press, 1990), 227.

9. Benedict Anderson, *Imagined Communities: Reflections on the Origin and Spread of Nationalism* (New York: Verso, 1991).

10. Williams, *Keywords*.

11. For a revealing critical analysis of the power of the "community" discourse within education, see Kathleen Knight Abowitz, "Reclaiming Community," *Educational Theory* 49, no. 2 (1999), 143–159.

12. I think that a marked change can be traced in my own work on this subject, from early enthusiastic works on dialogue, such as "Dialogue across Differences: Continuing the Conversation," *Harvard Educational Review*, 61, No. 4 (1991): 393–416 (with Suzanne Rice), to more recent works, such as "The Limits of Dialogue as a Critical Pedagogy," in *Revolutionary Pedagogies: Cultural Politics Education and the Discourse of Theory*, ed. Peter Trifonas (New York: Routledge, forthcoming).

13. Elizabeth Ellsworth, *Teaching Positions: Difference, Pedagogy, and the Power of Address* (New York: Teachers College Press, 1997).

14. For a helpful analysis of these concepts in the context of new technologies, see Michael R. Curry, "New Technologies and the Ontology of Places," available online at: http://baja.sscnet.ucla.edu/~curry.

15. Christian Norberg-Schulz, *Genius Loci: Toward a Phenomenology of Architecture* (New York: Rizzoli, 1980).

16. Rolland G. Paulston, *Social Cartography: Mapping Ways of Seeing Social and Educational Change* (New York: Garland, 1996).

17. For these examples I am grateful to Chip Bruce and Adrian Cussins.

18. Comfort is not a trivial or superficial dimension of how a space becomes a place. See, for example, Witold Rybczynski, who has written a series of popular meditations on architectural history, personal experiences of building, and the evolution of the idea of "home" in *Home: A Short History of an Idea* (New York: Penguin, 1987); and *The Most Beautiful House in the World* (New York: Penguin, 1989).

19. Henri Lefebvre, *The Production of Space* (New York: Blackwell, 1991).
20. See also Marc Smith and Peter Kollock, *Communities in Cyberspace* (New York: Routledge, 1998) and the Web site for the Center for the Study of Online Community at UCLA: http://www.sscnet.ucla.edu/soc/csoc. Other bibliographic resources can be found on-line at http://www.socio.demon.co.uk/topicVC.html, http://otal.umd.edu/~rccs/biblio.html,http://www.amherst.edu/~erreich/vircom.html, and http://home.navisoft.com/edg/communities.htm.
21. Barbara Duncan, a doctoral student at the University of Illinois at Urbana/Champaign, is completing her dissertation work on this subject, studying specifically how 'zines constitute focal points around which on-line communities are formed and identities established: *Feminist Grrl Zine Communities of Difference* (Ph.D. diss., University of Illinois at Urbana/Champaign).
22. For a discussion of some of the implications of these changes in academic publishing, see Nicholas C. Burbules, "Digital Texts and the Future of Scholarly Writing and Publication," *Journal of Curriculum Studies* 30, no. 1 (1997): 105–124.
23. See the exchange between Timothy Luke, "Digital Beings and Virtual Times: The Politics of Intersubjectivity," *Theory and Event* 1, no. 1 (1997), available on-line at http://muse.jhu.edu/journals/theory_&_event/v001/1.1r_luke.html; and Samira Kawash, "@, or Being on Line: A Reply to Timothy Luke," *Theory and Event* 1, no. 2 (1997), also on-line http://muse.jhu.edu/journals/theory_&_event/v001/1.2kawash.html.
24. Donna Haraway, "A Cyborg Manifesto," in *Simians, Cyborgs, and Women* (New York: Routledge, 1991).
25. Howard Rheingold, *The Virtual Community* (1993). Available on-line at http://www.rheingold.com/vc/book
26. David Shenk, *Data Smog: Surviving the Information Glut* (New York: HarperEdge, 1997), 174.
27. Alaina Kanfer and Christopher Kolar, "What Are Communities Doing On-Line?" (1995) Available on-line at http//www.ncsa.uiuc.edu/edu/trg/com_online.
28. David Johnson, "Community vs. Commerce," *Brill's Content* 2, No. 3 (1999): 86.
29. See Michael R. Curry, "New Technologies and the Ontology of Places."
30. See Samira Kawash, "@, or Being on Line." Kawash's analysis suggests a way of exploring the prepositions through which the *on*-line environment is discussed, as an important part of the "spatial practices" by which it is imagined and constituted.
31. The Swatch Corporation has just announced a new effort to define a standard, global "Internet Time," dividing the day up into 1,000 units ("beats") that do not correspond to seconds, minutes, or hours, and are not subject to time zones or other artifacts of physical location on the planet. The zero point of 12:00 midnight is, not surprisingly, set by the time at Biel, Switzerland, the home of the Swatch corporation. Internet Time is the same anywhere on the Internet, at any moment. The symbol for this temporal dimension of being online is also @, as in, "I will send this to you @ 472 Swatch beats." (See http://www.swatch.com/internettime/beatnik_fs_time.html) The commercial interests in bringing a standard measure of time for the transfer of banking and financial resources, information, or services should be clear, as is the benefit of having your corporation's name associated with that global standard!
32. Carmen Luke, "ekstasis@cyberia," *Discourse* 17, no. 2 (1996): 187–207.
33. Paul Virilio, *Open Sky*, trans. Julie Rose (New York: Verso, 1997).

34. This situation is akin to Dewey's idea of the *transactional* character of experience, in some respects.

35. My understanding of Arendt here owes a great deal to the work of my colleagues Melissa Orlie and Natasha Levinson.

36. Alaina Kanfer, "It's a Thin World: The Association Between Email Use and Patterns of Communication and Relationship," unpublished manuscript, National Center for Supercomputing Applications. Available on-line at http://www.ncsa.uiuc.edu/edu/trg/email.

37. Michael Fielding, "On Collegiality" (paper presented at the European Conference on Educational Research Frankfurt, Germany, autumn 1997).

38. This essay has benefited from conversations with, and feedback from, Geof Bowker, Chip Bruce, Tom Callister, Barbara Duncan, Caroline Haythornthwaite, Alaina Kanfer, and my colleagues in the Educational Policy Studies Department at the University of Illinois, Urbana/Champaign.

Contributors

Michael W. Apple is John Bascom Professor of Curriculum and Instruction and Educational Policy Studies at the University of Wisconsin—Madison. Among his many books are Official Knowledge (Routledge 1993), Cultural Politics and Education (Teacher's College Press 1996), and Power, Meaning, and Identity (Peter Lang 1999).

Jill Blackmore teaches Educational Administration and Policy Studies by distance education at Deakin University. She has published widely on gender equity reform, leadership, and educational restructuring. Her most recent publications include Troubling Women: Feminism, Leadership and Educational Change (Open University Press, 1999) and Answering Back: Girls, Boys and

Feminism in Schools written with Jane Kenway, Sue Willis, and Leonie Rennie (Routledge 1998).

Nicholas C. Burbules is Professor of Educational Policy Studies at the University of Illinois, Urbana-Champaign. His primary areas of scholarship include philosophy of education, critical, social, and political theory, and educational technology. His books include Dialogues in Teaching: Theory and Practice (Teachers College Press 1993) and Teaching and Its Predicaments, coedited with David Hansen (Westview Press 1997). He is the editor of the journal Educational Theory and series editor for the book series by Rowman and Littlefield Publishers entitled, "Philosophy, Theory, and Educational Research."

Juan-Ramón Capella is Professor of Philosophy of Law and the State at the University of Barcelona, Spain, where he is also Head of the Department of Sociology. He is the author of several books: El derecho como Lenguaje (Barcelona 1968), Los ciudadanos siervos (Madrid 1993), Fruta Prohibida (Madrid 1997), Marteriales para la crítica de la Filosofia del Estado (Barcelona 1975), Entre Sueño (Barcelona 1983) and Grandes esperanzas (Madrid 1995). He is the editor of Mientras Tanto, a social science quarterly.

Luiza Cortesão is Associate Professor of Education at the Faculty of Psychology and Education of the University of Oporto. Her interests include critical inter/multicultural education and action-research. She is also currently engaged in research on the impact of globalization on education in Portugal.

Greg Dimitriades is a doctoral candidate in the Department of Speech Communication at the University of Chicago, Urbana—Champaign. His work has appeared in journals including Popular Music, The Annals of the American Academy of Political and Social Science, and Educational Theory.

Patrick Fitzsimons is Researcher at the School of Education, the University of Auckland, New Zealand, where he also serves as a private consultant. He was Senior Researcher with the New Zealand Council of Educational Research and has published widely in the field of educational policy, including a forthcoming book from Bergin and Garvey on managerialism in education.

Douglas Kellner is George Kneller Chair in the Philosophy of Education at the University of California, Los Angeles. He is the author of many books on social theory, politics, history, and culture, including Herbert Marcuse and the Crisis of Marxism (California University Press 1984), Critical Theory, Marxism, and Modernity (Johns Hopkins University Press 1989), Jean Baudrillard: From Marxism to Postmodernism and Beyond (Stanford University Press 1989), Postmodern Theory: Critical Interrogations, with Steven Best (Macmillan 1991),

Television and the Crisis of Democracy (Westview Press 1990), The Persian Gulf TV War (Westview Press 1992), Media Culture (Routledge 1995), and The Postmodern Turn, with Steven Best (Guilford Press 1997).

Bob Lingard is Associate Professor in the Graduate School of Education at the University of Queensland where he teaches and researches the sociology of education and educational policy. His most recent book is Men Engaging Feminism (Open University Press 1999) and he is President of the Australian Association of Research in Education.

Allan Luke is Professor and Dean, Graduate School of Education, University of Queensland, Brisbane, Australia, where he teaches discourse analysis, literacy education, and sociology. He is author and editor of numerous books, including Constructing Critical Literacies (Hampton Press 1997), and his is currently working on research on antiracism in Australian schools and on Asian/Australian interethnic families.

Carmen Luke is Reader, Graduate School of Education, University of Queensland, Brisbane, Australia, where she teaches media and cultural studies, sociology, and gender studies. She is author and editor of numerous books, including Feminism and the Pedogogies of Everyday Life (State University of New York Press 1997), and she is currently completing a three-year study of Asian/Australian interethnic families and a comparative study of academic women in Asian higher education systems.

James Marshall is Professor of Education at the School of Education, the University of Auckland, New Zealand. His research interests are in educational philosophy and policy and he has published widely in these areas, including Wittgenstein: Philosophy, Postmodernism, Pedagogy with Michael Peters (1999) and Michel Foucault: Personal Autonomy and Education (1996).

Cameron McCarthy is Research Professor and University Scholar in the Institute of Communications Research at the University of Illinois. He is the author of The Uses of Culture published by Routledge in 1997. He is coeditor with Ram Mahalingham of Social Epistemology and Multiculturalism, a critical reader scheduled for publication by Routledge this fall.

Raymond A. Morrow is Professor of Sociology and Adjunct Professor of Educational Policy Studies, University of Alberta, Edmonton, Canada. He teaches primarily in the areas of social theory and culture. More recent publications include Critical Theory and Methodology (Sage 1994), Social Theory and Education with C. A. Torres (State University of New York Press 1995), and a forthcoming study Critical Social Theory and Education: Freire, Habermas and the Dialogical Subject with C. A. Torres (Teachers College Press).

Michael Peters is Associate Professor in the School of Education, the University of Auckland, New Zealand. His research interests are in educational philosophy and policy and his is the author/editor of twenty books, including most recently Wittgenstein: Philosophy, Postmodernism, Pedagogy with James Marshall (1999), After the Disciplines?: The Emergence of Cultural Studies (ed.) (1999), and University Futures and the Politics of Reform with Peter Roberts (1999).

Thomas S. Popkewitz is Professor of Curriculum and Instruction at the University of Wisconsin—Madison. His research is concerned with the relation of knowledge and power in education. His most recent publications are Struggling for the Soul (1998), Foucault's Challenge (1998), and Critical Theories in Education: Changing Terrains of Knowledge and Politics (Routledge).

Fazal Rizvi is Professor in Education at Monash University, Australia, where he is also the director of Monash Centre for Research in International Education. He has written extensively on globalization and educational policy, racism, and the politics of difference and problems of democratic reforms in education. In his current research, he is applying theories of cultural globalization to understand global flow of students, knowledges, and cultures. With Bob Lingard, he edits the journal Discourse: Studies in the Cultural Politics of Education.

Stephen R. Stoer is Professor of Education at the Faculty of Psychology and Education of the University of Oporto. He is also editor of the international journal Educação, Sociedades & Culturas. He is currently engaged in research on the impact of globalization on education in Portugal.

Carlos Alberto Torres is Professor of Social Sciences and Comparative Education, Graduate School of Education and Information Studies, and Director, Latin American Center, UCLA. He is the author of more than thirty books including Critical Theory and Education: Freire, Habermas and the Dialogical Subject with Raymond Morrow (Teachers College Press 1999) and Comparative Education: The Dialectics of the Global and the Local with coeditor Robert Arnove (Rowman and Littlefield 1999).

Index

discourse of, 175
the Enlightenment and, 3
feminist thinking in, 133
formulation of, 43
global, 85, 92, 100, 102
international presence in, 44
impact of globalism on, 44
in Malaysia, 211
movement to reform, 69
national tradition and, 3
in neoliberal framework, 20, 98
Post-Fordist neoliberal, 47
"postmodern" approaches in, 28
postnational, 91–92
production of, 85, 97–98
progressive agenda in, 73
and restructuring, 79, 103, 109
tendencies emerging in, 70
transformation of, 72
transnational, 91
in United States, 66
in the West, 71
Educational politics
in global context, 72, 96
postnational, 103
and practice, 74
Educational programs, 73
Educational reform, 48, 52, 70, 157, 168,
182, 193
critique of, 180
hybridity in, 172
movement, 62
in U.S., 161, 164
Educational standards, 42
"Education-for-employment," 61–62
Efficacy, 241
Efficiency, 260
Ellsworth, E., 330
Engels, 7
England, 44, 61, 72, 126, 147–48; See also
Great Britain; See also United Kingdom
English Labor Education Associations, 148
English-only movement, 68
the Enlightenment, 21–22, 120, 159, 164
contradictory universalism of, 28
Environment
on-line, 342, 350
"virtual," 337

Equal Opportunities (EO) Unit, 143
"Ethnoscapes"
definition of, 92
Eurocentrism, 195
Europe, 46, 68, 88, 94–95, 149, 158,
160, 162, 173–74, 194, 215, 222, 244,
254
social reform in, 159
European Commission, 261
European Economic Community (EEC), 33
Europeanization, 150, 261
European Network of Women, 143
European Union (EU), 8, 9, 10, 89, 93, 99,
137, 143, 151, 169, 172, 229, 256, 266,
269
national imaginary of, 173
European Union's Tacis, 179
European Women's Lobby, 143
Ewen, S., 196
Exchange relations, new
emergence of, 6
Falk, R., 10
Fanon, F., 279, 311
Federalism, 101
Feminism, 2, 18, 170
"Fictive ethnicities," 258, 267
Fielding, M., 351, 352
Finance
internationalization of, 9
Fine, M., 193, 200
Finland, 165
First world, 28, 49, 202
Fiske, J., 314
Fitzsimons, P., 18, 109
"Flexible production" model, 48, 52
Fordism, 14, 47, 255
Fordist model of production, 6
Foucauldian theory
post, 328
Foucault, M., 110–15, 119–21, 125, 158,
160, 175–76, 189, 202
Fourth world, 28, 49
rise of, 48, 52
critical pedagogy of, 50
France, 90
Fraser, N., 65
Freedom
social administration of, 158, 163, 170,